Essays in Honor of Burleigh Wilkins

American University Studies

Series V
Philosophy

Vol. 192

PETER LANG
New York • Washington, D.C./Baltimore • Bern
Frankfurt am Main • Berlin • Brussels • Vienna • Oxford

Essays in Honor of Burleigh Wilkins

From History to Justice

EDITED BY
Aleksandar Jokic

PETER LANG
New York • Washington, D.C./Baltimore • Bern
Frankfurt am Main • Berlin • Brussels • Vienna • Oxford

Library of Congress Cataloging-in-Publication Data

Essays in honor of Burleigh Wilkins:
from history to justice / edited by Aleksandar Jokic.
p. cm. — (American university studies.
Series V, Philosophy; vol. 192)
Includes bibliographical references.
1. Wilkins, Burleigh Taylor. 2. Political science—Philosophy.
3. History—Philosophy. I. Wilkins, Burleigh Taylor.
II. Jokic, Aleksandar. III. Series.
JA71 .E694 191—dc21 2001029040
ISBN 0-8204-5161-4
ISSN 0739-6392

Die Deutsche Bibliothek-CIP-Einheitsaufnahme

Essays in honor of Burleigh Wilkins:
from history to justice / ed. by: Aleksandar Jokic.
–New York; Washington, D.C./Baltimore; Bern;
Frankfurt am Main; Berlin; Brussels; Vienna; Oxford: Lang.
(American university studies: Ser. 5, Philosophy; Vol. 192)
ISBN 0-8204-5161-4

The paper in this book meets the guidelines for permanence and durability
of the Committee on Production Guidelines for Book Longevity
of the Council of Library Resources.

Printed in the United States of America

Contents

ALEKSANDAR JOKIC: Preface vii

BURLEIGH T. WILKINS: An Intellectual Autobiography 1

Part I: PHILOSOPHY OF HISTORY

JOHNATAN L. GORMAN: From History to Justice: Understanding Philosophy of History 19

PAUL REDDING: Wilkins, Hegel, and History 71

C. BEHAN MCCULLAGH: Understanding History 95

SUSAN MELD SHELL: Honor and the End of History: A Reading of Kant's "Renewed Question" 115

Part II: POLITICAL PHILOSOPHY

FREDERICK G. WHELAN: Taking Burke Seriously 135

KAI NIELSEN: The Crisis of Socialism and Analytical Marxism 155

Part III: APPLIED ETHICS

DAVID COOPER: An Introduction to Applied Ethics With References to Contributions by Burleigh Wilkins 193

ALEKSANDAR JOKIC: What is Wrong with Potentialism? 229

MARGARET GILBERT: Considerations on Collective Guilt 239

Part IV: PHILOSOPHY OF LAW

BRENDA M. BAKER: Wilkins on Intention and Responsibility, and the Obligation to Obey the Law 253

EDMUND WALL: Coercion, Voluntariness, and Valid Consent 269

Part V: THEORY OF JUSTICE

THOMAS POGGE: On the Third Principle of Justice Proposed by Burleigh Wilkins 287

J. ANGELO CORLETT: Collective Moral Responsibility 305

Part VI: REPLIES AND LITERARY POSTSCRIPT

BURLEIGH T. WILKINS: Replies and Reflections 321

BURLEIGH T. WILKINS: Epilogue.. 345

JOSPEH WHITE: Two Voices—Philosopher and Writer...........................347

List of Contributors 365

Preface

With this Festschrift we honor the philosophical career of Burleigh Taylor Wilkins. This collection is a celebration of his substantive contributions to a number of areas in analytical philosophy, his quiet literary career as well as a tribute to his generosity as a teacher and mentor. The group of contributors included here is comprised of both distinguished scholars as well as a coterie of younger philosophers who, as graduate students, had the good fortune of having Burleigh as a teacher and mentor.

Knowing Burleigh's modesty, I doubt that he would accept much responsibility for his pivotal role in helping so many young philosophers find "success" in the academic world. Rather, he would insist that our individual accomplishments are testimony to our own talents. If he is right, then he certainly has "a nose for talent." In any event, we all welcomed this opportunity to participate in a celebration of Burleigh's many contributions.

The idea for this festschrift came in late 1996, during a period in which Burleigh and I had regular Thursday lunches to discuss our current writing projects. Perhaps most significant to this particular project was Burleigh's writing at about this time on a third principle of justice which complemented John Rawls' first two well-known principles of justice. Realizing that Burleigh's early work in philosophy was focused upon philosophy of history, it struck me as a most attractive idea to trace his philosophical path from history to justice. And so, this festschrift was born. Burleigh became aware of the festschrift in 1998 thus allowing the inclusion of his intellectual autobiography and his replies to contributors.

The birth of this work importantly occurred within a uniquely dynamic milieu in which Burleigh played a prominent and very supportive role. During this period the Center for Philosophical Education (CPE) was created within the Department of Philosophy at Santa Barbara City College.

The creation of CPE marked an attempt to chart new territory for professional academic philosophy. Specifically, there was an intention to combine high-end research through regular and varied mini-conferences involving prominent philosophers as well as to publish a quality international journal, *Stoa*, for undergraduate students—two projects not usually associated with community colleges. The overriding goal of CPE was to take professional philosophy, with its ubiquitous sense of wonderment and pervasive academic value, beyond the narrow confines of traditional academia.

Without hesitating, Burleigh became one of the first members of the Advisory Board for CPE in addition to actively supported *Stoa* by mentoring and submitting one of the first student papers published in Volume 1 Issue 1. Within this same time period, Burleigh also served as a founding member of the International Law and Ethics Conference Series (ILECS) which was developed under the auspices of CPE. Burleigh's roles in securing initial funding as well as his moral support were crucial for the early stages of ILECS. Now in its fifth year, ILECS sponsors two conferences a year, one at Belgrade University and a follow-up conference in the U.S. This two-part strategy for conferencing has given leading moral, legal, and political philosophers—and increasingly, scholars from other disciplines—from both the U.S. and Western Europe an opportunity to meet with their Eastern European counterparts to discuss issues of global importance. Burleigh has made significant and substantive academic contributions to all of the ILECS conferences held thus far. Since this festschrift only covers Burleigh's writings up until 1997, his most recent work with ILECS will not appear here. This later work of his has focused upon several topics in international ethics and resulted in his papers on trials for war crimes, inter-ethnic reconciliation, secession, humanitarian intervention, and institutionalization of human rights.

In the end, let me thank Peter MacDougall, President of Santa Barbara City College, who had the vision to support its creation. Without CPE there probably wouldn't be this book either.

A.J.
Portland, OR
November, 2000

Burleigh T. Wilkins

An Intellectual Autobiography

I've been writing for a long time. I had my first publication when I was twelve. It was an essay in a scholastic publication for school children called *Young America*, and I won a contest "What To Do About Germany?." My essay was published on December 7, 1944. (I found a copy in the attic when I was home last summer so I'm sure of the date.) I received $25 in government saving stamps. I was an honored guest at the Rotary Club, and my visit was written up in the *Cape Charles Times*. The reporter/editor noted my embarrassment at being the center of attention. So much for the "Lifestyles of the Rich and Famous," but this story captures two things about me: I can't ever remember not being interested in current events, and I am still plagued by embarrassment whenever I am the center of attention. I'd rather be writing today about some other philosopher.

In high school I was on the debate team for three years. The first year my team won the state championship for rural high schools in Virginia. We supported universal health care insurance which over fifty years later is still not a reality for the United States (alone of all the industrial democracies). The second year we opposed the compulsory arbitration of labor disputes and the third year we supported the formation of a world government, and we lost both times. My support for world government represents a rare moment of utopianism on my part, and in retrospect I'm glad we lost. Our debate coach was also our history and government teacher. His name was George Baker Wynne, and it was mainly from him that I learned the conversational style of teaching which I use to this day. The impression he gave was that it was just a historical accident that he was old and we were young, and since some day we, too, would presumably become old it was his duty to help us grow up and to assist us in finding our own voice. Not that our own voice need be terribly original, but that we would have to pick and choose which of various conflicting opinions seemed most plausible. So, I tend to ask my students now that I am old questions that run along the following lines: What would Rawls or

Dworkin say about this problem, and what do you think? Philosophy majors are not surprised by these questions, but political science and law and society majors are sometimes taken back. In their other courses they are overwhelmed by empirical data and a profusion of court cases, so my "Socratic method" is something different. But, I assure them that unlike Socrates, I sometimes don't know what I think about a particular problem until after I have gone through the readings with them. My thoughts are often a response to their thoughts, and some of them find this challenging.

I was born in a farm house on the Eastern Shore of Virginia in 1932. My father paid the doctor and nurse to come to the farm and thus saved the fifty dollars the hospital would have charged for a room. There was no anesthesiology in those days, and in Church Neck there were no telephones. One of the neighbors recalled that the only time he ever saw my father drive fast was when he went to summon the doctor. Things were rough in those days, as old people are fond of saying to spoilt youth, and my father saw a number of his friends go broke and lose their farms in the Depression. My father was a dirt farmer (as opposed to a gentleman farmer), and my grandfather Taylor was a carpenter for the Pennsylvania Railroad for forty years. My mother was a bookkeeper for Wilson's Department Store in Cape Charles until she married my father and discovered hard times and rural isolation. I think my interest in politics stemmed in part from the hope that government could do something to alleviate the lot of farmers and workers. My father's farm was part of the original estate of Abel P. Upshur, who served as Secretary of State under President John Tyler in the 1840's and was the closest thing to a political philosopher the Whig Party ever had. John Wilkins, who came to Virginia from England in 1618, served in the House of Burgesses and, according to family legend, was a cousin of the eminent English philosopher Bishop John Wilkins. So perhaps it was preordained that I would become a political philosopher, but if so, I was unaware of it. Still, as Hegel and others have maintained, the end is in the beginning—where else could it be?

Anyone born in Virginia soon becomes aware of a legacy of great men and great events, and great problems. The greatest of the great men were George Washington, Thomas Jefferson, and James Madison. Under their leadership Virginia played a major role in the American Revolution and in the creation of the United States. Without their leadership Virginia played a major role in the South's unsuccessful attempt to secede from the Union, and Virginia was the scene of some of the bloodiest battles of the Civil War. But by far the greatest problem was race relations. Some of my ancestors, including John Wilkins, had owned slaves. I was born into a segregated society and attended segregated public schools, and when I attended Duke University it, too, was segregated.

Like many people my age, I tend to be an optimist. Our parents overcame the Depression, we saw the defeat of Germany and Japan in the Second World War, and we saw the end of racial segregation. I think our optimism was somehow essentially American, and that Jefferson, more than anyone, articulated the belief that there was no problem which could not be solved, though he had his doubts about the slavery problem. If I had a shrine or holy place, which I don't, it would be Monticello where Jefferson built his home. Actually, he never stopped building or remodeling it, which fact I think makes for a certain symbolic significance as a reminder both of a certain restlessness in the American spirit and of the fact that America, too, remains essentially unfinished.

There is, however, a downside to being born in the shadow of so much greatness. There is a sense of being overwhelmed at the historical memory of so many great men of practical reason solving so many problems, and there is also a certain sense of complacency. We had the Declaration of Independence and the Constitution, so what else was needed? If the American spirit is restless, Virginia as I remember it suffered from a sense of complacency and even a sense of collective self-congratulation. Virginia, alas, did not play a role of leadership in bringing about the end of segregation, quite the contrary; and when I ask myself why a state like Georgia did, while Virginia (so obviously, we thought, superior historically) did not, I believe the absence in Virginia of a great progressive newspaper like the *Atlanta Constitution* must be a large part of the explanation. We are, I think, what we read. Like Jefferson, I value a free press almost, but not quite, to the point of preferring, as Jefferson said he would, the benefits of a free press to those of having a government. Still, we have in America I think the best of two worlds: a free press and a government constrained *by law* from violating the freedom of speech and other rights of its citizens. And we have the Declaration of Independence which, though written by a slaveowner, proclaimed the moral equality of all persons, and we are still involved in working out the implications of this commitment to equality.

Although I've known some disappointments, I think that on the whole I've been very lucky. (Or "blessed", as my mother, who was a deeply religious person, might have put it.) I was lucky to grow up in a state with a great, though tragically flawed, history. I was lucky to have parents who encouraged my love of books and learning. I was lucky to grow up on a farm, though actually I preferred digging clams in the Chesapeake Bay. I was lucky when at two crucial moments, when I finished college and when I finished my first year of college teaching, my father refused to let me join him on the farm. There's no money in it, he said then, and there's even less now. First mechanized farming and now agricultural corporations have decimated our small farmers whom Jefferson regarded as the moral backbone of America. When my father was born over ninety percent of Americans were involved in farming, and now the number is less than five percent and shrinking. Some of my cousins are still hanging on. One of them rents the seventy-five acre farm I inherited from my parents and to which I make a kind of pilgrimage every summer. But he and his son have to farm six hundred acres to enjoy a standard of living not much higher than our parents had. Sixty acres used to support a farmer and his family and two "field hands" and their families, so you can gauge the size of the agricultural revolution that has occurred in my life time.

The story of my luck continues. I was lucky to have been too young for World War Two, and I was lucky to get a student deferment in the Korean War and an occupational deferment during the Vietnam War. My conscience bothered me, excessively I now think, about the student deferment, but not at all during the Vietnam War which, apart from the Civil War, was the most horrible mistake in our history. While on the subject of selfishness, I confess I was lucky to have been an only child; otherwise my parents couldn't have afforded to send me to Duke University for my undergraduate degree. I remember vividly the thirteen relatives, all but two dead by now, who drove down to Duke to see me graduate *summa cum laude* and Phi Beta Kappa. Over the years I was fortunate to receive fellowships for graduate study first in history and then in philosophy.

I've been fortunate to have stimulating teachers and responsive students. There were Harold T. Parker and Richard Watson in history at Duke University, and Arthur Schlesinger, Jr. in history at Harvard University, and Joel Feinberg, Carl Hempel, Walter Kaufmann, Richard Rorty, and Gregory Vlastos in philosophy at Princeton University. Of these, two in particular, Harold T. Parker and Joel Feinberg, have continued my "adult education" by writing in areas of special interest to me, Parker on the Napoleonic era and on historical method and Feinberg on ethics and legal philosophy. I may have left out some deserving teachers, and I'm not about to attempt a list of all the students, especially the graduate students, to whom I am indebted. Instead, I shall mention certain courses or seminars from which I've learned a lot: all of my classes in introductory humanities at the Massachusetts Institute of Technology, my course in the philosophy of history at Princeton University, my seminars in the philosophy of history and the philosophy of law at Rice University, and the following classes and seminars at the University of California at Santa Barbara: the philosophy of history, medical ethics, political philosophy, and the philosophy of law, and especially classes in the philosophy of Karl Popper, freedom and determinism, the right of privacy, and more recently problems in international law. That's a lot of courses and a lot of different interests, which, of course, were not entertained concurrently. I had a senior colleague at M.I.T. who said that a gentleman could teach anything; accordingly, one summer, he read some books on Chinese literature and gave a course on the subject that fall. I was never that big a dilettante, but I was intellectually restless. Perhaps I should have done better to follow the example of some of my most distinguished teachers and stick to one area, but I feel that I could not have done otherwise.

My first scholarly publications were a review of Isaiah Berlin's *The Hedgehog and the Fox* in *The South Atlantic Quarterly* in 1954, and an article, "James, Dewey, and Hegelian Idealism", in *The Journal of the History of Ideas* in 1956. In his letter of acceptance, John Herman Randall, Jr. wrote that my article on how the pragmatists reacted to Hegel was "extraordinarily faithful to the facts and spirit" of what I was examining, and that letter helped sustain me for years to come. I should perhaps mention that when I would tell my mother about various compliments my work had received, she would reply, "Some people know how to say the nicest things," which helped keep my ego in check. And then there was the example of a friend and teacher who almost ruined his career by boasting. But basically my rural Methodist upbringing made me wary of attaching too much significance to anything I might do, and there were always the writings of Jefferson and Madison to serve as a benchmark of excellence.

My first book was *Carl Becker: A Biographical Study in American Intellectual History*. One summer I went to Cornell University to look for materials on Becker's reflections on historical method, but here is what I found: the archivists had just finished assembling the Becker Papers in chronological order, and there was a book crying out to be written. Books can be harder to compose than articles, and first books can present formidable obstacles. In retrospect, I realize that in writing about Becker I was, without knowing it, also writing about myself. Like me, Becker grew up on a farm (in his case in Iowa), and in the Methodist Church, and like me he had his religious doubts. Like me, he was skeptical of grandiose theological and metaphysical theories; but he was sensitive to the residues of religious convictions in modern philosophy, hence his masterpiece, *The Heavenly City of the Eighteenth Century Philosophers.* He shared my fascination with Jefferson, and one of his best books was a study of the Declaration of Independence. Like me, he was a liberal, but one troubled by the application of liberal doctrine in an industrial society. Although I rejected his pragmatism, I found his "Everyman His Own Historian" and other papers on historical method to be among the most thoughtful essays I had ever read. His style of writing was clear and unpretentious, and just writing about his works helped improve my own style of composition. Lynwood Bryant of the M.I.T. Press helped immensely in securing its joint publication by the M.I.T. Press and by Harvard University Press, which meant that it went through two separate and independent reviewing processes. Probably it was my most successful work. Robert Palmer wrote in *The Journal of Modern History* that I had " the subtlety, the insight and the gift for elucidation of paradox that a full length study of Becker requires Some people know how to say the nicest things, and if my book on Becker was the one which I feel most confident about, I can truthfully say that as things turned out—no one in his right mind would have planned this—each successive book was on a more difficult topic and posed greater difficulties than the previous one.

If Becker was congenial, the subject of my next book, *The Problem of Burke's Political Philosophy*, published by Oxford University Press in 1967, was not. Edmund Burke wrote some of the most beautiful words in the English language, especially in his famous observation that society is indeed a compact but one between the living, the dead, and the unborn. But he was also at times a windbag, and he was also a well paid political henchman of the powerful Lord Rockingham. I had to read through dozens of florid speeches made for specific political occasions, and abstract from them a political philosophy, and the political philosophy, if there was one, expressed a hatred of abstract philosophizing about politics. No wonder that commentators were divided over whether Burke actually had a political philosophy and, if he did, whether it was a kind of utilitarianism or a kind of natural law theory. It was perhaps anti-climactic for me to argue that Burke only hated one kind of abstract thinking, the kind he associated with the *philosophes* and the French authors of the Rights of Man. Roughly put, Burke's argument was that the historical circumstances of a people must always be taken into account and that arguments from human nature alone were always vacuous. But I argued that Burke was also prepared to argue from human nature when it suited his purposes. It is true that Burke preferred to talk about historic rights in defending the English Revolution of 1648 and in defending the American colonists (they were, he said, fighting for their rights as Englishmen). But the distinction between the historic rights of Englishmen and the natural rights of man has been overblown by some commentators, who profess to see it as an exclusive disjunction. That's not the way that classical English jurists such as Blackstone saw it, and it's not the way that Burke, who was a keen student of English law, saw it either. So the upshot of my book was this: Burke located political philosophy in the domain of practical reasoning and not of theoretical reasoning; and the natural law tradition was rich enough in complexity (or ambiguity) to accommodate both a liberal interpretation such as Jefferson's and a conservative one such as Burke's.

The next two books I wrote were in the philosophy of history, though they were not intended as a pair and had quite different purposes. The first was *Hegel's Philosophy of History* (1974) and the second was *Has History Any Meaning? A Critique of Popper's Philosophy of History* (1978). Both were published by Cornell University Press. The book on Hegel was intended as a sympathetic historical reconstruction of Hegel's philosophy of history, and the second was a critical appraisal of Popper's philosophy of history. There is something of a paradox here, I suppose, as my own philosophical sympathies lay far more with Popper than with Hegel. The reason I wrote the historical reconstruction of Hegel was that although I taught Hegel's Introduction to his Lectures on the Philosophy of History, I simply did not understand his taxonomy of the different kinds of historical writing. Thus, I was confronted with a choice: either forget the most influential philosopher of history and focus entirely on the modern debate over the Popper-Hempel covering law model of historical explanation, or else try to make sense of Hegel. I chose the latter course of action, and I explained as best I could the ways in which Hegel's taxonomy was hierarchical in intent, culminating in philosophical history and its answer to the question, What is the ultimate purpose of the world? Other commentators had connected Hegel's philosophy of history to his *Phenomenology*, but I found the key to what he was after in his so-called *Science of Logic*. In this work Hegel sought to explain how mechanism, i.e. cause and effect relations, are "sublated" or taken up into teleological relations. All but the most mechanical human actions, which contemporary action theory would label "acts" as contrasted to bona fide "actions," were Hegel thought teleological or purposive in nature. In this Hegel was undoubtedly correct, but what was ambitious and controversial in Hegel was his claim that these individual actions all served a higher purpose, namely the advancement of human freedom. Hegel's "cunning of reason" resembled Adam Smith's "invisible hand" explanation of market economics in that both accounts focused on what Karl Popper would later describe as the unintended consequences of intentional human actions.

I was sympathetic, historically speaking, to Hegel, partly because in analytic circles one had only to mention his name to elicit a chuckle, and the statement "I don't understand Hegel" was guaranteed to produce laughter. I didn't find Hegel's teleology any more incomprehensible than Kant's transcendental deduction of the categories, but Kant was "on our side," being perceived as a precursor of the analytic movement. There was also the moral and political dimension of Hegel, which contributed to his unpopularity. Popper in his *The Open Society and Its Enemies* had labeled both Plato and Hegel as totalitarian. I'm afraid he was right about Plato, but I think he was dead wrong about Hegel, as Walter Kaufmann demonstrated in one of his articles. Conservatives like Hegel (and Burke) have fared badly at the hands of some scholars who have a litmus test for what would come to be called "political correctness." The result has been that we have neglected the contributions conservatives have made to the advancement of human freedom in their emphasis upon a complex of institutional settings. Human freedom can flourish in what Hegel called civil society and not just in political society, a fact which modern day liberals have neglected to their peril. In the past two decades I have noted with distress that the liberals' overemphasis on government as the solution has led to a populist reaction in which government is depicted as the problem. Popper was probably no more responsible for Ronald Reagan than Hegel was responsible for Hitler, but there is a danger in exaggeration, which may have its own unintended consequences.

I took the title of my book *Has History Any Meaning?* from the last chapter in Karl Popper's *The Open Society and Its Enemies.* I agreed with Popper that the question of whether history has any meaning is a self-referential question about the meaning we choose to give to history and not something to be "discovered" as Hegel seems to have thought in the historical process itself. I also agreed with Popper that the fact-value distinction is fundamental and cannot be collapsed as some contemporary philosophers have argued. As a conservative liberal I also agreed with Popper that piecemeal social engineering is closer to the experimental method of the natural sciences than "holistic" planning could possibly be, but I disagreed with Popper that holistic planning was, strictly speaking, impossible. This involved my only major difference with Popper, which turned on whether it is possible to speak intelligibly about the whole or totality of history or for that matter the whole or totality of any historical event. 'Whole', I argued, is ambiguous. If we take it to refer to every detail, including every true statement about an event or process, then obviously inquiry will necessarily remain incomplete. In this sense of 'whole' no account of the French Revolution could be complete which did not include my having just mentioned the French Revolution, and the same would obviously apply to any attempt to overcome this omission, and so on. For this reason definitive history is a chimera, but we can still speak intelligibly of the whole of history or an historical event if we use 'whole' to refer to the structure of processes or events, where 'structure' refers to the institutions around which historical events are organized and which affect the outcome of historical events. Thus, for example, a political history of the French Revolution would be holistic in the sense of explaining the course of events by references to changes in the government and its policies.

In retrospect, I think the upshot of my two books is the following. Speculative or metaphysical philosophy of history is not some fraudulent effort to achieve some superscientific account of the historical process but rather an attempt to discern the meaning of history. Meaning for Hegel, unlike for Popper (and for Kant before him) was constitutive of the historical process not in the sense of unveiling the efficient causes that determine the historical process, but in the sense of revealing the final end, or purpose, of the historical process. Both Hegel and Popper could be read as seeing freedom as the final end of history, though, of course, freedom was defined differently for the conservative Hegel and for the liberal Popper. And, of course, Popper did not speak of the final ends of history. Nevertheless, for Popper (and for Kant) the quest for the meaning of history could, perhaps, be seen as a regulative idea (to use Kant's terminology) around which historians, philosophers, and moralists could organize their inquiries. This is admittedly an overinterpretation of Popper, but one which is at least consistent with his emphasis upon the selectivity of points of view or interpretations of the past. Freedom, in this view, ought to be seen as the final end of history.

Hilary Putnam reviewed my book on Popper for *Clio*, and he wrote, "This is a valuable book. The exegesis of Popper is extremely good and the criticism is generally telling." However, in this book the exegesis was for the sake of evaluation, so not only was this my last effort in philosophy of history, it was also my last work in the history of ideas. In starting this intellectual autobiography, I didn't know how it would turn out, anymore than I knew how my life would turn out at the beginning. But one theme that emerges throughout is that of luck and a willingness to take chances.

Two graduate students who did their doctoral theses under me, in the philosophy of social and natural sciences respectively, set up a new course in medical ethics, and when they went on to take tenure track positions at other universities, I decided to teach this course and later added a course on advanced medical ethics. I published a paper "Does the Fetus Have a Right to Life?" in the *Journal of Social Philosophy* which managed to displease both the pro-life and pro-choice camps. The fetus, I claimed, was a potential human being, and I argued against Joel Feinberg that it is coherent, though it may be incorrect on substantive moral grounds, to say that a potential human being has a right to life where potentiality is understood in terms of what will normally be the case. Normally (and this is not a statistical point) the fetus will become a person, and for that reason it makes sense to accord the fetus a protection of its life. (Obviously, it's not interested in protecting its life, but that doesn't entail that it has no interest which requires protection.) However, I argued that a woman who is pregnant knows best whether bringing a pregnancy to term will impose an undue burden upon her health or life prospects. Not that her knowledge is incorrigible, but still on epistemological grounds she has a privileged position which we cannot ignore; and I concluded that we must allow a woman's right to choose to trump any right to life the fetus may have. I still think this is right, especially when we look at the alternatives. Justice Ruth Ginsburg's pro-choice position rests on the claim that to deny a woman's right to choose is to deny her equal rights as a citizen. Ronald Dworkin believes that the debate about abortion turns on a "religious" question, i.e. whether we hold the life of the fetus or the life of the woman who is pregnant sacred. If we take religious freedom seriously, neither version of what is sacred can be imposed as a matter of law. Then, of course, there's Judith Thomson's position that a woman can abort the fetus as if it were an unwelcome intruder. Where Ginsburg's position is concerned, if ever there was a justification which would in legal parlance stand the test of strict scrutiny for treating the sexes unequally, it would be where only one of the sexes can perform a given function, in this case of becoming pregnant and bringing a pregnancy to term. Dworkin's position has an element of truth, which helps explain the religious fervor surrounding the abortion controversy, but while one could argue that a mature woman's life is more sacred than the life of the fetus, this point seems decisive only where the life of the pregnant woman is literally at stake. However greatly we value the life of a mature woman possessing autonomy and rationality, the freedom to choose is limited in a large variety of ways in other areas of conduct where harm to others is involved so the question of the status of the fetus reemerges. Finally, the idea that the fetus may be regarded as an unwelcome intruder involves, as Thomson admits, the question of whether a pregnancy is planned. But should planned and unplanned pregnancies be treated differently so that in the case of a planned pregnancy a woman will not be permitted to change her mind? The entire metaphor of unwelcome intruder or unwelcome guest seems unacceptable when the life of the intruder or guest is at stake. We do not, or should not, ask whether someone seeking refuge is unwanted, and certainly we can't justify killing the intruder or guest on the ground that he or she was not invited (or is no longer welcome). So, I think the pro-choice position must turn upon the woman as uniquely qualified to decide whether to bring a pregnancy to term poses an unacceptable burden. The tragedy of the abortion controversy is that whether we embrace a pro-life or pro-choice public policy abuses will undoubtedly occur. If a pro-life policy is adopted, some women will be forced, presumably by public officials, to bear an intolerable burden; if a pro-choice policy prevails, then some pregnancies will be terminated unnecessarily or needlessly.

Back in the 1980's I had a graduate student ask if I would give a course on terrorism, and I said, yes, provided he would find the best articles on the topic. There weren't all that many. Consequentialists had tried to distance themselves from terrorism although a consequentialist justification of terrorism seems fairly easy to construct; and on the other hand deontologists were for the most part silent. For deontologists only the argument from necessity seemed to work, but I sought to provide a principled justification of terrorism under certain conditions. I cited the case of Jews in Nazi Germany, and argued that terrorism by the Jews against Nazi Germany would have been justified. Building on Joel Feinberg's work on collective responsibility, I tried to show how groups could be collectively responsible for actions done by their representatives on their behalf. And I explored cases of collective responsibility taken from military and corporate history. What got me interested in terrorism was the realization that while terrorists performed criminal actions, they could readily be distinguished from ordinary garden variety criminals. For one thing, they sought publicity for what they were doing, and almost without exception they believed that what they were doing was morally justified. In the criminal law, one finds lots of excuses and few justifications, and I tried to build upon the distinction between excuse and justification to construct a case for terrorism as a species of self-defense by groups against other groups which threaten their existence, analogous to an individual's plea of self-defense in the criminal law. I also argued that terrorism may or may not be random and that a definition of terrorism should not, by itself, serve as a condemnation of terrorism, as would obviously be the case if terrorism was defined as the random harming of innocent persons. It seems to me at times that work in applied ethics may be vulnerable to Hegel's objection to Fichte's proposal that passports bear the likenesses of their owner. What, Hegel asked, has this to do with philosophy, and this doubt haunted me occasionally as over a decade or so I wrote the essays which Routledge published in 1992 as *Terrorism and Collective Responsibility*. Accordingly, I was immensely relieved when the reviewer for *Ethics* began his review as follows: "Works in applied ethics all too frequently are superficial or deficient in analytical rigor. *Terrorism and Collective Responsibility* is a notable exception."

I try to help my students find their own voices, but when I found my own voice it was remarkably like John Rawls' voice. Rawls' *A Theory of Justice* and his *Political Liberalism* have had a profound influence upon my thinking, and that of an entire generation. Rawls recognized that the basic rights and liberties and the equality of opportunity championed by the historic liberal revolutions needed to be supplemented by what he called "the difference principle," which holds that inequalities in the distribution of primary goods, including wealth, are justifiable only if they benefit what Rawls called "the representative worst off man." I think that a liberalism which doesn't acknowledge this will end up as a kind of libertarianism which will be satisfied with Jefferson's claim that the best government is the one which governs least—shades of the nemesis of my youth, Senator Harry Byrd of Virginia. Such a political philosophy will fail to realize that questions of equality which emerge when we attempt to apply Jefferson's insights into the moral equality of all persons to modern day industrial society must take precedence over questions about the optimal size of government. Rawls' *A Theory of Justice* provided two principles of justice, lexically ordered, for the basic institutions of society: a principle protecting our basic rights and liberties, and a principle protecting equality of opportunity and incorporating provisions for the protection of the representative worst off man. Some commentators see the "difference principle" as separate from equality of opportunity, but I see it as being in part an indispensable means to securing substantive and not merely formal equality of opportunity.

In *A Theory*, Rawls confessed to being unable to provide lexically ordered principles for actions by individual persons. One of my happiest moments in philosophy was receiving a letter from Rawls acknowledging that I had succeeded in showing how this might be possible in a paper,

"Principles for Individual Actions," published in *Philosophia*. I argued that Rawls' recognition of the complexity of the subject matter of individual actions could be offset by his own point that a suitably high-powered theory could overcome complexity (a point which had seemed to me correct when I encountered it in the philosophy of history) and I argued that the considerations Rawls had used in constructing his two principles were applicable to the construction of lexically ordered principles for individual actions. I come now to a third principle of justice which I proposed after teaching Rawls' *Political Liberalism*, and which seems a way of overcoming the "strains of commitment" problem of how to secure the commitment of a multi-cultural society to the principles of political liberalism. Religious communities may fare badly in states where political liberalism prevails, so the problem is how to make the institutions of political liberalism more palatable to them. I argued for a third principle which, roughly speaking, provides that states should adopt laws or policies with harmful foreseeable consequences for such communities only if such policies serve a compelling state interest; and I tried to show that such a principle (like Rawls' first principle and the equality of opportunity part of his second principle) was consistent with American constitutional law. The arguments were presented in my "A Third Principle of Justice," which was published in *The Journal of Ethics* in 1997. Once again, Rawls replied graciously, agreeing that such a principle seemed reasonable to him.

From the problem of multi-culturalism in national or municipal law, it was a logical next step to problems of multi-culturalism in international relations which have concerned me over the last several years. I overcame my shyness at public appearances to read a paper on trials for war crimes and a paper on ethnic reconciliation at conferences at the University of Belgrade and at the Center for Philosophical Education in Santa Barbara, California. I suppose all of this comes under the heading "Works in Progress."

In the above sketch of an intellectual autobiography, I have tried to communicate my ongoing passion for philosophy which, gloriously, is just one problem after another. I have tried also to avoid the pitfalls of false modesty and self-importance. However, at the risk of seeming self-indulgent, I would like to end with a letter from a former student who is this year's editor of *The California Law Review*. I'm not as good a teacher as Kline thinks, but Kline has captured the kind of teacher, and the kind of person, I would like to be.

Matthew T. Kline
179 Dolores Street #5
San Francisco, CA 94103

April 28, 1997

Philosophy Department Chair
c/o Kathy McKinney, Office Mgr.
Philosophy Department
UC Santa Barbara
Santa Barbara, CA 93106

Dear Sir:

I graduated with a minor in Philosophy from your department in June of 1996. I received honors at graduation for my studies in Philosophy and I am slated to have a paper published that I wrote as a student in your department. I am currently a first year law student at Boalt Hall School of Law at UC Berkeley. I have received highest honors and the American Jurisprudence Award for my course work at Boalt and an award for my writing and advocacy in Boalt's moot court program. I will extern for Justice J. Anthony Kline (no relation) of the California Court of Appeals this summer. I am not writing this to sing my own accolades or impress you. Rather, I write to let you know that I feel I owe a great part of my success to one of your own faculty members, Professor Burleigh T. Wilkins.

I took four classes from Professor Wilkins in my last four quarters at UCSB. In the Spring of 1995, I took his Punishment seminar and was exposed to his theories regarding collective responsibility and terrorism as well as death penalty arguments, arguments over affirmative action, and several other contemporary controversial issues. On the last day of that class, Professor Wilkins, in the most brilliant ten minutes of logical, Constitutional and moral argument I have ever heard, articulated his opposition to the death penalty. To this day, as someone who hopes to do death penalty work in the Deep South, I wish I had taped that lecture. In the Fall of 1995, I took Professor Wilkins' Theories of Justice class. Under his tutelage, I wrote the most demanding paper of my academic career on Rawls' response to Hart in Rawls' *Political Liberalism.* The paper is supposed to be published in *Stoa International Undergraduate Journal of Philosophy* at the end of this year. In the Winter of 1997, I took Professor Wilkins' Philosophy of Law class. Exposed to mainstream and critical theories of law in Professor Wilkins' semi-Socratic style, I am today not only a better philosopher, but had a great advantage over my fellow classmates as a first year law student. In my last quarter at UCSB, Professor Wilkins and I had developed an enriching friendship that made his Advanced Legal Philosophy seminar on Privacy all the more challenging and entertaining.

I can imagine those critical of Professor Wilkins finding fault in his teaching style or in his approach to the subject matter. But as a student who always thrived in a challenging, engaging atmosphere of learning, I eagerly looked forward to the three hour sessions on Wednesday or Thursday nights. If Professor Wilkins' greatest fault is his hope and demand that students actually think and participate in class, it should not detract from his status as one of UCSB's most treasured teaching assets.

Some teachers are popular because they tell a lot of jokes or because their classes are easy or because they aim to please students at the expense of their scholarship. Professor Wilkins is popular among the top students that took his classes for his intellectual rigor, his belief in undergraduates as burgeoning scholars, and the time he has always taken to help students desiring a challenging education. As a long time student of his, I thank him for preparing me to be a good law student and lawyer and for being a friend and mentor.

Thank you for your time and consideration.

Sincerely,

Matthew T. Kline

cc: Burleigh Wilkins

Part I
Philosophy of History

JOHNATAN L. GORMAN

From History to Justice: Understanding Philosophy of History

Even among philosophers of history, who have regularly to think about the most distant implications of philosophical positions, Burleigh Taylor Wilkins' writings join his high intellectual achievements with a remarkably wide scholarly range. Yet what is counted as a wide range by one reader may not be counted so by another, and philosophy of history is particularly fertile ground for conflicting judgments. It is an area of study which exemplifies just how true Wilkins' comment in his *Hegel's Philosophy of History* is, that there has been "a breakdown, following Hegel's death, of a fairly general consensus concerning the proper tasks of philosophy."[1] Like history itself, the philosophy of history presents the student with a confusion in need of organization. As Wilkins notes in his *Carl Becker: A Biographical Study in American Intellectual History*, "The difficulties of explaining American history in terms of great families are well known... In political history it is a truism that the Byrds, Lees and Adamses, fascinating as they are, do not provide an adequate point of reference around which to organize events."[2] Moreover, however adequate or inadequate such a particular "point of reference" may be in structuring our understanding of a complex whole, we see from Wilkins' *Has History Any Meaning? A Critique of Popper's Philosophy of History*, that it is also possible that "the same thing or collection of things may be structured in more than one way."[3] Wilkins thus notes two very different types of hazard: first, that it may be extraordinarily difficult to find any way of organizing adequately a confused mass of material; second, that we may be able to find several adequate ways, and yet be unable to show which of them is best. Yet Wilkins has met the difficulties of organizing a complex whole. Those who wish to understand contemporary philosophy of history will find in Wilkins' own corpus of works a point of reference unmatched in its range of contributions, and one which overcomes both types of hazards.

What is philosophy of history? This question is grammatically similar to many others which philosophers have discussed, such as "what is history?", "what is science?" or "what is law?." The last three questions have stimulated many pages of philosophical discussion about the nature of each of these subjects, and yet more could be written comparing and contrasting the disciplines themselves. Apart from philosophical issues which may be specific to each subject, we can have philosophical worries about how far one subject could be in principle different from another at all, or whether a subject can have an "essence", or whether one subject is more fundamental than others, or what makes a subject a "discipline", or whether a subject is to be identified in terms of the logical and epistemological status of its theories, or in terms of its method, or its categories of explanation, or its subject matter, or the shared rules of its practitioners, and so forth.

Yet, while there is a multiplicity of approaches in each of these philosophical areas and many distinctions can be drawn between history, science and law, these three subjects have one thing in common: it is in practice clearly recognizable when we have an historian, when we have a scientist, and when we have a lawyer. Whatever is going on theoretically, and whatever borderline cases there may be, our educational, professional and research practices keep these subjects recognizably separate. A university degree in history is different from a university degree in science. Research in science is submitted to different academic journals from research in law. The practice of law is different from the practice of history. While a very few outstanding individuals can embrace more than one subject with sufficient mastery to appeal to the different audiences involved, there nevertheless are different audiences. While the practitioners of all subjects often have to explain themselves to lay people, at the practical professional academic level historians typically listen only to other historians, scientists typically listen only to other scientists, and lawyers typically listen only to other lawyers. So, no matter what philosophical difficulties we may find in attempting to answer a question like "what is history?", no matter what theoretical similarities we may find between subjects, in practice we can ignore these issues and can distinguish one subject from another in terms of its appropriately trained audience, an audience which shares at least a recognition of the distinctiveness of its own subject.

Unfortunately, the philosophy of history is not even in this minimally happy position. There is no accepted single place for the philosophy of history across the academic establishment. We can no more take the word "philosophy" in the expression "philosophy of history" to designate a subject which is essentially part of a philosophy curriculum than we can from its use in the expression "management philosophy." Trained professional philosophers know how widely the word "philosophy" is used outside their academic discipline. Apart from many other uses, the point can be illustrated by noting that "philosophy" can be taken to mean "theory" which can be taken to mean "science", and we see this in the familiar equivalence between political philosophy, political theory and political science, terms which are seen by some academics and some institutions as marking a single subject with a single audience and a single natural academic home, by others as concerned with three clearly distinct subject-matters with different methods, problems and audiences, and by others again as marking the presence of an "essentially contested concept."[4] In political philosophy or theory or science, however, there is—even considering them at their most diverse as subjects—a considerable overlap of understanding or subject matter between the interested audiences. It would be usual for the kind of political scientist or historian concerned, say, with the use of economic theory to explain political behavior to be familiar with the positions of the main authors in the philosophy of justice (Rawls or Nozick, perhaps), and also vice-versa (Arrow or Sen, perhaps). Yet in the case of the philosophy or theory of history, by contrast, contributions may be made by analytical philosophers of science, political theorists, "Continental" philosophers, historians of historiography, literary theorists and indeed other groups, where the traditions from which they contribute are distinct enough for a normal professional to be quite unfamiliar with the positions of the main authors in a different tradition. The philosophy of history is, in part, not a "philosophical" subject in the professional sense at all.

It is a consequence of this that a minimally adequate account of the philosophy of history will have to provide an outline of the main traditions and audiences involved in the subject, and also have to explain the assumed nature of the audience to which the account is itself primarily addressed. It is a measure of the range of Wilkins' academic accomplishments that the latter is not easy. In addition to his many articles in the best international philosophical journals, he has published also in journals which it is safe to say are mainly the preserve of historians. Nevertheless, while Wilkins is among the least narrowly classifiable of philosophers, he is a philosopher, and moreover a philosopher in the most honorific sense of that term. Just as his works address mostly—although hardly ever only—a professional philosophical audience, I shall do the same here, and will explain the place of other audiences relative to that philosophical center.

Even if we exclude those audiences who are not professional philosophers, this still does not solve the problem of understanding philosophy of history, for we have noted with Wilkins the absence of a post-Hegelian consensus and thus that there is more than one philosophical audience, and that this is so is again a centrally important feature of the philosophy of history. To resolve this, I shall begin by assuming that I share with the reader a certain particular tradition of current philosophy written primarily in English, a tradition which broadly characterises the first seventy-five years[5] of professional academic philosophy in the twentieth century, a tradition which is shared between North America, the British Isles, Australasia and some Scandinavian countries. It is often described as the "analytical" tradition—a term which is again particularly problematic for the philosophy of history.[6]

In this tradition university study in philosophy standardly covers a certain range of subjects. First, we may note the study of the history of philosophy, which initially takes as canonical texts and arguments drawn from at least the following philosophers: Descartes, Locke, Berkeley, Hume and Kant. It is a tradition which aims for the highest quality of logical reasoning and which makes epistemology foundational for the rest of philosophy. Earlier philosophers, particularly Plato and Aristotle, are read in the light of these interests.[7] Unlike other post-Kantian philosophical traditions, it is a tradition which takes as centrally problem-posing the empiricist scepticism most clearly expressed by Hume, although empiricist solutions are not insisted upon. Like Kant,[8] particular philosophers may take rationalist positions on the various issues, although the burden of proof in the tradition is such that arguments based on empiricist assumptions have a central place. The centrality of epistemology both reflects and expresses a concern with the limits of our understanding of the natural world, and in consequence the nature and limits of scientific understanding—usually assumed to be a successful enterprise—have set the agenda for many philosophers in this tradition. The theory of existence, or metaphysics, also has a central place, although it is often—but not exclusively—driven by the ontology of mathematics and science. In addition to studying its own canonical figures[9] in the history of philosophy, the university study of philosophy in this tradition stresses study in logical reasoning, epistemology and metaphysics. Moral philosophy is missing from the list so far, although it has always been—in a sense—a central part of the standard philosophy curriculum in this tradition. I shall not elaborate here the familiar point that, for the first seven decades of the twentieth century, it was standard to write as if—and sometimes to claim explicitly that—philosophers have no expertise in morality whatever.[10] In consequence moral philosophy in this tradition, until roughly 1970, was regarded only as a branch of epistemology and metaphysics, and in terms of practical moral advice was seen as merely transmitting to a new generation the older substantive positions, such as those of Kant or the Utilitarians.[11] Understanding these core philosophical subjects of logic, epistemology, metaphysics and ethics in the twentieth century has developed in a major way through a concentration on language deriving from American pragmatism and from the work of the later Wittgenstein. The outcome is that for this tradition there is also a post-Kantian canon in the history of philosophy: Mill, Frege, Russell, Wittgenstein and Quine, at least. The post-Kantian canon for this "analytical" tradition continues to be broadly empiricist in its agenda, although again it is not a condition of accepting the tradition that one should be an empiricist.[12]

This "analytical" tradition is one which had, until the 1940s, very little to say about history. Many philosophers accepted that history was not a mode of obtaining knowledge at all, and suggested that the role of the community of historians might perhaps be political, even purposely political.[13] After all, the identity of a nation may be supposed to be best preserved by, and indeed even created by, its history, and what its history is asserted to be might not, for some communities, be overly constrained by a regard for the truth—as, for instance, in Plato's "noble lie."[14] One of the most influential current philosophers of history, W.H. Dray, remarks that the antecedents of current philosophy of history—and he means by this what I have called the "analytical" tradition—"amount to little more than scattered observations in some of the lesser-known writings of Hume, some afterthoughts on the social sciences in J.S. Mill's *System of Logic* and a single essay by F.H. Bradley, published in 1874, perhaps"—he adds—"the first considerable piece of philosophical writing on history by an English philosopher."[15] although, as W.H. Walsh had earlier commented on Bradley, "there is nothing to show that he attached any special importance to history in the working out of his general metaphysical view."[16] History was, at best, a peripheral subject for the philosophers of this received "analytical" tradition.[17] Wilkins is one of the rare exceptions.

The peripherality of history as a subject of "analytical" philosophical study contrasts with what has been its much greater centrality for other philosophical traditions. The "analytical" tradition, until very recently, has rarely engaged with alternative post-Kantian traditions in philosophy. It has even more rarely engaged with alternative traditions in philosophy of history. It has merely observed them as a part of the history of philosophy, if it has connected with them at all. The difference between what I have described as the "analytical" tradition and alternative philosophical traditions in the philosophy of history begins to arise in an influential way with the work of Kant.[18] Kant shared with other great Enlightenment philosophers the conviction that humanity was no longer at the mercy of a barbaric nature. The world was a rational place, and we, being essentially rational ourselves, could expect both to understand it and to control it. The eternal and fixed characteristics of reason formed the essence of our being as human agents, it structured our personal and social morality, and it governed nature herself also. Kant showed us, in a series of great works, how all this was possible.[19]

Since history embodies an account of change over time, the eternal characteristics of reason initially allow no more than a peripheral place for philosophical thought about history. Almost as an afterthought, in 1784 Kant published an essay entitled "Idea of a Universal History from a Cosmopolitan Point of View."[20] an essay not much longer than its title. Kant reasoned here that, since the world was a rational place, everything in it must have its own purpose and also be perfectly fitted for its own purpose. Since perfection does not exist now, everything would therefore in the course of time achieve its own purpose and become perfectly what it was meant to be. That capacity of rationality which makes human beings what they essentially are would likewise achieve its own perfection in the course of time. Since being moral was essentially a matter of being rational, it followed that moral perfection would also be achieved in the course of time. Experience plainly showed that this development did not occur in the short lifetimes of the particular individuals around us, and so it had to occur in the human race as a whole over the course of the generations. We could therefore regard the history of the human race as the progressive realisation of a rational plan of nature to bring about a perfect moral community, embodying a perfect political constitution. Such a plan we, being rational, could work out; and the human race could help forward its own necessary political progress towards the final perfect state. A rational philosophy thus gives us a clue to the future pattern of historical development.

Kant's overall view, however, contained an unpleasant inconsistency which he missed. We learn from his writings how he linked morality both to reason and to human nature so closely that rational perfection was at the same time moral perfection and at the same time the perfection of human nature itself. His main moral philosophy, developed at length outside his short essay on universal history,[21] shows us the unchanging demands which morality makes on all of us as rational beings. There is an eternal and universal moral truth as absolute as Newton's laws, and it requires us to act from moral duty out of respect for other people as ends in themselves. We are never to use others as a means to our own selfish ends. The end never justifies the means.

But in his essay on universal history Kant explains for us how nature will use the natural capacities of human beings to bring about the final perfect state in the course of time. "Man wishes concord", he said; "but nature knows better what is good for his species, and she will have discord."[22] "Nature works through wars."[23] By a bloody route we will eventually arrive at the final perfect state, at a state of moral perfection which justifies the huge and hideous historical cost of getting there. Unlike the rest of Kant's philosophy, in this essay we find that all is in historical change. None of us, at our own point of historical time, is as fully moral, as fully rational, or even, it follows, as fully human as our descendants will be in the course of the generations. Moreover, the end justifies the means. There could hardly be a clearer denial of Kant's own eternal moral philosophy as he expressed it elsewhere. From the Enlightenment view that reason, morality and human nature are eternal and fixed, we see in this essay the first influential hints of change towards the view that reason, morality and human nature change over historical time.[24] History, far from being peripheral, becomes absolutely central to philosophical understanding, on such a view.

Yet the conclusion is based on the centrality of reason, and, given Newton's demonstration of the rational certainties of creation, this was not an easy position for an Enlightenment audience to deny, and Kant's successors Hegel[25] and Marx elaborated this approach to historical progress. The nature and ongoing development of rational enlightenment was argued through at great and difficult length by Hegel, and Wilkins in his *Hegel's Philosophy of History* explores and clarifies for us the claims Hegel makes about the relationships between philosophical reasoning and history. Hegel was politically conservative. Since at any given time historical progress has moved forward from what was necessarily a less rational and moral situation, it is incumbent on us to preserve the rational enlightenment which we have so far achieved, for fear of relapsing into that earlier barbarism. Hegel's younger followers used parallel reasoning to argue for a more radical response. Tomorrow must be better, so let us get rid of today as fast as possible. This revolutionary political response to the march of history was a major feature of Karl Marx's position, a position which, for all its "scientific" aspirations and distinctive features, did not escape the fundamental rationalism of the Kantian assumptions. However gentle and pious a man Kant himself was, much killing could be done in the name of historical "progress", and eventually it was.

Historical "progress" was not the only reason for killing people. For once one accepts, as Kant does in his essay on universal history, that human nature changes over time, then there is no theoretical bar to accepting that human nature may change with place also, and this was Kant's younger contemporary Herder's response.[26] Herder emphasized the importance of national character. On the Oxford philosopher R.G. Collingwood's interpretation, Herder showed that human nature is not unified but diversified, so that each race has a separate fixed set of fundamental characteristics. This dividing up of human nature "means that the task of creating or improving a culture is assimilated to that of creating or improving a breed of domestic animals. Once Herder's theory of race is accepted," Collingwood warned, "there is no escaping the Nazi marriage laws."[27]

While Kant effectively permitted in his essay a variety of imperfect human natures and thus a variety of imperfect values at different times, only one version of human nature and only one central point of view of value—that of the final perfect state—was truly right. Thus, even with so fundamental and novel a theory of historical change, he did not leave behind the main Enlightenment assumption that there is a single ultimately correct point of view. It was in this totalitarianism that the future dangers lay, and this feature that the Nazis and the Stalinists, among so many others, inherited. This fundamentally rationalist[28]—often called "historicist"—tradition in philosophy of historical "progress" speaks for itself in terms of its importance for and influence on the first part of the twentieth century. The approach defines one of the major philosophical traditions in philosophy of history, a tradition continuing in the Marxian and post-Marxian philosophies which are still strongly influential in continental Europe,[29] and a tradition opposed in particular to the Enlightenment-based empiricism of "analytical" philosophy.

A few otherwise "analytical" philosophers objected to the rationalist tradition in philosophy of history on substantive rather than "analytical" grounds. This involved not just an anti-speculative reaction on the part of empiricist philosophical minimalists against the historicist tradition's rationalist assumptions, but also a strongly felt reaction against the tradition's moral and political implications as they were in practice implemented. Thus Karl Popper dedicated his 1957 book *The Poverty of Historicism* to the "memory of the countless men and women of all creeds or nations or races who fell victims to the fascist and communist belief in Inexorable Laws of Historical Destiny."[30] One perhaps perverse effect of such objections was to keep alive on the fringes of the "analytical" tradition a place for discussion of substantive philosophy of history.[31]

A number of different grounds are available for the rejection of historicism. First, it should be noted that "historicism" has a range of meanings. Here "historicism" is taken in the rough but widely understood sense given to it by Popper, for whom it connotes in particular a belief in a pattern of historical development such that a degree of prediction of the historical future is possible, together with a belief that the historical future is a moral improvement over the present.[32] Popper makes it clear that historicism, conceived as describing the ongoing pattern of history, is objectionable as a factual historical description. As Wilkins notes, drawing on the Kant of *The Critique of Pure Reason* rather than on the Kant of "Idea of a Universal History."[33] "Popper, like Kant, denies that history taken as a whole is knowable: Popper denies that history taken as a whole 'exists', while in the Kantian terminology history in this sense is not an object of possible experience."[34] Thus it is not merely that historicism is a false historical story. For to claim that the historicist story is false would leave it open to the historicist to try to get the historicist story right, using, perhaps, Popper's own view of what can properly justify a claim to knowledge. Popper's objection is rather that the historicist kind of story cannot be provided at all. It is an impossible aim.

Wilkins shows us that one reason why history "does not exist", for Popper, is because the "realm of facts" is "infinitely rich", and thus cannot be conceived of as an existing whole which could be "considered as a legitimate object of inquiry."[35] "Of course", Wilkins continues, "strictly speaking, the most that Popper's thesis that description like all inquiry is necessarily selective could possibly yield in the present connection would be that we cannot know whether or not history taken as a whole exists."[36] "Whole" here is taken to involve expressing "the totality of all the properties or aspects of a thing", Wilkins notes. But it is not a very interesting failure of history that it cannot possibly discuss everything. Every science is in that position. Wilkins records, however, Popper's admission in *The Poverty of Historicism* that "whole" can also refer to those properties which make something an organized structure rather than a "mere heap."[37] Allowing, Wilkins continues, that a "whole" history cannot be known, does it follow that the history of mankind (say) is a "mere heap"?[38] Could it not be an organized structure? Wilkins believes that Popper holds the view that the history of mankind is indeed structured owing to its containing individuals. "Briefly I want to suggest that Popper has mistakenly assumed that history can have no moral meaning *because* it cannot be known as a whole or totality [in the sense of all its properties] when actually all that would be required in this connection to show that history could have moral meaning or significance would be to show that history could be a structured whole [in the sense of being an organized structure]."[39] "If we are to make any sense of Hegel's claim that he knows the whole of history, this claim must be construed as meaning that he knows certain properties, aspects, and relations of history, namely those which make it an organized structure."[40] In consequence, "...despair over finding a single overall moral meaning in history ('*the* meaning of history,' as it is sometimes called) is no reason to despair over history's having a plurality of moral meanings, (at least) as many moral meanings as it has structures."[41] Wilkins concedes "with some reluctance" that Popper cannot block the historicist who claims that history does exist as a structured whole, with moral significance.[42] Thus "the historicist may have erred...in not seeing sufficiently that [a structured whole] may be structured in many ways."[43] However, "...the greater the number of structures something may have, the more remote are the chances that all of these structures will be morally desirable...", and Popper is right to think that moral meaning cannot be inferred from historical reality.[44]

A further ground for the claimed impossibility of historicism is that, according to Popper, historicists are engaged in historical prediction, and it is here that the impossibility lies, for there can be no laws of history and consequently a predictive science of society is impossible.[45] Popper backs this up with a philosophy of science which explains the nature of the kind of laws which can warrant prediction. But whether or not this objection is effective against historicism,[46] a further ground for the impossibility of the historicist kind of story, according to Popper, is that the method underlying historicism is not a "critical" method.[47] For Popper, the ultimate ground for justifying claims to truth, including historical truth, is by "testing" those claims, and this is something which we *ought* to do.[48] We *ought* not to accept beliefs—and for that matter institutions—dogmatically. Dogma is a kind of moral error. There is for Popper (and indeed for many others) a perceived congruence between a properly structured scientific community and a democracy or "open society."[49] To get things scientifically right is also to get things politically right. As Wilkins puts it, "I believe that Popper would have been correct if he had argued that some approximation to the ideal of the open society is a necessary condition of scientific progress, at least in the long run."[50]

A corollary of Popper's position is that we are never entitled to certainty that we have achieved final truth. Our best scientific method can perhaps exclude the false account, but cannot guarantee that what remains is a unique and certain truth. We are not entitled to certainty about reality, although we may nevertheless have good reason to make some claims about reality rather than others. As Wilkins quotes from Popper, just because there is no general criterion—as opposed to definition—of truth, that does not mean "that the choice between competing theories is arbitrary."[51] Truth, for Popper, operates as a kind of unachievable yet controlling political ideal. By contrast, the absolute dogmatic certainty embodied in any kind of historicist position makes it completely unacceptable as a factual historical description. As such, historicism cannot in principle express the truth about historical reality.

While there is no doubt that Popper rejects historicism on deeply held moral grounds and indeed that this substantially motivates his application of his empiricist epistemology to historicism,[52] the foundations of his famous argument are not as explicitly moral as they might be. In principle the rejection of historicism could be purely moral: thus historicism—certainly of Kant's type—typically involves the claim that the end justifies the means. Moreover, whatever is, is right: "In short", Wilkins observes, "historicism tells us that the goal or end toward which history is moving is morally desirable *because* history is moving toward that goal or end."[53] It is therefore open to Popper to reject historicism explicitly on the ground of these immoral claims alone, independently of any reference to the epistemology of the matter. A different rejection of historicism is provided by Isaiah Berlin.[54] Historicism is rejected by Berlin primarily on the ground that it embodies a single comprehensive moral point of view, and this offends against Berlin's moral pluralism.[55] The essence of Berlin's moral pluralism is the belief that there are many different conflicting moral points of view, each offering a comprehensive view of life. Since each of these many different moral points of view is truly comprehensive, then each moral point of view must account also for the values of opposing moral points of view, either by explicitly denying the conflicting values, or by explaining those other values away, or at best by accepting those other values but holding them as essentially secondary to its own primary values. Conflicting moral points of view are therefore incompatible with each other at least in terms of what each point of view claims as the primary value or range of values. For example—to refer to one of Berlin's favorite conflicts—a comprehensive moral point of view which puts the value of political freedom first is incompatible with a comprehensive moral point of view which puts the value of political equality first.

Recognizing that there are many conflicting values is not an abstract "analytical" point of moral theory with no substantive implications, nor is it a claim merely expressing the obvious fact that people sometimes differ in their moral views. Berlin's pluralist position implies that it is substantively morally wrong to unify values. Any attempt to impose on the world a "unified" comprehensive moral point of view is totalitarianism, and this is in itself wrong. Similarly, any moral philosophy which seeks a single moral solution is inherently wrong. Such totalitarianism is bound to be wrong, for no comprehensive moral point of view is ever really unified, but is rather an improper triumph of some values over those others with which it is inconsistent.[56]

If we accept Kant's version of the claim that the world is a rational place, we can regard the history of the human race as the progressive—if bloody—realization of a rational plan of nature to bring about a final perfect moral state. As observed earlier, on this approach only one version of human nature and only one central point of view—that of the final perfect state—is supposed to be truly right. While this directly offends against Berlin's moral pluralism, this historicist position is not merely an expression of the totalitarian moral viewpoint of the final perfect state. Essentially involved with that viewpoint is a descriptive outline of the whole of human history. The totalitarianism which Berlin rejects is not merely the totalitarianism of a single comprehensive *moral* point of view. He rejects also the totalitarianism of a single *descriptive* point of view, and rejects in consequence the single whole moral and descriptive outline of history.[57]

Thus Berlin's rejection of historicism is not based solely on a moral pluralism, but also involves rejecting totalitarian description. In his essay "The purpose of philosophy"[58] he makes clear that the attitudes of people to each other differ profoundly, depending on their beliefs. "The world of a man who believes that God created him for a specific purpose, that he has an immortal soul, that there is an afterlife in which his sins will be visited upon him, is radically different from the world of a man who believes in none of these things; and the reasons for action, the moral codes, the political beliefs, the tastes, the personal relationships of the former will deeply and systematically differ from those of the latter." These beliefs are not just theological or moral but include factual beliefs: "the facts...are not at all identical for all men at all times."[59] for they are classified and arranged against the background of their general conception of the world. This general conception embodies not only ideas about good and evil, freedom and slavery, and similar moral or political notions, but also ideas about causation, truth and falsehood. The comprehensive point of view which forms a person's approach to the world therefore frames not merely their *moral* understanding but their *factual* understanding also. Berlin's pluralism embodies both moral pluralism and factual pluralism.

Berlin's factual pluralism is such that one central ground for rejecting historicism is precisely that historicism embodies a single comprehensive point of view, without the word "moral" (at one level of expression) needing to be attached to this.[60] Neither a moral nor a factual comprehensive point of view (supposing, possibly unreasonably at this point of the argument, that we were able to separate them) should be "totalitarian", for both the moral and the factual are structured in terms of background beliefs about which people may differ, and—more importantly for Berlin—differ not just legitimately but justifiably.[61] Pluralism lies at the heart of Berlin's political philosophy, just as criticism lies at the heart of Popper's.

The upshot of Popper's and Berlin's objections to historicism is that historicism is challenged by them on grounds which are in part substantively moral and political. Popper, for example, is praised by Wilkins for keeping alive professional philosophical recognition of big issues: "freedom and determinism, the role of institutions in scientific and political development, and the moral meaning or significance of the historical process."[62] Such important matters were being lost sight of by philosophers who thought, and who thought they had reason to think, that philosophers should not engage in matters of substance, moral or otherwise. In some ways more clearsighted than Popper, Berlin recognized that, just as historicism itself had no place in the insubstantial "analytical" linguistic philosophy as it was developing in the middle of the twentieth century, so his own moral and political interests, being equally substantive with historicism,[63] had no place also. The rights and wrongs of Hegel's or Marx's substantive philosophies of history, like other substantive moral and political judgments, were not matters on which philosophers, as philosophers, had any professional expertise. Political philosophy, as Peter Laslett commented in the middle of the twentieth century, was dead.[64] Rather than try to change the new direction of philosophy and in any event—perhaps unlike Popper—recognizing the intellectual quality at the centre of linguistic philosophy, Berlin gave up his academic position in "analytical" philosophy and turned to the history of political thought.[65] In conclusion at this point, substantive rationalist philosophy of history stimulated an opposing major anti-historicist tradition, exemplified most famously by Popper and Berlin, a tradition which is essentially to be understood as a certain kind of substantive political philosophy, and the discussion of which is standardly informed by political attitudes. Philosophy of history in the properly "analytical" tradition, by contrast, had to be something else entirely.[66]

Given the peripheral nature of philosophy of history on the "analytical" approach to philosophy, and given the political dangers of the subject when undertaken in an historicist way, why study it? In the middle of the twentieth century, after a world war fought in part against the totalitarian ideas derived from the rationalist tradition in philosophy of history, and facing a cold war against those committed to a certain Marxist theory of historical progress, many "analytical" philosophers interested in history unsurprisingly felt that they had to explain and defend the nature of their subject. Writing one of the first introductions to "analytical" philosophy of history in 1949, W.H. Walsh observed that he "must begin by justifying the very existence of his subject."[67] Even by 1967, Walsh still thought that "philosophy of history remains only marginally respectable in British universities."[68] This was partly because, as Walsh in particular saw it, there was no agreement among philosophers about whether history was a "legitimate undertaking", since it had been "expelled from the body of knowledge proper by Descartes."[69] Additionally, Walsh's acknowledgement of the subject's lowly status within the "analytical" tradition reflected his own view that philosophers should "reflect on the nature and conditions"[70] of knowledge and morality, rather than themselves speculate on matters of substance concerning the "secret of history", an approach which was "anathema to the cautious British mind."[71]

Apart from the uniquely influential contribution of Michael Oakeshott in 1933,[72] the interest in philosophy of history conceived as a branch of the tradition of "analytical" philosophy—what Walsh described as reflecting on the "nature and conditions" of historical knowledge[73]—surfaced in print in the 1940's in three very different works: 1942 saw the publication of "The Function of General Laws in History" by Carl G. Hempel,[74] and saw also the death of R.G. Collingwood, whose 1930's lectures at Oxford on philosophy of history formed his *The Idea of History*, which appeared posthumously in 1946.[75] 1945 saw the publication of Karl R. Popper's *The Open Society and Its Enemies*,[76] a work which drew on Popper's philosophy of science, which was published in its first form in his *The Logic of Scientific Discovery* of 1934.[77] As Wilkins observes, Popper should not be thought of "only or chiefly as a critic of Hegel and Marx,"[78] and he is not so treated here.[79]

Collingwood, an historian and archaeologist as well as a philosopher,[80] shared the empiricist tradition in a distinctive idealist way. It is a familiar feature of empiricism, first expressed most clearly by Bishop George Berkeley,[81] that reality can only be intelligibly conceived as it is experienced by us, rather than as it is "in itself." This was, in a way, also Hume's position, but Hume saw experience as delivering to us atomistic or simple impressions, accidentally combined with each other in complex ways. But a consistent empiricism, the empiricist idealist F.H. Bradley pointed out, should not assume such atomism, for experience comes "as a whole," and our factual judgments, in expressing only a part of experience, thereby alter what experience really delivers.[82] Bradley drew his idealism in part from Hegel (although Hegel was not an empiricist[83]), and Burleigh Taylor Wilkins in his discussion of Hegel describes the position under attack here as the "Myth of the Historically Given. The myth that something (direct awareness of physical objects? sense data?) is immediately given to us prior to the intervention of our cognitive faculties."[84] This myth, Wilkins continues, has a specific analog in historical understanding: "the belief that the historian must come to historical data or evidence without prior commitments or interpretative categories of any sort—that he must 'let the facts speak for themselves.'"[85] To describe experienced reality is inevitably to impose a conceptual structure upon it, a structure which does not copy any structure in reality.

Collingwood was strongly influenced by Bradley. It is reality as it is thought by us which is central, and this is most apparent in historical inquiry. History consists of human actions. To know the past is to know it as it was known by the historical agents involved. To know the past is therefore to know it as it was thought by those involved. Historians need to project themselves into the mental position of past agents and see things from their point of view, to think the very same thoughts. Historians understand past actions through seeing them in the terms in which the agents themselves saw them. History requires an imaginative reconstruction or re-enactment of the past, and it is this which provides the criterion of historical fact. The test of historical fact is the coherence of the imaginative reconstruction engaged in by the historian. All this is a way of making sense of so-called "empathetic understanding", an approach often thought distinctive of historical method.

The holistic idealism of Bradley and Collingwood did not affect Popper and Hempel. Their philosophical attitudes were particularly influenced by the general approach of the "analytical" tradition outlined above, and also specifically by the empiricism and positivism of the Vienna Circle, a group organized by Moritz Schlick which met from the 1920's until the late 1930's, and which expressed philosophical beliefs derived from the

Austrian physicist and philosopher Ernst Mach. On Mach's view, our best scientific theories are justifiable only by reference to our sensations, and are acceptable only in so far as they continue to apply successfully to the world. Mach's position was an extension of Hume's empiricism: everything we know must be derived from our experiences.[86] This approach involves attempting to build our entire understanding using only the building blocks of the immediately perceived data of the senses.

But Mach's—and so the Vienna Circle's—position was not only atomistically empiricist but also strongly positivist. They believed that science alone provides proper knowledge, but, more than this, they believed that science was the only proper way of saying anything at all. They attempted to show that only scientific statements are meaningful, because only scientific statements are verifiable. The point of this was to find a criterion which would distinguish proper science from metaphysical and other speculation by showing everything but scientific statements to be meaningless. Even philosophers should abide by the rules of language used in science. Since on the positivist view science alone achieves knowledge, philosophy can make no substantive contribution to knowledge,[87] and philosophers are left merely to analyze the meanings of sentences. The approach thereby sets for philosophy a standard of clarity and exactness of meaning, a standard modelled on the clarity and exactness of meaning to be found in scientific statements. "Analytical" philosophers thus tend to be more austere in their language than speculative historicists and even many historians. They are so in order to keep a tight rein on meaning and take less risk in saying something false. This approach—known as "Logical Positivism"—was afterwards notorious for its failure to find a self-consistent criterion of meaningfulness and also for its failure to find, in the theory of meaning, a criterion for science. Despite these failures, the general attitudes of the Vienna Circle, embodying empiricism, the philosophical centrality of science and the requirement for philosophy of a scientific exactness of meaning, have remained influential in the "analytical" tradition.

In the light of these details, the word "analytical", in the context of contemporary "analytical" philosophy, is ambiguous in a number of ways. It can mean merely that the philosophy in question is "analytical" just in so far as it insists on clarity of meaning, with no more being implied. It can mean more: that the "analytical" philosophy in question insists on clarity of meaning and also embodies a certain theory of "clarity" of meaning. Sometimes "analytical" in this context implies that the embodied theory of "clarity" of meaning is one that requires philosophical expression in a natural language (itself conceived as essentially vague) to be readily translatable into the terms of a formal—preferably classical—logical system.[88] Sometimes "analytical" in this context implies that the embodied theory of "clarity" of meaning is one that takes natural language, with all its subtleties and distinctions, as inherently exact, so that concentration on ordinary usage will resolve philosophical difficulties.[89] These are the main views, although there are others.[90] While a strong degree of attention to linguistic meaning is essential to the "analytical" approach, the term, apart from the implications just noted, can also be taken to imply in addition a belief in empiricism, which, as observed earlier, is very influential within the tradition, although often in an extremely weak sense.[91] Sometimes, however, the word "analytical" is taken to imply empiricism specifically of a Humean kind, and it is then assumed that an analytical philosopher believes particularly in mechanism[92] and atomism,[93] or even determinism.[94] Sometimes empiricism in a strong but more general sense is taken to be implied, permitting the non-Humean holistic empiricist pragmatist W.V.O. Quine, for example, to count as one paradigm of an analytical philosopher.[95]

Again, when contemporary philosophy is described as "analytical", it is sometimes the Logical Positivist characterization of philosophy, with all its presuppositions, which is referred to. Opponents—and indeed sometimes friends—of "analytical" philosophy often incorrectly assume that philosophers who take problems of meaning seriously and write and reason according to exact standards must thereby also believe that science alone achieves knowledge. Thus various degrees of weak or strong positivism are sometimes taken to be implied by the term "analytical." Moreover, some opponents of "analytical" philosophy specifically oppose what are asserted to be its positivist presuppositions and illegitimately derive from that a further opposition to any methodological requirement of exactness of meaning. Thus any insistence on clarity and exactness of meaning is often associated by opponents of "analytical" philosophy with the positivist view that science is central.[96] There are, then, a multiplicity of connotations of the term "analytical" in the expression "analytical philosophy." Within the analytical tradition, the attention which analytical philosophers pay to the exact understanding of what they are themselves doing is such that confusions about the many connotations of the word "analytical" do not arise too often. Philosophers of history, however, often ride roughshod over them, while opponents of analytical philosophy of history, often opposed to being exact, are happy to present history as essentially confused, so that any "clarification" made by analytical philosophy is just another confusion.

Popper's approach, while sharing the Logical Positivists' general attitude to the centrality of science, differed from theirs in seeking a criterion for science in the logic of scientific method rather than in the theory of meaning. In a little more detail than the outline given earlier, Popper's philosophy of science involves two elements: an account of the logical status of the statements of a scientific theory, and an account of scientific procedure. Familiarly now, a scientific theory is seen as essentially a collection of scientific laws, which are analyzed as having the logical form of generalizations, of universal conditionals. Popper stressed that these universal generalizations are, in Kant's terminology, synthetic rather than analytic. As such they cannot, against the Logical Positivists' position, be verified. They can in principle, however, be falsified, and it is falsifiability which provides the Popperian criterion for science. This is not merely a point of logic but also one of method, for the essence of scientific method, in the light of this logical fact about scientific laws, is to remove what may be false laws from the corpus of existing scientific beliefs by seeking out falsifications of them, by testing them. It is the critical attitude expressed in the practice of testing received beliefs which best characterizes the scientific approach. Assuming that this is correct, and assuming also the centrality of science, this critical attitude has application to other subjects also.

Hempel shares with Popper this broad understanding of the nature of science[97] and in particular he shares the Humean view that causation is to be understood in terms of generalizations. He therefore shares the view that scientific explanations, which are essentially causal explanations, can be analyzed in terms of the place within them of scientific laws. Yet while Hempel and Popper share so much of the tradition in philosophy of science ultimately derived from Hume's atomistic empiricism, their explicit applications of philosophy of science to areas outside the philosophy of science, and in particular to history, are very different, and this is apparent in the 1940's publications referred to above. Popper, as noted earlier, used his philosophy of science to attack historicism and in the course of doing so came to be seen as making a contribution to substantive political philosophy, a philosophy in which the theory of causal explanation, while essential, had a subordinate place. Hempel, whose writing in this area is not remotely political, was the first of the two to publish an explicit application of their Humean philosophy of science to history in his "The Function of General Laws in History." W.H. Dray introduced widely used terminology in describing this analysis of explanation as the "covering law model of explanation."[98] As Wilkins notes in his *Has History Any*

Meaning?, "the history of the covering law model remains unwritten, but while it is present in Hume and J.S. Mill and even, as I have argued elsewhere, in a passage in Aristotle's *Posterior Analytics*, its importance to contemporary philosophy of history derives from the treatment and refinement it has received first from Popper in *The Logic of Scientific Discovery* and later from Hempel in several articles."[99] "I believe that...contemporary philosophy of history is largely an extended commentary on arguments presented by Popper."[100] Who started covering law theory is contentious, at least for some. In consequence, the covering law model of explanation is often referred to also as the "Popper-Hempel theory of explanation" or, for reasons which will shortly be apparent, as the "deductive-nomological theory of explanation."

In his 1942 article, Hempel asserts that the explanation of an event of some specific kind *E* consists in indicating its causes, and, further, that "the assertion that a set of events—say, of the kinds C_1, C_2,..., C_n—have caused the event to be explained, amounts to the statement that, according to certain general laws, a set of events of the kinds mentioned is regularly accompanied by an event of kind *E*."[101] There is, he makes clear,[102] no difference between displaying the cause of some event and showing that universal scientific laws cover that event. A scientific law expresses a regularity which occurs in the world, and an event is "covered" by that scientific law in so far as a statement asserting the occurrence of that event can be deduced from that law and from statements which assert the occurrence of the "causes."

An explanation of some event E therefore has to have the following valid deductive form:

Whenever $C_1 \ldots C_n$ then E;
$C_1 \ldots C_n$;
Therefore, E.

Each of the statements in this deductive argument must be true, which means, in this context, that it must be empirically warranted, although in principle it would be possible to accept this theory of explanation without relying on the empiricism assumed by Hempel and Popper. Hempel stresses that the "*C*" and "*E*" in a scientific explanation mark *kinds* of things, rather than unique entities.[103] This has to be so, for the "*C*" and "*E*" in the generalization "whenever *C* then *E*" must be the sort of thing that can recur, so that the "whenever" in the universal statement can operate properly.

Hempel's view that an explanation "consists in" indicating its causes, and that a certain kind of assertion about the cause of something "amounts to" a certain kind of deduction involving regularity, makes it clear that three things, which other philosophers might wish to separate, are here regarded as fully equivalent: indicating causation is both necessary and sufficient for explanation, and each of these is similarly both necessary and sufficient for displaying a general law in the required way. It follows that a position such as Aristotle's, which in effect allows or even enjoins us to explain something other than by stating what we understand to be its cause,[104] is ruled out. It also follows that there is no way of stating the cause of something other than by displaying a general law in the required way. In summary, we have here an analysis of causation and of explanation and of the place of general laws in our understanding which identifies each of these three with the other two, and which is completely general in its application. It is therefore not merely an analysis of *scientific* explanations, causes and laws[105] but an analysis of explanations, causes and laws wherever those terms are used.

This analysis, in the light of its background Humean assumptions, and together with its later elaborations, the various responses to them and its consequential modifications, define what came to be seen as a standard tradition in philosophy of science.[106] In a similar way discussion of the application of this analysis of explanation to history came to define a particular tradition in philosophy of history.

The initial application of Hempel's analysis of explanation to history, which he made himself in his 1942 article, is straightforward. It follows directly from Hempel's analysis of explanation that anything that appears in historical writing which does not match the covering law model of explanation simply fails to explain at all. When we add, to this analysis of explanation, the positivist position that science is the only way of achieving knowledge, and add also the view that science consists of theories embodying laws which explain in the required way, then anything that appears in historical writing which does not match the covering law model of explanation is to be rejected, not merely as an explanation, but also as a contribution to knowledge. Philosophy of history, in one sense, then has to consist simply in measuring historical writing against the standard set and noting how far it falls short. This is not a particularly *philosophical* measurement, for simple inspection of historical texts will suffice. Such inspection unsurprisingly reveals a general failure on the part of historians to achieve the standard now set for them.

In principle the analytical philosophical discussion of history could stop right here, but, rather than judge the entire discipline of history to be a general explanatory failure—although that is a correct conclusion to draw on the basis of the premisses involved—Hempel himself judges that, while historical writing hardly ever takes the form of a valid deductive argument, it should be regarded as a form of rhetoric which is appropriate for sketching to an uninformed reader the bones of knowledge which are buried within. It is strictly true, then, that historians fail to explain, but they do provide "explanation sketches."[107] Some justification exists for such historical practice in so far as the laws in question are often familiar and therefore tacitly assumed,[108] but often the presupposed laws are only true to a degree of approximation, and sometimes only statistical.[109] The vagueness of historical writing which the word "sketch" implies is appropriate in the latter cases.

Hempel completes his article by very briefly analysing in terms of covering law theory several features which have sometimes been claimed as distinctive of history. First, the historian's supposed concern with the "meaning" of historical events requires no peculiar mode of knowledge since, for Hempel, it is to be understood entirely in terms of causal connections. Ascertaining the meaning of historical events "consists in determining what other events are relevantly connected with the event in question, be it as 'causes' or as 'effects.'"[110] Hempel's second application to history of covering law theory involves analysing "empathetic understanding", which is sometimes thought—in particular by Collingwood—to be essential to historical explanation. This is the idea that we can explain by empathising with others, by projecting ourselves into their mental position and seeing things from their point of view. According to Hempel, however, this is merely a heuristic device, suggesting "psychological hypotheses which might serve as explanatory principles."[111] Finally, any attempt by an historian merely to describe rather than explain the past does not remove covering law theory in history, for universal hypotheses would necessarily connect his present data with the past events.[112]

In conclusion at this point, one tradition in philosophy of history derives from Hempel's article, which by 1959 had "attained the status of a kind of classic in the field", as Patrick Gardiner noted.[113] Subsequent work within this analytical tradition took two approaches, which presupposed one or other of two views about the status of Hempel's model of scientific explanation. The first of these took Hempel's model as *prescrip-*

tive for historians, and the second took it as *descriptive*. These two approaches were founded on different conceptions of the nature of philosophical analysis. It was explained above that "analytical" philosophy requires at least clarity and exactness of meaning, and that there are two main views about how this should be understood. On one view, derived from Logical Positivism, it is assumed that ordinary language is inherently vague, and any claim to exact knowledge which is to be taken seriously needs to be readily translatable into the terms of a rational model, itself best expressed in terms of a formal deductive system. The "standard" philosophy of science models our necessarily scientific rationality. In analytical philosophy of history we should therefore "rationally reconstruct" what historians do. We should note the purpose of history, to describe and explain what happened in the past, and show how that rationally ought to be done in the light of the scientific model. This approach takes the "standard" philosophy of science as prescriptive for historians, and in his 1942 article Hempel exemplified in a small way how this might be applied to historical explanation. The analytical philosopher of history, on this approach, is concerned with what an historical explanation *ought* to look like.

On the second analytical approach to philosophy of history, deriving its conception of analysis—although very rarely with any explicitness—from the later work of Wittgenstein,[114] it is assumed that ordinary language has the fullest possible range of literal and rhetorical resources, and that concentration on ordinary usage will resolve philosophical difficulties. Analytical philosophy of history is then conceived as ordinary language analysis of what is meant by certain distinctively historical modes of expression, method, evidence, and so forth. On this view we need to grasp what an historical explanation *is* rather than what it *ought* to be. We need to grasp what actually counts as an historical explanation, and it is historians themselves who are the proper judges of this. As Alan Donagan put it, "The facts I consider concern what historians actually recognize as explanations."[115] After giving examples, he added, "The Hempelian theory, therefore, contradicts at least some good historians' opinions about their explanations."[116] On this approach analytical philosophy of history is supposed to provide a theoretical *description* of what historians do, and can be falsified by the linguistic "facts", facts which embody, for example, what is "correctly" called an historical explanation.

The difference between these two analytical approaches to philosophy of history can be seen in differing standards of "correctness" here. There is no doubt that covering law theory contradicts some historians' views about what counts as a good historical explanation. On the first approach, so much the worse for history, since the standard of correctness is set by the scientific model. On the second approach, so much the worse for covering law theory, since the standard of correctness is set by the best understanding of historians. A certain amount of subsequent philosophy of history has suffered from ignorance, on the part of some contributors, as to which side of the debate about the nature of philosophical analysis they were actually on. Curiously, it was philosophers who tended to suffer from this, rather than historians.[117]

These two approaches to historical explanation, by which an explanation is either judged by reference to good historical practice or by reference to a certain model of science, should not be confused with two other approaches to explanation which also ought to be noted.[118] One way of understanding a good explanation is to understand it as removing puzzlement on the part of those hearing it. If the explanation removes such puzzlement, then it is a success. If it does not, and such puzzlement continues, then the explanation is a failure. We often expect schoolteachers to be good at explaining things in this way. This understanding of the nature of explanation is perhaps best described in W. B. Gallie's philosophy of history, where he gave an account of the followability of an historical story.[119] Stories, Gallie said, should be self-explanatory in that they should be followable by the reader. If the reader's subjective puzzlement is removed or kept at a distance then the story is explanatory; otherwise not. A story thus has to pass a test for being an explanation which is set by the subjective capacity of a reader to follow it.[120]

By contrast, the physical sciences try to explain the way the world works, and if we accept the Popper-Hempel approach then we will accept that what makes a scientific explanation a good one is that it correctly gives the causes of things. On the other hand, if the explanation says something scientifically false, then it is a bad explanation. But the kind of explanation which gives the causes of things is in principle very different from the kind of explanation which successfully removes puzzlement. The kind of explanation which successfully removes puzzlement may or may not give the causes of things, while our best explanations of the way the world works may be impossible for most people to understand.

There are therefore two kinds of explanation. One kind of explanation is measured against the existing understanding of people. The other kind of explanation is measured against the way the world is. One kind of explanation is measured by a "subjective" test. The other is measured by an "objective" test. But it should not be assumed that historical explanation is to be measured in "subjective" terms and scientific explanation is to be measured in "objective" terms. It is an important advance to realize that the two theories of explanation cannot be opposed to each other, for each is doing a different job. Each theory of explanation involves two parts: a question, and an answer. One difference between the two theories of explanation is marked by the fact that each asks a different question. On the "subjective" theory of explanation the right question to ask is: what is it that removes subjective puzzlement on the part of an audience? On the "objective" theory of explanation the right question to ask is: what is it that objectively accounts for reality being the way that it is? It is begging the central question in the theory of historical knowledge merely to assume that this contrast of questions reflects, respectively, the contrast between history and science. It may be that, ultimately, "objectivity" of any kind is impossible, and that both scientific and historical explanations are to be measured against a "subjective" test. Conversely, a non-causal yet "objective" test may be suitable for both. In principle we might find history achieving an "objective" test better than science does, in giving a better account for reality being the way that it is.[121]

As noted, Hempel applied his covering law analysis in particular to three areas of history: "meaning" in history; empathetic understanding; and the use of general laws in connecting present data with past events. Among professional analytical philosophers discussion of the "meaning" of history was subsequently interpreted as discussion of the place and nature of causation in history. None argued in favor of the "meaning" of history in terms of the kind of religious teleology left over from speculative rationalist philosophy of history, and those philosophers still wedded to some kind of historicism tended to be Marxian in outlook, a position which did not need the concept of historical "meaning."[122] Other than with regard to the issue of causation, the "meaning" of history is now a matter to be analyzed away through clarification of the meaning of "meaning," and Wilkins provides a very useful summary of this in his *Has History Any Meaning?*[123]

The second area of history to which Hempel applied his covering law theory was that of empathetic understanding, and his contribution stimulated serious and lengthy further discussion, led in particular by W. H. Dray's *Laws and Explanation in History.*[124] Where Hempel had complained that historians typically do not spell out the laws and theories supporting what purported to be their explanations, Dray gave a response which developed Collingwood's approach: the reason why historians do not spell out the theory behind their explanations is that there is no theory, and hence no need. Historical explanations consist in giving reasons for actions, and the explanations are sufficient insofar as the reasons given are followable. Moreover, we can express this without the usual metaphor of "seeing things from other people's point of view." What we typically want as historians and as readers of history, Dray points out,[125] is a reconstruction of a person's calculation of the means to be adopted towards his chosen end in the light of the circumstances in which he found himself. This calculation gives the person's reasons for acting as he did, and it shows that what was done was the thing to have done for the reasons given. The action is thus displayed as having been an "appropriate" thing to have done, rather than the thing always done, and in this way the explanation contrasts with the requirements of covering law theory.[126] Covering law theory is nevertheless available for historians to use: "We give reasons if we can, and turn to empirical laws if we must."[127] Much discussion followed Dray's highly influential book, but the detail of the debate has moved to the philosophy of rational action as a subject area in its own right, and later advances have been consumed by philosophers of history rather than produced by them.[128]

Wilkins himself does not take Dray's position very seriously as an attack on covering law theory, however, and in effect assimilates it to the covering law model.[129] In *Has History Any Meaning?* he concludes that it seems reasonable to allow that reasons can be included among the causal conditions of human actions,[130] saying also that "while I remain troubled by the tensions between human agency and the prediction or explanation of human actions using general laws, I provisionally endorse the covering law model as the only model that satisfactorily accounts for both the generality and the factually informative nature of many explanations in both the physical and the social sciences."[131] Wilkins goes beyond the usual discussion of covering law theory by commenting on Popper's "situational logic," where an historical explanation tacitly uses "the trivial general law that sane persons as a rule act more or less rationally."[132] Approving Alan Donagan's position, Wilkins allows that an explanation may be trivial by being obvious without being trivial in the sense of unimportant,[133] while, however typical the use of trivial laws in history may be, this should not be taken as a defining characteristic of history.[134] Donagan also argues, however, that "analytic truths play an essential role in historical explanations."[135] At the centre of one of Donagan's examples is the following supposedly analytic truth: "All men who resolve to achieve a certain end at all costs, and who judge that only by doing a certain act can it be achieved, will do that act."[136] Wilkins rightly doubts just how far such examples really are analytic,[137] including in a footnote[138] Popper's important point that the analytic/synthetic distinction rests for real languages primarily on the attitudes of [say] physicists to their theories, since they may choose to interpret them as either factual or as consisting of implicit definitions. Wilkins understands Popper's situational logic in the following way: "we construct with reference to 'the logic of the situation' models of rationality by means of which we seek to assess the appropriateness or rational adequacy of an agent's response to what is to him a problematic situation calling for some decision or action on his part."[139] What we have, in Popper's situational logic, "is an appraisal of the rational adequacy of [a person's] behavior, given what we know about his situation and his beliefs about his situation."[140] An appraisal of rational appropriateness, however, is to be contrasted with an explanation.[141]

The third area of history to which Hempel applied his covering law theory was that of historical research. The use of general laws, in Hempel's way, to connect present data with past events has been rarely discussed by those later philosophers persuaded of the general correctness of the covering law approach, if only because it was not at all clear how it could be done. One problem here was what counted as an historical "fact."[142] Put simply, facts are normally understood in a Humean way to be the kinds of experienceable things which, according to standard Popperian philosophy of science, can be used to falsify universal generalizations. They are, relative to generalizations, epistemologically primary. But *historical* facts seem to be something different. Following Hempel's remarks,[143] historians would need generalizations in order to construct the "facts" themselves. Given this, generalizations are epistemologically primary relative to historical facts. In which direction is the epistemological primacy? Or is it in both directions at once? Is there a general answer at all? And how can any answer make Hempel's position consistent with Humean empiricism?[144] Popper gave some attention to this, of a kind.[145] Wilkins notes Popper's concern with such "circularity of evidence and theory."[146] and argues that "In cases where the theories the historian brings to the historical record are not the same as the theories initially used in the collection of the facts found in the record, there seems to be not even a prima facie reason to suppose that the facts in the records could not serve as an independent test of such theories, at least as independent, say, as the data used in crucial experiments in physics."[147] In a very valuable chapter Wilkins displays the many confusions in Popper's position, and also shows the larger issues of metaphysics and epistemology which are presupposed here.[148]

A particular contribution to the understanding of the epistemology of historical facts appears in recent work by C. A. J. Coady.[149] Coady notes that a vast amount of historical knowledge depends in practice on testimony, both written and oral, and argues that trust in the testimony of others is epistemologically fundamental. Coady quotes from David Hume's *Inquiry*: "there is no species of reasoning more common, more useful, and even necessary to human life, than that which is derived from the testimony of men and the reports of eye-witnesses and spectators."[150] Despite this, for Coady it is the Humean approach which is particularly at fault, although not only Hume's. Hume shared with Descartes, Kant and indeed most philosophers until the twentieth century the view that the first-person point of view was foundational for knowledge. On this approach the ultimate test of truth lies with the individual alone, whether in terms of Descartes' clearly and distinctly perceived ideas, or in terms of the empiricist's directly perceived sense data.

Hume's "reductionist" thesis was that the reason for believing the testimony of witnesses and historians is not that there is some *a priori* connection between testimony and reality, but because we are accustomed to find a conformity between them. Coady notes that, apart from being false to practice, this approach assumes that it is a mere contingency that we have found a conformity between testimony and reality, so that, as a result of my individual checking of other people's reports against reality, I might in principle find a total lack of correlation between the reports and the facts reported. But it is unintelligible to imagine a situation of no conformity between testimony and reality. If there were no conformity then we could never correct each other, since that would involve giving correct information, which is contrary to the supposition of no conformity. Since we do have a practice we call testimony, then we have a practice which is reliable in the face of checking, that is, we have a general correlation between testimony and reality. While it may be a mere contingency that we have testimony-cum-reality, that does not mean that the general conformity between testimony and reality is also contingent.[151] It is therefore false that our reliance upon testimony could be justified by personal observation. There is a general reliability of testimony which does not depend on observation. Coady's "fundamental insight," shared with Donald Davidson,[152] is that language-based communication is only possible between beings whose outlooks overlap to a great extent. As Wittgenstein put it, a language requires agreement not only in definitions but also in judgments.

Coady applies this epistemology to history, and in particular defends it against the position of R.G. Collingwood.[153] Coady characterizes Collingwood as thinking that, put into practice, such a method as Coady's would lead to what Collingwood called "scissors-and-paste history," where the historian receives a mass of reported facts from previous historical writers. From these he selects and edits excerpts.[154] Collingwood's position was rather that, in history properly undertaken, there is an imaginative reconstruction or re-enactment of the past, and it is this which provides the criterion of historical fact. Moreover, historians should take no statements on anyone else's authority.

Collingwood illustrated his own position with an example[155] in which, Coady tries to argue, Collingwood himself takes certain testimony for granted. Coady, however, fails to recognize that it was a *decision* by Collingwood to accept a certain report as testimony, and that it was that decision which gave the testimony in question the status of truth. Collingwood's position, quoted by Coady from *The Idea of History*, is that "there are for historical thought no fixed points...just as there are properly speaking no authorities, so there are properly speaking no data."[156] On Collingwood's approach, all evidence which purports to testify to the truth is in principle revisable, and the test of revisability is the coherence of the imaginative reconstruction engaged in by the historian. The result of that reconstruction will involve ascribing truth to some claims made by those "testifying."

What underlies Collingwood's idealist position is the view that no facts are interpretation-free, and there is the kind of circularity of evidence and theory mentioned earlier. Yet Collingwood's presentation of the historian's imaginative reconstruction of the past through empathetic understanding is, in the terms introduced earlier, an epistemologically first-person point of view. By contrast, the appeal to received historical tradition, to testimony, as being to some degree essentially authoritative of truth, is what might be called a third-person epistemological position, one which places us, in effect, in Wittgenstein's public space. In what sense can the authority of imaginative reconstruction be shared? Much work remains to be done in clarifying the issues here.

I have described Collingwood's position as "idealist." A number of philosophers of history did not accept the "realist" implications of Hempel's explicit position concerning the relationship between present data and past events, and argued that the past was "constructed" on the basis of present evidence rather than deduced in accordance with general laws.

These philosophers commonly tried to adopt an "idealist" metaphysics and analyzed historical knowledge in accordance with this, often very helpfully.[157] They were, however, rather overtaken by advances in metaphysics and epistemology taking place outside the philosophy of history, particularly in the understanding of realism and anti-realism.[158] Currently the discussion of such issues proceeds almost entirely outside the tradition of analytical philosophy of history.

While Hempel picked the three main areas already discussed for the application of covering law theory to history,[159] other philosophers gave particular attention to two further areas: "uniqueness" in history, and the place of "narrative" in history. As to the first of these, many historians take for granted a distinction (perhaps deriving from Aristotle) made by Windelband,[160] between "nomothetic" and "ideographic" sciences: the former are concerned to discover general laws for repeatable events and the latter are concerned with the unique and unrepeatable. History is then supposed to be an "ideographic" science.[161] However, the idea that historians attempt to cover essentially unique events is confused. Hempel made clear that "the symbols 'E,' 'C,' 'C_1,' 'C_2,' etc., stand for kinds or properties of events, not for what is sometimes called individual events."[162] This necessary reference to "kinds" of things in the account of covering law theory is not peculiar to Hempel's approach, but is a commitment which is shared by all who speak. The use of language is always more than the mere naming of things, and includes describing things, the application to them of kind-words. Hempel noted that historians rarely provide historical laws.[163] It is perhaps equally of note, from his point of view, that historians do not provide developed ways of classifying the kinds of historical matters with which they deal, so that laws may in principle be found to cover them. If physicists still used such everyday notions from the classification of experience as "table," "tree," and so forth, it is highly unlikely that their theories would have had even the most rudimentary form of existence. Historians have to describe and explain the past world, given assumptions as to what that world is. The many disagreements that there are between historians, and between historians and other human scientists, can be conceived by the covering law theorist to be, not necessarily disagreements about whether to use covering law theory at all, or disagreements about what laws lie behind their writings, but disagreements about what kinds of things people and historical events are. A proper historical science, on Hempel's approach, would sort out these things in ways which make plain the lawlike connections between them.

Against this approach, Dray rightly observes that "although historical enquiry may require generalization in the sense of bringing a subject matter under concepts, that is not equivalent to bringing it under laws."[164] While the application of general laws may presuppose the application of general concepts, the converse does not hold. Kinds of things may, despite being instances of general concepts, nevertheless have unique relationships with other things. The vague claim that historians are particularly concerned with the unique has been expressed for history, with some clarity, by Paul Veyne in his *Writing History: Essay on Epistemology*.[165] Veyne's position is that history is an ideographic science. In particular, history is a particular way of knowing things: that way of knowing things which, in contrast with science, involves concentrating upon those specific features which mark their difference from other things. It thus seeks the uniqueness of things.

There are other ways of knowing things besides concentrating upon their uniqueness. Things may be likened to other things with which they form a kind, and kinds of things are repeatable. The same thing may be known both as an instance of a generalization and as a unique individual. To know it as an instance of a generalization is to know it in the way that the sciences know it. To know it as a unique individual is to know it in the way that history knows it. The difference between science and history here is not a difference in subject matter, but a difference in the way of knowing, which amounts to a difference in the kinds of description which are given. To know something is always to know it under a description. To know something as an instance of a generalization is to know it under a description which abstracts from the many true details of that thing and picks out as relevant just those features which are, as kinds of features, repeatable. By contrast, to know something—the same thing—as a unique individual is to know it under a description which stresses the features which distinguish it from other things. Veyne understands history in terms of the concentration upon a type of description rather than upon a type of object, and any object—including those normally the province of the natural sciences—can be approached in this "historical" way.[166]

It follows that this definition of history, taken seriously, means that history is not essentially concerned with the study of human beings. Wilkins sees Popper as having a similar position: Popper extends the "use of the word 'historical' to include all the sciences interested in specific events."..“history has no distinctive subject matter; and if it did, this by itself would not make a history a distinctive discipline with its own special method; what history does have is an interest in specific or singular events."[167] If historians concentrate, as they obviously do, on human beings, then this is purely a contingent and therefore changeable interest. Naturally one may be interested in the reasons why historians are interested in, and use their detailed approach to, some things rather than others, but such reasons are themselves historical and changeable. Equally, this definition means that there is no essential reason why historians should concentrate on the past rather than on the present. Veyne's position extends to admitting doubt about whether the concentration upon the unique description is anything other than a temporary fashion. History may be no more than a temporary fashion in understanding the world.

To the covering law response that things, so described to a level of detail which stresses their difference from other things, cannot therefore be explained, Dray observes that bringing things under concepts is itself a way of explaining them.[168] "And when historians talk of giving explanations, this does appear sometimes to be what they mean."[169] Whether historians *ought* to mean this is another matter, as the covering law theorist could plausibly reply, adopting an alternative view of the nature of philosophical analysis. There the philosophical problem of uniqueness in history rests, at least for the present.

The second of the two post-Hempel areas for discussion among analytical philosophers regarding the application of covering law theory to history was the place of "narrative" in history. It was noted that the traditional rhetorical mode of expression in historical writing is that of the narrative story, although Wilkins observes that narrative "seems an unduly restrictive conception of what the historian does."[170] Narratives organise detailed descriptions for us in a chronologically ordered followable plot. Analytical philosophers who thought this feature of historical writing epistemologically important were, in part, commenting on Hempel's view of "meaning" in history. Hempel's replacement of the problem of "meaning" with the claim that it all came down to causal connections was addressed primarily through the question how far causal connections were present in historical narrative. Two works were of importance here:[171] Morton G. White's *Foundations of Historical Knowledge*[172] and Arthur C. Danto's *Analytical Philosophy of History*.[173] On White's and Danto's approach, narratives are texts which present in chronological order implicit causal explanations much as described by Hempel. It is the objective regularities involved in these explanations which alone give the narrative whatever objective explanatory force it may have.[174] Narrative as such is not a mode of explanation, but, in line with Hempel's approach, is part of the rhetorical presentation.

The issue was joined by the historian J.H. Hexter.[175] In his book Morton White considered that an historical "narrative" consisted primarily of descriptive and causal statements. For the narrative to be true, all the statements in it would have to be true.[176] The causal statements would be true in so far as implicit in them were well-confirmed valid covering law arguments of the kind spelt out by Hempel. Yet White recognized that historians' evaluations of historical works went beyond the mere assessment of the truth of all the constituent statements, and included also an assessment of whether the statements "ought" to have been included.[177] The justification of this latter assessment, White concluded, was ultimately a subjective one, a literary "fleshing out." In other words, we may read Morton White as having held that statements were selected in accordance with a narrative rhetorical structure, but that this fact was irrelevant to their truth, and thus irrelevant to the descriptive and explanatory function of an historical account.[178] Narratives, conceived as something other than their causal constituents, do not explain.

Hexter characterized this position of White's as one which falsely attempted to assimilate history to science.[179] White denied any assimilation of history to science, and pointed to the considerable room which his analysis allowed for historical writing to contain a subjective, literary, unscientific element. However, Hexter's complaint lay precisely against the fact that White did not allow those literary elements of historical writing outside the skeleton of explanatory and descriptive statements to be expressive of knowledge of the historical past. It was not White's claim that the literary elements were there which offended Hexter, but rather the implication that "literary" elements had nothing to do with knowledge, that any feature of historical writing outside White's "scientific" skeleton had no explanatory or truth-telling use. Such additional elements, which Hexter called elsewhere the "rhetoric" of history,[180] were themselves for Hexter an essential way of expressing historical knowledge. The unresolved question became this: does the rhetorical side of historical writing—the ordering or "employment"[181] of statements in a narrative, apart from any causal claims which may be involved—have an explanatory or truth-telling use?[182] Only a "fancy view of historical truth," claimed Morton White without argument,[183] would permit such a thing.

"A fancy view of historical truth" means any view of truth contrary to that presupposed by the "correct" model of science, the now "standard" empiricist model shared with Popper. Was that model correct? Had it been fully expressed? In a number of ways—for example, the lowly place given by Hempel to statistical generalizations in science,[184] or the nature of kinds and of classification in scientific theory[185]—the model needed further development. However, despite the remarkable clarity of Hempel's philosophy of scientific explanation when he outlined it for history, such development was nevertheless rightly understood as part of the ongoing philosophy of *science* rather than the philosophy of *history*. Hempel's very brief excursion into reflection on history was merely a useful way of explaining his position in philosophy of science, and it was in philosophy of science that the next important philosophical move occurred.

Quite independently of work in philosophy of history, a revolution in the philosophy of science began in 1962 with the publication of Thomas S. Kuhn's *The Structure of Scientific Revolutions*.[186] Kuhn, primarily an historian rather than a philosopher of science of the standard kind, noted that historical research revealed that science in the past had not operated in ways which accorded with the requirements of the standard empiricist model. "The more carefully [historians] study, say, Aristotelian dynamics, phlogistic chemistry, or caloric thermodynamics, the more certain they feel that those once current views of nature were, as a whole, neither less scientific nor more the product of human idiosyncrasy that those current today...myths can be produced by the same sorts of methods and held for the same sorts of reasons that now lead to scientific knowledge."[187] Kuhn suggested that scientists normally operated against the vague background of an accepted general understanding of the world or "paradigm", an understanding which framed not only the answers to scientific questions but also the questions which it was thought appropriate to ask. Part of the process of "normal" science was to articulate with explicit clarity the detailed implications of the paradigm, and this detailed development might well include in part Popperian-style falsifications of such theories as were offered as the latest expressions of the paradigm. However, the history of science disclosed that paradigms collapsed not generally because of Popperian falsifications but for a variety of pragmatic reasons. A period of "revolutionary" science followed the recognition that an existing paradigm did not command confidence, and in this period scientists cast around for a new approach which, despite being very poorly articulated in its initial form, might offer hope of further understanding in the future. The history of science therefore did not disclose the greater and greater accumulation of knowledge but rather a pattern of revolutionary changes between periods of normal science. Apart from a period of revolution, the best science at any time was produced against an unquestioned background of accepted presuppositions.

Kuhn's work was fascinating to many disciplines and widely influential, indeed more influential than most works of philosophy in the twentieth century, perhaps because it seemed to undermine long-established positivist attitudes in philosophy and to undermine in particular the standard empiricist philosophy of science.[188] A certain vagueness of expression allowed for a wide range of implications to be drawn.[189] Earlier it was noted that there were two different approaches to analytical philosophy. On one approach, analytical philosophy requires clarity of meaning in the sense that proper understanding is best expressed in the terms of a formal rational model. On the other approach, analytical philosophy takes natural languages as inherently exact, in such a way that ordinary language use is a paradigm case of correct use. The contrast between these two approaches yielded a contrast between two analytical approaches to philosophy of history. Where, for example, covering law theory conflicted with historians' judgments about good explanations, on the first approach it was so much the worse for history, since the standard of correctness was set by the scientific model, while on the second approach it was so much the worse for covering law theory, since the standard of correctness was set by the best understanding of historians. On the first approach, covering law theorists were taken to be speaking for science itself in trying to impose on historians the covering law model. The historians' position was rhetorically weak, given the generally undoubted successes of natural science.

But for those who accepted Kuhn's position—and even for those who did not—this approach could no longer be accepted. Covering law theorists were seen as speaking for themselves, not for science, since science—conceived as the real judgments of real scientists in the real world as disclosed by the history of science—did not fit their model any more than history—conceived as the real judgments of real historians in the real world—did. Covering law theorists were therefore forced to face a dilemma paralleling that which historians had hitherto faced: given a conflict between real science and their own rational model, which should be taken as pre-eminent? The rhetorical high ground which had previously been theirs was theirs no longer. Even the most obstinate covering law theorists could no longer rely on science itself for support, and they were in no position to rely on pure reason alone.

However one might respond to this problem, a powerful interest in the history of science was generated. Surely Kuhn was wrong about the reality of the history of science? Surely scientific practice did accord with the standard model? Turn to history and find out. On the other hand, one might interpret Kuhn's position as a straightforward Popperian falsification of philosophy of science by an appeal to the facts of the history of science. Either way the history of science became center stage for philosophers of science. Historical understanding suddenly became necessary.

Philosophers of history, aware of these developments, could no longer impose on history a well-founded model of *science*, whatever abstract philosophical justification there might be for the model itself independently of actual scientific practice. It became widely recognized that our understanding of scientific knowledge required understanding the actual historical development of scientific knowledge. And as for science, so for history; but here there is a vacuum where there should have been effort. Philosophers of history are aware that most historians[190] do not engage in the philosophy of their subject. Perhaps surprisingly for philosophers, most historians do not engage in the history of their subject either, and often regard the history of historiography as a way of undermining "real" history by drawing our attention to historians themselves rather than to what they write about, as if the problem of historical objectivity could be solved by closing one's eyes to any actual subjective input.[191] The tradition among historians of writing their own theory of history has always been a haphazard one. However, historians are at last beginning to think about their own procedures in a systematic way, drawing on what are for them the user-friendly writings of postmodernists and poststructuralists, and it is here that most current writing on the theory of history is published.[192] Yet there is no doubt that there is a present intellectual need for more philosophical work in the history of historiography. Such work as there is is often not well-informed theoretically.[193] Just as, following Kuhn, there was massive intellectual investment in the history of science, so attention should be given by philosophers of history to the history of historiography. Yet very few philosophers have ever given serious attention to the historyof historiography, and perhaps only one has devoted a complete scholarly volume to a single historian: Burleigh Taylor Wilkins, anticipating the current needs with his critical and analytical study of the historian Carl Becker, who was so powerfully influential in his relativistic understanding of the nature of the historical construction of the past.[194]

Relativism, a very old philosophical problem, is also a very new one in the postmodern world, and it is continually fuelled by disagreements among the plurality of historical approaches which the ongoing history of historiography discloses. Whatever the importance of history either to philosophy of science or to philosophy of history, no philosopher could for long think that the study of history involved an appeal to historical *facts.* Even Kuhn's position, it was eventually seen, did not involve an appeal to "facts" from the history of science, but involved the development of a model for understanding the history of science. Kuhn's was an historicist model, and moreover a plausible one, maybe a better model of the realities of scientific practice over the historical period of successful science than the Popperian model. Evaluating the comparative merits of Kuhn's and Popper's models for science was therefore at the same time evaluating the comparative merits of these models as *interpretations of the history of science.*

Accepting this, a similar approach might be taken to the philosophy of history. Perhaps a contrast should not be drawn between philosophy of history as *prescriptive for* and as *descriptive of* historical practice, as if the facts of historical practice were independent of the theories about it. The contrast should perhaps be seen as being between models of history: one—not necessarily covering law theory—based on successful natural science, and the other—"best historians' judgments"—expressing the historical profession's own model, its *interpretation* of its own practice over time. Nor is there any reason to think that there are merely two choices here. On this approach, the widespread suspicion of models on the part of historians is misplaced, since models, or otherwise "interpretations", are unavoidable.[195] Yet the epistemological status and use of models in the social and historical world is not yet well understood, and further exposition is required. One area in which the matter is becoming a little clearer is that of cliometric history. In this subject historians use models of rational action derived from economic theory. It is assumed that we may treat individual people "as if" they were so-called "rational economic men," and construct the behavior of their institutions on the basis of this.[196] The upshot of Kuhn's approach at this point is that it is a pragmatic question which model is the most appropriate to historical understanding, and moreover that it should not be assumed that only one model should be used. There may be a multiplicity of historical approaches, or paradigms.[197]

Once we are aware of the existence of different paradigms, frameworks, models, or interpretations,[198] then we immediately face the question of *choice,* with the implications of relativism which lie behind it. Wilkins notes that "...both Kant and Popper believe there are real alternatives or choices open to us when we confront the questions of what we ought to do...[although] such alternatives or choices are not open to us where questions of science and empirical fact are concerned."[199] However, given Kuhn's position, there is even choice where questions of science and empirical fact are concerned. "History and science alike require interpretations or frameworks for the selection and explanation of data," Wilkins observes.[200] Wilkins in consequence asks an important question: although Popper is against the view that our scientific theories are relative to a background framework, "is Popper an enemy of the Myth of the Framework in general only to become in effect its champion where the writing of history is concerned?" Popper's "error really consists in not having gone far enough in recognizing the incommensurability of frameworks."[201] We should note that it is not even clear that a choice has to be made between conflicting approaches to history, for perhaps it is right to live with alternatives. We then face the problem of making sense of Berlin's factual pluralism.

In conclusion, while the possibility of choice between systems does not imply that one system is no better than another, "Popper ultimately fails to provide us with an adequate, rational basis for preferring one system to another or to provide us with a rational demonstration that his preferred system of norms is superior to other systems of norms."[202] However, we should at least "applaud [Popper's] intention of avoiding both an absolutistic historicism that dogmatically claims to infer the moral meaning of history from the facts of history and a historicist relativism that tends to transform questions of fact into questions of value or meaning and that urges us not to worry about choosing rationally among a plurality of historical interpretations and 'meanings' of history. ...we give moral meaning to history and...we can do this legitimately because...we make history."[203]

"Pressed hard," Wilkins says, "Popper might perhaps concede that the asymmetry between facts and standards is ultimately a *moral* asymmetry in the sense of reflecting our *decision* not to allow facts about sociology, psychology, or language usage to usurp our moral autonomy."[204] In effect, distinguishing between facts and values is itself a *moral* decision. It is we who give meaning to history, but it is not thereby arbitrary how we do it. It is a moral decision how we do it. Getting history right is a matter of justice.

Notes

1 Burleigh Taylor Wilkins, *Hegel's Philosophy of History*, Ithaca: Cornell University Press, 1974, p. 16.

2 Burleigh Taylor Wilkins, *Carl Becker: A Biographical Study in American Intellectual History*, Cambridge, Mass: The M.I.T. Press and Harvard University Press, 1961, p. 1.

3 Burleigh Taylor Wilkins, *Has History Any Meaning? A Critique of Popper's Philosophy of History.* Hassocks, Sussex: The Harvester Press, 1978, p. 162.

4 See W.B. Gallie, *Philosophy and the Historical Understanding*, London: Chatto & Windus, 1964.

5 In recent years there has been a marked increase in discussion between different traditions in philosophy, sufficient to require a professional philosopher to understand more than his own tradition.

6 The term is so problematic that I shall continue to use it within inverted commas until it has itself been properly analyzed, below.

7 It is common in this tradition to study no philosophers between Aristotle and Descartes.

8 Whose "dogmatic slumber" was roused by Hume. Immanuel Kant, *Prolegomena to Any Future Metaphysics* [1783] (trans. Peter G. Lucas), Manchester: Manchester University Press, 1953, p. 9.

9 The canonical figures involved overlap with the canonical lists of other traditions in philosophy, although the same philosophers are often read in different ways.

10 Wilkins reminds us that even Hegel believed that "detailed recommendation as to how the world ought to be was...unsuited to the task of philosophy". Burleigh Taylor Wilkins, *Hegel's Philosophy of History*, Ithaca: Cornell University Press, 1974, p. 82.

11 The substantive moral and political philosophies beginning with John Rawls' *A Theory of Justice* become influential from the 1970's onwards.

12 This outline historical account of the "analytical" tradition in philosophy is supplemented by a more exact analysis given below.

13 A full account of the nature of history would go back at least to Herodotus' *Histories* in about 425 BCE. (Philosophers may not know that, among historians, BCE—"Before the Common Era"—is coming to replace BC—"Before Christ"—to avoid an inappropriate Christian perspective on ancient history. See Paul Cartledge, "Introduction", in *Companion to Historiography*, Michael Bentley (ed.), London and New York: Routledge, 1997, p. 4.) For a useful discussion of Herodotus' and other classical historians' presuppositions of their historiography see Paul Cartledge, "Historiography and Ancient Greek Self-definition", *ibid.*, pp. 23-42, and Michael Bentley, "Introduction: Approaches to Modernity: Western Historiography since the Enlightenment", *ibid.*, pp. 395-506, particularly at pp. 405-410.

14 Plato, *The Republic*, Book 3.

15 W.H. Dray, "Philosophy and Historiography", in Michael Bentley (ed.), *Companion to Historiography*, London and New York: Routledge, 1997, pp. 763-782 at p. 764.

16 W.H. Walsh, *An Introduction to Philosophy of History*, 3rd ed., London: Hutchinson, 1967, p. 15. The lack of any special importance of history for Bradley contrasts with the position of Hegel, by whose idealism Bradley was influenced. Bradley

was, unlike Hegel, an empiricist. Bradley's holism is instructively similar to that of the pragmatist W.V.O. Quine.

17 Alan Donagan remarks, "Few philosophers have accepted the opinion of the late R.G. Collingwood that "the chief business of twentieth-century philosophy is to reckon with twentieth-century history". Alan Donagan, "Explanation in History", reprinted in P. Gardiner (ed.), *Theories of History*, New York: The Free Press, 1959, pp. 428-443, at p. 428. Donagan is referring to philosophers of the "analytical" tradition.

18 A precursor was Giambattista Vico, *Scienza Nuova*, the first edition of which was published in 1725 and the third in 1744. His work was not at the time influential, becoming so through the writings of the French historian Michelet, *Principes de la philosophie de l'histoire*, 1833.

19 In particular *The Critique of Pure Reason* (1781 and 1787) and *The Critique of Practical Reason* (1787), in various translations.

20 Reprinted in *Theories of History*, Patrick Gardiner (ed.), New York: The Free Press, 1959, pp. 22-34. Michael Bentley remarks that Kant writes history "like a Voltairean schoolboy", in his "Introduction: Approaches to Modernity: Western Historiography since the Enlightenment" in Michael Bentley (ed.), *Companion to Historiography*, London and New York: Routledge, 1997, pp. 395-506 at p. 409.

21 For Kant's own elementary introduction to his moral philosophy, see his *Fundamental Principles of the Metaphysic of Ethics*, trans. T.K. Abbott, 10th edn., London: Longmans, 1962.

22 "Idea of a Universal History from a Cosmopolitan Point of View", in *Theories of History*, Patrick Gardiner (ed.), New York: The Free Press, 1959, pp. 22-34 at p. 26.

23 "Idea of a Universal History from a Cosmopolitan Point of View", in *Theories of History*, Patrick Gardiner (ed.), New York: The Free Press, 1959, pp. 22-34 at p. 28.

24 Michael Bentley contrasts Kant with Herder, ascribing to the latter the understanding of reality as "a process of becoming through time" in his "Introduction: Approaches to Modernity: Western Historiography since the Enlightenment" in Michael Bentley (ed.), *Companion to Historiography*, London and New York: Routledge, 1997, pp. 395-506 at p. 410. However, I think this is appropriate only for Kant's *Critique of Pure Reason* and associated writings, and not for his "Idea of a Universal History".

25 "Hegel, however, was not a Kantian", Wilkins reminds us. "Hegel denies that the Ideas of Reason are merely regulative". Burleigh Taylor Wilkins, *Hegel's Philosophy of History*, Ithaca: Cornell University Press, 1974, pp. 63, 86.

26 Some extracts from J.G. Herder's *Ideas Toward a Philosophy of the History of Man* appear in Patrick Gardiner (ed.), *Theories of History*, New York: The Free Press, 1959, pp. 35-49. See also Isaiah Berlin, *Vico and Herder: Two Studies in the History of Ideas*, London: Hogarth Press, 1976, and Michael Bentley, "Introduction: Approaches to Modernity: Western Historiography since the Enlightenment" in Michael Bentley (ed.), *Companion to Historiography*, London and New York: Routledge, 1997, pp. 395-506 at pp. 405-410.

27 *The Idea of History*, R.G. Collingwood, London: Oxford University Press, 1946, p. 92.

28 Kant and Hegel are clearly rationalists, but Marx saw his position as "scientific" and his "materialist" metaphysics has sometimes been confused with empiricism. If Marx was an empiricist, which is perhaps doubtful, then he is open to criticism based on empiricist theories of science. See the discussion of Karl Popper, below.

29 And perhaps not just in Europe, for there is more to historicism than Marxism. Wilkins observes, "I do believe that historicism is a recognizable trend or aspect of contemporary philosophy", Burleigh Taylor Wilkins, *Has History Any Meaning? A Critique of Popper's Philosophy of History*, Hassocks, Sussex: The Harvester Press, 1978, p. 12.

30 Karl R. Popper, *The Poverty of Historicism*, London: Routledge and Kegan Paul, 1957. The historian Maurice Cowling suggests that this claim is simply a wholly inadequate explanation of an historical problem. Maurice Cowling, *The Nature and Limits of Political Science*, Cambridge: Cambridge University Press, 1963, p. 117.

31 Popper contributed to what are in effect two different traditions in philosophy of history, first to that subject as, in its anti-historicist form, it is a branch of substantive political philosophy, and secondly to that subject as it concentrates on the analytical philosophy of historical explanation. Each contribution is outlined here in the appropriate place.

32 Robert D'Amico distinguishes two senses of "historicism": first, that "history obeys a lawful order or logic and knowing its 'laws of emergence' allows for historical predictions"; second, that "historicism emphasizes that ways of reasoning are entrenched or embedded in contexts that can be judged either internally or retrospectively from the present. Rationality is inseparable from and judged internally to changing problem situations". While Popper rejects historicism in the first sense, he is an historicist in the second sense. Robert D'Amico, *Historicism and Knowledge*, New York and London: Routledge, 1989, pp. 20-21 and *passim*. See the discussion of Popper's "situational logic" below. See also Arnaldo Momigliano, "Historicism in Contemporary Thought" [1961], rep. in his *Studies in Historiography*, London: Weidenfeld and Nicolson, 1966, pp. 221-238.

33 As Wilkins puts it, Kant believed that the final end of history is "not constitutive of the nature of historical reality" but "is important as a regulative idea or concept which reflects our moral concern with the course of historical development and which may also be of some heuristic value as an organizing principle in our inquiries concerning past events". Burleigh Taylor Wilkins, *Has History Any Meaning? A Critique of Popper's Philosophy of History*, Hassocks, Sussex: The Harvester Press, 1978, pp. 20-21. This applies to history the approach of Kant's *Critique of Pure Reason*, and seems to me to contrast markedly with some of the factual theses in Kant's "Idea of a Universal History", as explained above. But it may be that I make more of this contrast than I should.

34 Burleigh Taylor Wilkins, *Has History Any Meaning? A Critique of Popper's Philosophy of History*, Hassocks, Sussex: The Harvester Press, 1978, p. 21.

35 Ibid., p. 124.

36 Ibid., p. 125.

37 Ibid., p. 125-126.

38 Ibid., p. 131.

39 Ibid., p. 141.

40 Burleigh Taylor Wilkins, *Hegel's Philosophy of History*, Ithaca: Cornell University Press, 1974, p. 174. [Passage originally in italics.]

41 Burleigh Taylor Wilkins, *Has History Any Meaning? A Critique of Popper's Philosophy of History*, Hassocks, Sussex: The Harvester Press, 1978, p. 143.

42 Ibid., p. 143.

43 Ibid., p. 162.

44 Ibid., p. 163, 167.

45 Wilkins reminds us that "Hegel's philosophy of history is not predictive", and analyzes the reasons why. Burleigh Taylor Wilkins, *Hegel's Philosophy of History*, pp. 74, 80ff.

46 Wilkins hints at doubts about whether Popper's own studies of Hegel and Marx are accurate. Burleigh Taylor Wilkins, *Has History Any Meaning? A Critique of Popper's Philosophy of History*, p. 12. That the objection is not "fatal to Hegel" is also made clear: Burleigh Taylor Wilkins, *Hegel's Philosophy of History*, p. 74.

47 See Burleigh Taylor Wilkins, *Hegel's Philosophy of History*, pp. 176-177.

48 It is plain that Popper understands this as what Kant would have called a "categorical" imperative, rather than a "hypothetical" one. Popper is not merely offering us a way of being scientifically rational, on the off-chance that some of us might have an arbitrary taste for that pursuit. However, whether this position is defensible, given the rest of Popper's epistemology, is doubtful. See Burleigh Taylor Wilkins, *Has History Any Meaning? A Critique of Popper's Philosophy of History*, pp. 219-239.

49 The allusion is to Karl R. Popper, *The Open Society and its Enemies*, vol. 1, *Plato*, and vol. 2, *Hegel and Marx*, London: Routledge and Kegan Paul, 1945. See also Burleigh Taylor Wilkins, *Has History Any Meaning? A Critique of Popper's Philosophy of History*, pp. 218-219.

50 Burleigh Taylor Wilkins, *Has History Any Meaning? A Critique of Popper's Philosophy of History*, p. 117.

51 Ibid., p. 196.

52 This point is not to deny the intellectual merit of the empiricist epistemology itself.

53 Burleigh Taylor Wilkins, *Has History Any Meaning? A Critique of Popper's Philosophy of History*, p. 22.

54 Wilkins observes that Popper's attacks on historicism "clearly anticipate" Berlin's position: Burleigh Taylor Wilkins, *Has History Any Meaning? A Critique of Popper's Philosophy of History*, p. 14. Much of Berlin's philosophy is usefully presented in a collection of his best-known essays: Henry Hardy and Roger Hausheer (eds.), *The Proper Study of Mankind*, London: Chatto & Windus, 1997.

55 Kant's younger contemporary Herder was arguably a pluralist despite being an historicist, and this reminds us that the rationalist tradition of substantive philosophy of history embodied a number of different philosophical positions, not all of which had to be accepted by everyone in the tradition. There is much confusion among philosophers about what, exactly, historicism involves. Wilkins anticipates a "future A.O. Lovejoy who may someday distinguish thirteen varieties of historicism (as Lovejoy once distinguished thirteen varieties of pragmatism)", Burleigh Taylor Wilkins, *Has History Any Meaning? A Critique of Popper's Philosophy of History*, p. 12.

56 Totalitarianism is not a simple matter of the state refusing to allow for freedom of association, as Roger Scruton has it in his *A Dictionary of Political Thought*, London: Macmillan/Pan, 1983, p. 466.

57 This need have nothing to do with the issue of the possibility of historical prediction. Wilkins describes the relationships between historical determinism and political

totalitarianism as "alleged connections". Burleigh Taylor Wilkins, *Has History Any Meaning? A Critique of Popper's Philosophy of History*, p. 14. If descriptive totalitarianism is false then deterministic historical prediction is false; but not necessarily vice-versa.

58 From selection published on the date of his obituary, *The Daily Telegraph*, Friday, November 7th, 1997, p. 21. Originally in Berlin's "The Purpose of Philosophy", *Concepts and Categories: Philosophical Essays*, Oxford: Oxford University Press, 1980, p. 8.

59 Isaiah Berlin, "The Purpose of Philosophy", *Concepts and Categories: Philosophical Essays*, Oxford: Oxford University Press, 1980, p. 8.

60 The rejection of successful historical prediction is a consequence of this.

61 "And not only values. Propositions too. Truth is not a unity." Noel Annan, "Foreword" to Henry Hardy and Roger Hausheer (eds.), *The Proper Study of Mankind: An Anthology of Essays*, London: Chatto & Windus, 1997, p. xiii.

62 Burleigh Taylor Wilkins, *Has History Any Meaning? A Critique of Popper's Philosophy of History*, p. 14.

63 Although not equally speculative; Berlin, like Popper, was an empiricist.

64 Peter Laslett, "Introduction", to *Philosophy, Politics and Society*, First Series, Peter Laslett (ed.), Oxford: Basil Blackwell, 1970, p. vii. While substantive political philosophy resurfaced in the analytical tradition in the 1970s, it did not bring with it much renewed discussion of substantive philosophy of history. Indeed, I believe the political philosophies of Popper and Berlin have yet to be satisfactorily digested by the rest of "analytical" philosophy. Wilkins is one of the few who have made a contribution in this area. Just as the rejection of substantive moral philosophy in the 1950s in fact embodied a suppressed utilitarianism on the part of the philosophers concerned, so in an analogous way the present rejection of substantive philosophy of history in fact embodies a general acceptance that history can be predictively structured in terms of the principles of neoclassical microeconomic theory. See Francis Fukuyama *The End of History and the Last Man*, London: Penguin, 1992. There is, furthermore, some theoretical recognition that rational criteria may be essentially, rather than accidentally, subject to change over time: see, for example, Nozick's distinction between historical and end-result principles of justice, Robert Nozick, *Anarchy, State and Utopia*, New York, Basic Books, 1974, chap. 7.

65 Berlin explains why in more detail in the "Author's Preface" to his *Concepts and Categories: Philosophical Essays*, Henry Hardy (ed.), Oxford: Oxford University Press, 1980, p. vii.

66 It is noteworthy that a symposium on philosophy and history held in New York in 1962 organized some of its papers under the heading "Patterns in History". Nothing whatever on patterns in history appeared there. See Sidney Hook (ed.), *Philosophy and History: A Symposium*, New York: New York University Press, 1963. Various terms have been used to contrast "substantive" and "analytical" philosophy of history, but all are problematic since there is more than one distinction here, as will be explained below. Instead of "substantive" and "analytical", the terms "speculative" and "critical" are used by W.H. Walsh, *An Introduction to Philosophy of History*, London: Hutchinson, 1967, pp. 15ff, and by W.H. Dray, *Philosophy of History*, Englewood Cliffs, N.J.: Prentice-Hall, 1964, p. 1. Dray notes also Maurice Mandelbaum's words "material" and "formal" respectively, p. 1. In addition, W.H. Walsh distinguishes, again respectively, between "meaning *of* history" and "meaning *in* history". This is very helpfully summarised and further analysed in Burleigh Taylor

Wilkins *Has History Any Meaning? A Critique of Popper's Philosophy of History*, chap. 1. For a brief history of the meaning of "history" see Paul Cartledge, "Historiography and ancient Greek self-definition", in Michael Bentley (ed.), *Companion to Historiography*, London and New York: Routledge, pp. 23-42 at pp. 23ff.

67 W.H. Walsh, *An Introduction to Philosophy of History*, [1951] London: Hutchinson, 1967, p. 11.

68 Ibid., p. 11, footnote 1 in square brackets. This comment by Walsh was added in the 3rd edition, as the new Preface made clear.

69 Ibid., p. 12.

70 Ibid., p. 13.

71 Ibid., p. 14. Walsh proceeded in a footnote to observe that Romanticism has made a poor showing in British philosophy.

72 Michael Oakeshott, *Experience and Its Modes*, Cambridge: Cambridge University Press, 1933.

73 W.H. Walsh, *An Introduction to Philosophy of History*, p. 13.

74 Carl G. Hempel, "The Function of General Laws in History", *Journal of Philosophy* 39, 1942, p. 35. Reprinted in Patrick Gardiner (ed.), *Theories of History*, New York: The Free Press, 1959, pp. 344-356.

75 R.G. Collingwood, *The Idea of History*, T.M. Knox (ed.), Oxford: Clarendon Press, 1946.

76 Karl R. Popper, *The Open Society and its Enemies,* vol. 1, *Plato*, and vol. 2, *Hegel and Marx*, London: Routledge and Kegan Paul, 1945.

77 Karl R. Popper, *The Logic of Scientific Discovery*, [1934] London: Routledge and Kegan Paul, 1959.

78 Burleigh Taylor Wilkins, *Has History Any Meaning? A Critique of Popper's Philosophy of History*, p. 13.

79 Although the Professor of Modern History at Cambridge describes Popper as having "dedicated much of his life to disputing the claims of Marxism to be a scientific doctrine". Richard J. Evans, *In Defence of History*, London: Granta, 1997, p. 36.

80 Collingwood's *The Idea of History* and *Oxford History of Roman Britain* "might have been written by two different people", remarks Richard J. Evans, *In Defence of History*, London: Granta, 1977, p. 11. See the first few paragraphs, above.

81 George Berkeley, *The Principles of Human Knowledge*, 1710.

82 F.H. Bradley *The Principles of Logic,* Oxford: Oxford University Press, 2nd edn. 1922, vols. 1 and 2.

83 Wilkins remarks that Hegel "is most afraid of contingency", although contingency is not removed in Hegel's philosophy: "the discovery of necessity presupposes the presence rather than the absence of contingency". Burleigh Taylor Wilkins, *Hegel's Philosophy of History*, Ithaca: Cornell University Press, 1974, pp. 143, 171.

84 Burleigh Taylor Wilkins, *Hegel's Philosophy of History*, p. 23.

85 Ibid., p. 23.

86 Hume's "atomism" was rather unthinkingly assumed by positivist philosophers of science until the work of W.V.O. Quine.

87 The supposition that philosophy is not substantive ignores the fact that it is a substantive philosophical claim, necessarily associated with the positivist position,

that science alone—and indeed science conceived in a particular way—achieves knowledge. The metaphysical presuppositions of the empiricist position are spelt out in J.L. Gorman, *Understanding History: An Introduction to Analytical Philosophy of History*, Ottawa: University of Ottawa Press, 1992.

88 This is broadly Hempel's view. Popper avoids the discussion of meaning. Isaiah Berlin, while an empiricist, consistently rejected the philosophical desire to "translate many *prima facie* different types of proposition into a single type", as he put it in his essay "Logical Translation", *Concepts and Categories*, Oxford: Oxford University Press, 1980, pp. 56-80 at p. 57.

89 This is the position of J.L. Austin.

90 R.G. Collingwood, who was strongly against positivism, suggested that philosophers should choose their vocabulary according to the rules of literature. See his *An Essay on Philosophical Method*, Oxford: Clarendon Press, 1933, p. 207. Philosophers in the analytical tradition have nevertheless rarely warmed to the suggestion that one cannot be literal and must therefore embrace the metaphorical. See for an insistence on the literal and an explanation of the metaphorical Donald Davidson [1978], "What Metaphors Mean", in his *Inquiries into Truth and Interpretation*, Oxford: Clarendon Press, 1984, pp. 245-264. Metaphors have, however, been taken much more seriously in recent analytical work in philosophy of history.

91 For example, most philosophers in the "analytical" tradition would require knowledge claims to be justifiable, so in a minimal sense they are sceptical, and their scepticism would be a consequence of an empiricist attitude rather than, for example, being driven by a Cartesian and rationalist "method of doubt".

92 Hume's "mechanism" involved the claim that, space and time apart, the only fundamental relation which exists between all the things that exist is a causal relation. The view is that the world consists of many things in causal relationship with each other, a world which we are supposed to know about on the basis of experience. One needs to leave the analytical tradition to find serious philosophical criticism of this idea. Hegel's philosophy is a useful corrective, and Hegel's treatment of mechanism is carefully examined at length in Burleigh Taylor Wilkins, *Hegel's Philosophy of History*, Ithaca: Cornell University Press, 1974, chap. 2.

93 Frank Ankersmit, for example, characterizes "analytical" philosophy, as used by philosophers of history from that tradition, as assuming "that language is the principal condition for the possibility of all knowledge and meaningful thinking" and that philosophers should accept "the so-called *resoluto-compositional* method", that is, that "philosophy of language ought to start with an investigation of the behavior of logical constants, proper names, et cetera, and of the meaning of words and propositions," and work up to the solution of complex issues on these atomistic foundations. F.R. Ankersmit, *History and Tropology: The Rise and Fall of Metaphor*, Berkeley and Los Angeles, California: University of California Press, 1994, p. 2.

94 Both Hempel and Popper deny being determinists, as Wilkins notes in his *Has History Any Meaning? A Critique of Popper's Philosophy of History*, p. 48.

95 Unsurprisingly, in view of what has been said earlier about holistic empiricism, there are many interesting similarities between the philosophies of F.H. Bradley and W.V.O. Quine.

96 "Postmodern" attacks on analytical philosophy often embody this view.

97 See Carl G. Hempel, *Philosophy of Natural Science*, Englewood Cliffs, N.J.: Prentice-Hall, 1966.

98 "...what the theory maintains is that explanation is achieved, and only achieved, *by subsuming what is to be explained under a general law* " [Dray's italics]. W.H. Dray, *Laws and Explanation in History*, Oxford: Clarendon Press, 1957, p. 1. "Covering law" is not the terminology originally used by Hempel or Popper.

99 Burleigh Taylor Wilkins, *Has History Any Meaning? A Critique of Popper's Philosophy of History*, p. 13. See also Burleigh Taylor Wilkins, "Aristotle on Scientific Explanation", *Dialogue* IX, 1970, pp. 337-355.

100 Burleigh Taylor Wilkins, *Has History Any Meaning? A Critique of Popper's Philosophy of History*, p. 13.

101 C.G. Hempel, "The Function of General Laws in History", in Patrick Gardiner (ed.), *Theories of History*, New York: The Free Press, 1959, p. 345.

102 C.G. Hempel, "The Function of General Laws in History", in Patrick Gardiner (ed.), *Theories of History*, New York: The Free Press, 1959, p. 347 note 1. There are theories of causation different from Hempel's Humean "Regularity" conception. See, for example, R.G. Collingwood, "On the So-called Idea of Causation", *Proceedings of the Aristotelian Society* 38, 1937-38 p. 85; D. Gasking, "Causation and recipes", *Mind* 64, 1955, p. 479; J.L. Mackie, "Causes and Conditions", *American Philosophical Quarterly* 2, 1965, p. 245; J.L. Mackie, "The Direction of Causation", *Philosophical Review* 75, 1966, p. 441, and essays in T. L. Beauchamp (ed.), *Philosophical Problems of Causation*, Encino: Dickenson, 1974.

103 C.G. Hempel, "The Function of General Laws in History", in Patrick Gardiner (ed.), *Theories of History*, New York: The Free Press, 1959, p. 346.

104 What we now understand to be the cause of something would be Aristotle's "efficient" cause. What is ruled out is, among other things and for example, explaining a human action by reference to its "purpose," or "final cause" in Aristotle's terms.

105 It is a model of scientific testing and prediction also, but these are of lesser relevance to the philosophy of history.

106 While the tradition continues, some will deny that it is any longer the "standard" position, after the publication of Thomas S. Kuhn's *The Structure of Scientific Revolutions*, Chicago: The University of Chicago Press, 1962. A source of reading in the standard approach to philosophy of science is Carl G. Hempel, *Philosophy of Natural Science*, Englewood Cliffs, N.J.: Prentice-Hall, 1966. Another is Ernest Nagel, *The Structure of Science*, London: Routledge and Kegan Paul, 1961.

107 C.G. Hempel, "The Function of General Laws in History", in Patrick Gardiner (ed.), *Theories of History*, New York: The Free Press, 1959, p. 351.

108 Ibid., p. 349.

109 Ibid., p. 350.

110 Ibid., p. 354.

111 Ibid., p. 352. The nature of "empathetic understanding" will be discussed further below.

112 C.G. Hempel, "The Function of General Laws in History", in Patrick Gardiner (ed.), *Theories of History*, New York: The Free Press, 1959, p. 355.

113 "Recent Views Concerning Historical Knowledge and Explanation: Introduction", in Patrick Gardiner (ed.) *Theories of History*, New York: The Free Press, 1959, pp. 265-274 at p. 269.

114 That is, from his *Philosophical Investigations*, rather than from his *Tractatus Logico-Philosophicus*. Only in more recent studies of Wittgenstein does the view of him as having expressed two distinct philosophies begin to break down.

115 Alan Donagan, "Explanation in History,",reprinted in Patrick Gardiner (ed.), *Theories of History*, New York: The Free Press, 1959, pp. 428-443, at p. 430.

116 Ibid., pp. 428-443, at p. 433. Hempel would have agreed with this.

117 This will be briefly illustrated below in the public discussion between Morton G. White and J.H. Hexter. For an excellent summary from an historian's point of view, see Richard J. Evans, *In Defence of History*, London: Granta, 1997. Historians in general have rarely suffered from doubt about the proper nature of the philosophical analysis of history: it has to describe what historians do.

118 I have expressed this elsewhere, in particular in "Kellner on language and historical representation", *History and Theory* 30, 1991, 356-368.

119 W. B. Gallie, *Philosophy and the Historical Understanding*, London: Chatto & Windus, 1964. The connections which make a story followable are often causal in form, Gallie says, and he analyses historical causes as necessary connections.

120 A further part of Gallie's position is that it is the narrative story which most people in our culture find particularly followable and understandable. The place of narratives in philosophical understanding will be discussed further below.

121 Vico, *Scienza Nuova*, suggested the "verum factum" principle, that we can only truly understand that which we make. People make the social and historical world, and therefore they can have full understanding of it. But only God can understand the natural world, since He alone made it. A related Marxist position would be that scientific theories, far from describing truly the natural world, are just social constructions based on the epistemologically foundational historical understanding of the reality of dialectical materialism.

122 I shall not discuss here the view which is of particular importance to the history of ideas, that historical understanding essentially involves the recovery of meaning in accordance with a certain view of the nature of interpretation, translation or conversation. See Q.R.D. Skinner, "Meaning and Understanding in the History of Ideas", *History and Theory* 8, 1969, pp. 3-53.

123 Burleigh Taylor Wilkins, *Has History Any Meaning? A Critique of Popper's Philosophy of History*, chap. 1. The issue about whether history can be given "meaning" in terms of being given an intelligible structure is discussed below. Wilkins approves W. H. Walsh in saying that one could inquire into the meaning of history in the sense that one might in principle be able to find laws of historical development, but that would not necessarily involve telling us where history as a whole is going or whether it is going in a morally desirable way, pp. 18-19.

124 William Dray, *Laws and Explanation in History*, Oxford: Clarendon Press, 1957.

125 Ibid., pp. 122-124.

126 It is arguable that, with the help of the so-called "rational economic man assumptions" of neoclassical microeconomic theory, further analytical detail for Dray's notion of a "calculation" can be provided. On this approach we are able to empathise with another person, because we can work through a calculation which displays the net preference and consequent choice as appropriate, given that person's desires and beliefs as to his circumstances. These desires and beliefs characterise the calculation

as being a cost-benefit analysis. Economic history, on this approach, is then "scientific" and uses the "laws" of economic theory, despite being consistent with Dray's position. The use of economic theory in the epistemology of history is examined at length in J.L. Gorman, *Understanding History: An Introduction to Analytical Philosophy of History*, Ottawa: University of Ottawa Press, 1992.

127 William Dray, *Laws and Explanation in History*, Oxford: Clarendon Press, 1957, p. 138.

128 For some subsequent thinking on the relationship between causes and reasons, begin with Donald Davidson, "Actions, Reasons and Causes", reprinted in his *Essays on Actions and Events*, Oxford: Oxford University Press, 1980. See also T. Abel, "The Operation Called *Verstehen*", and other essays in M. Truzzi (ed.), *Verstehen: Subjective Understanding in the Social Sciences*, Reading, Mass.: Addison-Wesley, 1974.

129 Although Wilkins notes Hegel's position, "that an ever-increasing self-consciousness in man involves an ever-decreasing applicability of the category of causality and the mechanical point of view to his actions." Burleigh Taylor Wilkins, *Hegel's Philosophy of History*, p. 133.

130 Burleigh Taylor Wilkins, *Has History Any Meaning? A Critique of Popper's Philosophy of History*, p. 47.

131 Ibid., p. 49.

132 Ibid., p. 51.

133 Ibid., p. 35.

134 Ibid., p. 26.

135 Ibid., p. 36. Hegel believed that "propositions about the cause-effect relation are 'tautological'". Burleigh Taylor Wilkins, *Hegel's Philosophy of History*, Ithaca: Cornell University Press, 1974, p. 184.

136 Ibid., p. 38.

137 Burleigh Taylor Wilkins, *Hegel's Philosophy of History*, p. 185.

138 Burleigh Taylor Wilkins, *Has History Any Meaning? A Critique of Popper's Philosophy of History*, p. 43 note 18.

139 Ibid., p. 52.

140 Ibid., p. 55.

141 Ibid., p. 55. It is doubtful how far this contrast would hold with regard to so-called "cliometric" history, where models of rational behavior are used in economic explanations. This is discussed at length in J.L. Gorman, *Understanding History: An Introduction to Analytical Philosophy of History*, Ottawa: University of Ottawa Press, 1992.

142 Collingwood's criteria for the acceptability of an historical "fact", outlined above, are not relevant here.

143 C.G. Hempel, "The Function of General Laws in History", in Patrick Gardiner (ed.), *Theories of History*, p. 355.

144 The place of generalizations in history is examined at careful length in C. Behan McCullagh, *Justifying Historical Descriptions*, Cambridge: Cambridge University Press, 1984. One of his justifications here consists in "Arguments to the Best Expla-

nation", chap. 2. This idea is examined at still more careful length in Peter Lipton, *Inference to the Best Explanation*, London: Routledge, 1991: "Beginning with the evidence available to us, we infer what would, if true, provide the best explanation of that evidence", p. 1.

145 Karl R. Popper, *The Open Society and its Enemies,* vol. 2, *Hegel and Marx*, London: Routledge and Kegan Paul, chap. 25.

146 Burleigh Taylor Wilkins, *Has History Any Meaning? A Critique of Popper's Philosophy of History.* p. 86.

147 Ibid., pp. 69-70.

148 Ibid., chap. 2, "Historical Interpretations".

149 C.A.J. Coady, *Testimony: A Philosophical Study*, Oxford: Clarendon Press, 1992.

150 C.A.J. Coady, *Testimony: A Philosophical Study*, Oxford: Clarendon Press, 1992, p. 7.

151 The expression of Coady's position here derives from J.L. Gorman, "Coady on Testimony", *History and Theory* 33, 1994, 230-241.

152 C.A.J. Coady, *Testimony: A Philosophical Study*, Oxford: Clarendon Press, 1992, p. 154.

153 R.G. Collingwood, *The Idea of History*, Oxford: Clarendon Press, 1946.

154 Ibid., p. 33.

155 Supposedly an example of historical method, but in fact a fictional detective story.

156 C.A.J. Coady, *Testimony: A Philosophical Study*, Oxford: Clarendon Press, 1992, p. 238.

157 Apart from Collingwood, Leon J. Goldstein made a particularly powerful contribution here: *Historical Knowing*, Austin, Texas and London: University of Texas Press, 1976. See also *History and Theory* Beiheft 16, 1977.

158 Some discussion of the issues of realism and anti-realism in history is given in J.L. Gorman, *The Expression of Historical Knowledge*, New York: Columbia University Press and Edinburgh: Edinburgh University Press, 1982. More advanced sources for study of realism and anti-realism, although without any particular application to historical understanding, are Crispin Wright, *Truth and Objectivity*, Cambridge, Mass.: Harvard University Press, 1992, and Simon Blackburn, *Essays in Quasi-Realism*, New York and Oxford: Oxford University Press, 1993.

159 That is, the use of general laws in connecting present data with past events; empathetic understanding; and "meaning" in history.

160 Wilhelm Windelband [1894], "History and Natural Science," trans. Guy Oakes, *History and Theory* 19, 1980, pp. 169-185.

161 However, W.H. Dray notes that the "objection that the uniqueness of what historians characteristically study makes it impossible for them to explain things in the law-instantiating way is associated especially with the name of Oakeshott". W.H. Dray, "Philosophy and Historiography", in Michael Bentley (ed.), *Companion to Historiography*, London and New York: Routledge, 1997, pp. 763-782 at p. 768, referring to Michael Oakeshott's *Experience and Its Modes*, Cambridge: Cambridge University Press, 1933. Oakeshott was writing before Hempel explained the details of the application of covering law theory to history.

162 C.G. Hempel, "The Function of General Laws in History", in Patrick Gardiner (ed.), *Theories of History*, p. 346.

163 Ibid., pp. 345, 349.

164 W.H. Dray, "Philosophy and Historiography", in Michael Bentley (ed.), *Companion to Historiography*, London and New York: Routledge, 1997, pp. 763-782 at p. 768.

165 *Writing History: Essay on Epistemology*, Paul Veyne (trans. Mina Moore-Rinvolucri), Middletown, Connecticut: Wesleyan University Press, 1984. What follows is derived from J.L. Gorman, "Veyne on Writing History," *History and Theory* 26, 1987, 99-114.

166 "Empathetic Understanding" is neither necessary nor sufficient for this.

167 Burleigh Taylor Wilkins, *Has History Any Meaning? A Critique of Popper's Philosophy of History*, p. 32.

168 W.H. Dray, "'Explaining What' in History", in Patrick Gardiner (ed.), *Theories of History*, New York: The Free Press, 1959, pp. 403-408.

169 W.H. Dray, "Philosophy and Historiography", in Michael Bentley (ed.), *Companion to Historiography*, London and New York: Routledge, 1997, pp. 763-782 at p. 768.

170 Burleigh Taylor Wilkins, *Has History Any Meaning? A Critique of Popper's Philosophy of History*, p. 46. See also Richard G. Ely, Rolf Gruner and William Dray, in a discussion in *History and Theory* 6, 1967, who point to other modes of writing history. While narrative is not the only way of writing history, at least at the level of the surface structure of the historical text, it may nevertheless be argued that the narrative mode of understanding is presupposed by all historical knowledge. That narrative understanding may be presented or "written up" in some other rhetorical form is merely a superficial point. See Hayden V. White, *Metahistory: The Historical Imagination in Nineteenth-Century Europe*, Baltimore and London: The Johns Hopkins University Press, 1973.

171 W.B. Gallie made an important contribution to the analysis of narrative, and his position, expressed in terms of subjective followability, has already been explained.

172 M.G. White, *Foundations of Historical Knowledge*, New York: Harper and Row, 1965.

173 A.C. Danto, *Analytical Philosophy of History*, London: Cambridge University Press, 1965. Published later with amendments under the title *Narration and Knowledge*.

174 For a useful and more wide-ranging discussion of the place of narratives in historical understanding see W.H. Dray, "Philosophy and Historiography", in Michael Bentley (ed.), *Companion to Historiography*, London and New York: Routledge, 1997, pp. 763-782 at pp. 774-779.

175 J. H. Hexter reviewed White's *Foundations of Historical Knowledge* in "The One That Got Away", *New York Review of Books*, 9 February 1967, p. 24. See also A.C. Danto, letter, *New York Review of Books*, 18 May 1967, p. 41.

176 Although it is not the main issue, assessing statements as true would be made on what most historians would regard as scientific grounds.

177 The epistemology of narrative selection of statements is dealt with in J.L. Gorman, *The Expression of Historical Knowledge*, New York: Columbia University Press and Edinburgh: Edinburgh University Press, 1982.

178 This description of the issues between White and Hexter appears also in J.L. Gorman, *Understanding History: An Introduction to Analytical Philosophy of History*, Ottawa: University of Ottawa Press, 1992.

179 It should not be thought that Hexter was speaking on behalf of all historians here. Historians may recall the Bury-Trevelyan debate, the former asserting that history was a science, and the latter denying it. See "The Science of History" and "Clio, A Muse", in Fritz Stern (ed.), *The Varieties of History*, Cleveland: Meridian, 1956, p. 223 and p. 235 respectively. See also Richard J. Evans, *In Defence of History*, London: Granta, 1997, chap. 1.

180 J. H. Hexter, "The Rhetoric of History," in *The International Encyclopedia of the Social Sciences*, D. L. Sills (ed.), New York, 1968, VI, pp. 368-394.

181 This is Hayden V. White's word: *Metahistory: The Historical Imagination in Nineteenth-Century Europe*, Baltimore and London: The Johns Hopkins University Press, 1973.

182 An attempt at making sense of this appears in J.L. Gorman, "Objectivity and Truth in History", *Inquiry* 17, 1974, pp. 373-397.

183 M. G. White, letter, *New York Review of Books*, 23 March 1967, p. 28.

184 Despite some earlier remarks allowing statistical generalizations some place, p. 350, "Only the establishment of concrete laws can fill the general thesis with scientific content...", C.G. Hempel, "The Function of General Laws in History.",

185 Raising the so-called "New Riddle of Induction." See Nelson Goodman, *Fact, Fiction and Forecast*, Cambridge, Mass., 1955.

186 Thomas S. Kuhn, *The Structure of Scientific Revolutions*, Chicago: The University of Chicago Press, 1962.

187 Ibid., p. 2.

188 Ironically, Kuhn's work was also issued as a volume in the *International Encyclopedia of Unified Science*. The "unity" of science was normally taken to involve the acceptance of positivism and the consequent imposition on, for example, history, of covering law theory.

189 Thus Margaret Masterman claimed that twenty-one different senses of the word "paradigm" appeared in Kuhn's book. Kuhn himself was not the best judge of what he had said it really meant.

190 Philosophically low-grade texts appreciated by historians traditionally include E.H. Carr, *What is History?* London: Macmillan, 1961, and G.R. Elton, *The Practice of History*, London, Collins, 1969. The most influential historian in postmodern philosophy by far is Hayden V. White, *Metahistory: The Historical Imagination in Nineteenth-Century Europe*, Baltimore and London: The Johns Hopkins University Press, 1973. The journal *History and Theory* gives space to articles of a high professional philosophical standard, although it covers a much wider range of interests also. However, the small number of historians with a serious interest in philosophy is increasing, with a new journal, *Rethinking History*, published in 1997. Yet even those historians who claim a serious interest do not always follow philosophy of history at the appropriate level. For example, in an otherwise very sound and valuable work, one claims that E.H. Carr was "correct" in saying that the question whether history is a science was largely discussed because of "an eccentricity of the English language," and would not happen in German. Richard J. Evans, *In Defence of History*, London: Granta, 1997, p. 45.

191 The various attitudes of historians to the theory of history are described in Richard J. Evans, *In Defence of History*, London: Granta, 1997. A useful collection of material is Fritz Stern (ed.), *The Varieties of History From Voltaire to the Present*, Cleveland and New York: Meridian, 1956.

192 See, for example, Hayden V. White, *Metahistory: The Historical Imagination in Nineteenth-Century Europe*, Baltimore and London: The Johns Hopkins University Press, 1973; Hans Kellner, *Language and Historical Representation: Getting the Story Crooked*, Madison, Wisconsin: University of Wisconsin Press, 1989; Keith Jenkins, *Re-Thinking History*, London and New York: Routledge, 1991; Keith Jenkins, *On "What is History?" From Carr and Elton to Rorty and White*, London and New York: Routledge, 1995; Alun Munslow, *Deconstructing History*, London and New York: Routledge, 1997.

193 One very useful volume is Michael Bentley (ed.), *Companion to Historiography*, London and New York: Routledge, 1997, which contains thirty-nine contributions to the subject in almost one thousand pages, covering a wide range of historical approaches from the ancient Chinese until the present day. Yet even here, however, the "historiography" sometimes does little more than chronicle a bibliography in continuous prose, without any attempt at explanation or justification of the approaches taken. Furthermore, the material is organized by date of subject matter rather than date of writing. There is no doubt that the subject needs more attention.

194 Burleigh Taylor Wilkins, *Carl Becker: A Biographical Study in American Intellectual History*.

195 A valuable contribution to the understanding of historical interpretations is made by Burleigh Taylor Wilkins, *Has History Any Meaning? A Critique of Popper's Philosophy of History*, chap. 2.

196 This is analysed at length in J.L. Gorman, *Understanding History: An Introduction to Analytical Philosophy of History*, Ottawa: University of Ottawa Press, 1992. For the "as if" approach see Milton Friedman, "The Methodology of Positive Economics", originally in his *Essays in Positive Economics*, Chicago: The University of Chicago Press, 1953, reprinted in Frank Hahn and Martin Hollis (eds.) *Philosophy and Economic Theory*, Oxford: Oxford University Press, 1979. For an excellent introduction to the philosophy of economic theory, see M. Blaug, *The Methodology of Economics*, Cambridge: Cambridge University Press, 1980.

197 Wilkins notes that Hegel "gave us a definitive list of the basic *kinds* of points of view adopted by historians." Burleigh Taylor Wilkins, *Hegel's Philosophy of History*, p. 28.

198 These should not be assumed to be the same thing.

199 Burleigh Taylor Wilkins, *Has History Any Meaning? A Critique of Popper's Philosophy of History*, p. 174.

200 Ibid., p. 28.

201 Ibid., p. 29.

202 Ibid., pp. 228-229.

203 Ibid., pp. 184-185.

204 Ibid., pp. 207-208.

Paul Redding

Wilkins, Hegel, and History

In 1975, a year after Burleigh Taylor Wilkins had published *Hegel's Philosophy of History*, a work on Hegel appeared which would introduce many to his philosophy: this was Charles Taylor's comprehensive and simply-titled, *Hegel*.[1] Both books sought to re-introduce to an English-speaking philosophical world a philosopher who had largely disappeared long before, but they were very different books. Taylor's book set Hegel's philosophy against the background of what he described as a dilemma at the heart of late eighteenth-century European cultural life: on the one hand, a yearning for the recovery of a perceived loss of unity with the world, on the other, a simultaneous desire to maintain the individual autonomy that enlightened thought of that century had promised. Utilising Aristotelian hylomorphic ontology, a romantic "expressivist" theory of the mind, and a dose of Kantian philosophy, Hegel had produced the most serious attempt to solve that dilemma, and at the centre of this attempt was a conception of the universe as a "cosmic subject" or "self-positing God" called "spirit" (*Geist*).

On the subject matter that Taylor shares with Wilkins, Taylor presents Hegel's philosophical history as the story of this spiritual self-positing, a type of divine biography. While acknowledging that Hegel was no "theist in the ordinary sense,"[2] Taylor frequently employs formulae that suggest that *Geist* can be conceived as an individual embodied, acting and self-aware subject writ large, a subject whose activities could be described from the external or third-person point of view of philosophy.[3] Hegel, we are told, had adopted a radically anti-dualistic conception of the human subject from earlier expressivist theorists like Herder, and when his earlier more humanist views came to be replaced by his later strongly theo-centric perspective, this divine subject was dealt with in the same strongly anti-dualist way.[4] As the divine mind needed a body, God's infinite life had to supervene on the collective lives of humans; in fact, human history simply was the process in which *Geist* posits itself and comes to reflective awareness of itself in the world.

Given this account, it is not surprising then that now "no one actually believes [Hegel's] central ontological thesis." Despite the wide variety of extant views about the world, today "no one holds the Hegelian ontology."[5]

Wilkins's much shorter "sympathetic account of Hegel's philosophy of history [presented] in the light of Hegel's overall system, with special reference to his *Science of Logic*" is relatively free of this overarching, unbelievable "metanarrative" approach to the history of the West as the vehicle for a divine biography.[6] Rather, Wilkins's orientation seems more to start from the presupposition that it is in fact far from clear *how* we are meant to take Hegel's broad interpretative claims. Consequently, Wilkins attempts to clarify exactly what is at issue here by proceeding *via* the investigation of three topics: Hegel's understanding of the relation of his own philosophical approach to history to other, non-philosophical, historical genres; his conception of immanent teleology; and the issue of contingency and necessity in history.

In the quarter century since the appearance of these two books, one of the most significant features of English-speaking Hegel scholarship has been the increasing questioning of that familiar understanding of Hegel as presenting some bizarre *ontological* thesis in the way assumed by Taylor, and in various types of "non-metaphysical" readings a different picture of Hegel to that of the unbelievable ontologist has taken shape. In particular, it is now often argued that, despite his criticisms of Kant, Hegel in fact inherited Kant's critical attitude towards all "dogmatic" metaphysics, and so, towards the sort of "ontological thesis" with which he is burdened by Taylor. Indeed, Wilkins's small book, by its very reluctance to recycle old verities on Hegel's attitude to history, may be read as an early expression of this non-metaphysical orientation.

In this essay I reflect on those three areas on which Wilkins focuses as providing clues for a non-metaphysical Hegelian conception of history, and do so against the background of two strands within contemporary non-metaphysical accounts—on the one hand the strand which stresses the continuity with Kant's critical philosophy, and on the other, a strand which emphasises the centrality on Hegel's notion of recognition or *Anerkennung*.[7]

Hegel's Account of the Varieties of History

Wilkins draws attention to Hegel's brief comments on historical methodology in the "Introduction" to his *Lectures on the Philosophy of History*. The Kantian hue of Wilkins' Hegel is clearly apparent in the nature of his criticism of an empiricist understanding of the nature of historical knowledge—specifically his criticism in the context of history of what Wilfrid Sellars pilloried as the "myth of the given."

According to Wilkins, Hegel's criticism of the "myth of the historically given" is directed to the assumption that historians can come to historical data "without prior commitment or interpretative categories of any sort,"[8] that is, that the story they aim to tell is one that is somehow found ready-made in history as it actually happened. But to emphasise Hegel's critique of the myth of the given does not mean that he had no room in his theory of historiography for "the facts;" rather, "Hegel claimed in effect ...that historical facts themselves are not so much given as selected in accordance with various points of view."[9]

Neither does the recognition that history can in no way be freed from the historian's interpretative schemes in any way imply skepticism or relativism.[10] Rather, the outlook it exemplifies might be characterised as a type of "realism," we might say, a "perspectival realism."[11] There is a certain "perspectivism" in Hegel's attitude to historical knowledge in that to be a finite knowing subject is to know the past on the basis of some determinate epistemic conditions which simultaneously limit and enable knowledge, conditions which constitute that "point of view" from which one grasps history as it appears. Clearly, an important aspect of one's point of view here is going to be one's temporal place *within* the flow of history. The only alternative would be a view of history from some position outside of it, but as Wilkins points out, "Hegel is not claiming to have any special extra-historical vantage point from which he can survey the whole of historical progress."[12] What allows Hegel to both acknowledge the situatedness of finite knowers and yet simultaneously be a realist rather a sceptic or a relativist is his willingness to forego the "Kantian" idea of a "world in-itself," and subsequently any idea of a "history-in-itself" behind the veil of appearance.[13] Thus to know history from within is in no way to reduce such knowledge to the status of knowledge of "mere appearance" as this notion relies on the contrast with an underlying reality.

Wilkins's way of capturing this perspectival realist reply to relativism is by stressing the difference between being "responsive" to facts and, like the empiricist's ideal knower, being "merely receptive" of facts. We might say that in appealing to "the facts" we necessarily appeal to them "under a description:" without this interpretation (or "determination") the very concept of "the facts" would remain empty. Because it is interpretation that brings a fact into the Sellarsian "space of reasons," it is precisely by putting facts into words that a knower can be "responsive" to them. But if *all* history-telling is situated or perspectival, what then can be special about philosophical history?

Clearly philosophical history is not on the same level as the forms of empirical history with which Hegel deals, nor can the "perspective" of philosophy be thought of in the same way as those of non-philosophical history. For Hegel it is "reason" itself that articulates the point of view of philosophy, and from *this* point of view history will appear in a very particular way—i.e., as "rational:" "To him who looks at the world rationally the world looks rationally back."[14] This is, of course, precisely the sort of idea that leads advocates of the at times metaphysical Hegel to see him as aiming at a "God's-eye view" of history as the evolution of a self-knowing "cosmic spirit." Wilkins, however, regards the very meaning of what it is to be "philosophical" history as understandable *only* in its relation to the varieties of non-philosophical history. "Only when these points of view are compared and contrasted with one another and then with that of the philosophical historian—the philosopher of history—can we adequately understand what it is that Hegel thought philosophy brings to and learns from the study of history."[15] In terms of the familiar and recurring cognitive triad in Hegel's thought, philosophical history will involve the "*Aufhebung,*" the negation but preservation of, the other two forms. To understand the internal structure of the *philosophically* historical perspective, we will then need to know something of the other two non-philosophical historical perspectives *aufgehoben* within it.

The Non-Philosophical Historical Perspectives

Hegel's two major categories of non-philosophical historiography correspond broadly to its ancient and modern modes. "Original historians" such as Herodotus and Thucydides narrated contemporary deeds, events and situations which they had "witnessed, experienced and lived through." Furthermore, the historian had "participated in … the *spirit* which informed them."[16] That is, original historians had been immersed in the culture within which events and situations were described and reacted to in certain ways and had thereby gained their significance; these historians were at one with those values, aspirations, drives, and outlooks which the historical agents expressed in their actions. In contrast, in terms of historical *content* the modern "reflective historian" is not so restricted to his or her own time but can write about events of distant and foreign historical epochs.

As a result of this, the scope of historical inquiry can expand, with the result that one of the types of reflective history Hegel describes is "universal" history. But the reflective historian is still not without a perspective constituted by his or her own time: with reflective history "the writer approaches [the past] in his own spirit, which is different from the spirit of the object itself."[17]

This immediate difference tells us something about how the two types of historical narrative are constructed. For their historical narratives original historians could take over those agents' own descriptions of their intentions and actions such that much original history consists of the reporting of speeches in which central protagonists "express the maxims of their nation and of their own personality, their consciousness of their own political position and of their moral and spiritual nature, and the principles which underlie their designs and conduct."[18] With the reflective historian's loss of direct contact with the events narrated historiography is now, by necessity, a second order activity. What are synthesized are no longer perceptions and random "vivid" recollections, but *accounts* such as those of the first order original historians. This process in which original rich descriptions are reduced to abstractions—"a battle was fought, a great victory was won, a town was unsuccessfully besieged"—results in narratives which "portray the central interests of states" in which the "particulars of individual lives disappear altogether."[19] Where particular traits remain they "should be characteristic, and of significance for the spirit of the age" under examination.[20]

The distinction within non-philosophical historiography between an immediate form of knowledge, immersed somehow in the world of its objects, and another more mediated form "reflected" out of this world, exemplifies a more general distinction between experiential or cognitive styles which runs throughout Hegel's philosophy. Hegel's distinction between the three forms of historical writing maps pretty directly onto the three "moments" of theoretical knowledge—intuition (*Anschauung*), representation (*Vorstellung*), and thought (*Denken*), described in the *Encyclopaedia*.[21] While it is clear that all forms of historiography involve "representation,"[22] the first two forms of historiography reflect the differences between the moments of intuition and representation (while, of course, philosophical history will exemplify the structure of *thought*). And so, just as in the form of intuition "intelligence is immersed in the external material, is one with it, and has no other content."[23] We might say that the original historian is immersed in the events themselves, is at one with the meanings expressed in the historical actions. And as typical of its representational phase, intelligence as manifested in the reflective historian "withdraws into itself from the relationship in which it is related to the *singleness* of the object and relates the object to a universal."[24]

Clearly, for Hegel the reflective viewpoint of the modern historian is one that is intimately bound up with the nature of modern society. Specifically, it is bound up with the existence of a realm of intersubjectivity peculiar to it, a "reflective" form of life which is centred on the interactions of the modern market: "civil society."[25] While in ancient societies the family alone provided the model on which all public institutions were mapped, in the modern world, civil society comes to exist alongside the family as a fundamental institutional form. Elsewhere I have argued that family and civil society for Hegel typified opposed cognitive contexts, spheres of peculiar forms of "education" within which subjects are formed and giving rise to distinct "epistemic and moral styles."[26] The key to understanding such distinctions is to understand these institutional realms in terms of the different ways that individual subjects are "recognised" or "acknowledged" (*anerkennt*) within them. To see how this works requires a short digression into what for a number of recent Hegel interpreters is one of his key concepts, that of recognition or "*Anerkennung*."

Hegel's Concept of *Anerkennung*

The idea behind Hegel's use of the notion of *Anerkennung* might be traced back to post-Kantian attempts to do away with the Kantian notion of the "noumenon" or "thing in itself." Kant had needed the notion of the noumenon to prevent transcendental idealism from collapsing into Berkeleian metaphysical (or "material") idealism; but to say *anything* about noumena, even that they exist or are unknowable, seemed to transgress the critical prohibition on applying concepts beyond the realm of empirical appearances.[27] Fichte's answer to this problem of what limited the "positing" activity of the subject once the "noumenon" was given up was to claim that intelligence was somehow *self-limiting*. In his practical philosophy, specifically in his theory of rights, this idea of the ego's setting boundaries to its own conceptualising activities was linked to the self-limitation that an ego enacted in the context of the demands of *another ego.* To recognise the right of another was precisely to limit one's activity such that it did not intrude upon their sphere of activity.[28] Further, Fichte seemed also to make this form of intersubjective recognition of the right of another a necessary condition of self-consciousness. Thus, as from the

Kantian point of view "transcendental" self-consciousness was the condition of the objectivity of any conscious experience, it now seemed that Fichte had made what we now think of as the subject's "intentionality" dependent on its recognitive intersubjective relations to other subjects.

Hegel introduces this recognitive intersubjective structure as a necessary context for the existence of self-consciousness in chapter 4 of the *Phenomenology of Spirit*: "Self-consciousness" he there asserts, "exists in and for itself when, and by the fact that, it so exists for another; that is, it exist only in being acknowledged." [29] This recognitive relation is at the heart of what Hegel calls "spirit."[30] Thus, as Terry Pinkard points out, "'Spirit' ...denotes for Hegel not a metaphysical entity but a fundamental *relation* among persons that mediates their self-consciousness."[31] Throughout the *Phenomenology* Hegel will trace various structures of spirit terminating the "absolute knowing" of philosophy—the highest form of "absolute spirit." The recognitive relation at the heart of spirit is perhaps most explicit, however, in Hegel's account of the form of religious life and consciousness immediately anterior to philosophy. It is the form of recognition of *mutual forgiveness* which is at the heart of the religious relation: "The word of reconciliation is the *objectively* existent spirit, which intuits the pure knowledge of itself qua universal essence, in its opposite ...—a reciprocal recognition which is *absolute* spirit." [32] This "reconciling *Yea*" between two mutually recognising subjects is also described as "god manifested in the midst of those who know themselves in the form of pure knowledge."[33]

If we read this last sentence alongside a notorious series of sentences concerning history from the *Philosophy of Right*, then the latter might be seen in a different light. In discussing the state, Hegel says of it that it "consists in the march of god in the world, and its basis is the power of reason actualizing itself as will. In considering the Idea of the state, we must not have any particular states or institutions in mind; instead, we should consider the Idea, this actual God, in its own right." [34]

Clearly formulations such as this latter one appear to give credence to the picture of Hegel as divine biographer. But if the manifestation of God in the world *is* simply the act or event of reciprocal recognition, the reconciling "yea" of mutual forgiveness which establishes some complex form of community, then the identification of the "march of God in the world" with the *development* of a certain type of sociality—that which Hegel calls "the state" but which in no way is identical to "any particular states or institutions"—takes on a quite different hue.[35]

We see an alternative, non-metaphysical, account of what Hegel means by the historical development of a particular type of sociality conducive to freedom in approaches to Hegel such as those of Robert Pippin and Terry Pinkard. In these accounts Hegel's philosophy of history is understood in terms of the development of those structures of freely communicative sociality within which questions concerning the validity of our epistemic and moral claims come to be posed and answered in ways which neither rely on existing bodies of dogma (religion, for example) nor which collapse into scepticism.

> The general theme of Hegel's narrative of political history—the development of freedom—does not ...express any metaphysical assumptions about God's directing history ....The teleology of history is the movement from self-undermining conceptions of what is authoritative for human beings to a fully rational form of self-understanding which is capable of resolving its own skepticism about itself. ...It is thus not implausible to interpret Hegel as taking this to be the end of that particular story, to have as a result a sustainable self-understanding of who we are and what we are about.[36]

According to Pinkard modernity is "that stage of history in which the accounts of what is authoritative are capable of satisfactorily answering the kinds of skeptical objections which are generated against them."[37] This is perhaps most obvious in the growth of the culture of empirical science from the early modern period, but this style of cognition needs to be integrated with much broader changes taking place within social life, which crucially include changes in individuals' self-conceptions within that life. The characteristic change here is the development of "reflective" forms of self-identification from a more immediate form in which the individual is socially recognised primarily in terms of interlocking social roles modelled on those of the family. In Hegel's synopsis of European history the development of the *legally* defined citizen was a significant development in this regard, but this in turn needed the support of more fundamental forms of interaction in which individuals recognise each other in abstract or reflective ways. In the modern period it was the emergence of *market* relations in which contractees in practical ways "*recognise* [*anerkennen*] each other as persons and owners of property" that reflective subjectivity could gain a proper foothold in social life.[38]

A clear account of the polarity between familial relations on the one hand and market relations on the other is provided in *Principles of the Philosophy of Right* where Hegel characterises family and civil society as two "masses" into which modern "ethical life" (*Sittlichkeit*) divides itself. These two institutional forms are differentiated in terms of the different structures of mutual recognition at their respective centers. The form of recognition characterising the family, constituting its members in their relations to each other is that of love. "Love means in general terms the consciousness of my unity with another, so that I am not in selfish isolation." [39] But love is a one-sided form of recognition in as much as the emphasis falls on the unification of the individuals involved at the expense of the recognition of their separateness and particularity. Contrariwise, in the market-based realm of civic society the emphasis falls on the separation and particularity at the expense of unity.

In civil society recognition has become particularised to the extent that social differentiation now reaches its limit and coincides with natural, biological particularisation. This is what is behind both the felt loss of unity with the world and the blossoming of the autonomy of the individual that Taylor identifies as key concerns of the late eighteenth century. It is this polarity of emphasis between unification and separation that characterises the epistemic and moral styles typifying such forms of life. While the family is the world of unquestioned, unreflectively shared interpretations, the modern institutions of civil society introduce a different style in which the familiar can be reflectively held up for questioning. Reflectively recognised the cognitive subject of civil society tends to the divestment of all those assumptions, values and so on, characteristic of the more "substantive" identity they have in the immediate context of intimates and family.

We can now see something about the distinctive peculiarity of the non-philosophical historical styles. Original historians of the ancient world display a cognitive style which goes along with the familial nature of the recognitive relations within which they are formed. Here the historical narrative is marked by a unity between the historian's own meaning-conferring perspective with that of both his audience and the world of the historical protagonists themselves. Integration and immediacy are the hallmarks of the original history as a cultural or communicative form as such communicative acts forge links between the outlooks of the historian, the historical agents represented in the history, and the historian's original audience.

In contrast, the modern, reflective historian is necessarily cut off from the collective spiritual world of the ancient Greeks informing the original historian's narrative: we moderns "will never be able to sympathise with the Greeks and ...share their feelings in the most important issues of all."[40] Nevertheless a type of interpretative orientation towards the original agents can be achieved in virtue of the fact that reflective thought can "disregard the differences and isolate the common factor which can be expected to behave in the same way and to show itself in the same light under all circumstances." [41]

It is the modern historian's reflective perspective that allows him or her to abstract the *form* of the original actions from their culturally-given contents or objects. Thus *states* with their own characteristic "spirits" now come forward as the real agents of these narratives, while the actions of individuals come to be captured by quasi-mechanical forms of explanation in which motivations are reduced to *passion,* "the subjective or formal aspect of the energy of active volition [which is] irrespective of its actual content or end." [42] In short, it is the reflective abstraction of form from content which allows the spirits of individual human communities to be understood as providing the new "content" of the narration.

Clearly Hegel's philosophical history is meant to retain some of characteristics of each of these historical modes while shedding others. Like original history it will involve a type of identification with the spirit revealed in the narrative, but this identification will be re-established on a higher level given the plurality of forms of objectified spirit revealed by reflective history. By abstracting a socially-constituted *content* from the form of individual actions, the reflective historian can appeal to a type of supra-individual meaningfulness which shows through the mechanically understood individual actions. Appealing to something "supra-individual" here doesn't look too threatening since we can simply identify this with that fabric of cultural meaning characterising the particular society. But what is going to be put in its place in philosophical history? Hegel identifies a purpose manifested here, and surely this would seem to be so wedded to the idea of a God being realised in history that the familiar ontological interpretation of Hegel is hard to circumvent. What we need to get clearer on then is Hegel's understanding of purpose, and it is purposiveness that Wilkins turns to in the second part of his study of Hegel on history.

Purpose in History

Hegel was, Wilkins points out, "the last philosopher to ask the question of the ultimate purpose of the world."[43] But such purpose was not to be conceived as located in the mind of some transcendent God: for Hegel, the teleological process revealed in history and involving the realisation of freedom and self-consciousness was an *immanent* teleology. This concept of teleology was, Wilkins's believes, central in Hegel's philosophy: it was not only the key to understanding his philosophy of history, it was the key to understanding his entire system.[44]

This issue of teleology provides us with a suitable focus around which the question of whether or not Hegel is a dogmatic metaphysician might be addressed because it will allow us to raise the crucial question of Hegel's relation to Kant: as Wilkins points out, it was Kant's distinction between external or relative purposiveness and internal purposiveness that Hegel regarded as his greatest service to philosophy.[45] With this idea of internal purposiveness, claimed Hegel, Kant "has opened up the concept of life, the Idea, and by so doing has done positively for philosophy what the *Critique of Reason* did but imperfectly, equivocally and only *negatively* namely, raised it above the determinations of reflection and the relative world of metaphysics."[46] And yet although teleology had "opened up" this concept of life—the "Idea"—a problem still adhered to Kant's treatment of the "ideas of reason," Hegel believed, in that Kant had treated these ideas as merely "regulative" rather than "constitutive"—that is, as *directing* the systematic employment of the understanding, but as producing no knowledge themselves.[47]

The treatment of teleology Hegel praised in Kant was, of course, to be found in the third of Kant's three critiques, the *Critique of Judgment*.[48] And there, paralleling his restriction of the ideas of reason to regulative status in the first critique, Kant restricted those judgments attributing *purpose* to the organic realm to "reflective" status. Reflective judgments, unlike the "determinative" judgments of understanding of the first critique, were judgments for which no rule-governed application of a concept could be found. The other instance of this was the judgment of taste, in which the ascription of beauty to some presentation could not be grounded in any rule justifying that ascription.

Thus we could not attribute "purpose" to the organism in the straightforward way in which we attributed, say, *mass* to it: biological thought approached the organism *as if* it manifested purpose, and purpose was thought of as read into the organism *via* a heuristic move which compensated for the fact that the categories of *our* mechanistic understanding could not capture the complex patterns of reciprocal causality manifest in its functional structure.[49] In contrast, Hegel made teleology here the "higher principle," a relation reflected in the development, as Wilkins traces it, of categories of mechanism, chemism, and teleology in Hegel's *Logic*.

But is not the rejection of the merely regulative status of ideas here together with the promotion of the reflective judgment *precisely* the type of move that typifies Hegel's lapse into pre-critical dogmatic stance? For Kant, our inability to utilise ideas constitutively was central to his critique of dogmatic metaphysics. Concepts were always applied to appearances as presented through non-conceptual representations—intuitions—rather than to "things in themselves." But pure reason essentially applied to *judgments* as bearers of logical form, not to objects. Thus its concepts, "ideas," were experience-transcendent: to think that they could yield knowledge was to attribute to human beings the "intellectual intuition" of which only an infinite, divine mind would be capable.

This is the standard picture of the "metaphysical" Hegel, and yet to gain some overall idea of what is at issue here, more needs to be said about the way logic is conceived in Kant and Hegel.

Kant and Hegel on the Logical Grounds of Judgment

It is misleading to think of the syllogistic logic that Kant adopted from Aristotle as functioning in the critical philosophy as merely articulating truth functional relations between judgments. Kant distinguishes *reason* as the faculty of inferences and principles from the *understanding* as the faculty of judgments and concepts, and in places construes the constitutive structures of the former on the analogy with those of the latter. That is, reason unifies *judgments* within its larger inferential structures in a way parallel to that in which the understanding unifies *appearances* within its judgments. The syllogism itself thus displays the relation between the judgment and its "principle" or "ground."[50]

Kant's idea might be illustrated with a familiar example. Starting with an empirical judgment like "Gaius is mortal," the faculty of reason allows us to construct a syllogism of which this initial judgment is the conclusion. For example, we can construct the syllogism: "All men are mortal, Gaius is a man, therefore Gaius is mortal." But while we set out such a syllogism as a movement from premisses to conclusion, Kant is interested in thought's movement in the reverse direction, that is in the "ascending" movement from the conclusion to a major premiss which will reveal the principle or ground of that judgment: it is Gaius' humanity that explains the fact of his mortality. In Kant's words, "reason, in its logical employment, seeks to discover the universal condition of its judgment (the conclusion) and the syllogism is itself nothing but a judgment made by means of the subsumption of its condition under a universal rule (the major premiss)."[51]

Of course, any principle so discovered will itself have the form of a judgment and so reason can now pose the question of *its* grounds—that is, pose the question of the "condition of the condition"—and in answering this reason will now construct a further syllogism on top of the first such that the conclusion of the new syllogism is the major premiss of the original. We can see then that the activity of reason can issue in an ascending "prosyllogistic" chain and the question will naturally arise as to whether thought will ever reach an end of this ascent, will ever reach the ultimate *unconditioned* condition of all that is represented "below" it. It is consistent with the Platonic imagery of all this Kant will identify the termini of such ascending prosyllogisms as the "ideas" of reason.[52]

Given the fundamental premisses of the critical philosophy we can see why for Kant "ideas" can only have regulative status. To think of them as presenting some ultimate objects to our mind—Platonic archetypes—would be to lapse back into thinking that we can know objects from concepts alone and so circumvent the realm of empirical appearance. Nevertheless, despite the fact that we can never know the "unconditioned" ultimate conditions of our experientially-sourced knowledge, reason demands that we think of our understanding as unified: it demands that we strive to find "for the conditioned knowledge obtained through the understanding the unconditioned whereby its unity is brought to completion."[53]

It is plain that a certain parallelism exists between *this* search, initiated by reason, for the higher principle for a given judgment in the first critique, and the nature of teleological judgment in the third. As has been said, teleological judgments are merely "reflective" rather than "determinative," and Kant further describes this distinction such that while a determinative judgment involves the application of a given concept to intuitions, reflective judgments involve the search *for* the relevant concept which would apply to the intuition.[54] That is, in the latter the *judgment itself* is non-conceptual: it predates, and guides the search to find the right concept. We can see why Hegel could see Kant's teleological reflective judgment as opening up the path to the "ideas." But here Hegel would give Kant's Platonic schema an Aristotelian twist.

What at first seems perplexing about Hegel's use of the notion of the "syllogism" is that he typically uses it, as in the *Phenomenology of Spirit*, for example, not to describe anything like a relation between judgments in the conventional sense, but to characterise the structure of recognitive relations constituting "spirit."[55] In a sense, the reason for this is apparent:

Hegel appeals to the syllogism as the model for a structure in which a particular term "mediates" the opposition between universal and singular terms. Thus, in his well-known example of the dialectical relation between master and slave, the master provides for the singular slave consciousness, a "particular" presentation of an otherwise unrepresentable universal—death. At first this seems little more than a metaphor, but if what I have said so far concerning the fundamental role played by recognition in Hegel's philosophy is on the right track, then we might see more at stake than this. Hegel's reference to "syllogisms" in such cases seems entirely consistent with the idea of a structure that grounds or conditions an intentional relation to the world (as the capacity for judgment)—but this "grounding" is now understood in a *pragmatic* way. It is in virtue of belonging to normative social practices involving mutual recognition that individuals have the capacity for intentionality and judgment. To put this in a more recent way, Hegel has construed the "conditions" of my cognitive claims in terms of my belonging to a linguistic community with immanent intersubjective norms regulating those claims and the appropriate responses of others to them. "Recognition"—my recognition of others as participants within these practices and their reciprocal recognition of me, together with the implicit recognition by all of us of the normativity of those practices themselves—is precisely what constitutes this "belonging." These practical recognitive infrastructures of our lives might then be described as the "unconditioned conditions" of our cognitive abilities—our capacity for judgment. The "ideas" are no longer in any Platonic realm but are now, following Aristotle, understood as at the center of a living process.

The complicated relationships existing among the topics of reflective versus determinative judgment, natural and aesthetic teleology, the relation of judgments to "syllogisms," and so on, in the respective philosophies of Kant and Hegel deserves much more elaboration than can be provided here.[56] Nevertheless, a few markers suggesting how these issues might be pursued in a non-metaphysical reading of Hegel's idea of philosophically comprehended history as teleological might be roughly staked out. As we have seen, along with Fichte and Schelling, Hegel had abandoned the problematic transcendental idealist dichotomy of phenomena and noumena, and with it, that between concept and intuition as epistemologically distinct sources of knowledge (eliminating any residual "myth of the given"). Along with this Hegel abandoned the ultimacy of the distinction between the understanding and its judgments on the one hand, and reason and its inferences on the other, a distinction already implicitly problematised by Kant himself with his conception of the syllogism as a type of higher-order judgment, and his idea of reflective judgment as a syllogism-like search for, rather than application of, a grounding universal. And just as the life of the organism could be thought of as teleological in the sense of self-productive, processes within the cognitive life of "spirit" could be conceived of as involving self-generation in some analogous but "higher" way. But how exactly *are we* to think of this spiritual teleology in general and as a teleology of history in particular?

It is commonly believed that a teleological approach is relevant to historical thought in *some* way. At the most basic level, historical narratives are, as Wilkins points out, teleological in the sense that actions are understood as end-directed. But the teleology typically presupposed is of an "extrinsic" nature: subjects of these accounts are understood as agents whose actions flow from their individual intentional states, their consciously held beliefs and desires, and clearly the teleology that Hegel sees operative in history cannot be simply reduced to this. Thus Hegel is often critical of this sense of teleology, noting in the *Encyclopaedia Logic* that "in dealing with the purpose, we must not think at once (or merely) of the form in which it appears in consciousness as a determination that is present in representation."[57] Such an extrinsic approach to teleology sees purpose as *imposed upon* the external world, and as such it is to be contrasted with the intrinsic or "functional" purposiveness that the Kantian teleological judgment attributes to the organism as immanent within its self-organising structure.[58] Clearly, for Hegel, the latter is in some way more basic: human agents can have and act on subjective goals only because they are first *living* beings with real, objective ends. But, of course, to be an intentional agent capable of subjective goals requires belonging to a further realm, that "second nature" of objectified spirit consisting of those recognitive and normative practices of some distinctively human form of sociality.[59] Thus on the one hand such intentional beings must be instantiated in organisms, understood in terms of a natural teleology, and on the other, within recognitive and normative practices of a social community. But while we might follow Hegel in thinking of these latter structures as necessary *conditions* for the existence of the teleology of individual human agency, what does it amount to think of these structures as *themselves* teleological? It is precisely *that* that Hegel thinks is manifested in history.

Perhaps we can start here by considering how the idea of a teleology belonging to such spiritual structures gets into more conventional eighteenth- and nineteenth-century approaches to history. The type of triumphalist enlightenment universal history as found in Schiller, for example, is clearly teleological in the sense that the modern period is seen as the flowering of freedom and reason thought of as the essential attributes of "man." Romantic, nationalist historians, more sensitive to the singularity of different cultures reacted against this, but nevertheless still attributed a type of teleology to individual nations by conceiving them on the model of organisms. Hegel does not follow either of these paths, each of which can be thought of as involving a reduction of spiritual to natural teleology. While the enlightenment story of progress of "man" to maturity in the present was modeled on the growth and maturation of an individual human being, romantics saw the quasi-organic spirits of the community as functionally borne by individual members regarded as organs of a complete social body. In contrast to each, Hegel insists on the *distinctly* spiritual character of the teleology revealed in history.

Again we might appeal to the notion of recognition to learn something about the peculiarity of spiritual teleology here. One obvious difference from Hegel's point of view between the inter-relation of organs in an organism and the inter-relation of members in a society is that the latter exists only *through* the acknowledgment of all the participants involved, an acknowledgment manifested in their cognitive interaction. This is the glue of a distinctly human sociality and so must also apply to the unity of communities across time, the unity assumed, for example, by the universalist concept of teleological progress. Thus the teleology ascribed to "spirit" running from the Greeks, say, to modern European society could not be a process that could be thought of as occurring *independently* of the acts of recognition of the members of that community, including ourselves. Without that recognition there would be no properly spiritual community within which there could be a teleological moment.

Clearly, the historiographical act itself can be seen as containing an implicit act of recognition—recognition of the cognitive or "spiritual" status of both the object revealed in the account and the addressee to whom it is directed. The original historian can, in an immediate and implicit way, so acknowledge both the agents described and the audience addressed because all belong to the one substantive culture. The type of recognition involved in the reflective historian's act is less straightforward. The distant historical agents are understood in a universal but abstract and quasi-mechanical way because they belong to different configurations of "objective spirit," and in turn these different configurations of national spirit can come into focus as particulars. If we were to think of these national spirits simply as quasi-organismic particulars, this might be all there would be to say here. But spirit itself is that whose identity can persist *through* these types of changes in a way analogous to that in which the organism retains its identity throughout the assimilation of that which is foreign to it.[60] This reflective historian and his or her audience can still understand the distant agents, but not as a member of a determinate community, rather, as a member of the historical community of "spirit" *per se*. That is, the historian must grasp that the spirit of his or her own time stands in a type of continuity, despite the differences, with the spirit of the agents whose actions are described. While many nostalgic romantic historians would have regarded the modern world with its "reflective" dimension as the *loss* of some earlier community, Hegel sees the modern world as the "negative form" of such an earlier substantive community.

As always, then, Hegel tries to move to a position in which rival perspectives, here those of the enlightenment progressivist and the nostalgic romantic historicist, are "*aufgehoben*." We must understand ourselves as located in a realm of spirit such that we can look back and understand earlier societies as containing the seed, as it were, out of which we have developed. But this cant be understood in a quasi-natural way, because it is only in our act of retrospectively understanding the earlier society as an earlier form of our own that we thereby establish, or re-establish, the community which can be characterised as having this teleological dimension.[61]

This is a teleological conception of spirit, but given its perspectival rooting in what, in fact, it *has* become, and given that its teleological character is *dependent on* it being recognised as such, it is not at all obvious that it is an ontologically *weighty* form of teleology. But surely Hegel's teleology cannot be as weak as this, because he conceives of this development as *necessary*. What we have to look at then is how Hegel understands necessity.

Necessity, Necessity, and More Necessity

To gain some sense of what is at issue here we might again look to Hegel's logic and in particular to his relation to Kant on key logical issues. Towards the end of book two of the *Science of Logic*, "The Doctrine of Essence," Hegel gives his own exposition of the modal categories of possibility, actuality and necessity. In fact he there derives three *different* versions of this modal triad and so has three different categories of necessity—formal necessity, real or relative necessity, and absolute necessity. As might be expected, the third involves the *Aufhebung* of the first two, and in understanding these two presupposed conceptions of necessity we might usefully turn to Kant's discussion of the modality of necessity in the first critique.

Early in the transcendental analytic of the *Critique of Pure Reason* Kant claims to derive the modal categories of possibility, existence, and necessity from the three logical forms (problematic, assertoric and apodeictic) of modal judgment; but one gains a fuller sense of his approach to modality in his treatment of the "postulates of empirical thought" in the "Analytic of Principles." There we find possibility treated as "that which agrees with the formal conditions of experience," actuality as "that which agrees with the material conditions of experience, that is, with sensation," and necessity as "that which in its connection with the actual is determined in accordance with universal conditions of experience." Kant follows this with a gloss which relates directly to his later critique in the "Transcendental Dialectic" of the ontological proof of God: the categories "do not in the least enlarge the concept to which they are attached as predicates. They only express the relation of the concept to the faculty of knowledge."[62]

Kant's refutation of the ontological argument can be regarded as an instance of his general criticism of dogmatically metaphysical thought, which tries to derive knowledge of the world from the resources of concepts alone. Dogmatic metaphysics had taken necessity as pertaining to objects. But what necessity pertains to are judgments—the application of concepts to appearances given in intuition—and "the unconditioned necessity of judgments is not an absolute necessity of things."[63]

We might consider the two contrasting concepts of necessity here, the older "metaphysical" notion as pertaining to objects, the newer "critical" notion as pertaining to judgments, that is, to some experienceable fact caught under the determinate form of conceptualisation, as reflected in Hegel's first two conceptions of necessity, formal and relative. Clearly, these differing concepts are meant to coincide in some way with what I have described earlier as the differing cognitive styles characterising the realms of immediate and reflective social relations, the paradigms of which being family and civil society. A cognitive style whose resources were limited to simple characterisations of immediately given objects would have no other way to try to capture the sense of necessity than by treating it as some immediate determination of those objects. "The necessary *is*, and this that simply is, is *itself the necessary*."[64] The notion of *relative or real* necessity, on the other hand, requires more complete and "reflective" resources. Relative necessity is not marked by any simple distinction to possibility or actuality as with the formal categories. Real possibility constitutes the "totality of conditions" of something which "enters into actuality" when those conditions are completely present.[65] That is, possibility understood in *this* way is sublated, "*aufgehoben*," into real actuality, and real necessity here pertains to this identity in difference of an actuality and its conditions. "But this necessity is at the same time relative [because] it has a *presupposition* from which it begins, it has its starting point in the contingent," that is, in the formally considered "actuality" of those conditions themselves.[66] As Wilkins points out, this is the type of necessity that Hegel takes as relevant for non-philosophical history. It simply says that the occurrence of a certain phenomenon necessarily followed upon certain others, constituting the conditions of that phenomenon.[67] Such a conception of historical necessity hardly seems to be particularly worrying, but of course it is Hegel's *further* notion of absolute necessity into which the other two notions are "*aufgehoben*" that is relevant to history conceived philosophically. What can we say about this third notion?

It can be expected that absolute necessity will have sublated characteristics of the other two, the necessity that immediate thought applies to simple "beings" and that which reflective thought applies to the relation of beings to their conditions, a necessity pertaining more to facts cognised in judgments. It is further apparent that this is the proper modality pertaining to "spirit." We are to think of spirit not as having the simple necessity of a "thing," as behind the ontological proof of God, nor are we to think of it as having the relative necessity of that which follows necessarily upon the existence of its own conditions of existence. But again, elements of these modalities will be contained in some negated way within it.

In the text of Hegel's *Science of Logic* at this point one encounters a bewildering barrage of conceptual relations, but some things emerge clearly enough. Absolute necessity, the modality of spirit, will, like relative necessity, have preconditions upon which its existence supervenes, but the difference to relative necessity inheres in the fact that absolute necessity somehow "posits" these conditions of its own existence.[68]

We get some help with exactly what Hegel is trying to get at here in the additions to the parallel section of the *Encyclopaedia Logic* where he reflects on the proverb "Everyone is the smith who forges his own fortune." This proverb is directed against the temptation to blame others or external circumstances for what befalls us, an attitude which is the "standpoint of unfreedom" and the "source of discontent." "By contrast, when we recognise (*anerkennt*) that whatever happens to us is only an evolution of our own selves, and that we carry only the burden of our own debts, we behave as free men, and whatever may befall us, we keep the firm faith that nothing unjust can happen to us. ...Now certainly, there is much that is contingent in what happens to us. But this contingency is grounded in the natural dimension of man. And since we also have the consciousness of our freedom, the harmony of our souls and our peace of mind will not be destroyed by the misfortunes that befall us. Thus, it is our own view of necessity that determines our human contentment and discontent, and thereby our very destiny."[69]

This necessity then, is akin to the type of necessity which one might attribute to the circumstances and conditions that have contributed to making one *who one is*, and Hegel is concerned with the act in which one recognises or acknowledges (*anerkennt*) the necessity of those conditions. If the circumstances of my birth, my upbringing, and so on had been different, then the being who would have resulted from that altered nexus of circumstances just would not have been *me*. It is the recognition or affirmation of one's conditions *as* one's own that amounts to the "positing" of those conditions that Hegel refers to in the *Science of Logic*.

Hegel's immense act of philosophical imagination amounts to projecting this schema onto the conditions of our collective existence as distinctly modern human beings. Again it is the idea of "*Anerkennung*" at the core of spirit which is the relevant concept. From a non-philosophical point of view, we are the products of some historically given set of circumstances from which we have emerged. Necessity here can be understood "relatively": *given* those conditions we had to turn out the way we are. But from a philosophical point of view, we are no passive products: we have become formed into the beings we are within a community but we become ourselves only to the extent that we acknowledge that community, with its internal differences, its reflective possibilities, and its developmental tendencies, as our own.

Hegel was a philosopher belonging to a particular period of European history, and each individual—and thus the individual philosopher—is, as he taught us "a *child of his time*."[70] It is undeniable that Hegel shared in many of the elements of the spirit of that time that are regarded today with justifiable suspicion, and many have come to see his philosophy of history as the mere attempt to confer a type of divine right on social arrangements built on a set of systematic exclusions rather than the universality of freedom. Along with other "sympathetic approaches," Wilkins's book has helped in retrieving Hegel's *philosophy* as a mode of thought and as an approach to history which can be reduced neither to the individual philosopher nor to his age.

Notes

1 Burleigh Taylor Wilkins, *Hegel's Philosophy of History*, (Ithaca: Cornell University Press, 1974), Charles Taylor, *Hegel*, (Cambridge: Cambridge University Press, 1975).

2 Taylor, *Hegel*, 102.

3 Thus Taylor sometimes describes *Geist* as if it is somehow constructed on the model of the finite subject: "this theory of the subject applies not only to man, but to cosmic spirit, or *Geist* as well" (*Hegel*, 87); "now let us transfer this from man onto Geist ..." (ibid., 89); "the universe must be grasped as something analogous to a life form" (ibid., 88); "Hegel's Geist thus seems to be the original existentialist, choosing his own nature in radical freedom from anything merely given" (ibid., 92).

4 Ibid., 80-3.

5 Ibid., 538.

6 Wilkins, *Hegel's Philosophy of History*, 13.

7 Among the recent non-metaphysical readings of Hegel which stress the Kantian dimension of his project, see especially, Pippin Robert, *Hegel's Idealism: The Satisfactions of Self-Consciousness*, (Cambridge: Cambridge University Press, 1989) and Terry Pinkard, *Hegel's Phenomenology: The Sociality of Reason*, (Cambridge: Cambridge University Press, 1994). Robert R. Williams treats Hegel's concept of recognition in *Recognition: Fichte and Hegel on the Other*, (Albany: State University of New York Press, 1992). I argue for the complementarity of these approaches in *Hegel's Hermeneutics*, (Ithaca: Cornell University Press, 1996).

8 Wilkins, *Hegel's Philosophy of History*, 23.

9 Ibid., 27-8.

10 Ibid., 24.

11 I take this term from Wachterhauser who uses it to capture the Hegelian approach of Hans-Georg Gadamer in "Gadamer's Realism: The 'Belongingness' of Word and Reality", in Brice R. Wachterhauser (ed.), *Hermeneutics and Truth*, (Evanston: Northwestern University Press, 1994).

12 Wilkins, *Hegel's Philosophy of History*, 175.

13 "Kantian" because like most Kant interpreters Hegel subscribed to the contestable "two world" interpretation of Kant's phenomena-noumena distinction. On the distinction and for a defence of the rival "two aspect" interpretation, see, for example, Henry E. Allison, *Kant's Transcendental Idealism: An Interpretation and Defense*, (New Haven: Yale University Press, 1983. This latter interpretation of Kant makes Hegel more of a Kantian by making Kant more Hegelian.

14 Quoted in Wilkins, *Hegel's Philosophy of History*, 24. We might hear Hegel's sentence here as a variant of Kant's well-known claim that "reason has insight only into that which it produces after a plan of its own". Immanuel Kant, *Critique of Pure Reason*, trans. N. Kemp Smith, (New York: Macmillan, 1929), B xiii.

15 Wilkins, *Hegel's Philosophy of History*, 28.

16 G. W. F. Hegel, *Lectures on the Philosophy of World History: Introduction*, translated by H. B. Nisbet, with an introduction by Duncan Forbes, (Cambridge: Cambridge University Press, 1975), 12, emphasis added.

17 Hegel, *Lectures on the Philosophy of World History: Introduction*, 16.

18 Ibid., 14.

19 Ibid., 18-9.

20 Ibid., 19.

21 G. W. F. Hegel, *Hegel's Philosophy of Mind: Being Part Three of The Encyclopaedia of The Philosophical Sciences*, trans. W. Wallace and A. V. Miller, (Oxford: Oxford University Press, 1971), §§ 440-468.

22 "They have compiled a written record of these deeds and events, thereby transferring what were previously mere extraneous happenings into the realm of intellectual representation. What was mere existence thereby takes on an intellectual aspect and becomes a representation of the internal and external faculties of the mind." (Hegel, *Lectures on the Philosophy of World History: Introduction*, 12); and further: "original historians transmute the events, deeds and situations they have witnessed into a work of representational thinking for the representational faculty" (Ibid., 13).

23 *Hegel's Philosophy of Mind*, § 450, *Zusatz.*

24 *Hegel's Philosophy of Mind*, § 445, *Zusatz.*

25 I have explored some of the ramifications of this in "Absorbed in the Spectacle of the World: Hegel's Criticism of Romantic Historiography", *Clio*, 16 (1987): 297-315.

26 Redding, *Hegel's Hermeneutics*, 191-203.

27 Kant himself was clearly aware of this problem and suggested that the concept "noumena" be used entirely "negatively" as a "limit concept". It was as if he conceived of "noumena" as a word bereft of its own cognitive content – a non-concept to be used somehow simply to signal the limitedness of our knowledge as knowledge of "phenomena". Kant, *Critique of Pure Reason*, A 256/B311-2.

28 For a helpful account of Fichte's complex thought on these issues see Williams, *Recognition*, part 2.

29 G. W. F. Hegel, *Hegel's Phenomenology of Spirit*, trans. A. V. Miller, (Oxford: Oxford University Press, 1977), § 178.

30 "A self-consciousness, in being an object [i.e., for another], is just as much 'I' 'object'. With this we have already before us the concept of *Spirit*." (Ibid.)

31 Pinkard, *Hegel's Phenomenology*, 9. Cf., Pippin, *Hegel's Idealism*, 152-4.

32 Ibid., 670, translation modified.

33 Ibid., 671.

34 G. W. F. Hegel, *Elements of the Philosophy of Right*, edited by Allen W. Wood, translated by H. B. Nisbet, (Cambridge: Cambridge University Press, 1991), § 258.

35 Mutual forgiveness might be thought of as some complex "performative" which relates subjects in a certain way which, paradoxically, simultaneously absolves or frees them from relations of a different and presupposed sort (from being bound by some debt or sanction, say).

36 Terry Pinkard, "Hegel on History, Self-Determination, and the Absolute", in Arthur M. Melzer, Jerry Weinberger, and M. Richard Zinman (eds.), *History and the Idea of Progress* (Ithaca: Cornell University Press, 1995), pp. 53-4.

37 Ibid., 54.

38 PR, 71, remark.

39 Hegel, *Elements of the Philosophy of Right*, 158 addition.

40 Hegel, *Lectures on the Philosophy of World History: Introduction*, 17.

41 Ibid., 44. Hegel brings this to bear on the vexed question of knowing "what it is like to be" a member of another community. We can no more know what it is like to be an ancient Greek than we can a dog ("we cannot share their (ie., the Ancient Greek's) feelings when they prostrate themselves before Zeus, Minerva, etc., ... just as we cannot share the sensations of a dog." (Ibid., 18)) but we can reflectively know them just as we "can predict [the dog's] mannerisms, attachments, and idiosyncrasies". (Ibid.)

42 Ibid., 73. It is precisely reflective abstraction which makes use of "this distinction between form and content" which can be applied "to all personal convictions, opinions, and conscience." Ibid.

43 Wilkins, *Hegel's Philosophy of History*, 56.

44 Ibid., 91-2.

45 Ibid., 86.

46 G. W. F. Hegel, *Hegel's Science of Logic*, translated by A. V. Miller (London: Allen and Unwin, 1969), 737, quoted by Wilkins, *Hegel's Philosophy of History*, 87.

47 Hegel, *Science of Logic*, 590.

48 Immanuel Kant, *Critique of Judgment*, trans. Werner S. Pluhar, (Indianapolis: Hackett, 1987).

49 Similarly for Kant, there is a certain "as if" character to nature with respect to its aesthetic appreciation: it is as if it had been designed to elicit a response of disinterested pleasure.

50 "Knowledge from principles is ... that knowledge alone in which I apprehend the particular in the universal through concepts. Thus every syllogism is a mode of deducing knowledge from a principle." Kant, *Critique of Pure Reason*, A 300/B357.

51 Ibid., A 307/B364.

52 "Now since this rule is itself subject to the same requirement of reason, and the condition of the condition must be sought (by means of a prosyllogism) whenever practicable, obviously the principle peculiar to reason in general, in its logical employment is: – to find for the conditioned knowledge obtained through the understanding the unconditioned whereby its unity is brought to completion." Ibid., A 307/B364.

53 Ibid., A 307/B364.

54 In the *Science of Logic* Hegel brings together the reflective judgment and the syllogism by describing the former as "a connecting *middle term* between the *universal of reason* and the *individual of intuition*". (Hegel, *Science of Logic*, 739.)

55 See, for example, 184 and 227.

56 For a non-metaphysical reading see, Robert B. Pippin, "Avoiding German Idealism: Kant, Hegel, and the Reflective Judgment Problem", *Proceedings of the 8th International Kant Congress*, vol 1, (Milwaukee: Marquette University Press, 1996), reprinted in *Idealism as Modernism: Hegelian Variations*, (Cambridge: Cambridge University Press, 1997).

57 G. W. F. Hegel, *The Encyclopedia Logic* trans. T. F. Geraets, W. A. Suchting, and H. S. Harris, (Hackett, Indianapolis, 1991), 204, remark.

58 On this see especially Willem deVries, "The Dialectic of Teleology", *Philosophical Topics*, 19, 2 (1991): 51-70.

59 Hegel invokes the idea of a "second nature" in *Elements of the Philosophy of Right*, 151.

60 For a detailed account of the analogy between organic and spiritual processes in Hegel's philosophy see Klaus Brinkmann, "Hegel on the Animal Organism", *Leval théologique et philosophique*, 52, 1 (1996): p. 140.

61 Brinkmann points to the retrospective nature of Hegel's concept of teleology. Ibid., p. 148.

62 Kant, *Critique of Pure Reason*, A 218-9/B 265-6. Kant's critique of the ontological proof is in book 2, chapter 3, section IV of the *Transcendental Dialectic.*

63 Ibid., A 593/B 621.

64 Hegel, *Science of Logic*, p. 546.

65 Ibid., pp. 547-8.

66 Ibid., p. 549.

67 Wilkins, *Hegel's Philosophy of History*, pp. 154-6.

68 "It is thus the necessity which is equally the sublating of this positedness or the positing of immediacy and the in-itself, and in this same act is a determining of this sublating as positedness. It is therefore necessity itself which determines itself as contingency ...." Hegel, *Science of Logic*, 551.

69 Hegel, *Encyclopaedia Logic*, 147, addition.

70 Hegel, *Elements of the Philosophy of Right*, p. 21.

C. BEHAN MCCULLAGH

Understanding History

B.T. Wilkins published *Has History Any Meaning?* in 1978. The title of this book is the title of chapter 25, the Conclusion to Popper's *The Open Society and Its Enemies.* In that book Popper attacked those who have argued that history has a meaning, an inevitable outcome, and that we should consequently act so as to promote that end. This 'historicist' thesis, as he called it, espoused by Hegel and Marx, was a threat to the 'open society' which Popper argued was necessary for human flourishing. He wrote:

> History has no meaning, I contend. ...[Nevertheless] We can interpret the history of power politics from the point of view of our fight for the open society, for a rule of reason, for justice, freedom, equality, and for the control of international crime. Although history has no ends, we can impose these ends of ours upon it; and *although history has no meaning, we can give it a meaning.* [1]

Note the word 'fight'. Historicists, said Popper, by claiming that history will achieve its end no matter what our individual decisions may be, imply that we have no responsibility for the outcome.[2] That is false, according to Popper. Rationality, justice, freedom and equality have to be fought for, or they will not be achieved. We can interpret history as a 'fight for the open society and against its enemies' if we wish, and join that fight ourselves.[3]

The subtitle of Wilkins' book is *A Critique of Popper's Philosophy of History*. Wilkins wholeheartedly applauds Popper's praise of open societies, where freedom, reason and justice prevail. This will be no surprise to those who have read his earlier books on Becker, Burke and Hegel. His relief when Carl Becker during the Second World War regained his faith in 'the intrinsic worth of liberal democracy,' is quite manifest.[4] He remarks that 'Critics have often complained that Americans still live in the eighteenth century,[5] but he, like Becker, is quite content to do so. Jefferson is undoubtedly his hero.[6] In his biography of Burke, Wilkins uncritically accepts the importance of natural law as justifying the defence of life, liberty and property, so that people can flourish according to their nature.[7] Noting that Burke like Popper approved of only those traditions which he judged rational, Wilkins said 'Popper is in my judgment a Burkian or conservative liberal,'[8] like Wilkins himself. Then, in the final paragraph of his little book on Hegel, one cannot be sure whether it is Wilkins or Hegel who is speaking:

> Indeed it is freedom which binds together the actions of individual agents pursuing their private interests and the world historical process. Historical men are, however imperfectly, free men deliberately and freely pursuing their own subjective ends, and in the process of doing so they help, unintentionally, to advance the development of freedom in the world historical process.[9]

While Wilkins approves of Popper's moral and political values, he does not agree with several of his opinions about the nature of historical explanation and interpretation. He approves of the covering law model of explanation which Popper proposed even before Hempel, which Wilkins judges to be 'Popper's most important contribution to philosophy of history' (p. 13).[10] This model says that particular events are explained by being inferred as the consequence of other events according to a law which covers both kinds of events.[11] Popper said that historians employ 'trivial' covering laws in explaining particular events in the past, and are incapable of discovering any laws of history. The examples he gives are generalizations from folk knowledge of sociology and psychology.[12] Wilkins disagrees that the generalizations used by historians are always trivial; and even more important he disagrees that historians are incapable of establishing laws of history. It is a major concern of Wilkins' book to argue that there can be laws of history, and even to suggest what an important law of history might be. This law is not a teleological one, like those proposed by historicists, stipulating what the outcome of history must be. Rather it states sufficient conditions for the achievement of scientific progress. More of that shortly.

A second matter on which Wilkins disagrees with Popper is in his assessment of the importance of 'situational logic' in explaining human behaviour. Popper said that historians frequently explain human behaviour by referring to people's beliefs and hopes about their situation, showing that what they did was the rational thing to have done in the circumstances.[13] Popper considered this analysis of historical explanation to be more important than his covering law model, but Wilkins disagrees (p. 13). He denies that it is a form of explanation, preferring to call it a method of rational appraisal (pp. 52-6).[14]

The third major point of contention between Popper and Wilkins concerns Popper's analysis of historical interpretations.[15] Popper said that theories of historical change are not testable, as scientific theories are, but represent a point of view, and should be regarded as just interpretations. It is often possible to find evidence in support of various different interpretations, even apparently contradictory ones, he said. For example one can find evidence of progress and of retrogression in history. Such interpretations do not really conflict, he said; 'rather, they may be complementary to each other, as would be two views of the same landscape seen from two different points'.[16] Wilkins objects that historical theories can indeed be tested, just like scientific theories, to see whether or not they provide the best explanation of a body of information. It is pretty clear that Wilkins is not defending functional laws, which explain events by saying they were necessary for certain outcomes, such as Marx and perhaps Hegel proposed. Rather, the laws he defends are those which explain historical trends, such as a tendency towards enlightenment being explained by a law stating the conditions necessary and sufficient for such progress to occur. Wilkins agrees with Popper that there is no self-evident end of history, and no value of history which can be directly inferred from the historical facts. We have to decide what is valuable in history, and draw attention to that. However, there could well be laws of historical change.

In defending the possibility of laws of history and their importance in explaining historical change, as well as in setting aside situational logic as mere rational appraisal, Wilkins believes he is refuting Popper's claim that there is a significant difference between scientific and historical methods of inquiry (p. 89). Scientific method, said Popper, involves the testing of theories by observation of their implications.[17] Historians do not test their theories like this. Rather their theories are simply kinds of interpretation, patterns in the past detected from a certain point of view.[18] As I have said, Wilkins argues that this difference is not as profound as Popper asserts. He also points out that Popper thinks the covering law model of explanation applies to both science and history alike, so there really is a unity of method between them (p. 110).

Wilkins' main concern in this book is to defend a generalization about the conditions which make for scientific progress, which he has derived from Popper. It is not his aim to provide a careful analysis of historical understanding, for he skips through the sections on the covering law model and on situational logic quite quickly, and says nothing about functional explanation, which is at the heart of historicist theories (though admittedly Popper did not notice that either). He says that a generalization like his theory of the conditions of scientific progress is a 'law of history' which states 'the meaning of history,' where history is 'taken as a whole' (p. 166), and so provides one answer to the question which is the title of this book. That question could be taken to ask about not just the law of history but the end of history. The advancement of science, he goes on, cannot be proved to be the end of history, since history has not yet ended, but we can apply it to history, seeing history as if it were working towards that end (p. 190). He admits that the advancement of science is a value he holds dear. If we hold this to be the meaning of history, Wilkins says it becomes 'regulative of our ways of looking at, and behaving in, the world' (p. 189).

My discussion of the ideas Wilklins has presented in *Has History Any Meaning?* will take the following course. First I will examine the general theory about the causes and conditions of scientific progress which Wilkins proposes as an example of a law of history. I am quite sympathetic to this generalization, but have a few questions to ask about it. Precisely how are the conditions related to the outcome? Wilkins appears to say that they necessitate the outcome, but that cannot be right.

My second task will be to consider explanations which refer to the logic of the situation, to see whether they are explanatory at all. Wilkins thinks they provide a way of appraising the rationality of actions, but denies that they explain actions, assuming no doubt that explanations require covering laws. I think that particular desires and beliefs can explain human actions without further reference to covering laws.

Third, I shall suggest that the whole covering law approach to historical explanation needs to be replaced with a theory in terms of causal powers and tendencies, which properly acknowledges the role of contingencies in bringing about historical outcomes.

Finally I shall consider the central question posed by this book: has history any meaning? Wilkins argues that although we cannot discover the meaning of history, we can and should ascribe a meaning to it. I suggest that one can find several different meanings in history, and to declare just one of those to be 'the' meaning of history, as Wilkins does, is very misleading.

First, then, let us look at the law of history which Wilkins derives from Popper's 'Institutional Theory of Progress,'[19] and assess its status. The law is as follows:

> given the presence of the institutional factors he [Popper] cites (including democratic political institutions [which safeguard freedom of thought, expression and discussion]), the ability of science to continue to attract able champions and

> imaginative investigators with the "knack" of inventing new hypotheses..., and the absence of certain cultural variables (such as the triumph of mysticism or the decision, democratically arrived at, that science is too dangerous to be permitted any longer), science will continue to be a progressive enterprise. (p. 117)

Wilkins claims that it is reasonable to believe 'that scientific progress is contingently necessary in this fairly precise sense' (p. 117). He adds that this theory raises the 'exciting possibility' of providing 'a partial basis for a new substantive philosophy of history that might be able to show that virtually all continuous progress within a society depends upon institutional, and methodological, factors such as the ones he [Popper] has mentioned' (p. 118).

Popper had denied that the presence of appropriate institutional arrangements would be sufficient to guarantee scientific progress. He said that all kinds of things could disrupt the process, such as 'an epidemic of mysticism,' or a dearth of imaginative scientists.[20] Wilkins remarks that he has accommodated these factors in his theory (p. 118), as indeed he has. But as Wilkins himself observes, his theory claims more 'than Popper himself might find acceptable,' because human behaviour is not entirely predictable (pp. 117-8). As Popper wrote: 'the human factor is *the* ultimately uncertain and wayward element in social life and in all social institutions.'[21]

There are two things which Wilkins claims for his theory. The first is that under the conditions he states, scientific progress is 'contingently necessary,' meaning inevitable. Second, he claims that virtually all cases of scientific progress depend upon the conditions he has listed. In short those conditions are both sufficient and necessary for scientific progress. Unfortunately Wilkins does not defend this claim. Having made it, he just moves on. Yet it is at the heart of his disagreement with Popper. Popper says there are no laws of history, for people's behaviour is not entirely predictable. Wilkins says there are, but does not discuss the problem of human unpredictability.

Given the conditions Wilkins lists, is scientific progress inevitable? It is certainly very probable, assuming that people continue to form scientific hypotheses with the freedom, skill and enthusiasm he stipulates. However, consider the following scenario. Suppose science is funded only by industries which want proof that their products are safe and effective, and which dismiss any scientists who suggest otherwise. Then scientists might be motivated to look for results which please their pay-masters, rather than deepen their understanding of nature. They would still be free to say and publish what they wish, given the normal constraints of prudence, and to pursue their inquiries with imagination and vigour. Yet I doubt much scientific progress would result from such work.

Wilkins could add another exclusion clause from his generalization to meet this objection, but Popper's point is that there is no knowing when all the possible contingencies have been covered. Suppose environmental toxins became so strong that they inhibited scientific research, preventing scientists from having the energy to complete their work, or interfering with their ability to think rationally. We can hardly say that scientific progress is 'necessary' given the conditions mentioned by Wilkins. The most we can say is that it is very probable, in communities like ours.

Nor can Wilkins prove that the conditions he lists are necessary for scientific progress. Scientists under dictatorial regimes have been immensely successful, as the achievements of those in the U.S.S.R. demonstrate. Popper should have seen this was the case even in Nazi Germany, which developed tanks, planes and rockets with remarkable efficiency. Indeed a case could be made for saying that wise dictators will foster military science in their own interests. Democracy is certainly not a necessary condition of scientific progress.

All this is not to deny that Wilkins' generalization is useful in explaining some cases of scientific progress. It can help explain, for instance, why progress in science was so much greater during and after the Renaissance than in medieval Europe. Jacob Burckhardt draws upon a generalization like Wilkins' to explain the burgeoning of scientific inquiry during the Italian Renaissance:

> When once the veil of illusion was torn asunder, when once the dread of nature and the slavery to books and tradition were overcome, countless problems lay before them for solution. It is another matter when a whole people takes a natural delight in the study and investigation of nature, at a time when other nations are indifferent, that is to say, when the discoverer is not threatened or wholly ignored, but can count on the friendly support of congenial spirits. That this was the case in Italy is unquestionable. (p. 174)

Generalizations like Wilkins' are particularly useful as here for contrastive explanations, in which historians explain why one outcome was more probable than another.

Wilkins, however, claims more for his generalization than its occasional relevance to scientific progress. Having detected a trend towards scientific progress throughout history, this law is meant to explain it. Wilkins likens what he is doing to the function of evolutionary theory. Evolutionary theory can explain particular instances of evolution from one species to another; and it can also explain the development of humankind from very primitive organisms, that is the history of animals taken as a whole (pp. 154-5). Likewise, Wilkins suggests his law of scientific progress can explain particular instances of such progress, and the trend as a whole.

Popper doubted that generalizations like Wilkins' could be proved true, but Wilkins is not so sceptical: 'my intuition [is] that general historical theories....are testable often enough to resemble scientific theories' (p. 89), and he explains a little later on that 'a theory is confirmed, or probably true, when it explains all we know' (p. 92). Popper's reasons for doubting that historical theories can be proved are easily stated.[22] He says that historians can usually find some evidence in support of the trends they detect in the past, even for apparently contradictory trends, and these trends represent their views of the past. Causal theories may explain instances of these trends quite convincingly, but that does not make them true. They are true only if they can be tested by examining all relevant instances, and if no observations are inconsistent with them. The fact that a theory is supported by a few instances which it is designed to explain is not enough to establish its truth.

Unfortunately Wilkins does not put his general theory about the causes of scientific progress to the test. We have seen that the conditions of scientific progress which he identifies are neither necessary nor sufficient for such progress. Indeed the failure of Wilkins' generalization to pass scrutiny illustrates precisely the argument Popper was putting. The generalization seems plausible while one focuses upon those instances which it is designed to explain, but that is not sufficient reason for thinking it true.

Popper and Wilkins both believe that historical explanations, like scientific ones, conform to the covering law model, and that when historians consider a person's reasons for acting, they are not explaining the action but are trying to understand or appraise its rationality, in the circumstances. Popper defers to Weber in claiming that a psychological explanation of an action in terms of its motives 'presupposes' judgments about the rationality of the action in the circumstances.[23] The idea is that historians assume people act rationally, and if they can see why an action was a reasonable thing for a person to do in the circumstances, they then attribute those reasons to the agent. In *The Poverty of Historicism* Popper calls this a 'method of logical or rational construction,'[24] and insists that it 'is *not* a psychological but rather a logical method'.[25] Only if they cannot think of any good reason why the agent would have acted as they did, will historians start looking for irrational motives for what was done.

Wilkins, to his credit, sees that when historians appraise the rationality of someone's action, they are interested in whether it was rational from the agent's point of view. That is, they want to know whether, given the agent's desires, beliefs, values and so on it was rational for the agent to act as he or she did in the circumstances (pp. 56-60). In other words, judgement about the rationality of an action presupposes knowledge of the agent's psychological state, of their reasons for acting. It seems that what Popper described was how historians would judge whether an action was rational from *their* point of view, whether they would have thought it reasonable to act as the agent did in the circumstances. Despite Weber's opinion, historians do not automatically ascribe their reasons for acting to the agent, knowing that the agent might have had other reasons for what they did. As Collingwood said, the reconstruction of a person's reasons for acting requires careful and critical examination of the relevant evidence, to see what hypothesis best explains it all.[26]

Wilkins does not notice the difference between values and beliefs which would rationally justify an action, and those which not only justify but also caused an action. In assessing the rationality of an action from the agent's point of view, historians are usually interested in the reasons for which the agent acted, rather than other reasons the agent had which might have justified it. The reasons for which an agent acted are those which significantly increased the probability that the agent would act as he or she did.

Wilkins notes that when Popper says that a person's reasons for acting explain their action, he explicitly appeals to the trivial generalization that sane people act rationally. It seems that Wilkins regards this as both vague and false, and not much value in warranting a causal explanation (p. 51). Because Wilkins holds that explanations require covering laws, he is led to conclude that when historians examine people's reasons for acting they cannot be explaining their actions, since no adequate covering law relating reasons and actions is available, so they must be just appraising their rationality.

I am uncomfortable with Popper's analysis of rational explanations, which was later adopted by C.G.Hempel, because you do not find historians assessing the rationality of people when explaining their actions as this model requires. Rather they note the agent's state of mind, and show how the action followed naturally from that. Let me illustrate the difference between these two ways of explaining actions with an artificially simple example. Suppose the British Prime Minister Neville Chamberlain signed the Munich Agreement with Hitler permitting German occupation of Czechoslovakia in September 1938 because he wanted to preserve peace in Europe and believed that signing this was the best way of doing so. Hempel would say that this explanation is satisfactory if Chamberlain was acting rationally at the time, so that he would do what his reason dictated. If he were rational it was very probable that he would act according to his reasons. An alternative model examines the implications of Chamberlain's desires and beliefs. The historian would note that Chamberlain was absolutely passionate about preserving peace, and believed that by giving Hitler much of what he wanted, war would be averted. If someone wants a particular outcome very strongly, and believes a certain action will produce it, then it is very probable that they will act accordingly. Why? Because to want something is to be disposed to pursue it in what one believes the most advantageous manner. Mental states such as wants and beliefs are dispositions which imply the probability of certain actions in certain circumstances. One does not need to mention the rationality of the agent to infer what they will probably do. Knowing their state of mind is enough. Indeed it is not entirely clear that Chamberlain was rational at Munich. Some think his passion for peace clouded his judgement.

Wilkins at one point considers Alan Donagan's claim that certain mental states necessitate corresponding actions, which Donagan argued is an analytic truth (pp. 35-40). He notes that people do not always act in accordance with their desires and beliefs when it is convenient to do so, as Donagan supposed. He hints that to predict people's behaviour you would have to know almost everything going on in their minds (pp. 41-2), which is impractical (p. 49).

It is certainly wrong to say that people will act in accordance with their reasons whenever they can, as some do not if only from weakness of will. However, it is not a mistake to say that if people have certain desires and beliefs it is more probable that they will act according to them, and if the desire is a strong one it is much more probable that they will do so, than if they did not have those mental states. The last sentence has to be qualified: it is only more probable that they will act according to their reasons *assuming that nothing else influences them to act otherwise.* That is, the consequence follows only in an ideal world, where there are no interfering factors. Philosophers call probabilities of this kind 'objective chances'. They are theoretical rather than observational truths. It is natural to speak of mental states producing a tendency to act in a certain way, a tendency which would be fulfilled with a certain degree of probability so long as nothing interfered.

Once we see that mental states produce tendencies to act in a certain way, it is easy to understand how different desires can produce conflicting tendencies. In the actual world people do not by any means always act upon their desires. What they do depends among other things on what other desires they have. I might wish to celebrate your birthday with an extravagant gift, but also fear being unable to pay my bills, so end up buying you something for a moderate price. What we do is a function of the various tendencies acting within us. It is also affected by our ability and opportunity to act. So, people often have reasons to perform an action yet not perform it.

Popper thought that 'most historical explanation' refers to people's reasons for acting ,[27] but Wilkins disagrees, saying that historians refer to the logic of the situation only to assess the rationality of actions, as no adequate covering law relating reasons to actions is available (p. 57). I have shown that if reasons are regarded as intentional mental states, more precisely as dispositions, it is easy to see that they produce tendencies in people to act in accordance with their rational implications. In this way reasons can be seen to cause actions without having to appeal to a generalization about the way in which rational people behave.

If my analysis of rational explanations is along the right lines, then it is already clear that historical explanations do not all conform to the covering law model as Wilkins supposed. In fact it seems that most other historical explanations do not fit the covering law model either. The analysis of causation in terms of objective chances and active tendencies which I have just outlined can be extended to all kinds of causal explanation. It is easy to see that all causes increase the objective chance of a certain kind of outcome, but that what actually occurs is the product of all the various tendencies at work in the situation

The trouble with the covering law model is that it is just too crude. It asserts that certain consequences follow certain antecedent conditions if not always then very frequently, whereas in fact first, the frequency is far from regular, and second, the outcome depends upon what are usually called contingencies, that is, upon what other causes are operating which affect the probability of the predicted outcome. The only way in which a covering law model can handle contingencies is by trying to exclude them in its list of antecedent conditions. Notice how Wilkins, in his generalization about the conditions of scientific progress, excluded 'certain cultural variables (such as the triumph of mysticism or the decision...that science is too dangerous to be permitted any longer)' (p. 117). As I pointed out, one can never be sure that all contingencies have been excluded, which is why one cannot know for certain that the outcome will occur given the stated conditions. What must now be added is that in the real world interfering contingencies are seldom if ever absent, in which case it would seem that such generalizations are of little relevance. What we need is a form of explanation which allows us to take account of interfering contingencies, and estimate their effect on the outcome. That is precisely what the present account does.

There is no doubt that this approach to causal explanation is especially useful in accounting for individual events. For instance, to explain why particular scientists made the discoveries they did, it enjoins us to consider both the scientists' desires and beliefs, and the circumstances which either facilitated or impeded their work. There is no need to look for some covering law relating conditions of scientific inquiry to productive outcomes in order to explain their work.

Wilkins' generalization, however, was intended to explain a general trend across the reaches of history. I think Wilkins assumed that if it applied to individual cases of scientific progress, it could then be thought to apply to all such cases, and so to explain scientific progress in general. At one point Wilkins says this:

> I propose that historicism can be regarded as a three-stage affair in which the success of our explaining particular events by subsuming them under laws is taken to be a good or even conclusive reason for believing that the entire historical process can be explained by subsuming it under either these same laws or some other laws of greater generality, and this in turn is taken to be a good or even conclusive reason to believe that we can discover the moral meaning of history taken as a whole. (pp. 76-7)

Wilkins denies the validity of the third step, that the moral meaning of history is implied by any law of historical process. People have no obligation to further the trends which historians find in history. But it seems he does not deny the connection between the first and second stages. Indeed, whereas Popper thought any general processes found by historians to be merely personal interpretations, Wilkins holds that they may well have more objective significance (pp. 79-80, 89, 105-7, 112). His general law of the conditions of scientific progress is thought to explain both particular instances of such progress and the progress of science in general.

In fact there are two ways of explaining scientific progress in general. One is to list the kinds of event which have usually promoted such progress, and the kinds of event which have impeded it. This provides knowledge of what generally produces scientific progress, and might even have counterfactual force in certain contexts. The second kind of explanation is a contrastive explanation, mentioned above, in which one identifies the conditions which make the difference between one case of scientific progress and another case in which such progress did not occur. Popper presented his explanation of scientific progress as an answer to the first kind of question. He said, suppose, with Comte and Mill, that humans by nature will apply their minds to the improvement of their lot, even so scientific inquiry could be impeded by governments which close laboratories, ban books and conferences, and suppress theories which depart from the official line. So, scientific progress requires a supportive political and social environment, such as is found in Western democracies.[28] He did not consider that dictatorships might allow scientific freedom but not political freedom, probably because Popper was committed to the defence of open societies, and wished to extol only their virtues. Interestingly, Popper does not support his theory with case studies, for its truth seems self-evident to people who live in Western societies. Everyone knows you need laboratories, books and conferences to do good science. That is an instance of what Popper said are the trivial generalizations upon which historical explanations depend.[29] Had Popper considered a contrastive explanation, and asked why there has been more scientific progress in Europe than in, say, India, he might have discovered other important conditions which contribute to it. These may include education in certain methods of investigation, as well as a culture which values material pleasures very highly. Wilkins did not notice the value of comparative studies in checking causal theories, because although he thought causal generalizations could be rationally justified, he said little about what form that justification should take. It is one thing to notice what facilitates scientific progress in a given society; it is quite another to list all the conditions necessary for such progress to occur in any society. A generalization about the causes of scientific progress throughout the whole of history would surely need to be of the second, comprehensive kind. It would be no use giving an Indian community a raft of laboratories, books and conference facilities if the people had neither the skill nor the inclination to use them. Wilkins' generalization simply does not apply to all countries in the world, and so can scarcely be accepted as of general historical significance.

It is sometimes argued that causal explanations in terms of covering laws are better than those which refer to dispositions and tendencies. The argument is most easily understood by means of an example. Compare two different accounts of what it is for something to be red. One says an object is red if it is disposed to reflect just those light waves which appear red in normal circumstances. To explain why a tomato appears red to me,

I would say that the tomato had this disposition, and that it was triggered by light falling on the tomato and being reflected into my eyes. The second account says that a tomato is red if its surface is composed of a substance such that it normally appears red to those who look at it. To explain why it seems red to me, I say that the tomato is made of substance X, and such substances normally appear red. In this case I appeal not to a disposition but to a covering law. The reason why the second explanation is better, people say, is that it is ontologically simpler, for it makes no reference to dispositions at all. Those who say that red things are disposed to look red admit that this disposition is caused by the substances of which they are composed, which absorb some light waves and reflect others. But it seems that there is no need to mention any dispositions in order to explain why a thing looks red. It is enough to say that things made of such substances regularly appear red. A covering law is all you need.

Strictly speaking, such laws express the objective chance of their consequence occurring given the antecedent. So the covering law is not the kind which Popper and Hempel had in mind. Their laws implied that given the antecedents the consequence would occur, either necessarily or at least very probably. Laws of objective chance do not imply that the consequence will occur, only that when the antecedents exist then there is a tendency for the outcome to occur; but that tendency can be offset by other tendencies operating in the situation. Thus the tendency for a ruler to look straight can be offset by the tendency for it to look bent when dipped into water. The tendency of a see-saw to dip if you sit on one end of it can be offset by a counteracting force if someone of equal weight sits on the other. What happens is always the product of all the relevant tendencies operating at the time.

Problems arise for even this version of the covering law theory when we consider how mental states are related to actions. Mental states are defined as dispositions: for instance to want to achieve a goal G means to be disposed to do what is believed necessary to achieve G in appropriate circumstances. We simply do not know what grounds mental states. Probably brain states do, but we are quite unable to identify them. Even if we could, whenever we relate mental states to actions, it is not because we correlate such brain states with such actions. Rather it is because we know the mental disposition has been triggered to produce the action. We explain that Chamberlain signed the Munich agreement because he was disposed to seek peace at almost any price, and believed this was an effective way of securing it, not by trying to correlate certain of his brain states with such behaviour. This is a vastly simpler and subtler way of explaining actions than trying to relate them to the brain states which caused them.

There is no doubt that most of the generalizations used in historical explanations report the objective chance of a certain kind of effect, given certain kinds of conditions. Nevertheless, generalizations listing all the conditions sufficient to make a certain kind of effect very probable are possible, so long as they exclude all the kinds of contingencies which could prevent that effect from happening. In other words, a generalization like the one Wilkins put forward is certainly possible. The question is, should we agree with Wilkins that it provides the meaning of history? Suppose it listed all the conditions necessary for scientific progress. Would it enlighten us as to the meaning of history? Wilkins argues that such a generalization could be rationally defended. Why does he think it could provide the meaning of history?

Popper roundly declared: '*History has no meaning*'.[30] It cannot have meaning, Popper explained, because history consists of the 'hopes, struggles, and sufferings' of all people, and such a history 'cannot be written'.[30] We can select various topics in history, but none deserves precedence. Some have thought the history of political power to be central, but those who celebrate power pay little heed to the people who suffer under it. To trace the history of the establishment of the state, as Hegel did, is to diminish the importance of the individual. In writing history, Popper suggests, we focus upon 'our fight for the open society, for a rule of reason, for justice, freedom, equality, and for the control of international crime. Although history has no ends, we can impose these ends of ours upon it; and *although history has no meaning, we can give it a meaning*.'[32]

In response to Popper, Wilkins draws attention to a passage in *The Poverty of Historicism* in which Popper contrasts two kinds of wholes: (*a*) the totality of all the properties or aspects of a thing, and especially of all the relations holding between its constituent parts, and (*b*) certain special properties or aspects of the thing in question, namely those which make it appear an organized structure rather than a 'mere heap.'[33] Only the latter, he said, can be studied scientifically[33] and historically.[33] Wilkins suggests that although history taken as a whole in the first sense as the totality of all that has happened has no meaning, there might be structured wholes of the second kind which could be said to constitute the meaning of history (pp. 136-43). History, he concludes, has as many moral meanings as it has structures (p. 143).

Let us pause for a moment to note the implication of this position. The title of Wilkins' book is *Has History Any Meaning?*, not 'are there meaningful structures in history?' He writes: all that would be required in this connection to show that history could have moral meaning or significance would be to show that history could be a structured whole in his sense (b). (p. 141) The natural reading of 'history' here is everything that people have done and suffered in the past, which is history in Popper's first sense of a heap. That history is not, and cannot be, a structured whole. Any structure, any trend found through the events of history must be selective, and leave out of account an immense number of historical facts. Wilkins does not show that 'history' has a meaning. The most he argues for is the existence of 'structured wholes' in history.

To discover the structures of history, Wilkins follows the recipe Popper provided in *The Poverty of History*:[36] first discover the broad trends of historical change, and then look for the causes of these processes of change (pp. 145-60). Wilkins' proposal that there is a general trend in history towards improvement in science and technology is worrying as an account of 'the meaning of history' for two reasons. First, there seem to have great stretches of history in which such progress is not manifest. Australian aboriginals are thought to have inhabited Australia for about forty thousand years, yet achieved very little advance in science and technology in that time. The trend is true of our Western culture, especially since the Renaissance, but does not represent a trend throughout the whole of history. Second, as has been said, every trend an historian discovers in history is selective, and leaves out of account many historical facts, even regarding those societies which manifest it. Movements in art, philosophy and religion, for instance, find little place in the history of science.

I have discussed the truth of Wilkins' explanation of this trend above. Popper warned how easy it is to suppose that the causes of a trend which seem conspicuous in our own community might not be so important in another. People too readily think that the regularities which they observe around them are universal laws of social life, holding good for all societies.[37] The conditions which foster progress in science and technology in Europe are not as important as others which do so in India. Popper had an interesting further point in this regard. He said that the causes which operate in one society might not be the important ones which operate in a later one, and the philosopher of history should find the laws which govern the shift from one set of causes to another. He wrote:

> there can be no social uniformities which hold good beyond single periods. Thus

> the only universally valid laws of society must be the laws which *link up the successive periods.* They must be *laws of historical development* which determine the transition from one period to another.[38]

I do not doubt that he had the work of Arnold Toynbee in mind, whose work *The Study of History* explained the rise and fall of civilizations, and is briefly discussed by Popper.[38] In fact Popper went on to argue that the causes of historical change are so numerous that no laws could be formulated to represent them.[39]

Wilkins claims that he has shown, *contra* Popper, that there could be laws of history, meaning laws governing historical trends. The most one could allow, I think, is that there could be laws governing trends within certain societies for certain periods. These are scarcely 'laws of history'.

Wilkins admits that even the trend of scientific progress which he identifies in history can not be known to continue, as we have no knowledge of the future (p. 190). He denies any inevitability to historical progress, such as Hegel and other historicists assumed. Why then does he offer scientific progress as the key to the meaning of history? Both in the present book, and more fully in a previous article,[41] Wilkins endorses elements of Kant's approach to the philosophy of history. Kant believed that people's reason would ultimately drive them to overcome their conflicts by establishing a rule of law, both within and between states. His faith in human reason grounded his faith in progress towards a more liberal society. Wilkins is less optimistic about inevitable progress, either political or scientific, allowing that scientific progress depends upon the presence of the facilitating conditions set out in his law of history. If the trend to scientific progress is so uncertain, why does Wilkins make it the key to the meaning of history?

With Kant, Wilkins claims that there is a moral justification for proposing an historical trend as providing the meaning of history (pp. 184-91). In doing so he is encouraging people to both recognize and value that trend, and perhaps work to achieve the conditions which will enable it to continue. The question of whether history conceived of as a whole has certain ends must… be treated as a question about final ends and as such must be answered from the moral point of view (p. 190). Although we cannot know what the final end of history will be, there are some ends worth pursuing. For Wilkins presumably the growth of science and technology is such an end, and he values the open society which furthers it.

Two questions immediately arise. First, is there any reason for preferring Wilkins' interpretation of history to, say, Hegel's or any other? Second, is it not misleading to say that one trend is the key to the meaning of history, when there is no way of knowing whether it will continue in the future and there are other trends which could equally well be mentioned? It would be more honest to call this 'an interpretation' of history, which suggests there could be others.

Wilkins takes Popper to task for failing to provide us with an adequate, rational basis for preferring one system to another (pp. 228-9), but offers no rational defence of his own moral convictions. He clearly approves of Popper's criticism of the theory that an open society can be justified in the pursuit of happiness. This could be a goal of private morality, he said, but in the public sphere it can lead to utopian social engineering with some very inhumane consequences. Consequently Wilkins and Popper prefer the reduction of avoidable misery by means of piecemeal social engineering as the aim of public policy (p. 215-8, 222-4). Presumably Wilkins values progress in science and technology for providing the means of relieving human misery more and more efficiently.

Wilkins is aware that he has presented no argument for preferring his interpretation of the meaning of history to others, such as Hegel's. Hegel saw history as a process by which human freedom, rationality and self-consciousness were increased. Wilkins concludes his book by saying that the question whether history has meaning is a self-referential question, or in other words a question about what meaning *we* decide or choose to give to history (p. 247). There is no objective truth about the meaning of history. Its meaning is a matter of individual choice.

If we cannot know the future, and cannot establish the superiority of one reading of history over another, why claim to know 'the meaning of history' (p. 19) at all? These are the reasons why most people deny that history can be said to have any single meaning. There have been several trends in universal history up to the present, though none has been observable in every society at every period of time. It would be more accurate to write of an interpretation of universal history rather than 'the meaning of history' when describing one of these.

Wilkins does not want merely to suggest an interpretation of history. Rather he wants to impose an interpretation upon us, so that we will see history in terms of the values and processes which his interpretation presents. Wilkins wants to use history as propaganda, as a conservative liberal, and would probably justify doing so on moral grounds. If people focus upon the growth of science and technology, life will become less miserable in due course.

The trouble is that Wilkins also applauds the open society, which involves as a central tenet the free, rational, critical pursuit of truth. He acknowledges that such a society is most likely to produce scientific and technological discoveries. Yet surely such a society would disapprove of assertions which are known to be misleading, such as the assertion that the growth of science and technology is 'the' meaning of history. One is reminded of E.H. Carr's claim that

> The absolute in history ...is something still incomplete and in process of becoming —something in the future towards which we move, which begins to take shape only as we move towards it, and in the light of which, as we move forward, we gradually shape our interpretation of the past....It rejects the relativist view that one interpretation is as good as another....It enables us...to liberate and organize human energies in the present with a view to the future...[42]
>
> (What is History? pp. 121-2)

Like Carr, Wilkins wants to present one view of historical progress as though no other view were equally valid, though Carr looks forward to greater equality of freedom and prosperity than Wilkins envisages. Both, like Marx, present a theory of historical progress which will inspire political action. In an open society, however, critics would point out that they mislead readers by suggesting there is only one meaning to history.

Notes

1 K.R. Popper, *The Open Society and Its Enemies*, vol. 2. Hegel and Marx. Fifth ed. Routledge and Kegan Paul, London, 1966, p. 278.

2 p. 274.

3 p. 278.

4 B.T. Wilkins, *Carl Becker: A Biographical Study in American Intellectual History.* MIT Press, Cambridge, 1961, p. 216.

5 *Ibid.*, p. 225.

6 *Ibid.*, pp. 222-3.

7 B.T. Wilkins, *The Problems of Burke's Political Philosophy.* Clarendon Press, Oxford, 1967. See especially pp. 149-53, 250-2.

8 *Ibid.*, p. 213.

9 B.T. Wilkins, *Hegel's Philosophy of History.* Cornell U.P., 1974, p. 190.

10 All page references given in the text are to B.T.Wilkins' *Has History Any Meaning? A Critique of Popper's Philosophy of History.* Cornell U. P., Ithica, 1978.

11 Popper, *The Open Society and Its Enemies,* vol. 2, pp. 262-5.

12 See also K.R. Popper, *The Poverty of Historicism*, second ed. Routledge and Kegan

Paul, London, 1961, pp. 144-6.

13 Popper, *The Open Society and Its Enemies* vol.2, pp. 96-8; *The Poverty of Historicism*, pp. 147-9.

14 Compare W.H. Dray, *Laws and Explanation in History*. Oxford U.P., Oxford, 1957, p. 214.

15 Popper, *The Open Society and Its Enemies*, vol. 2, pp. 265-9; see also *The Poverty of Historicism*, pp. 150-2.

16 Popper, *The Open Society and Its Enemies*, vol. 2., p. 267.

17 Popper, *The Open Society and Its Enemies*, vol. 2, pp. 259-60.

18 *Ibid.*, pp. 265-6.

19 Popper, *The Poverty of Historicism*, pp. 152-9.

20 Popper, *The Poverty of Historicism*, pp. 156-7.

21 Popper, *The Poverty of Historicism*, p. 158.

22 See Popper, *The Open Society and Its Enemies*, vol. 2, pp. 265-9.

23 Popper, *The Open Society and Its Enemies*, vol. 2, p. 97.

24 *Ibid.*, p. 141.

25 *Ibid.*, p. 158.

26 R.G. Collingwood, *The Idea of History*, Oxford U.P., Oxford, 1946, Part V, section 3.

27 Popper, *The Open Society and Its Enemies*, vol. 2, p. 265.

28 Popper, *The Poverty of Historicism*, pp. 152-5.

29 Popper, *The Open Society and Its Enemies*, vol. 2, pp. 264-5.

30 Popper, *The Open Society and Its Enemies*, vol. 2, p. 269.

31 *Ibid.*, p. 270.

32 *Ibid.*, p. 278.

33 Popper, *The Poverty of Historicism*, p. 76.

34 *Ibid.*, p. 77.

35 *Ibid.*, pp. 80-1.

36 Popper, *The Poverty of Historicism*, p. 45.

37 Popper, *The Poverty of Historicism*, p. 99.

38 *Ibid*, p. 41.

39 *Ibid.*, pp. 110-2.

40 *Ibid.*, pp. 117-8.

41 B.T. Wilkins, 'Teleology in Kant's Philosophy of History', *History and Theory*, vol.V, No. 2 (1966), pp. 172-85.

42 E.H. Carr, *What is History?* Penguin, Harmondsworth, 1964, pp. 121-2.

Susan Meld Shell

Honor and the End of History: A Reading of Kant's "Renewed Question"

Burleigh Taylor Wilkins' "Teleology in Kant's Philosophy of History" is a model of its kind. Not only is Wilkins among the first to mount a thoughtful defense of Kant's treatment of history against Popperian attack; Wilkins also reads Kant with an unusually sympathetic ear, treating the manifest complexities of his argument, not dismissively, as evidence of simple-minded error or confusion, but as welcome invitations to further inquiry. Wilkins is always alert to the various roles Kant plays—as "moralist," "philosopher," and "scientist"—as well as to their subtle and often shifting boundaries. In particular, Wilkins draws new attention to the role of teleology in historical explanation, showing, in a manner free of jargon or special pleading, the impossibility of doing away with teleological guidance entirely, if only for identifying facts relevant to the historian's own purposes.

Wilkins' study of Kant's philosophy of history centers on a reading of the well-known (and relatively early) *Idea for a Universal History from a Cosmopolitan Standpoint* (1784). In what follows I will try to read, with similar rhetorical sympathy, a later essay in which Kant revisits the question of history from the other side of the French Revolution, and in which he claims, for the first time, to be able to predict in a manner sufficient "for the most rigorous theory" that the human race is constantly progressing.[1]

To better understand Kant's striking claim, it will be helpful to examine in some detail the discussion that proceeds it. The title of Kant's work, *Renewed Question: Whether the Human Race is in Constant Progress toward the Better* [*Erneuerte Frage: Ob das menschliche Geschlecht im beständigen Fortschreiten zum Besseren sei*], asks a question raised before but, it seems, in need of repetition. *What* is wanted (or demanded) [*verlangen*] by that question, according to section one, is a predictive [*vorhersagende*] ethical history, not of individual men but of mankind as a *whole*, hence, as apportioned into peoples, and united socially on earth.

Such an effort is called prophecy [*weissagen*], Kant says, when it exceeds, *with* supernatural aid, what can be known on the basis of natural laws. When it does so *without* supernatural aid, it is called soothsaying [*wahrsagen*; literally, "truthsaying."][2] One who would foretell the future by exceeding what can be known on the basis of natural laws, yet without supernatural aid , should, it seems, anticipate being scorned.

Still, according to section two, it is *wahrsagen* and not *weissagen* that Kant is after: if a fragment of future history is to be known at all, it will be as a "soothsaying [*wahrsagende*] historical narrative [*Geschichtserzählung*]" and "exhibition" [*Darstellung*] "of what is immanent in future time."

Such soothsaying history is possible, Kant says, but only "if the foreteller of the future himself makes [*macht*] and arranges [*veranstaltet*] the events that he announces in advance [*zum Voraus verkündigt*]" [VII 80; 143]. The Jewish prophets [*Propheten*] of old, for example, could easily prophecy [*weissagen*] the destruction of their state, since they themselves as national leaders [*Volksleiten*], by stubbornly clinging to an untenable [*unhaltbar*] constitution [*Verfassung*] of their own making, burdened [*beschwert*] it with so much ecclesiastical and civil freight as to render their state unfit [*untauglich*]. Similarly, "our politicians," who claim to take men as they are rather than as they should be, and who urge that liberal policies will have mournful [*trauig*] consequences, are likewise lucky [*glücklich*] in their soothsaying [*Wahrsagen*], for these consequences are the outcome of their own previous oppression of the people. Finally, [*Christian*] ecclesiastics, sometimes prophecy [*weissagen*] the complete destruction of religion and immanent appearance of the Antichrist, and in so doing help to bring about the end they warn of. For instead of attending to the moral improvement of the people directly, they fabricate duties that are supposed to work indirectly, and thus employ the mechanical constraints appropriate to secure civil, but not moral, unanimity. [VII 80; 143] The ancient prophets, then, who, as "leaders of their people," combined the functions of ruler and priest (and who, in New Testament terms, spoke better than they knew) are here the model for modern politicians and pious enthusiasts alike, machiavellian contrivance [*wahrsagen*] and religious divination [*weissagen*] amounting, in the end, to the same (bad) thing.

On this troubling note, Kant turns, in section three, to a "division [*Eintheilung*] of the concept of that concerning the future which we would know before hand." The cases, he says, under which a prediction may fall are three: either the human race is in continual regress or in constant progress or eternally stagnant at its present stage of ethical value [*sittlichen Werths*].

Each case, however, poses a difficulty. Moral decline cannot be incessant, since at some point of dissolution the human race, and hence human wickedness, will necessarily destroy itself. (Hence, what Kant calls the "terroristic way of presenting history" looks forward to a cataclysmic end [*jüngste Tag*], followed, in the dreams of "pious enthusiasts," by a restoration and renewal of the world [*erneuerten Welt*].) Continual moral improvement, on the other hand, contradicts the assumption, basic to the notion of a morally imputable act, that the quantity of good and evil in an individual cannot be augmented or diminished. (If I had it in me to make myself worse or better in a moral sense I would already be so.) Hence, the "eudaimonistic way presenting history," "with its sanguine hopes," seems "untenable" [*unhaltbar*] and to promise little to favor a prophetic [*weissagen*] history of progress. (Kant silently leaves open the possibility that eudaimonistic *wahrsagen* might, in this regard, be more successful.) [VII 81-2; 145-7]

We are thus left with case number three, or perpetual oscillation between improvement and decline: unlike the previous two, this opinion, which may well garner, Kant observes, the most votes (*Stimme*), is not a "way of representing human history [*Vorstellungsart der Menschengeschichte*]" at all, but a "hypothesis" for its determination beforehand. According to this "Abderitic"[3] hypothesis:

> Busy folly is the character of our species; people hastily set off on the path of the good but do not persevere, instead, if only for the sake of not being bound to a single end, indeed, if only so that there may be diversion/alternation [*Abwechselung*], they reverse the plan of progress...and lay upon themselves hopeless exertion [*hoffnungslose Bemühung*]....The principle of evil in the natural disposition of the human race and that of the good seem here to be not so much amalgamated (melted down together) as to be mutually neutralizing, which would result in inactivity [or "deedlessness" =*Thatlosigkeit*][4] (which is here called stasis [*Stillstand*]): an empty business, to so alternate/exchange [*abwechseln*] the good with the bad through going forwards and backwards, that the entire game of commerce [*Spiel des Verkehrs*] of our species with itself on this globe would have to be regarded [*angesehen*] as a mere farce [*Possenspiel*], which can endow our species with no greater value, in the eyes of reason, than that of animal species , who carry on [*treiben*] this game with fewer costs and without expenditure of understanding. [VII 82; 147]

What is wrong in this third case—leaving momentarily aside its own mirror-like capacity to induce the folly it portrays—is a lack of genuine activity, all the more disturbing, given Kant's definition elsewhere of persons as agents to whom acts [Thäten] can be imputed. Mankind as a whole, on this view, enters into commerce with itself to no effect, rather like a top that spins in place. It does so, moreover, in a way that makes us more contemptible "to the eyes of reason" than other species, "who drive the play/game" at lesser cost and without "expenditure of understanding" (the faculty that Kant especially associates with worldly knowledge, or experience). The Abderitic hypothesis, in other words—whether despite or owing to its popularity—calls into question the value of man's natural existence.

Experience, we learn in section four, "cannot directly resolve the problem/task [*Aufgabe*] of progress." [VII 83; 149] Given the fact of human freedom, what looks so far like progress might be the beginning of a fatal downturn; while what looks like a decline might be the beginning of what hereafter is improvement. Human action, in short, as free "cannot be predicted [*vorhersagen*]."

The seeming senselessness of human affairs (which like the Tychonic heavens appear to move backwards, forwards, or both together [and hence not at all]), raises a certain hope, by calling to mind the astronomical confusion of cycles and epicycles—"entangled to the point of absurdity"—that Copernicus replaced with lawful order, through a transposition of standpoint from earth to sun. It is, however, our misfortune [*Unglück*] that predicting human actions (unlike predicting the movements of the stars) calls for a providential standpoint "beyond human wisdom."[5] A man can see but not *foresee* free actions (even his own), because he does not (and as a free worldly being cannot) know the proportion of the mixture of good and evil in his own disposition . [VII 84; 151]

What is wanted, then, is a place to stand within experience (analogous to the Copernican removal from earth to sun), on which hope for mankind's future can be grounded. Such a, a soothsaying [*wahrsagende*] history of the human race must (as Kant insists in section five) be connected to experience *in some way.* An experience

> must come forward [*vorkommen*] that as an event [*Begebenheit*] points out [*hinweiset*] a human endowment and capacity to be the cause and (since this is the deed [*That*] of a being endowed with freedom [*eines mit Freiheit begabten Wesen*]) author of its own progress toward the better. But from a given [*gegebenen*] cause an event as effect [*Wirkung*] can be predicted [*vorhersagen*] only if cooperating [*mitwirkend*] circumstances come about/to sight [*eräugnen*]. That these latter must sometime come about can well be generally predicted, as with calculations of probability in a game [*Spiel*]...without my knowing whether I will have the experience of it in my own lifetime. [VII 84; 151]

What is sought, then, is an event [*Begebenhiet*] from which progress would follow as an inevitable consequence—an event that points out [*hinweisen*] both the existence [*Dasein*] of an operative moral cause [*Ursache*] and the act of its causality [*Act iherer Causalität*] in the human race, an act indeterminate with respect to time. But if the human race begins at any time constantly to progress, it has done so all along. Thus this event would have to be regarded [*ansehen*] as an historical sign or indication [*hindeuten*] of a tendency of the human race at large—the human race, that is to say, not as a sum of individuals, but as "the whole divided into nations and states that we encounter on earth." [84; 151] (As such, this event would do for human affairs what natural laws, which guided [*Hinweisung*] Copernicus, did for the movements of the stars [see VII 83-84; 149-51].)

Kant's repeated reference throughout the essay to "Spielen" (understood both as dramatic spectacles and as games [as in games of chance]) highlights mankind's discomforting resemblance to the fabled citizens of Abdera, whose madness lay, precisely, in a failure to distinguish between spectacle and spectator. (All the world, as Shakespeare might say, is but a stage, and we but players.) We too—all of us—cannot avoid being actors in the play of which we are, just as inevitably, the audience. What Kant seeks, then, is a place to stand *within* experience from which one can regard mankind's doings as intelligible—a vantage point that (like the Copernican hypothesis) substitutes order for absurd entanglement, without reducing history to a pointless mechanism.[6]

The sought for event "in our time" which demonstrates "the moral tendency of the human race" is described in section six. It consists:

> neither in important deeds or misdeeds directed by men, whereby what was great among men is made small or what is small among men made great, nor in ancient splendid [*glänzende*] state structures that vanish as if by magic as others come forth in their place as if from the depths of the earth....It is merely the way of thinking [*Denkungsart*] of the spectators which publicly betrays itself by this game [*Spiele*] of these great transformations/metamorphoses [*Umwandlungen*], and manifests such a universal and yet unselfish [*uneigennützige*] sympathy [*Theilnehmung*] for players of one side over those of the other, despite the danger [*Gefahr*] that such partiality could be very disadvantageous [*nachtheilig*] for them if it should become known; so [there] is demonstrated a character (owing to its universality) of the human race as a whole and at the same time a moral character (owing to its unselfishness), at least in disposition, a character that not only permits hope in progress toward the better, but is already itself such progress, in so far as the capacity for progress succeeds/suffices for now. ...The revolution of a people rich in spirit [*geistreichen*], which we have seen going forth in our day, may succeed or fail....this revolution, I say, still finds in the

> hearts [*Gemüthern*] of all spectators (who are not themselves entangled [*verwickelt*] in the game/play [*Spiel*]) a wishful participation [*eine Theilnehmung dem Wunsche nach*], bordering on enthusiasm, and whose utterance/externalization [*fusserung*] is itself bound up with danger, [and] which thus can have no cause other than a moral disposition [*Anlage*] in the human race. [VII 85-6, 153-5]

This morally inflowing cause (the republican "idea") manifests itself both as the "*right* of a people not to be hindered...by other powers when it seeks to give itself a civil constitution" and the *duty* that this constitution be "just and morally good."

But how can enthusiasm for revolution prove mankind's moral tendency, if revolution as such is contrary to duty (as Kant elsewhere claims) and enthusiasm (as he here insists) not altogether praiseworthy [VII 86; 155]? The answer comes in a remark, "weighty [*wichtig*] for anthropology," which "enthusiastic participation in the good...gives occasion [*giebt Anlass*] through [the] history [previously cited]":

> True enthusiasm always goes toward what is ideal, and, indeed, purely moral, as is the concept of right, and it cannot be grafted onto self-interest [*Eignennutz*]. Monetary rewards could not pitch the adversaries of the revolutionaries to the zeal and greatness of soul which the sheer concept of right produced in them, and *even the concept of honor [Ehrbegriffe] of the old martial nobility [kriegerischen Adels] (an analogue of enthusiasm) vanished [verschwand] before the weapons of those who kept before their eyes the right of the people to whom they belonged and of which they thought themselves the guardians.* With what exaltation [*Exaltation*] the external, onlooking public [*Publicum*] then sympathized [*sympathisirte*] without the least intention [*Absicht*] of cooperating [*Mitwirkung*]. [VII 86-7, 155-7 {emphasis added}]

Kant's public onlookers, who "take part" (by taking the revolutionaries' part) without intending to cooperate, are exalted by the sight of one concept of honor disappearing before the weapons of another. Like the shimmering political structures that also vanish [*verschwinden*], warlike pride (which is not, as Kant elsewhere puts it, "nothing") gives way before the even more fearless, but ultimately peace-loving, zeal that animates the guardians of and for the people. What is crucial here is not the revolutionaries' success (their plans may miscarry or succeed at such cost that no reasonable person would embark on them anew [VII 85, 152]), but the uplifting feeling they engender in those not "entangled" in a *Spiel* whose stake is the honor of the human race as such. If Kant's ploy does not succeed—if no sign of constant progress is to be found—history is a "deedless" treadmill in which "our species' entire play of commerce with itself on this globe would have to be considered a mere farce [*Possenspiel*]," endowing us "with no greater value, in the eyes of reason," than that of other animal species "who carry on this game with fewer costs and without expenditure of understanding." [VII 82, 147] Human understanding—our very power to conceive—would on this view have to be reckoned a dead loss. The alternative, for Kant, is history as a spectacle (neither tragedy nor farce) that communicates enthusiasm (without which, as Kant puts it in an early essay, "nothing great can be achieved") without entangling its audience in a revolutionary breach of justice.

How the (non-revolutionary) feelings of this audience signal progress is taken up in section seven, entitled "soothsaying [*wahrsagene*] history of humanity." There must in principle [*Grundsatz*], says Kant:

> be something moral, which reason presents before the eyes as pure but also, because of its great and epoch-making influence, as the recognized duty thereto of the soul of human beings, and which pertains to the human race as a whole..., something the hoped for and attempted [*Versuchen*] success of which...[the human soul] jubilates over [*jujauchzt*] with so much universal and unuseful/selfless [*uneigenützige*r] participation. [VII 87, 157]

That event, which Kant identifies with the "phenomenon" of the "evolution" (*not* revolution) of a republican constitution, reveals mankind's evolving institution of a right "exalted above all price (of utility [*Nützlichkeit*])" [VII 87n; 157n] and thus represents, or, literally, "sets before mankind's eyes," [VII 87; 157] man's elevation, and hence removal from the economy of negative value earlier referred to. (The value of life lived for the sake of happiness alone sinks, as Kant elsewhere puts it, below zero.[7])

But what the jubilating onlookers of Kant's time had in view, as we earlier learned, was the overpowering of an undeveloped and barbaric code of honor by the weapons of a modern citizen army—i.e., the "vanishing" of a "concept," flawed but real, before a popularly embodied and empowered "idea." [cf. VII 86, 155][8] That jubilant onlooking is the invisible yet palpable event Kant here describes as the "phenomenon" [*Phenomenon*] of the "evolution" of a constitution according to natural right (or, alternatively, of a constitution that is both natural and just [*einer naturrechtlichen Verfassung*]). [VII 87, 157]

If a prophetic history of man's advance, Kant earlier suggested, were to be possible at all:

> Some experience in the human race must come forth which, as an event points to its disposition [*Beschaffenheit*] and capacity [*Vermögen*] to be the cause of its own advance toward the better; and ...to be the author of that advance. [VII 84, 151]

Accordingly, Kant sought an event that points to such a cause—an event that signals a tendency of the human race taken as a whole, or in its essential species character (thus getting round the difficulty that surrounds the notion of individual moral progress.) [See VII 81-2; 146-7]

But this, precisely, is the public betrayal [*verräthen*] of a way of thinking characterized above—that of spectators who observe the "game of great upheavals/revolutions [*Umwandlungen*])" without intending to cooperate [*mitwerken*] (and whose activity is to this extent removed from the machinery of ordinary effectuating [*mitwerkende*] circumstance [VII 85, 153]).[9] The distinct avoidance, by such spectators, of all "entanglement in the game" calls to mind the Tychonic "entanglements" bordering on absurdity of those, "otherwise not stupid" [*Unweis*], whose stubborn way of interpreting [*Erklärungsart*] astronomical appearances led them to reject the standpoint of Copernicus—a standpoint only reason can assume. [VII 83, 149]). The worldly standing of Kant's spectators, on the basis of whose way of thinking [*Denkungsart*] one can predict free actions without presuming supernatural guidance, is the sought for equivalent, within the realm of human affairs, of that Copernican hypothesis.

The felt appearance, so to speak, to an international audience, of the idea of right (figured in the *disappearance* of honor aristocratically and martially conceived) is the sought for connection between experience and a self-authored cause from which a progressive history of the human race can be deduced. The spectacle of revolution in France is evidently to do for others what Rousseau's egalitarian transformation of honor did for Kant.[10] (There is a nice symmetry, then, in the famous story of Kant interrupting his regular afternoon walk on only two occasions—once to read Rousseau's *Emile*, the other time to read late breaking news concerning revolution in France.)

If the argument presented here is correct, it is this consideration, above all, that lies behind the power Kant now claims to predict, "even without a seer's spirit,"[11] human attainment of the republican goal. Even if the French Revolution should founder, the enthusiasm felt by its audience "is too great [*gross*], too interwoven with the interests of mankind, and its influence too widely disseminated" not to be "brought to memory by peoples on the occasion [*Veranlassung*] of any favoring circumstance," thus arousing "a repetition of new efforts of this kind [*Art*] [VII 88, 159]. Accordingly, "the intended constitution [*beasichtige Verfassung*] must [eventually] attain the constancy [*Festigkeit*] that the instruction [*Belehrung*] of repeated experience cannot fail to effect [*bewirken*] in the minds [*Gemüthen*] of all." [VII 88, 159].

Kant's prediction, in short, derives its own undiminishable force [*Kraft*] [VII 88; 159] less from politics in the usual sense (which may succeed or fail, and, as an exercise of power over others, is, an any case, always suspect)[12] than a kind of renewable instruction to which Kant's essay. through the history thereby provided, "gives occasion."

But what sort of instruction or teaching can this be? A clue is to be found in a remarkable footnote, appended to the passage, previously cited, on the "disappearance" of the old warlike concept of honor. "Why," Kant there asks:

> has no ruler ever dared to freely proclaim that he recognizes no right on the people's part against him; that the people owe their happiness entirely to the beneficence of a government that confers it on them, and that all presumption on the subjects' part to a right against the government...is absurd and even punishable?— The answer is: because such a public declaration would rouse all of his subjects against him; although, as docile sheep, led by a benevolent and sensible master, well-fed and forcefully guarded, their well-being would lack nothing of which to complain.—For a being endowed with freedom is not satisfied with enjoyment of life's comforts that falls to his lot [*Theil*] through someone else; what matters is rather the principle according to which he provides it for himself. [VII 87n., 157n.] [13]

The perverse result of this refusal on the part of unjust rulers to publicize their maxims is the real danger that the people's sense of honor will continue to lie dormant. So long as rulers do not publicly declare a right to govern autocratically *on principle*, their subjects need never face up to the stark choice of either (passively) resisting (at whatever danger to themselves) or utterly renouncing their claim to be valued as other than mere means. Absent that public declaration, ordinary men (not schooled as knights of old) need never face that choice and thus come to recognize their own preference, at once natural and in keeping with the moral law, for freedom over mere enjoyment. Absent such a proclamation [*aussagen*]—which, according to Kant, no ruler has ever made or ever will—ordinary men might never become conscious of what is for Kant a kind of *naturrechtlich* fact, namely, that "a being endowed with freedom is not satisfied" with a happiness for which he is dependent on someone else; what matters is rather the "principle" according to which he gains it for himself.

But:

> a being endowed with freedom, in the consciousness of his privilege [*Vorzug*] over the reasonless animal, *can and should demand* [*verlangen*], according to

> the formal principle of his will, no other government for the people to whom he belongs than one in which they are co-legislative. (Emphasis added.) [VII 87n.; 157n.]

Prior to Kant's epoch making "event," which arouses, in all who call it to mind, an exaltation that bears witness to their own preference for freedom over mere enjoyment, nothing would have permitted an observer to maintain "despite all unbelievers" and "for the most rigorous theory" that the human race was genuinely advancing. Unlike the religious prophecy [*weissagen*] based on supernatural communication [*übernatürliche Mittheilung*], which Kant earlier rejected, the prophecy at hand rests on a participation, or sympathy [*Theilnehmung*], within the limits of human experience. Such communicable enthusiasm, which though not entirely estimable, participates [*theilnehmen*] in the good [VII 86, 155], bears witness to the human preference for freedom over mere enjoyment, recognition of which itself gives value to existence.[16]

Practical education succeeds by eliciting the student's own supersensible awareness of absolute value (the ultimate or inner source of all true honor).[16] In doing so it imparts a feeling that directly registers, and on a basis of equality, that student's (natural? moral?) preference for freedom over mere enjoyment. Interpreted in this way, the spectacular occasion of the French Revolution turns the play of human affairs (a play that could not otherwise be viewed by wise observers as other than a farce) into the comedy, or "eudaimonistic way of representing human history [*Vorstellungsart der Menschengeschichte*]," that Kant had seemed earlier to reject. 'Eudaimonism" with its "sanguine hopes," seems "untenable" [unhaltbar], as Kant there put it, and to do "little to favor a supernaturally [*weis*sagenen] prophetic human history in regard to ever enduring progress toward the good." [VII 81-2; 146-7] (Emphasis added.)

And yet, in so foreclosing *supernatural* eudaimonistic prophecy (prophecy, literally, "of lucky genius"), Kant left out the possibility of eudaimonistic soothsaying (or fortune telling *within the limits of human experience*), a possibility that Kant 's discussion of a prophetic history of humanity ["wahrsagende Geschichte der Menscheit" (VII 87, 157)] now explicitly "opens up" (or makes public") [*eröffnet*] (VII 89, 161):

> Here, thus, is a proposition that is not just well-meaning and sufficiently valuable from a practical standpoint, but also maintainable [*haltbarer*] despite all unbelievers, and for the strictest theory: namely, that the human race has always been in progress to/toward the better and will be so henceforth, [a consideration which], if one has regard not only to what happens to one people, but also to the spreading over all peoples of the earth, that little by little come to take part/partic-

ipate [*Theil nehmen*] in it, opens up the outlook/prospect of an unpredictable/immeasurable/unforeseeable [*unabsehliche*] time. [VII 89, 161]

In this way, supernatural communication, which is knowably beyond the limits of human experience, gives way to spiritual participation by a public [*Publikum*] interested in political happenings without being entangled in the mechanism of ordinary politics.

That "opening" of an outlook [*Aussicht*] onto a "unabsehliche Zeit" [VII 89, 161]—a time that cannot be foreseen because its end, literally, cannot be seen, and hence is not subject to calculative prediction[16]—calls to mind the "end of time" prophesied [*weissagen*] in the Book of Revelation [*Offenbarung*], in which the heavens departed and every mountain and island were moved out of their places.[17] Kant continues, however, with the following qualifying disclaimer:

> The prospect of an immeasurable/endless time opens up] unless, that is, there does not, after the first epoch of a natural revolution, which (according to Camper and Blumenbach) buried the plant and animal kingdoms, before there were yet men, follow a second, which plays with/mistreats [*mitspielt*][18] the human race in the same way, in order to let other creatures strut[19] upon the stage, etc. For before [*vor*] the omnipotence of nature, or, even more, its highest cause, which for us cannot be arrived at, the human being is, in turn, but a trifle [*eine Kleinigkeit*]. But for rulers [*Herrscher*] of his own species to take a human being for such—that is no trifle but the overturning [*Umkehrung*] of the final purpose of creation itself. [VII 889, 161]

The proposition that man always has been and always will be progressing toward the good,[20] a proposition maintainable [*haltbarer*] despite all unbelief [21] and for the strictest theory, opens up (and opens up upon) the prospect of an incalculable time—except that allowance must be made for nature's power to bury us.[22] Nothing could more forcefully bring home the contrast between nature's revolutionary epoch and the "epochal" event that is properly human—the former making "the small great and the great small," the latter weighty [*wichtig*] in a way literally beyond measurement [cf. VII 85, 155; 87, 157].[23] Hence the cataclysmic uncertainties to which our species, like every other, is subjected do not lessen the rigor of Kant's happy prophecy, because the power of nature touches what is here at stake—the worth of existence—only insofar as it is natural for human beings to value and be valued. The natural/juridical [*naturrechtlich*] fact that human beings (and they alone) take honor seriously mediates between a natural realm in which we hardly reckon (and in which the eventual physical destruction of the species is a virtual certainty) and a moral one in which we count absolutely.

The demand [*Verlangen*] for government that is republican in principle—like the demand [*Verlangen*] for a eudaimonistic history of the human race [See VII 140, 141]—is the articulation of what Kant later calls a "rightful need"—a necessity, that is to say, both natural and honor-loving. "To one accustomed [*gewohnt*] to freedom," as Kant once put it, "there can be no more horror-filled misfortune than to see oneself subjected to a creature of one's kind." Kant's fragment of the future, alternately chiliastic and terroristic, can thus be read as an instructive wake-up signal for "our time"—one in which mankind's love of honor, poised to emerge, is also, and perhaps fatally, at risk.[24]

The means of such instruction is taken up in section eight, "on the difficulty of maxims laid down [*angelegten*][25] for [*auf*] progress toward world good [*Weltbesten*], with regard to their publicity." Here Kant urges that philosophers—i.e., those "free professors of law" [*freie Rechtslehrer*][26] among the people who, as "natural announcers[27] and interpreters [*Verkündiger und Ausleger*]" [VII 89, 161], can bring about the people's public instruction [*öffentliche Belehrung*], or civic enlightenment [*Volksaufklärung*] as to the people's "shear natural right"—be allowed to publicize their teaching without governmental hindrance. Such teachers, wrongly decried as public dangers, address their voice [*Stimme*],[28] not confidentially [*vertraulich*], to the people (who, Kant says, take little if any notice of their writings), but respectfully and with all honor [*ehrerbietig*][29] to the state itself, so that, when an entire people brings forward [*vortragen*] its grievances [*Beschwerde*], the latter may take to heart the people's rightful/juridical need [*rechtliche Bedürfniss*].

The natural educators of the people, then, do not speak to them directly, but rather to the state, whose human instruments the state sets up universities to train. [VII 18; 25] [Free] universities, it seems reasonable to conclude, are the special home of civic education of the sort Kant has in mind.[30] Rightly instructed, those invested with the offices of government would not treat the people's grievances paternalistically, but as *demands* for what is just. (Hence, the vital importance of establishing the independence of philosophy *vis a vis* the other faculties).

The crucial importance of education in this narrow sense becomes clear from Kant's subsequent discussion of the British state, where a public constitution, formally committed to representative government, disguises the autocratic truth. Such 'lying publicity" [*lügenhafte Publicität*], Kant says, deceives the people with the illusion of representative government, while their representatives [*Stellvertreter*], won over by bribery, secretly subject them to what is in fact an absolute monarchy. As a result of this deception , a "true constitution according to right," which people think they already have, "is no longer sought at all." [VII 90, 163]

That this "representation" [*Vorstellung*], which "has in itself something of the deceptive [*Trügliche*]" is, in fact, "easily penetrated [*leicht durchzuschauende*]," suggests the moral use of an external "observing public" [*zuschauende Publikum*], who can point out to those directly involved their fatal error. It also serves us, Kant's readers, as an instructive counterpart to the uplifting "disappearance" earlier described: whereas in the case of France, honor martially conceived gave way to the enthusiasm of the people's guardians, in England eagerness on the part of the people's representatives for "offices and dignities [*Amter und Würden*]" "wins them over" to carrying out the king's unrestricted warlike bidding. [VII 90, 163] Hence the central role of honor, properly conceived, to national enlightenment and, with it, the civil progress of the species. It is not enough, or even necessary, that government immediately assume the formal trappings of a republican constitution: unless the people's representatives love honor in the appropriate republican sense, such legal forms amount to nothing. What most serves the cause of freedom is not revolution but education, by the people's "natural teachers," of the nation's leaders to a true understanding of honor—a task crucially advanced, in Kant's own time, by the lucky occurrence [*eraügnen*] of a people rich in spirit.[31]

Section nine, on "the profit yielded [*Ertrag ...abwerfen*][32] by progress to/toward the better" [VII 91, 165], reconsiders the possibility of a eudaimonistic history *immune* to reasonable/well-grounded ridicule [*Spott...mit Grunde*] (especially by politicians). Although, for the reasons earlier cited, an increase in the quantum [*Quantum*] of morality as it pertains to our attitude [*Gesinnung*] would contradict human freedom (and would require, Kant now adds, "supernatural influence" and a kind of "new creation" [VII 92, 167]), no comparable difficulty stands in the way of a change in the "phenomena" or appearances of the ethical makeup [*Beschaffenheit*] of the human race, phenomena which is all that the civil evolution here traced amounts to.

Nothing in Kant's prophetic representation [*Vorstellung*] of history [*Geschichte*], in other words, depends on more than is available on the basis of "the empirically given," or "experience"—that is to say, the physical causes of our actions, "insofar as they happen [*geschehe*]," and which are themselves appearances [*Erscheinungen*], rather than the moral cause, establishable [*aufstellen*] a priori on the basis of the concept of duty, or what "ought to happen [*geschehen sollte*]." Nothing in the evolutionary growth or increase here described requires what Kant elsewhere calls "engraftment on a new, morally good *Gesinnung*."[33]

What, then, are the physical, experientially available causes on which Kant relies? In part [*theils*], "love of honor" [*Ehrliebe*], in part, "well-understood self-interest" [*Vorteil*]. [VII 92, 167] On this basis, he predicts a gradual decrease in violence and increase in trustworthy behavior, eventually reaching even the relations among states, without this requiring any augmentation in the moral foundations [*Grundlage*] of the human race. That love of honor, elsewhere treated as a synonym for virtue, is here identified as *physical*, underscores the centrality, for understanding human history, of the human experience of valuing and seeking to be valued .[34]

The order in which such progress may be expected, according to section ten, is from the "top down" rather than "the bottom up." The latter plan is hardly to be hoped for, inasmuch as the people (still themselves uneducated) refuse the burden of educating their children, while governments, which spend everything on war, have nothing left for the able teachers [*Lehrer*] who are "devotedly desirous of office [*Amte*]." Instead:

> the entire mechanism [*Maschinenwesen*] of this education [*Bildung*] lacks coherence, for it is not designed [*entworfen*] according an underlying plan of the highest state power and, put into play [*Spiel*] according to that intention, consistently maintained therein. [VII 93, 169]

To be sure, government might pursue reform directly. And yet, given that education must be effected [*bewirken*] by men themselves in need of education, such an outcome can be hoped for (not to say predicted) only if contingent circumstances produce a "favoring effect [*Effect*]," i.e., only by an appeal to "providence [*Vorsehung*]" (or "wisdom from above that is invisible to us"). There remains, then (if we wish to depend only on what is to be expected of men as men [i.e., on human nature]) only the "negative wisdom" of rulers who "see themselves compelled [*sich genöthigt sehen werden*]" to gradually put an end to war. Rulers, to whose honor and self-interest Kant specifically appeals [VII 21-36; 31-61], can, then, be counted on to further progress toward the better, whether by positive intention or (more likely) by allowing such circumsances to arise as that to which Kant's own "announcement and interpretation" gives "favoring occasion." [cf. VII 86-7; 155-7. VII 88; 159]

We thus return to the cosmopolitan question with which Kant's essay begins—how to assume a viewpoint [*Ansicht*] for predicting "the course of human things" equivalent to the self-displacement of Copernicus from earth to sun for purposes of predicting the movement of the stars. Kant makes or finds it in the "outlook" [*Absicht*] that his interpretation of a certain event opens up within the realm of human experience—an event resembling the moment, in which, thanks to Rousseau, Kant was himself "set right." (That Kant describes this event in almost the same terms he employed forty years earlier to depict that personally transformative moment—each involving the "disappearance" [*verschwinden*] of an illusory concept of honor before its republican rival—further emphasizes the resemblance.) Thanks to this event [*Begebenheit*], to which Kant's own (fortuitous) education would seem to give privileged access, man is brought face to face with his own nature as a being given to be free. [*Ein mit Freiheit begabtes Wesen*], forestalling rulers' ongoing abuse of others of their kind. Foremost among *Volkserklären* is thus Kant himself, who publishes a representation of history in which men see themselves freely compelled to peace before the fact—an "announcement in advance"[35] that (for once) knowledgably and honorably fulfills the condition that alone makes thinkable the possibility of soothsaying—or foretelling the end of human history—without supernatural guidance.[36]

Notes

1 Honor, which, as we shall see, is central to this claim, also figures importantly in the historical essays of the 1780's – from the first moment of "release" from nature's womb, as sketched out in the *Conjectural Beginnings of Human History*, a moment Kant characterizes as both "dangerous [*gefahrvoll*]" and "honorable [*ehrend*]" [VIII 114,], to Kant's designation of the "the political ambition [*Ehrbegierde*] of rulers," at the end of *The Idea for a Universal History with a Cosmopolitan Intention*, as one reason for attempting such a history in the first place [VIII 31,].

2 As Kant's note makes clear, the usual sense of "wahrsagen" is pejorative (something like "fortune telling"): "From Pythia to the gypsy girl, of one who meddles [*pfuschert*] in foretelling the future [*Wahrsagen*] (doing it without either knowledge or honesty [*Ehrlichkeit*]) it is said: he *engages in soothsaying* [*er wahrsagert*]." [VII 79n.; 141n.]. (Pythia, the priestess of the Pythian Apollo, delivered the oracles at Delphi.) According to the Bible, false prophecy (or soothsaying ["Wahrsagerei" in Luther's translation]) is deserving of death; see Deuteronomy: 18; 10-22.

3 On the meaning of this term, see Alexis Philonenko, *La theorie kantienne de l' histoire* (Paris: Vrin, 1986), pp. 47-51. Kant's use of the term remains somewhat mysterious. Abdera was known in ancient times as a city of folly, owing especially to the tendency of its inhabitants to assume the persona of characters they had witnessed on the stage. Cicero, who uses the term "abderitic project" for one without prudence or direction, ascribes to the Abderites the qualities of vain agitation and extreme susceptibility to spectacles. Abdera was also the home of Democritus, the atomist. Kant may also have in mind Christoph Martin Wieland's *Geschichte der*

Abderiten (1774-80). See especially Wieland's description of this dramatic susceptibility [the so-called "Abderite sickness"](Book Three, chapter twelve). Kant also associates Abderitism with the thought of Moses Mendelssohn, who famously argued, in defending Judaism, that the human species as a whole is subject neither to moral progress nor to moral regress. On the latter point, see Peter Fenves, *A Peculiar Fate* (Ithaca: Cornell University Press, 1991), p. 192.

4 Kant elsewhere defines "deeds" as actions that are morally imputable. (See his "Introduction" to the *Metaphysics of Morals.*)

5 The relevant passage reads as follows:

> That the course of human things seems so senseless [*widersinnisch*] to us lies, perhaps, in the incorrect [*unrecht*] choice of standpoint from which we regard [*ansehen*] it. Viewed from the earth, the planets sometimes move backward, sometimes stand still, sometimes move forward. If the standpoint assumed is that of the sun, however, which only reason can do, they move, according to the Copernican hypothesis, with constant forward regularity. Some [people], however, who are otherwise not stupid, like to persist stubbornly in their way of interpreting appearances, and to maintain the standpoint they have once taken, even if they entangle themselves thereby in Tychonic cycles and epicycles to the point of absurdity.—But this is precisely the misfortune [*Unglück*]: we lack the ability [*Vermögen*] to place ourselves in this standpoint, when it is a matter of predicting free actions. For that would be the standpoint of providence, which lies outside of all human wisdom [*Weisheit*], and which stretches also to the free actions of man, which human beings can certainly *see* but not *foresee* with certainty (for the divine eye there is no difference here)... [VII 83-4; 149-51]

6 Kant's image of the *Possenspiel* calls to mind Georg Buchner's *Woczek*, with its dark vision of the world as puppet show without a puppetmaster.

7 See, for example, *Critique of Judgment* [V 433n.], tr. Werner S. Pluhar (Indianapolis: Hackett, 1987), p. 321n.

8 Which is not to say that the individual members of that army were themselves behaving morally.

9 The irony involved in characterizing this morally crucial, yet strangely a-political event as a "betrayal" (cf. "Verträter" = traitor) should not go unnoticed. So long as it is unaccompanied by (further) practical intention, such public betrayal of feelings escapes the culpability that otherwise condemns all public expressions of political disloyalty. (That the event in question involves neither activity [*Täthen*] susceptible to imputation in the ordinary sense nor action reducible to physical causality marks its status as moment in which morality "flows into" nature.

10 See p. 1 above.

11 "Sehergeist" (cf. "Geisterseher [Ghostseer]," the subject of an early essay by Kant).

12 See *Idea for a Universal History*, thesis six; and *Perpetual Peace*, second supplement: "the possession of power inevitably corrupts the free judgment of reason." [VIII 369; 115]

13 Compare *Perpetual Peace*, Appendix I: men "only need to realize consciously that they are not free beings for them to become in their own eyes the most wretched of all earthly creatures."

14 See [VII 89; 161]

15 Cf. *Metaphysics of Morals* [VII 482; 270]

16 "Absehen" means "to see [to] the end of."

17 See Rev. 6. 13-14: und schwur bei dem, der da lebt von Ewigkeit zu Ewigkeit, der den Himmel geschaffen hat und was darinnen ist, und die Erde und was darinnen ist, und das Meer und was darinnen ist, dafl hinfort keine Zeit mehr sein soll. (Luther translation)
[And sware by him that liveth for ever and ever, who created heaven, and the things that therein are, and the earth, and the things that therein are, and the sea, and the things that are therein, that there should be time no longer.] (For a thematic discussion of the passage, see Kant's essay "The End of All Things.") The entire Book of Revelation is relevant to Kant's argument.

18 "Mitspielen" means "to play with in a game or play (as with actors) but also, figuratively, "to use" (in a pejorative sense) as in the phrase "das Schicksal spielte ihm hart mit" [fate used him very ill].

19 "Treten." Kant's usage here contrasts ironically with his discussion of human progress [Fortschreit], which literally means a "stepping forward."

20 Cf. Rev. 22.11.

21 Cf. Rev. 21.8.

22 Cf. Rev. 20.1: "And I saw an angel come down from heaven, having the key of the bottomless pit." ("Abgrund" in Luther's translation)

23 That "epoch" literally denotes a fixed point in time (from the Greek *epochal*, meaning "stoppage, station, or position," as in the position of a planet) is worth pondering: the "epoch-making event Kant claims to uncover marks the moment, or determinate point of transition, between temporal and moral revolutions.

24 See [VII 80, 143].

25 Compare the moral disposition "anlage" in the human race, a disposition whose existence is certified by the event in question, associated as it is with what Kant characterizes as a humanly weighty affair [für das Menschengeschlecht so wichtigen Anlegenheit]. [VII 88, 159] These verbal variations on the term "anlegen" draw attention to the deposit-like status of man's capacity for improvement. ("Anlage" can also be translated as "investment.")

26 Kant's essay was published as part two ("On the Conflict of the Faculty of Philosophy with that of Law [*Recht*]) of a work (the *Conflict of the Faculties*), concerned with establishing the authority of philosophy (the so-called "lower faculty") with respect to the faculties of theology, law and medicine.

27 Cf. VII 80; 143.

28 Cf. VII 82; 147.

29 See VII 19; 27: for the state to pursue scholarship directly would undermine the respect it is owed. Kant "honors" the state by warning it not to interfere with the freedom of the "lower" faculty (i.e., philosophy), whose public "role" [*spielen*] is to "examine everything" without commanding anything.

30 This is particularly so, given the new restrictions on publication with which Kant was forced to contend during this period of his life. On the special role of the university, see the Preface to *The Conflict of the Faculties* [VII 5-11; 9-21]. Among university graduates Kant distinguishes between scholars proper and tools of government (clergymen, magistrates and physicians) who deal directly with the people (who are themselves incompetent [Idiotes]). Because possession of a civil office

does not itself insure that such graduates possess an understanding of the theoretical principles underlying their specialty, they are not "free to make public use of their reason as they see fit," but are subject to government control in the form of censorship by the faculties. In a properly functioning system of *Volkserklärung*, popular education is mediated by a class of government officials, themselves trained by and subject to scholars who command, or are directed by, a wisdom that is "principled" in the precise Kantian sense.

31 The French are "spirit-rich" [*geistreich*] in a way that the British (and the German) evidently are not. "Reich" in German (as well as Old English) originally connoted power or rule (as in "Reich" or "kingdom"), hence also "overflowing and abundant." That the French people are (naturally) rich in spirit has, then, both a political and an economic register, implying both resources of spirit and the power of spirit to rule.

32 "Ertrag," which means "product, or yield," as with farm crops (hence by extension, profit in a financial sense) is related to the term "erträgen," meaning "to bear a burden or endure." The title of the section might also be translated as "What burden will the human race's progress to/toward the better throw off?"

33 Cf. *Idea for a Universal History from/with a Cosmopolitan Standpoint/Intention* [VIII ; trans. Hans Reiss, *Kant's Political Writings*, p. 49]: "Everything good that is not engrafted onto a morally-good attitude [*Gesinnung*], is nothing other than empty appearance [*lauter Schein*] and glittering misery [*schimmerndes Elend*]." The evolutionary "event" (which Kant's essay of 1784 does not and cannot into take account) evidently provides Kant with a new way to save the appearances.

34 See *Idea for a Universal History*, which attributes the "happening" [*geschehen*] of the "first true steps from rudeness to culture" -- steps that consist in what Kant calls "the social value [*gesellschaftlichen Werth*] of man – to men's effort to be "more [than] human [*mehr als Mensch*]," a verbal ambiguity that neatly captures the dialectical character of honor in its undeveloped (i.e., non-egalitarian) state. [VIII 21; 44] Man initiates the process of his own cultivation, and thus becomes more fully human, by (wrongly) claiming superiority over other men. Kant's designation of "social value" as the activator of historical progress anticipates in broad outline Kojeve's famous "dialectic of master and slave." (Readers familiar only with Kojeve's earlier work may be surprised to find his monumental, posthumously published *Phenomenologie du droit* more Kantian in flavor and substance than Hegelian.)

35 Compare Kant's characterization of "free professors of law" as "natural announcers [*Verkündiger*] and interpreters [*Ausleger*]" of "natural rights and rights arising from common human understanding." [VII 89; 161]

36 See Kant's reference to himself as a "teacher of the people" [*Volkslehrer*] at VII 8; 15; see also [VII 80, 79n.; 143, 141n.]. Kant's representation [*Darstellung*] of history calls to mind representations of the aesthetic sublime, which evoke similar affects of "enthusiasm." According to the *Critique of Judgment*: "Even war has something sublime about it" if it is carried out with due respect for citizens' rights. "At the same time, it makes the way of thinking [*Denkungsart*] of a people that carries it on in this way [*Art*] all the more sublime in proportion to the number of dangers before which was able to stand its ground." The same "way of thinking" is debased, however, by the merely "commercial spirit" that arises from a prolonged peace. [V 263; 122] These remarks, which contrast dramatically with the views later expressed in *Perpetual Peace*, suggest Kant's own ambivalence as to the ultimate possibility of peace with honor.

Part II
Political Philosophy

FREDERICK G. WHELAN

Taking Burke Seriously

The preparation of this *Festschrift* for Burleigh Taylor Wilkins provides a welcome occasion for reflection on the development of Burke scholarship over the past generation and for a reassessment of Professor Wilkins' notable contribution to this field in *The Problem of Burke's Political Philosophy* (1967).[1]

One's first impression on rereading this book is the high level of scholarly rigor that Wilkins applies to Burke. This approach reflects the exacting standards of Anglo-American analytic philosophy of the 1950s and 1960s. When applied to historical political philosophers—one thinks, for example, of Warrender's *Political Philosophy of Hobbes* (1957) as a comparable work in this respect—this approach was one of the strands that produced the extraordinary flourishing of the study of political theory in the English-speaking world over the past thirty years or so. This flourishing embraces both the detailed study and interpretation of historical political thought and the revitalization of political philosophy as such. A glance at the titles of Wilkins' publications readily shows that he has been active in both of these areas. This in turn suggests—and I would argue—that the two areas are always symbiotic: contemporary political philosophy (e.g., reworkings of the principles of liberalism), if it is done well, draws upon the intellectual heritage of the past, just as the questions we take to the study of past thinkers (e.g., Wilkins in his study of Burke) in part reflect the moral and political concerns of the present. The former point is of course itself a Burkean one: we are not flies of a summer and, if we hope to make any progress, we do not begin our inquiries as if in a vacuum, but with a lively sense of the contributions of our predecessors. As we shall see in the following survey, Burke perhaps more than other thinkers has often been read through the lenses of the present, though in many different ways.

Wilkins' rigorous, philosophical approach to Burke also indicates that he takes Burke seriously as a political philosopher. Doing so is of course not a given in Burke scholarship and is therefore noteworthy. Burke's thought is unsystematic, and most of it was expressed in *ad hoc*, usually controversial writings and speeches that were tied to specific political events, and he composed no treatise on political philosophy. This of course does not mean that he cannot be a philosopher or a theorist of comprehensive scope; rather, it means that students of his works must undertake the task of selecting and organizing his main principles and arguments as well as interpreting and criticizing them. Some readers of Burke, both in the past and in the present, have doubted that this can be done in a non-arbitrary way, or in a way that is plausible as an account of Burke's own intentions and beliefs, and have accordingly denied that he should be regarded as a political philosopher. Wilkins is of course aware of what he calls the "Question of Consistency" and indeed takes the construction and presentation of a consistent and coherent system to be the central exegetical enterprise in the study of Burke's texts. His conviction that this can be done is stated in a way that is both provocative and compelling: "No criteria can be produced which would demote [Burke's *Reflections* or *Appeal*] from the ranks of philosophy which would not also affect adversely Plato's *Republic* or Aristotle's *Politics*" (*Problem*, p. 6).

In presenting Burke as a political philosopher Wilkins takes the central issue to be the underlying moral basis of his political thought. He of course defends the thesis that Burke adheres to natural law, grounded—like other major traditional expressions of this doctrine—in Christian faith, reason, and a conception of human nature. The "problem" as he encountered it was to make this case against the contrary view that Burke was basically a utilitarian. Formulating the problem in this way appears to date Wilkins' book to a degree, since no one today (that I know of) is making the case that Burke should be read as a utilitarian, at least in any strict and meaningful sense of the term. Some earlier writers, themselves adherents or admirers of nineteenth-century utilitarianism, had sought to make this case and thus recruit Burke to their cause; they did this by emphasizing Burke's opposition to abstract doctrine (today's "deontological" principles) in political life and his frequent invocations of utility, prudence, and expediency in his efforts to achieve workable and generally beneficial political outcomes. Today it is clearer than it perhaps used to be that "utility" in a loose (pre-Benthamite) sense was common currency in eighteenth-century British thought, that the natural law tradition itself often made a large place for context-oriented prudence or practical wisdom in decision-making and governance, and that utilitarianism does not have a monopoly on a moral concern with consequences and the common good. Burke like other non-utilitarian moralists believed in promoting "the good," but—if Wilkins and others are correct—held that this enterprise was morally constrained in various ways, in addition to having a non-subjectivist conception of "the good" itself that was informed by Christian beliefs and a view of human nature. Another important difference between Burke and the followers of Bentham is that the latter were energetic re- formers with contempt for the past, whereas Burke's sense of social complexity and the resulting likelihood of pernicious unintended consequences led him to embrace cautious reform grounded in respect for the past.

Both the natural law and the utilitarian readings of Burke sought the philosophical dimension that was assumed to be present below the surface of his writings. In addition to opposing the older utilitarian interpretation, Wilkins and others were constructing a Burke who contrasted with other earlier images as well. Two influential older views implicitly denied that Burke was a philosopher at all, but rather understood him as a politician of note—as a parliamentarian, party man, political tactician, statesman, or rhetorician as the case may have been. The predominant view of Burke among most of his admirers in the later nineteenth and early twentieth centuries—from Macaulay to Trevelyan—took him largely in his own terms as a Whig of the constitutionally crucial reign of George III. This meant that Burke became a key player in the "Whig interpretation of history," that is, the celebratory, if one-sided and partisan, reconstruction of the achievements of those earlier Whigs by their Liberal political and intellectual descendants.[2] Burke was admired for having played a major role in upholding and strengthening constitutional government, the place of Parliament within the Constitution, the House of Commons within Parliament, principled parties within the House of Commons, and the concept and practice of ministerial responsibility to the party-structured legislature rather than to the monarch. He had sought enlightened imperial policies in America, Ireland, and India; he had led reform of executive offices; and he had revealed and thereby thwarted schemes by the king and his personal advisors to exercise surreptitious influence over the government. Not all of these causes had been equally successful, but they had all pointed in the direction of progress towards liberal-democratic and responsible government as understood in subsequent generations. Burke was accordingly admired as a statesman and for his teachings on statesmanship and related practical political matters, rather than as a philosopher.

Burke the distinguished politician of the Whig interpretation was abruptly dismissed by Lewis Namier, whose books of 1929-30 initiated a major revision in the historiography of eighteenth-century British politics and in English approaches to history more generally.[3] For Namier and his followers, whose influence was strong into the 1960s, Burke, far from being a political philosopher, was not even a principled politician; rather, he was a typical (or worse than average) politician of that era, motivated only by a desire for the perquisites and patronage of office in the context of personalistic and clientelistic factionalism, and one who merely rationalized through his grandiose eloquence the narrow interests of self or party. Although prominent Namierites did not carry out studies of Burke himself—and their methodological assumptions ruled out the study of political ideas except as reflecting ulterior, self-seeking motives—this did not prevent their conveying a disparaging assessment of his career.[4]

Although the Namierite view was never as strong in the United States as in England and was probably receding by 1967, Wilkins begins his book somewhat defensively with an allusion to Burke's low reputation among historians (*Problem*, p. 4). Namierite cynicism about Burke is scarcely an issue any more,[5] but scholars who wish to take Burke seriously today as a political theorist must confront analogous criticisms and approaches—whether Marxist, psychological, feminist, post-modern, or post-imperialist—who are more interested in his hidden (usually disreputable) motivation than the content of his thought. As for the pre-Namier Whig view, Wilkins brackets off the older claims (and some modern doubts) about Burke's contributions as a statesman in order to proceed with his philosophical study; but these are less troubling in any case, since the Whig interpretation of his principles and actions would seem to be compatible, at the level of political practice, with the natural law interpretation of Burke at a more foundational level.

Wilkins was preceded in his natural law interpretation of Burke's political thought by the important works of Leo Strauss (1953), Peter J. Stanlis (1958), and Francis P. Canavan (1960).[6] Wilkins takes Strauss's scholarship to be decisive in initiating this line of investigation, although we should take note of the remark of Harvey C. Mansfield, Jr., a knowledgeable commentator, that Strauss was on the sidelines of this debate, only *seeming* to endorse the natural law view.[7] Strauss actually portrayed Burke's thought as ambivalent: on the one hand he is said to have attempted a last-ditch defense or revival of "classical" natural right, but on the other he paved the way toward Hegelian and subsequent historicism (which displaced natural law doctrine) by means of his traditionalism and his doctrine of prescription. Wilkins like most students of Burke addresses the important topic of prescription, analyzing at length the relation between "historic rights" and natural rights in Burke's philosophy (*Problem*, Part

III); he appears to endorse Burke's own view that prescriptive rights (with respect both to property and to political authority) can be accommodated within a natural law perspective—though Burke is unusual in his emphasis on this point.[8] However, although Wilkins went on to write a book on *Hegel's Philosophy of History* (1974), he unfortunately did not address at any length Strauss's charge that Burke contained the seeds of historicism or his suggestion of an affinity between Burke and Hegel (cf. *Problem*, pp. 82-83).

Strauss's assertion of Burke's adherence to natural law was set within his well-known distinction between classic (ancient and Medieval) and modern versions of natural right; Burke was said to have embraced the older tradition, in its Christian or Thomist variant, which not only was soon to be challenged by nineteenth-century positivism and historicism, but had also been largely pushed aside by modern Hobbesian or liberal versions of natural right.[9] Although Wilkins' prediction of the "highly probable demise" of this Straussian framework (*Problem*, p. 25) has not materialized, some of his criticisms of it seem to me to carry weight. Wilkins essentially posits a single natural law tradition extending from Aristotle through Burke, with many variations within it, but without the decisive classic-modern break. The differences—as well as the family resemblances—among the doctrines of Aristotle, Cicero, and Aquinas, for example, are plausibly said to be as great as those between, say, Aquinas and Locke (*Problem*, p. 18); hence Burke's natural law beliefs can be said to be as much in the tradition of Locke as in that of St. Thomas—as Burke himself presumably believed them to be.[10] More substantially, Strauss argued that "premodern natural law doctrines taught the duties of man," whereas in the modern version—equivalent to liberalism, as founded by Hobbes—"the fundamental political fact" was the "rights, as distinguished from the duties," of man; the greater prominence of rights over duties in modern doctrines was not, as Gierke had taught, a shift of emphasis, but a fundamental turning point, a difference in kind.[11] Wilkins, in contrast, aligns himself with Gierke: Medieval natural right protected rights, even individual rights, whereas Locke's theory is more attentive to moral duties, more concerned with the common good, and premised on a greater degree of natural human sociability, than Strauss was willing to grant (*Problem*, pp. 24-25). On the issue of the traditional elements, and indeed the fundamental theism, of Locke's doctrine (though not necessarily Hobbes'), as well as on the point that in a system of law, including natural law, rights and duties are generally correlative, I believe that recent scholarship by and large supports Wilkins' positions. One can then agree that Burke's natural law expresses a Christian outlook with a lineage extending to the distant past, without worrying about his also being a Whig of more proximate Lockean pedigree. I would add that Wilkins' view of natural law as a complex and evolving but single tradition, extending back to the Middle Ages and beyond, corresponds both to a Burkean conception of traditions and to Burke's view of a common moral heritage of Europe which, though somewhat variable in its manifestations, was not seriously broken until the French Revolution.

The natural law interpretation of Burke that was first enunciated in the 1950s coincided with several other developments in philosophy and political thought, developments with which it can reasonably be associated. In the first place, it corresponded to the more general revival of natural law and related forms of moral and political philosophy in the same period. In the English-speaking world this movement countered the utilitarianism that was still prevalent among moral philosophers—not to mention the view, briefly taken seriously in some positivist circles, that moral utterances should be relegated to the category of "emotivism." More broadly, this revival appears to have been a response to the 1914-45 crisis of European civilization that many came to see as the product of the nihilistic implications in nineteenth-century thought—a diagnosis in which Strauss was far from alone. Various initiatives in secular ethics—including human rights doctrine, renewed appreciation of Kant, and analyses of the autonomy of the "moral point of view"—reaffirmed in a philosophically rigorous fashion the possibility of reasoned and objective moral judgments in the face of the previous relativism, subjectivism, and historicism. Revitalized religious versions of natural law, especially among Catholic scholars, concurrently repudiated the thesis regarding the inexorable disenchantment of the modern world that Weber had announced early in the century, and in which numerous skepticial and agnostic intellectuals had concurred.[12] The interpretation of Burke's underlying doctrine as theistic—whether Anglican or specifically Thomist—natural law must ultimately rest on the evidence that can be presented for it. The decision to emphasize this theme in Burke's multifaceted works, however, instead of, for example, the Whiggish themes on which some of his earlier admirers had fastened, had the effect of recruiting Burke to the larger natural law revival—and may have reflected a wish on the part of some scholars (Stanlis, Canavan) to do so. Wilkins wrote later, more dispassionately, and evidently at something of a distance from this movement; but his claim that "for Burke the ultimate source of original justice is in the Creator and the intermediate source … is the rational nature of man as created by God"

(*Problem*, p. 14)—and his detailed exposition of the coherence of this doctrine—have the effect of adding to the foundations of the Christian natural law perspective.

Second, it was in the 1950s that Burke was firmly identified as a conservative political theorist, indeed the decisive founder of modern conservatism.[13] This label has been so frequently reiterated in the teaching of Burke over the past two generations that one must make an effort to recall that central elements in his political philosophy (e.g., his checks-and-balances constitutionalism) are well within the classical liberal paradigm, and that he was once a hero of Liberals for his reformist causes and his pragmatic ("utilitarian") statesmanship. While Burke's respect for the past and his endorsement of reform within traditional constraints have always been apparent, the centerpiece of the new conservative Burke was of course his attack on the French Revolution and on ideologically militant, anti-religious, and internationalist Jacobinism. The parallels to the Russian Revolution and international Communism were obvious and sometimes explicit, and Burkean theory no doubt contains powerful teachings concerning the destructive and self-defeating tendencies of such movements that are at least as plausible in the twentieth as they were in the eighteenth century. Burke's recruitment to the vociferously anti-Communist right in the post-war period, however, had the unfortunate effect of stereotyping and constricting students' understanding of his thought. Since anti-Communism was doubtlessly consistent with adherence to natural law philosophy and with the political opinions of its modern proponents, the entire natural law revival—and the natural law interpretation of Burke—were sometimes dismissed as ideological products of "cold warriors" in the ranks of American scholarship.[14] This charge is surely excessive, and in the case of Burke scholarship it overlooks the point that a scholar's motivation may and should be separated from his arguments and evidence. In any case, it is a relief that a preoccupation with Burke's conservatism in the sense of anti-revolutionism, and the "cold war" overtones of some such discourses, are by and large absent from Wilkins' *Problem*, which can clearly claim to be a philosophical rather than an ideological analysis of Burke's thought.

Finally, the revival of natural law and other substantive ethical doctrines in the post-war generation paralleled and sometimes overlapped with both the reworking of philosophical liberalism in this period (in which Burke's "conservative" image at this time disqualified him from participating, so to speak) as well as with appreciative scholarship on the Enlightenment by scholars such as Judith Shklar and Peter Gay. Although Wilkins does not dwell on this, interpreting Burke as a natural law theorist may bring out his affinities to the Enlightenment (e.g., to Locke), in contrast to the older view that made him a (post-Enlightenment) utilitarian, and to another older view (expressed by Alfred Cobban as late as 1929[15]) that he was part of the romantic reaction against the Enlightenment. The fact that Shklar, Gay, and others did not include Burke in their teachings on the Enlightenment suggests that they remained doubtful about his credentials in this respect.[16]

Burke's life and thought fall entirely within the eighteenth century, however, and he can be excluded from the Enlightenment only through an arbitrarily narrow definition of that movement; rather, it seems to me, interpretations of Burke's thought ought to serve to open our eyes to the diversity of Enlightenment political theory and lead us to question simplistic generalizations about it. One simplistic view, for example, equates Enlightenment political thought with classical liberalism, from which Burke is excluded if he is seen primarily as a traditionalistic and religious conservative; another view takes Enlightenment theorizing to rest on abstract universalism and rationalism, in contrast to Burke's defense of what Wilkins calls "historic rights" or what today might be called "contextualized" rights and institutions, as well as prejudice, prescription, and so forth. Clearly both of these views express only partial accounts of eighteenth-century thought. A major scholarly initiative since 1967, for example, has been the documentation (by Pocock and others) of a civic humanist or republican tradition of political thought extending well into the eighteenth century, paralleling but distinct from the development of liberalism.[17] Burke exhibits little if any affiliation with classical republicanism, but once we begin to think of Enlightenment political theory in terms of a number of alternative theoretical traditions, paradigms, discourses, or languages—several of which may be combined in the works of a single writer—we may be in a better position to study what Wilkins calls the "problem of correspondence" among the ideas of different thinkers and their period as a whole. Burke's conviction that a polity embodying limited government, the rule of law, individual rights, and liberty could be stable only if it rested on a cohesive moral foundation resembles the republicans' claim that civic virtue is a necessary condition of free government, although Burke's historical or traditionalist conception of the foundation perhaps distinguishes his theory from theirs. Burke clearly was adept at drawing—for rhetorical as well as theoretical purposes—on a number of the political languages available to him; nevertheless, a sense that there is something original and distinctive about his central ideas—adding up to a comprehensive alternative to both liberalism and republicanism—is what underlies the modern impulse to see him as the founder of the new political outlook of conservatism.

Wilkins' book preceded the methodological focus on languages as well as the "republican revival" in political theory, and his comparison of Burke to other figures is old-fashioned in its straightforward juxtaposition of arguments from the principal texts. Interestingly, he concentrates on Burke's similarities to Hume, Smith, and Beattie, thus in a way anticipating the renewed attention to the Scottish Enlightenment that has been stimulated in recent years by interest in the republicanism-*vs.*-commercial society debates of the period. Of these figures, Wilkins' claims regarding similarities in political philosophy between Burke and Hume are the most interesting.[18] Wilkins argues convincing, for example, that Burke's defense of "prejudice"—which can be worked out more systematically as the claim that social norms embodied in custom and habit are more reliable as a guide to most ordinary moral judgments and moral conduct than individual reasoning—draws on psychological materials and the theory of moral sentiments developed by Hume and Smith (*Problem*, p. 110). One might argue that Burke was distinctive in emphasizing how the Scots' "moral sense" had to be thoroughly socialized, preferably within a stable tradition in which many elements of a complex moral heritage were preserved and passed on; it seems to me, however, that the germ of this argument may be found in Hume's inability to find a satisfactory motive in self-interest for uniform compliance with what he terms the artificial moral virtues, and his ensuing claim that an adequate sense of moral duty attending these virtues therefore must develop through experience, education, and habituation (see *Problem*, pp. 59-60). Hume's epigram that "Custom, then, is the great guide of human life,"[19] which has moral and social as well as psychological and epistemological meanings, sounds Burkean; and Hume, like Burke, was led in consequence to recommend caution is disturbing the social and political institutions within which stable moral practices flourish. Wilkins remarks in passing that Burke's "political conservatism" is "substantially the same" as Hume's (*Problem*, p. 54), but he does not develop this claim as far as he might have, for example by exploring the extent to which Hume anticipated Burke in transferring the idea of prescriptive right from the sphere of property law to that of political legitimacy. Wilkins accepts too readily the old view, forcefully expressed by Dr. Johnson, that Hume was a "Tory," if only "by chance" (*Problem*, p. 55).[20] In my view this causes him to overlook both the deeper philosophical sense in which Hume legitimately may be called conservative—his arguments to the effect that moral and social order depend on rules, artifices, and authority—as well as the manner in which Hume (like Burke) maintained many relatively liberal (or Whiggish) political positions on this conservative foundation.[21]

Wilkins' finding of important similarities between Burke and Hume was asserted in opposition to the view of other scholars, notably Stanlis and Canavan. Arguing (like Wilkins) that Burke adhered to the natural law, but taking Hume to be simply a skeptical empiricist and hence an anti-natural law thinker, they accordingly denied any affinity between the two, at least on the central issue. Equally importantly, in terms of the history of scholarship on political theory, Wilkins was opposing the view of George H. Sabine in his extremely influential survey of the history of political thought. Sabine had been one of the principal targets of Stanlis and Canavan, since he regarded Hume and Burke as so similar that he treats them together in the same chapter of his text, a chapter entitled "Convention and Tradition: Hume and Burke." Sabine embraced the older view that Burke was a traditionalistic conservative, that is, a theorist whose evaluative standard was the principle of "expediency" (or utility) but who applied this standard with deep respect, even "awe" and "reverence" for the experience of the past, a presumption in favor of evolved institutions, and an acceptance of the psychological importance of custom in moral life—all themes that he inherited from Hume. Sabine anticipated Stanlis and Canavan in arguing that Hume's philosophy "destroyed all the pretensions of natural law to scientific validity;" indeed, reading the history of political theory teleologically, with his eye on nineteenth century trends, he appears to have regarded the "gradual elimination of the system of natural law" as Hume's main contribution.[22] Burke is said to have "accepted Hume's negations of reason and the law of nature," and thus to have been Hume's successor in this respect also.[23]

Against this background, then, Wilkins stakes out a third position, agreeing with Sabine on the Burke-Hume link, and with Stanlis and Canavan on Burke's acceptance of the natural law. The problem here of course is: what about Hume's supposed undermining of natural law, and, if his doing so is central to his philosophy as Sabine and others assumed, how could Burke be in any way a Humean and consistent? One might of course simply argue that there are numerous themes of importance in Hume's moral psychology and political theory that are separable from whatever it is in his epistemology that undermines natural law, just as they are separable from his irreligion, and that were thus available for appropriation by Burke the religious natural law adherent. Wilkins instead takes what seems to me to be a more interesting tack, criticizing Sabine and others (including those who read Hume strictly as a utilitarian) for overstating Hume's opposition to natural law: while not an ethical rationalist, Hume nevertheless made a substantial place for practical reason in moral life, and his argument that the rules of justice are, in any determinate form, "artificial" inventions of this reason, is not inconsistent with their also being, in another sense. "natural" to human beings and (in some form) universal, and thus, as Hume also says, not improperly called "laws of nature" (*Problem*, pp. 52-53).[24] With these suggestions Wilkins anticipated subsequent scholarship on Hume, in particular Duncan Forbes' argument that Hume's moral theory constituted a "modern theory of natural law," that is, one that was secular, without final causes, and tied to the empirical study of social needs and historical development—but well within the framework of Scottish and continental natural jurisprudence of the period.[25] Ongoing research into natural law, especially in the work of jurists, suggests that this tradition was indeed more complex than Sabine, Stanlis, or even Strauss imagined. I would add one reservation: Hume's version of natural law, on any account, is "naturalistic" in the sense of arising entirely from the natural necessities of human society, and is completely non-theistic; in this respect it appears to differ foundationally—though not necessarily in many of its practical teachings—from the Thomist version, and hence from Burke's version, insofar as this is interpreted (as Wilkins interprets it) as Thomist.[26]

Wilkins' *Problem* represented the high water mark of the natural law question as the central issue in the interpretation of Burke; it is the most detailed and judicious treatment of a problem that had been prominent for the preceding decade and a half. I will conclude by surveying some of the post-Wilkins Burke scholarship, including some who have dissented from the natural law interpretation as well as some who have accepted it. I defer to another occasion any discussion of the latest, current wave in Burke studies: those who bypass this interpretative problem (as a serious philosophical issue) in the pursuit of literary and rhetorical studies of Burke's texts, rather than of his thought.

Shortly after Wilkins' *Problem*, Conor Cruise O'Brien published his influential Introduction to Burke's *Reflections*, in which he rejected out of hand the notion that Burke was a philosopher and scorned as "pedants" those who try to construct a "system of political philosophy ... out of the hollower components of his rhetoric and the commonplaces of his education."[27] O'Brien does not name any culprits, but the context implies that he has the natural law interpreters in mind, and that he associates this interpretation with the right-wing "counter-revolutionary" appropriation of Burke, which he also denounces.[28] O'Brien's Burke was rather a concretely political writer and actor, one who brought to his astute political analysis heartfelt moral concerns about power and oppression that reflected his formative experiences and consciousness as an Irishman. This approach is continued and expanded in O'Brien's recent, magisterial study, in which it is evident that O'Brien is in a way reviving the old Whig-Liberal view of Burke as primarily a principled statesman active in reformist causes; the opponent now is not the philosophizers, but the cynical Namierite view of Burke's career and motives.[29] The underlying consistency and the underlying moral impetus in Burke's writings is said to be his opposition to what he perceived as oppression and the misuse of political power, with colonial matters (Ireland, America, and India) receiving more attention than either the French Revolution or English constitutional disputes. Natural law goes unmentioned in two extensive indexes.[30]

Frank O'Gorman and James Conniff may be included among scholars who share O'Brien's view that Burke should be seen as a statesman or politician and whose political theory should be read as perceptive political analysis rather than philosophy.[31] O'Gorman's title is misleading, since he treats Burke entirely as a practical politician, and indeed one whose ideas are taken to be rationalizations of political interests, whereas Conniff complements O'Brien in regarding Burke as a reforming statesman. Neither makes a serious effort to address the natural law interpretation, thus tacitly rejecting it.

A more complex case is that of Harvey C. Mansfield, Jr., whom O'Brien claims as an ally (and predecessor) in his campaign against the Namierite view of Burke. Mansfield's major work on Burke, which preceded Wilkins', was a detailed study of Burke's political thought that focused on his ideas about statesmanship and political parties. These sound like the kinds of practical topics that earlier Liberals appreciated in Burke, but Mansfield's analysis of them sets Burke's views in a classical philosophical framework. Burke's endorsement of the rule of "gentlemen" acting through parties, within a stable system of constitutional government, is seen as a safer and more feasible alternative to the rule of philosophers—an alternative that is not only appropriate to the modern world, but one that had been anticipated by the ancients (especially Aristotle): "When the classical political philosophers applied the principle of the rule of the wise to ordinary circumstances, they concluded that the rule of gentlemen who had been favored by such advantages as Burke recounts would be usually the best, because probably the wisest."[32] Burke defends government based on a plurality of principled parties, relies on the "presumptive" virtue of men of settled property, and upholds prescriptive institutions; all this, Mansfield remarks, is "at first sight contrary" to traditional natural law, which might be supposed to indicate a unitary set of correct moral principles, call for actual virtue, and prefer reason to custom. Nevertheless, as implied by "at first sight," Mansfield acknowledges Burke's clear—though neither frequent nor detailed—statements of allegiance to natural law; but his unusual manner of reconciling these statements with other leading themes in Burke's thought amounts to a denial of the natural law interpretation as advanced by others. Mansfield concludes both that Burke's natural law is strictly of the modern variety, and that it reduces to "two rules of prudence, prescription and political economy," both arising from natural processes. This rather restricted understanding of Burke's natural law rests in turn on Mansfield's serious doubts about the genuineness of Burke's Christian faith, doubts that separate Mansfield not only from O'Brien but also from Wilkins and Stanlis and indeed nearly all other readers of Burke.[33]

In his subsequent introduction to a volume of Burke's correspondence Mansfield returns briefly to this issue. Still keeping his distance from the natural law interpretation, Mansfield comments that "at the least it was a public service to rescue Burke from the disgrace of being mistaken for a utilitarian," but that the attribution of a philosophical theory to a thinker who often rejected theory in politics is questionable. Burke's first principles, suitable for a man of an essentially practical orientation, were prudence and the British constitution. But these commitments are of course perfectly compatible, as Burke maintained, with belief in natural law, and Mansfield goes on to concede again that, formally, Burke embraced this concept, along with a related conception of moral elements in human nature; Burke's natural law is said to be non-Thomist, though not non-Christian.[34] In general, although the scholarship establishing Burke's natural law credentials is not repudiated, Mansfield both questions the usual interpretation of this position and appears to doubt whether natural law plays a very large or direct role in Burke's political theory. To be applicable in a particular setting, perhaps, natural law must be mediated (in Burkean theory) both by practical reason or prudence and by a complex network of social, legal, and customary institutions and practices, such as constitutional government and its prescriptive foundation, and it was on these that Burke concentrated most of his attention as a political theorist.

The centrality of the question of natural law in Burke scholarship came to an end with Wilkins' *Problem*, presumably because there was little more to be said—or, since this is never a safe assumption, little more until the passage of time opens up new perspectives in which to approach the question. A number of scholars who have accepted the natural law thesis in some form, however, may be mentioned. Frederick A. Dreyer affirms the importance of natural law to Burke; but, endorsing Burke's own self-identification as a Whig, Dreyer sees Burke's beliefs as basically Lockean, in opposition to the predominant tendency to place him in the Christian-Aristotelian tradition of Aquinas and Hooker.[35] Michael Freeman grants that Christian natural law constitutes Burke's ethical foundation, while denying (what is not really in dispute) that he made any notable contributions to this doctrine.[36] Joseph L. Pappin III, a student of Canavan's, has gone further than others in attributing a systematic natural law philosophy to Burke.[37]

I would finally add my own work, in which I relate Burke's views on India, Hastings, and the Indian empire to a wide range of themes in his political theory, including both concrete analyses of institutional dynamics and more abstract issues of political ethics.[38] I endorse the Christian natural law reading of Burke's ethics, largely accepting Wilkins' account, and of course the Indian speeches contain some of Burke's most important assertions on the subject—texts that I explore in some detail. The attempt to interpret the natural law elements within Burke's larger political theory, however, leads me to emphasize a different problem from the one Wilkins addressed. For Wilkins, the central problem in Burke was the tension between his evident appeals to natural law and those passages that had led others to label him a utilitarian, sometimes in conjunction with the positivism and historicism that led Sabine to pair Burke with Hume as destroyers of the epistemological foundations of natural law. In arguing for a natural law Burke against a utilitarian Burke, Wilkins' scholarship on Burke's texts reflected debates that were taking place between utilitarians and rights theorists in Anglo-American moral philosophy of the 1950s and 1960s—a good example of how the guiding questions in historical political theory often stem from issues contemporary to the investigator. My decision to study Burke's Indian campaigns no doubt similarly reflects contemporary issues—perhaps the coming to terms with legacies of the bygone era of Western empires, and the growing sense that we need to learn more about the other civilizations of the world. In any case, the focus on India made it natural to see the central problem of Burke's political philosophy as a tension between natural law and traditionalism, two ingredients in Burke that are not easy to reconcile.

This is not, of course, a problem to which Wilkins was oblivious, since it is connected to the historicism that both Strauss and Sabine, for example, detected in Burke's thought, and to the conservatism that was the usual label applied to him in the post-World War II period. Wilkins uses the term "traditionalism" (e.g., *Problem*, p. 15), but he analyzes at length, under this rubric, only Burke's doctrine of prescription, or the generation of right by history and usage. Prescription surely sometimes expresses Burke's deep sense of the moral importance of temporal continuity and history, and in his notion of England's "prescriptive constitution" it is nearly equated with custom; but Wilkins does not sufficiently recognize how, even for Burke, prescription can also function to foreclose inquiries into origins in favor of the claims of present possession. Burke's traditionalism goes beyond the specialized matter of prescriptive right to the conviction that reliable moral conduct and well-functioning political institutions are more likely if they are embedded in practices and customs that are relatively stable over time, and that in the best cases they form interrelated parts of a coherent social tradition that is received by the present generation as a heritage from its predecessors. Such traditions are concrete and particularistic, at varying levels: Burke defended English constitutional practices ("our" entailed inheritance) in England, Catholic society in Ireland, the rights of Englishmen for the Americans, and "the old common law of Europe" against the French revolutionaries. Likewise, his study of Indian affairs convinced him that India possessed a similarly rich tradition embracing adequate, even admirable, conceptions and practices in law, morals, and politics. One of his major charges against the East India Company was that it had disregarded and violated Indian customs which it ought to have respected in its rule over that country, with destructive results for the social fabric comparable to those inflicted by the Jacobins in France.

The dispute between natural law and utilitarianism is a dispute within European philosophy; Burke's traditionalism as applied to India raises questions of a different order: the value of non-European practices and beliefs, and the meaning of cultural differences on a world scale. The "problem" with traditionalism is that it seems to be culturally relativistic and therefore in conflict with a universalistic scheme of moral values or justice such as is set forth in natural law. This problem arises conspicuously in Burke's speeches on India, since his other general charge, sometimes expressed side by side with his defense of Indian traditions, was that Hastings and his colleagues had violated higher-law norms of justice and human rights in their dealings with their Indian subjects; Burke notably denounced the (relativistic) "geographical morality" that he attributed to

Hastings—the view that moral standards differ in different cultures, that while lawful rule was morally required in Europe, despotism was permissible in Asia.

If Burke is read as a pure traditionalist, these passages must be disregarded, as they are, for example, by Alasdair MacIntyre, who asserts such an interpretation. As a leading proponent of the view that a coherent and satisfactory moral life can be led only in the context of a moral-intellectual tradition and a community defined by tradition, one might have expected MacIntyre to embrace Burke as a kindred spirit. For MacIntyre, however, vital traditions are ones that contain self-critical or reflective potentialities and hence are always open to change; Burke, in his view, defends established orders solely by reference to values already acknowledged within them (strictly "internal justifications"), and is thus the kind of reactionary who defends only the past.[39] To make this case, of course, MacIntyre must deny that Burke believes in the natural law or any other moral standard transcending actual past practice, and he might be right, if Burke were a pure traditionalist and nothing else. Wilkins argued persuasively, however, that notwithstanding Burke's respect for the past, natural law provided him with a standard for evaluating laws and customs, however venerable, and prejudices, however trustworthy they might usually be. Indian affairs, moreover, offer clear cases where Burke repudiated "bad customs" and calls for reform—whether the prescriptive chartered rights of the Company, or in some specific cases, Indian practices. The older Liberal argument that has recently resurfaced in O'Brien to the effect that Burke was frequently on the side of reform would make no sense if Burke could offer nothing beyond internal justifications for ossified practices. Rather, Burke sought a balance between the general norms of the moral law and traditions (including diverse cultural traditions), and he focused his theoretical attention on the complex processes by which abstract values come to be embodied and stabilized in concrete institutions and in habitual moral conduct. Whether he solved it satisfactorily or not, this was his problem, one that is a problem only because of the natural law background to which he brought the claims of history and traditional practice.

Notes

1 Burleigh Taylor Wilkins, *The Problem of Burke's Political Philosophy* (Oxford: Clarendon Press, 1967); cited in the text as *Problem*. I regret that I am not personally

acquainted with Professor Wilkins. I thank Professor Aleksandar Jokic for his invitation to contribute this essay.

2 See George Macaulay Trevelyan, *History of England* (London: Longmans, 1926), esp. p. 557. Although Trevelyan calls Burke a "political philosopher," he appears to be thinking of "sagacious insight" of a more practical variety, and he singles out for praise Burke's quite practical Economic Reform Bill, which ended the "bribery" of Parliament by the executive through patronage and sinecures. Trevelyan mildly chastises Burke and his contemporaries for their "undue admiration of things as they were": "Because James II had attempted to destroy the institutions of the country, it long remained impossible for anyone else to attempt their reform" (p. 475). The destiny of Old Whiggism was to become modern Liberalism.

3 Sir Lewis Namier, *England in the Age of the American Revolution* (London, 1929); *The Structure of Politics at the Accession of George III* (London, 1930).

4 The most extreme case seems to be Richard Pares, *King George III and the Politicians* (Oxford: Clarendon Press, 1953), whose numerous references to Burke are so unrelentingly hostile that they take on the appearance of self-caricature. See Conor Cruise O'Brien, *The Great Melody: A Thematic Biography and Commented Anthology of Edmund Burke* (Chicago: University of Chicago Press, 1992), p. xlix.

5 In this tradition, however, see L. G. Mitchell, Introduction, *The Writings and Speeches of Edmund Burke* (Oxford: Clarendon Press, 1989), vol. VIII. My impression is that this essay has been criticized by many reviewers as irresponsible in its one-sidedness.

6 Leo Strauss, *Natural Right and History* (Chicago: University of Chicago Press, 1953); Peter J. Stanlis, *Edmund Burke and the Natural Law* (Ann Arbor: University of Michigan Press, 1958); Francis P. Canavan, *The Political Reason of Edmund Burke* (Durham: Duke University Press, 1960).

7 Harvey C. Mansfield, Jr., ed., *Selected Letters of Edmund Burke* (Chicago: University of Chicago Press, 1984), p. 4n.

8 Wilkins' discussion of prescription reproduces some of the ambiguities in Burke's own statements. Sometimes prescription is equated with "immemorial" custom (*Problem*, p. 201); elsewhere he recognizes that its usual purpose as a legal principle was to validate titles to property based on stable possession over a certain period of time, even if their origin was indeterminate or clearly irregular (*Problem*, p. 208). Wilkins does not sufficiently emphasize Burke's originality in transforming a principle of property law into a principle of political legitimacy. I have explored this matter, and its Humean background, in "Time, Revolution, and Prescriptive Right in Hume's Theory of Government," *Utilitas* 7:1 (1995) 97-119.

9 Stanlis asserts the classical-modern distinction as forcefully as Strauss, saying that both Hobbes' and Locke's "natural rights" are no more than disguised assertions of power, given their "egocentric" view of human nature; *Edmund Burke and the Natural Law*, p. 22. On this view, of course, Burke cannot in any way be a Lockean any more than a Hobbesian.

10 Burke explicitly appeals to Hooker rather than to Aquinas, but the point is the same. Locke also of course appeals to the authority of Hooker – disingenuously, on the Straussian interpretation.

11 Strauss, *Natural Right and History*, pp. 181-82.

12 Catholic jurists had been invoking natural law as part of a more general critique of legal realism, in the context of a broader offensive against totalitarianism, from the 1930s. See Edward A. Purcell, Jr., *The Crisis of Democratic Theory* (Lexington:

University Press of Kentucky, 1973), chap. III.9.

13 This label probably goes back to efforts in the interwar period to refurbish the credentials of the Conservative Party: Burke was available due to the decline of the Liberals, his former patrons, and was a suitable standard-bearer against the rising Labour Party, which was full of "Tom Paine people;" O"Brien, *Great Melody*, p. xlvii

14 O'Brien, *Great Melody*, p. lxv, for example.

15 Alfred Cobban, *Edmund Burke and the Revolt against the Eighteenth Century* (London: George Allen and Unwin, 1929).

16 Gay understood the Enlightenment as a "pagan" movement, which clearly would exclude Burke. In the case of Shklar, I am thinking of her oral teaching, and the omission of Burke from her Enlightenment seminar at Harvard.

17 Liberalism and republicanism are not symmetrical concepts in the study of historical political theory. Unlike "republican" discourse, "liberal" is an anachronistic term as applied to eighteenth-century thought, and classical "liberalism" therefore a construct that we impose on a cluster of assumptions and arguments made by various thinkers in the period. I believe that this procedure is legitimate and can be illuminating, though one must be conscious of the nature of one's interpretative methods. To be a follower of Locke (or not) was of course a contemporary possibility, and to be so was to embrace some "liberal" positions. On the other hand, the fact that both Burke and, say, Richard Price were both Lockeans in different ways and in different degrees suggests the complexities involved in the transmission of different discourses.

18 I believe this to be true in a substantive, philosophical sense. I should add that this relationship is of special interest to me personally, since I posited such a connection in my *Order and Artifice in Hume's Political Philosophy* (Princeton: Princeton University Press, 1986), without any (conscious) indebtedness to Wilkins at the time.

19 David Hume, *Enquiries*, ed. L. A. Selby-Bigge, 3rd ed. (Oxford: Clarendon Press, 1975), p. 44.

20 "By chance," because Hume's political outlook lacked the religious dimension essential to normal Toryism. Burke's agreement with Johnson here prevented his ever aligning himself openly with Hume's thought, and certainly the issue of religion remains a crucial difference between Hume and Burke.

21 Hume himself claimed to be a "sceptical Whig;" the old charge of his "Toryism," as put forward by figures such as Thomas Jefferson or John Stuart Mill, arose largely from Hume's effort to provide a non-ideological, balanced account of the earlier Stuart kings in his *History*. If one were to stipulate a model of classical liberalism, Hume would probably be found to conform to it more closely than Burke, although many of its elements could be found in Burke as well.

22 George H. Sabine, *A History of Political Theory*, revised ed., (New York, Henry Holt, 1959), p. 598. The chapter on Hume and Burke remained unchanged from the first edition in 1937 to subsequent editions. In his preface, Sabine announces his own philosophical preferences as being "in general agreement with the results of Hume's criticism of natural law," p. xii.

23 Sabine, *History*, p. 607. Sabine at times equates natural law with natural rights, about which it is easy to show that Burke had certain reservations.

24 Burke's "art is man's nature" (*Problem*, p. 105) is very Humean.

25 Duncan Forbes, *Hume's Philosophical Politics* (Cambridge: Cambridge University Press, 1975), chap. 2. Wilkins says that natural law doctrine was usually tied to a "teleological perspective" that was in decline (*Problem*, pp. 47-48). In this light, the Humean version is nonstandard and perhaps should be seen as Hume's reworking of the formal categories of natural jurisprudence on a different philosophical basis.

26 In Hume's account, the rules of justice and other artificial virtues are empirically grounded, and so his argument proceeds from *is* to *ought*. Wilkins argues that there is a close relation between fact and value in Thomist natural law as well, in addition to its grounding in the divine will and in reason (*Problem*, p. 47). Hume and Thomists (including Burke) negotiate the transition from is to ought somewhat differently, but both provide the additional premises and arguments that are required to satisfy Hume's own stricture against the naturalistic fallacy.

27 Conor Cruise O'Brien, Introduction to Edmund Burke, *Reflections on the Revolution in France* (Harmondsworth: Penguin, 1969), p. 70.

28 O'Brien appears to speak here as a man of the left chastising his fellow leftists for their habit of ignoring and underestimating their opponents: "In fact, the left should devote to the *Reflections* not less thought than the right has long given to *The Communist Manifesto*" (Introduction, p. 70). Although O'Brien's Burke was a refreshing alternative to the "cold war Burke," it was perhaps unfortunate that he couched the alternatives in such ideological terms.

29 O'Brien, *Great Melody*, Introduction. One would have thought that such an attack on Namier was scarcely needed today, though perhaps his influence lingers on in Great Britain, where the natural law view of Burke correspondingly never seems to have taken hold. O'Brien's ideological positioning seems to have shifted somewhat in the later work: Burke's view of the French Revolution is praised (contra ongoing Paineite leftism) as "the first great act of intellectual resistance to the first great experiment in totalitarian innovation;" Marxist revolutionaries are then denounced as "clones" of the Jacobins and compared to Hitler in their employment of mass terror to realize a grand social design; *Great Melody*, pp. 596-602.

30 The only allusion to "natural law" tht I find treats it dismissively, as in the earlier text, as a cold war ideology; *Great Melody*, p. lxv. This stance jars – at least from an American perspective – with O'Brien's sympathetic view of Burke as a Catholic in a broad sense and as spiritually close to Roman Catholicism.

31 Frank O'Gorman, *Edmund Burke: His Political Philosophy* (Bloomington: Indiana University Press, 1973); James Conniff, *The Useful Cobbler: Edmund Burke and the Politics of Progress* (Albany: State University of New York Press, 1994).

32 Harvey C. Mansfield, Jr., *Statesmanship and Party Government: A Study of Burke and Bolingbroke* (Chicago: University of Chicago Press, 1965), p. 210. Mansfield may or may not be as glad to accept O'Brien as an ally as O'Brien is to have him, but in any case O'Brien's remarks suggest that he has not grasped all the nuances of Mansfield's work, which in its own distinctive way builds on that of Strauss.

33 Mansfield, *Statesmanship and Party Government*, pp. 208, 212, 230-35. This position also appears to reject Strauss's suggestion that Burke was a Thomist, since, according to Mansfield, one cannot believe in Christian (including Thomist) natural law if one does not believe in the Chrstian revelation. Nevertheless, Mansfield's association of modern natural law with both Hobbes and Locke is Straussian, and his doubts about Burke's religion parallel those that both he and Strauss express about Locke's.

34 Mansfield, *Selected Letters*, pp. 4, 18-19.

35 Frederick A. Dreyer, *Burke's Politics: A Study in Whig Orthodoxy* (Waterloo: Wilfrid Laurier University Press, 1979). As has been mentioned, Wilkins denied the significance of the alleged break between Thomism and Locke. As has also been noted, Mansfield argued that Burke's version of natural law was in a modern Hobbes-Locke tradition, which for Mansfield, though not for Dreyer, implies it is non-Christian.

36 Michael Freeman, *Edmund Burke and the Critique of Political Radicalism* (Chicago: University of Chicago Press, 1980), esp. chap. 2, 3.

37 Joseph L. Pappin III, *The Metaphysics of Edmund Burke* (New York: Fordham University Press, 1993)

38 Frederick G. Whelan, *Edmund Burke and India: Political Morality and Empire* (Pittsburgh: University of Pittsburgh Press, 1996).

39 MacIntyre says enough just to indicate the direction his argument about Burke might take; he makes his hostility perfectly clear, saying that Burke was an "agent of positive harm." MacIntyre seems to assume that Burke has been decisively captured by modern reactionaries, who give tradition a bad name, and does not choose to contest this capture; or, as with Hume, he may simply have an aversion to Burke as one who abandoned his native tradition to become the spokesman for another. Alasdair MacIntyre, *Whose Justice? Which Rationality?* (Notre Dame: University of Notre Dame Press, 1988), pp. 229, 353, 217. The equation of Burke with reaction is also suggested in MacIntyre's *After Virtue*, 2nd ed. (Notre Dame: University of Notre Dame Press, 1984), p. 222: "Traditions, when vital, embody continuities of conflict. Indeed when a tradition becomes Burkean, it is always dying or dead." Perhaps MacIntyre thinks that participants in a vital tradition would not be self-consciously traditionalistic. But Burke looks forward as well as back; the efforts he expended on behalf of India make no sense otherwise.

Kai Nielsen

The Crisis of Socialism and Analytical Marxism

> One of the errors of the postmortems of communism has been the identification of central planning with command/administrative allocation systems. These terms are not co-extensive; it is only the latter that have been shown not to function.
>
> John Roemer

1

Socialism and communism, to understate it, are, and have been for some time, in a crisis. Indeed, not a few would say both socialism and communism have not merely broken down, they have collapsed. After years of bitter struggle, the claim goes, capitalism has won. Reversing Marx's predictions, and Kruschev's proclamations, the capitalist world order has prevailed over the rising socialist world order. We have gone not from capitalism to socialism but in some considerable parts of the world from socialism to capitalism. Of course, it could still be maintained that we remain in the midst of a long struggle between the two social orders and two classes and that while for now the capitalists have won some crucial battles the class war is not over yet. The consolidation of capitalism was slow with many setbacks, why should it be different for socialism? Perhaps this is so, but it looks at least as if really existing socialisms have either collapsed or are collapsing on all fronts and that the fundamental claims of Marxism, and indeed even of socialism more generally, have been shown by our historical experience to be, to understate it, very problematic indeed.

As a Marxian (albeit an analytical one) and a socialist, to speak personally for a moment, this at least ideological collapse of socialism is dismaying. As a moderately observant person of world affairs from the Bolshevik Revolution to our time and as a reader of Leon Trotsky, I had no illusions about the Russian thermidor or the other 'Marxist' social orders that emerged in its wake. They were clearly, though in varying degrees, authoritarian elitist states with poorly functioning economies. They were hardly bastions of freedom and equality or of democracy. One could be without illusions about the radical inadequacies of capitalist democracies and still appreciate the rottenness of those Soviet and Chinese regimes and have a sense of the betrayal of socialism that they represented or, in some instances, still continue to represent.

All of that to the contrary notwithstanding, the depth and thoroughness of the rejection of socialism when the citizenry of some of these societies had the chance came as a shock and frankly dismayed me. That they should reject their *ersatz* socialist statist authoritarian regimes was one thing; that they should so thoroughly reject socialist ideas, including democratic socialism, was another. Trying to make sense of this, let us begin at the beginning and try, indirectly at first, to gain a purchase on this by saying something about what socialism is.

At rather a minimum—though even here not a bedrock minimum—for a social order to be a socialist one there (a) must be a public ownership and control of at least the major means of production and (b) it must not be a society with an extensive labor market where most citizens sell their labor power as a commodity and own or control little, if any, of the of the means of production and where others purchase their labor power and, directly or indirectly, control what is to be done with it and determine how its products are to be distributed. To have such commitments, to be for public ownership and to be against treating labor as a commodity, or at least purely as a commodity, is—or so at least it seems—at a minimum what it is to be a socialist. But it is these very things that citizens in the actually existing socialisms, or the once existing socialisms, particularly where there is any democratic choice in the matter, seem in mass to be repudiating or to have already repudiated and that after years of actually existing socialism with its distinctive socialization. I expected, and indeed welcomed, a reaction against the authoritarian political model and against command theory economics, but I did not expect with democratization such a thorough root and branch rejection of Marxian theory and practice. Particularly, given Marxian conceptions of the intimate connection of theory and practice, it behooves Marxians and socialists such as myself to think through again their socialism in a very thorough manner. Beyond what old socialists should do, why should—or indeed should—anyone else be interested in socialism and Marxian theory? I shall in the course of this essay give some reasons why they should but I should not be at all surprised if what I say falls on deaf ears. But I shall persist, for while the Soviet block social systems have been shown to be thoroughly unjust and repressive, as well as inefficient, it is also the case that the paradigmatically capitalist states (the United States, the United Kingdom, Canada, Germany, France, South Korea, Japan, and the South American states) have also been shown to be hardly models of just and democratic social orders where life, for most people, is flourishing, and freedom and equality prevail. To speak of social equality in the United States, for example, is a bad joke. And to speak, as President Clinton did in addressing the South African parliament, of the United States having "a government of the people by the people and for the people" is another. The social perceptions of the inhumanity of our societies, widely felt and voiced in the sixties, have been lost, or at least extensively submerged, in Yuppiedom and a complacent liberal conservatism or sometimes just conservatism. But, though as we saw in Seattle, London, and Washington, some pointed resistance is returning, there remains the challenge (though it is not clear that many are listening) that these social orders—the capitalist social orders of the rich capitalist democracies—must be deeply altered if we are to achieve anything like a just and flourishing social order. Socialism, or at least a radical social democracy, may still have an important voice here. There remains, when we look at the matter with tolerable care, the very deep question about how (if at all) a social order can, under conditions of social wealth, such as the world is now capable of producing, be both capitalist and just. Convinced—and rightly so—of the historic failures of what were "actually existing socialisms", people in our societies have turned their eyes away from such questions. I shall make a modest attempt to induce people to look again and to take socialism seriously.

2

There is, to my mind, a kind of irony, from a theoretician's point of view, about this at least apparent collapse of socialism. The collapse is occurring just at the time when a powerful form of Marxian theory has emerged, principally in the English-speaking and Scandinavian worlds and, on the economic theory side, in Japan, through the combined efforts of social scientists with various disciplinary backgrounds and philosophers. By contrast with classical Marxism and even more so with Continental forms, say Marxisms under the influence of Lukács, existentialism, Althusser or the Frankfurt school, it is a form of Marxian theory that is clearly articulated, vigorously argued, philosophically sophisticated, historically conscious, undogmatic, at the cutting edge of current developments in the social sciences, and yet politically relevant and engaged. It has, by some of its practitioners, dubbed itself "analytical Marxism." More crudely (if tendentiously) put by some 'No bullshit Marxism', it is important to recognize it is a diverse movement unified only by (a) the belief that Marxian ideas remain important to present day social theory, social critique and political practice and to (b) a commitment to clarity, rigor of argument and to using the best philosophical and social science tools available. There is, however, a not inconsiderable difference concerning what they are. There is a considerable theoretical difference, both in methodology and substantive claims, between, for example, John Roemer and Richard Miller (both major players here).[1]

What is ironical here, and in many ways depressing, is that just where the *subject* for Marxian theory seems at least to have disappeared and public interest in socialism is rapidly dwindling, a form of Marxian theory has emerged which made true what both Western Marxism and Soviet Marxism had both claimed, but in fact had also long put in disrepute, namely a scientific socialism.[2] With analytical Marxism, at least with some of its practioners, a non-scientistic form of scientific socialism has emerged capable of competing with the best extant social theories and capable of guiding socialist practice and providing a basis for critiquing capitalism.[3] Again it seems that the Owl of Minerva flies only at dusk. This is deeply disturbing to me as a socialist. Yet socialists would be sticking their heads in the sand if they did not face it.

3

I want in the next three sections to consider some of the reasons why socialism is thought to have collapsed or at least to have so sufficiently broken down so as to be in crisis. I will then, in the remaining sections (VI-X) discuss whether there are theoretical resources of a reasonably plausible sort which will enable Marxians and socialists more generally to respond and to rebuild the ship at sea. The ship to be rebuilt at sea is not, of course, just Marxian theory but renewed socialist practices and the achievement of a socialist society that could, and rightly so, win the allegiance of the mass of the population.

Michael Buraway succinctly summarizes the standard set of liberal and conservative grounds for saying—they would have it definitively—that Communism has collapsed and Marxism is dead.

> Marxism is dead.... It has shown itself to be morally, politically, and economically bankrupt: it justified the gulag, the Soviet-Nazi pact; it provided the foundation of totalitarianism, the decimation of the peasantry, the denial of civil rights to its working class and oppressed nations, as well as armed invasions of its colonies in Eastern Europe; through its advocacy of planning it promoted proverbial inefficiency, waste, shortages and low standards of living. The bankruptcy of Marxism as ideology spells its death as science. The prediction of a socialist future is its most fundamental flaw. The failure of communism proves that there can be no future after capitalism. Communism is only a nightmarish detour: the longest road from capitalism to capitalism. The scourge of Marxism has finally been laid to rest.[4]

In the same issue in which Michael Buraway's essay appears, the editors of the *Socialist Review* (an American socialist journal) remark of American socialists—and I think the remark could be reasonably extended to other Western socialists as well—that the collapse of communism has left them "feeling unmoored, ill at ease, and at times uncertain of their own convictions."[5] And this comes from socialists, and typically Marxists or Marxians, who have long been opponents of Stalinism and very frequently even of Leninist models for society and surely of the Marxism-Leninism of Soviet block and Chinese societies. This sense of uncertainty and defeat is pervasive, and deeply felt, with socialists who have consistently and for a long time "denounced the state socialist countries for their perversion of socialist ideals."[6] Some might find it strange and indeed somewhat irrational that such an unmooring, such a sense of loss, such a pessimism about a socialist future, should obtain among such socialists. Rather, it might be said, there should be a sense of new beginnings with new opportunities to be taken advantage of. Thermidor—the old Soviet Leviathan—has finally come apart. Moreover, and importantly, it has come apart—or so it could be argued—from struggle from within. It is not something, at least in any obvious way, that has been imposed by the capitalist order. And it should also be noted that this collapse of communism cannot help but have reverberations in the capitalist world. Among other things, capitalist nation-states will have to find new societies to hate and to blame for the ills in their own societies. They will have to find, with the end of the Cold War, new excuses for the plain injustices of their societies. That is particularly true for the rich capitalist societies. Why shouldn't these changes—principally the end of the old Soviet block—be unambivalently welcomed by socialists and taken as a source of hope?

I think that all of that notwithstanding, the unmooring and pessimism of Western socialists is most centrally rooted in the fact that, before the collapse, there was a hope and indeed an expectation—now seen to have been utterly unrealistic—that these Soviet societies, given a chance to in a democratic way decide their own future, would not turn their backs on the whole of the socialist past—the whole socialist project—and that there would be something left in their consciousness of a genuinely Marxist tradition and that there would continue to be something of a socialist consciousness in those societies,, and that there would remain blocks of industrialized nations that would provide us with alternatives to capitalism. There was, of course, on the part of such Western Marxists, an awareness that many in the East had illusions about the West. But there was not the expectation that there would be such an extensive taking on in such an uncritical and holus-bolus way of the conceptions and ideals of *laissez faire* capitalism with Ludwig von Mises and F. H. Hayek becoming the new heroes rather than Rosa Luxemburg and Karl Korsch or even, at a minimum, Swedish style social democracy. But this uncritical acceptance of *laissez faire* capitalist models is what seems at least to have happened.

However sound the arguments of such dissident Eastern European Marxists as Ferenc Fehér and Agnes Heller that the Soviet societies were neither socialist nor capitalist societies but had developed a distinctive mode of production of their own, it is still a well entrenched and, I suspect, a propagandistically fixed fact of ideological perception in the West that these are or were the socialist societies.[7] In *popular consciousness* this is what socialism means. More politically sophisticated people in Western societies realized that there were models, perhaps even plausible models, of genuinely democratic socialist societies, but they also recognized they were only models. They were not exemplified anywhere. Actually existing socialism, statist though it was, was these Soviet and Chinese societies and their satellites and the like and they have collapsed or are on their way to collapsing. And in collapsing they are moving back to capitalism again and sometimes to its cruder forms at that, with at least the possibility—and in Russia the reality—of all the inhumanities and injustices of which Western socialists are keenly conscious. The fate of these societies seems to be to go from one system of horrible injustice to another.

This is happening in the East while there is nothing even remotely like a mass movement to socialism in the industrial developed societies of the West. Moreover, if the socialists in question take Marx and Engels seriously and in particular historical materialism seriously, they will have little confidence in Third World strategies. Socialists had hoped that if not the term "socialism" at least the concept of socialism would have had a social embedding in such formerly Soviet societies. It would be something in some respects, though not all, like the socialism that existed in the USSR before the Stalinist deformation, though with less vanguardism and more stress on "All power to the soviets" than obtained there. It was hoped that such conceptions would have retained some foothold in those societies and that, with democratization and power returning to the workers, something could have been built on that that was not the old capitalist jungle all over again. But that appears at least to be a pipe dream. The removal (particularly when it came from within) of the totalitarian hierarchy was plainly a very good thing. But the undermining of democratic socialism is another thing again. We must not confuse Rosa Luxemburg with Josef Stalin. But something like that seems at least to be happening. The debacle of bureaucratic communism has generated the loss of socialist aspiration in such societies. "Socialism" there has become a dirty word. This, taken along with the non-existence of significant socialist movements in the West, makes the situation very bleak for Western socialists. Our pessimism and unmooring is understandable. But it does not follow from that that we should acquiesce in becoming unmoored. As Michel Foucault well realized, that is a living death. We should not forget Antonio Gramsci's slogan concerning the pessimism of the intellect and the optimism of the will. And if this is moralism then so be it.

4

I shall turn now from such a lament to a statement of the principal at least putative grounds for failure, grounds that go more into socialist theory than into socialist practice. Socialism could, and indeed would, fail here if these grounds are good grounds, even if the socialist regimes were not tyrannical or corrupt. With those defects—or alleged defects—before us I shall turn to considering possibilities for the righting within the framework of socialism of these defects. Some of these corrective proposals emanate from some conceptions of analytical Marxism. They all, I hope, reflect its respect for being non-partisan, for clarity of articulation and for reliance on evidence and argument.

I shall focus on five principal defects (or at least putative defects) that have been taken to be pervasive in Soviet and similar societies and have been thought with at least some plausibility to be attached both to Marxist and Marxian theory and socialist practice itself, particularly, but not exclusively, to its Leninist developments. Two are economic and two political-ethical defects and one is a bit of both.

First the economic ones:

1. Marxists not unreasonably wished to overcome the anarchy of capitalist production in market societies and to have a rationally planned economy where the underlying point of production would be both to maximally and equitably meet the needs of everyone alike. But experience has shown, the claim goes, that such economic rationalism will not work. A planned economy without markets, planned no matter how carefully and intelligently, will not work for complex societies except perhaps temporarily where those societies are in a wartime situation. To maximally achieve the meeting of people's needs we need a market economy. Directly to try to produce to meet needs circumventing market mechanisms will not work.

2. We cannot move to a full employment society where everyone works and securely has a job, where the ideal, as the springs of social wealth flow more fully, is for us to distribute "From each according to her ability and to each according to her needs." We need incentives and a certain amount of insecurity, the claim goes, for people to work at all efficiently and effectively. With guaranteed secure jobs, only a few will work effectively. We need, to achieve this, a labor market where labor power is bought and sold as a commodity and where people can lose their jobs if their work does not prove beneficial, i.e. cost effective.

Now for the mixed economic/normative one:

3. A necessary condition for a society being socialist is that there be public ownership of at least the major means of production. In Soviet societies and the like this came to a state ownership and control of the means of production. But this, as far as public ownership goes, is little more than a legal fiction. The effective control of the means of production was not in the hands of the workers but in the hands of a very circumscribed group and the major benefits of the use of the means of production go to an even smaller elite, who were very privileged and very powerful, while in the society at large people lived spartanly and had very little control over their own lives. They neither had autonomy nor an adequate meeting of their material needs. Non-statist socialists want industrial democracy and a form of public ownership and control that is distinct from such a Soviet style state ownership and control. But we have, the claim goes, no feasible non-utopian conception of that. Moreover, where public ownership comes simply to worker owned and controlled firms, we would have many of the difficulties of *laissez faire* capitalism.

Now for the political-ethical defects:

4. Soviet practice used fundamental normative conceptions such as democracy, freedom, equality, social justice, rights, and legality opportunistically, moralistically and manipulatively, while Marxian theory conceptualizes them as ideological constructions distortive of social reality, conceptions that in effect do not liberate people but shore up the *status quo*. These moral conceptions, these ideological slogans, Marxian theory has it, are impediments to socialism rather than fundamental conceptions essential to both socialist theory and practice. But, against Marxist orthodoxy here, it needs to be recognized that these normative notions have a real life in society. They are essential to the attaining and sustaining of what the young Marx called a truly human society. They are, that is, essential to a socialism with a human face as they are to any society that can rightly claim to be a good society. By treating such normative notions as ideological twaddle, Marxian theory, when it does so, impoverishes itself. Such thinking is and has been disastrous for socialist practice as, to take the other side of the coin, has Soviet-style moralistic socialistic preaching and exhortation. Moreover, Marxist theory and Soviet practice clearly clash here.

5. Marxian theory and socialist practice have offered us no adequate theories of or models of or practices of democracy. While often making trenchant criticisms of capitalist democracy, showing that in practice it is not infrequently farcical, socialist theory affords us no adequate alternative to the liberal democratic theory of the social democracies.[8] Even Leninist and Trotskyian conceptions of a vanguard party playing a legally protected leading and decisive role in social life lead to elite paternalistic control undermining both freedom and equality and certainly not leading to workers' self-emancipation or any other kind of emancipation. Moreover, it is not a conception which is compatible with a genuinely democratic society. But from democratic socialists we have no conception of democracy which is clearly socialist and which takes us beyond social democratic, liberal pluralism.[9]

5

Let us start by examining the first noted economic defect of traditional Soviet societies, namely their economic rationalism where the economy is a central and bureaucratically planned economy, thoroughly planned from commanding heights and *without competitive markets*. The

Soviet economic system was such a system of state ownership and central planning with a bureaucratic administrative management of the economy ostensibly to satisfy the needs of its citizens. An attempt at such a direct meeting of needs was at least ostensibly an instrument of state policy. It, whatever the intentions of its architects, has resulted in incre- dible and at least seemingly ineradicable inefficiencies, shortages of many goods and services, oversupply of others, shoddy quality of goods and services, intractable coordination problems where resources or parts needed for production do not arrive or do not arrive where and when they are needed, and the like. The Soviet economy was a permanently ailing economy.[10]

In this economy bureaucracies compete with each other fiercely for scarce resources. This leads to bureaucratic bargaining in which a paternalistic state allocates resources and distributes resources according to political criteria. Inefficient enterprises are rarely closed down, though, if things go very badly, their managers may be removed. Such Soviet-type economic systems lack the economic discipline of the threat of bankruptcy. Their firms in gaining credits and the like from the state have only soft-budget constraints not the hard-budget constraints required for them to run efficiently. Managers of the state enterprises in order to protect and advance their "interests...seek to garner more resources, particularly investment resources, from the state. Their demands become insatiable, equaled only by the intense bureaucratic rivalry for those resources."[11] Inevitably this leads to shortages, which in turn leads to hoarding, which, of course, makes the shortages even worse. Shortages and the unreliable quality of inputs are very disruptive of and sometimes even crippling to complex production processes. Such things in Soviet societies—all the good intentions of Oscar Lange to the contrary notwithstanding—have resulted in a very badly functioning economy.

This has led, along with a radical shifting in the political climate, to an abandonment in the former Soviet block societies and in China and Vietnam of such a planned command economy. Indeed in many of these societies, they are rapidly, sometimes chaotically, turning themselves into capitalist social orders. One of the more influential models for change in the fading days of the Soviet Union was the Shatalin Program, named after the very influential and powerfully placed Soviet economist Stanislav Shatalin.[12] It aimed at replacing state ownership, central planning and administrative management with private property, market forces and entrepreneurship. But this, of course, whatever it is called, just comes to replacing socialism with capitalism. Shatalin aimed to privatize, within a year of putting his program into place, 70% of Soviet industry, an even greater proportion of agriculture, virtually all commerce, and the entire service sector of the Soviet economy.[13] Economic rationality, capitalist style, was to be introduced using the market forces of supply and demand to bring growth. With this prices will be deregulated and state subsidies eliminated in order to bring in what he anticipated to be a dynamic economy that would flow with supply and demand.

Shatalin, deeply influenced by Frederich Hayek, argued that this economic transformation would also require a political transformation and reorientation in social philosophy. It would require, he tells us, a social philosophy which puts the individual center-stage ahead of the collectivity. "Any attempt to put 'us' ahead of 'myself'," Shatalin contends, "is flawed, essentially and fatally flawed."[14] We can only form a *gemeinschaft*, a community that is ethically adequate, on an individualism which stresses the sovereignty of the individual person where the "we" of community does not develop at the expense of "I": where the "I", as he puts it, must come first. This runs firmly against the collectivism of Lenin as well as against earlier pre-communist forms of collectivism in Russia. But, like Hayek and Nozick, Shatalin thinks that the Soviet economy and with it the Soviet society could only be healthy and prosperous when its ideology of egalitarianism and collectivism is set aside and such an individualism is embraced instead. Asked if this means abandoning socialism, Shatalin responds, "It is perhaps a pity, but we never had socialism."[15] He goes on to say, even more significantly, that he doubts that anyone can ever have socialism. Asked if that means he is actually a capitalist roader, he responds, somewhat evasively, "So what? Who wouldn't prefer the quality of life enjoyed in America or Sweden or Italy or France to that led in the Soviet Union?"[16]

Faced with the criticism that taking such a capitalist road would create millionaires and even billionaires and thus exploitation, sharp inequalities and long lines of unemployment, Shatalin responds that that, unfortunately, is the price one has to pay for a prosperous society. Millionaires and perhaps even billionaires are essential, he believes, for developing the productive forces. Without such entrepreneurs there will only be an equality of poverty. This would lead to a barracks communism that no one should want. (We should add, parenthetically, that in what was the Soviet Union there is that poverty but it was not, with its privileged and powerful elites, an *equality* of poverty.) Shatalin is interested not in such abstract and perhaps ideological matters as equality, but in seeing, as he puts it, the Soviet people live better. If that, he has it, requires great inequalities of wealth, so be it.[17] These Hayekian views come from an economist who was not, as I remarked, on the fringe of Soviet society. He was a member of the presidential council which was the Soviet Union's highest policy-making body, the head of the economics section of the Soviet Academy of Sciences, and a member of the Community Party's Central Committee.[18]

6

In response to this and more generally in response to the widely perceived ills of a Soviet-style planned economy *sans* markets or even, though less generally, to models of a democratic socialist planned command economy without markets, such as that advocated by Ernest Mandel, the response from a considerable number of socialists, including some Marxian socialists, East and West, has been to argue for some form of a market socialism.[19] This can mean and has meant several different things. In speaking of market socialism I shall, somewhat prescriptively, define it and then distinguish four importantly different varieties. But in offering such a prescriptive and even *persuasive* definition, I do not mean to be covering everything that could reasonably be meant by "market socialism." Moreover, within my types there are further subdivisions I shall not note.

A market socialism is, in my conceptualizing of it, a *socialism*. That means that there is a public ownership of at least the major means of production and this comes to, on my reading of it, a workers' ownership of at least the major means of production in a society where a very able-bodied person is, was or will be a worker. It also will be a society in which there will be no labor markets or at least the labor markets will be very circumscribed.[20] It will, of course, have markets in the sense that there will be free competition for the supply of many goods and services. There will, as Alec Nove puts it, be competition in the plain sense "that there are several suppliers of any particular good or service, that customers can choose, with knowledge among alternative sources of supply and that the bargaining process includes prices, quality, delivery dates, after-sales services, and other relevant dimensions."[21]

A market socialism, in line with the characterization I gave of socialism, will in some considerable measure be at least a system of labor cooperatives. This may or may not, depending on how far the *market* extends, cover all economic activities and, depending on how far the *public ownership* extends and how it works, it may include all market economic activities. On the one hand, there may remain some centrally planned economic organizations not subject to market constraints in a market socialist society and there may, as well, in a market socialist society, be some (probably very small) privately owned and controlled market enterprises. But for it to be a market *socialism* a "large part of the economy" will be *both* publicly owned and "subject to the control and criteria of the market."[22] As we shall see, it is vital which parts are and are not in the market system. Finally, in its pure form, as a system of labor cooperatives, the enterprises will, whether or not they are owned by their workers, be controlled by their workers subject only to the further constraint that in the interests of the society of workers at large their control of the workplace will be limited in certain respects by the decisions of an industrial parliament and a political parliament, elected by the citizens at large and subject to democratic control, operating in the usual way by majority decisions and where the delegates or representatives are all elected, and are subject to recall and dismissal by a majority vote of the citizens.

In this very fundamental way, a market socialism is a democratic socialism. But what is distinctive about it, from a socialist point of view, is that it is a system of worker cooperatives *and* that it relies on market mechanisms. The above makes it distinctive for, as we have seen in speaking of the Mandel models, we could have with them, unlike the traditional Soviet system, a *democratic* socialism which was still a centrally planned economy *without markets*. In that form of democratic socialism there would, as in the Soviet system, be central planning and soft budget constraints for firms, but there would as well be worker control of enterprise decision-making. Further, unlike Soviet-style bureaucratic centralized planning, the officials of the central planning and ministry level planning bodies would be elected and be recallable by the workers. The workers assemble and vote and if they want them out, they are out. This model, unlike the Soviet model, is, as a model of a genuinely *democratic socialism*, a socialism that is as genuinely democratic as market socialism usually is, but it does opt, at least in its pure form, for an economy that is as centrally planned and as much a publically owned economy without markets as it used to be in the Soviet Union. The crucial question, in assessing Mandel's model, is not to challenge its democratic character but to ask whether (a) it would be any more efficient, or even significantly more efficient, than Soviet-style bureaucratic central planning and (b) be more efficient than or as efficient as market socialism.

Even within the above general characterization of market socialism there are several varieties, some more plausible than others. While all of these forms have markets, they differ about the form and sometimes the extent of public ownership and about the nature of the control of the means of production.

1. State ownership with cooperative control of *all* enterprises, where that control for each enterprise is located in the *particular enterprise* in which the worker works, but where market mechanisms are in place for the allocation of goods and services.

2. Cooperative ownership of *all* enterprises by the workers and control by them of *all* enterprises, where both that ownership and that control for each enterprise is located in the particular enterprise in which the worker works, but where market mechanisms are in place for the allocation of goods and services.

3. State ownership of certain enterprises with worker control of those enterprises and some private ownership and control of some enterprises and some private ownership and control of some enterprises.

All four varieties of what could be market socialism overcome the ills of a completely centrally planned command economy without competitive markets and without democratic control. All allow market mechanisms, though the first two, as thorough socialisms, do not allow a labor market. The last two are mixed economies, partly socialist and partly capitalist, and they allow in some areas for a labor market. Depending on how many and which kind of enterprises are privately owned and controlled, a society, with such a mixed economy, would be properly called socialist or capitalist. Where the major and strategic enterprises are owned by the state or by workers and, further, where it is the case that *most* work is under the control of workers, though the society still has small enterprises, e.g. family restaurants, farms, boutiques and the like in private hands, the society would plainly be a socialist one, though if it has market allocations for some goods and services, it is a market socialism.

It is these last two forms that I shall discuss. Let us preeminently assume 3, where there is state ownership of most of the enterprises—most means of production—including the strategic ones, with worker control of these enterprises but with some sectors remaining in private hands. *Some* sectors, including both worker controlled ones and privately owned ones, compete with each other and are subject to collapse, if they do not remain competitive and profitable. Others are not so competitive, are not subject to competitive defeat and are centrally planned, though, on these models, the central planners are democratically elected and controlled as in Ernest Mandel's model of democratic central planning. But these no-market sectors aside, such a form of market socialism would overcome the ills of Soviet-style economies without introducing the ills of a capitalist economy. *Perhaps* this would be true of Mandel's model as well if it were put in practice. My point above was to underscore its difference from market socialism, while stressing that it is a democratic model of a centrally planned economy. (It should be noted that a market socialism need not be democratic. The Soviet state could have introduced market mechanisms while remaining non-democratic and keeping central planning.)

However, while I will primarily have 3 in mind, the differences between 3 and 4 can be safely overlooked in the discussion that immediately follows. With either model, if it was to be exemplified by a society, and I think both could be, we would have something which is, its limited private ownership to the contrary notwithstanding, recognizably socialist and free of both the inefficiencies and authoritarianism of the Soviet model. In this discussion I am deeply indebted to Alec Nove's *The Economics of Feasible Socialism* as well as to some of his essays and exchanges (including his exchange with Mandel). The model he proposes for a market socialism is something like my 3 but more complex and more nuanced and, for really laying out a blueprint, more adequate than my own models. I avoid Nosve's complications for purely simplifying and pedagogical purposes for I believe my conceptualizations, though inadequate in certain ways, show in a reasonably straightforward and easily graspable manner how we could have socialism without inefficiency or tyranny.

In both 3 and 4 some private property and entrepreneurship are countenanced, but, following Nove, we keep firmly the *socialist* character of our economy and society by not allowing the scope of private property to be such that it generates a capitalist class with a class of people (namely capitalists) that hire labor and can live off their capital without work. Private property ownership is small scale. A person or family that runs a restaurant may hire a cook or waiters, a family farm may hire a few farm laborers, an owner of a boutique may hire sales personnel or a tailor, a writer may hire a typist, an artist a model, and so on. No capitalist class emerges from such hirings for the people hiring labor themselves remain workers in the enterprise or in the activities in which they are engaged such as being a carpenter who hires a helper. They both are workers. The scale of the operation where there is a private sector is strictly and distinctly limited in a way that prevents capitalist class formation or the sustaining of it where it is a holdover from the old capitalist order. If a restaurant or boutique or book store or grocery store gets too large (i.e., large enough to generate capitalist class formation), it will have to become either a state enterprise or (more likely) a workers' cooperative with the former owner properly compensated for having to sell. She will, as well, have the option of remaining a worker in the newly socialized enterprise and/or a partial owner if it is a workers' cooperative where the workers own shares in their own enterprise. What is morally troublesome about hiring labor is not a farmer hiring someone to help him bring in his crops or a pianist a page turner or a restaurant owner, who works in his own restaurant, hiring a chef, but the great disparities in wealth, whole life prospects, power, and control that go with one person or a few persons hiring large number of people and with that gaining a vast wealth that will give them power and control over others so that there emerges a class of owners who *need* not be workers themselves—who need not themselves, even in a managerial role, work—but who hire workers and control workers in central aspects of their lives and live off their labor. (However, we should remember that things are a matter of degree here. Haledór Laxness shows vividly in his *Independent People* how small landowning farmers in nineteenth century Iceland exploited and lorded it over their hired laborers.)

There can, of course, be no algorithm for how big is too big to be legitimately private. However, the only enterprises that could plausibly be up for being private enterprises in a market socialist society would be small scale operations. But how large a restaurant or clothing store could be before it would be up for socialization would have to be decided pragmatically and should be democratically determined by legislation. The crucial thing to guard against is extensive disparities of wealth and influence that would allow for domination by one class of another class and with that, for contemporary industrial societies, the reemergence or continued existence of a capitalist class ruling over labor and living off the labor of others, i.e. the situation we have now in capitalist societies.

The advantage of such petty entrepreneurship and private property owning is that it makes readily available the production of goods and services that state enterprises or labor cooperatives would have little incentive to produce or supply. Suppose some few people in Calgary or Regina would like the *New York Times* delivered on Sunday to their doorstep before breakfast. If they can find someone willing and able to perform that service at a price they can agree on, what is wrong with it? There is nothing wrong with such capitalist acts—if that is what they should be called—between consenting adults. What is bad is when, à la

Nozick, Hayek or Friedman, there are no political or ethical constraints on the market and where it would be the case that the market would not generate an equilibrium and vast disparities in power and control would emerge thus undermining both autonomy and equality. But this is just what happens in the real world though not in the models of some economists. This is a social world in which people are deeply exploited or in other ways harmed. But small scale entrepreneurship can be and predictably often will be a benefit all around and will not sustain or generate a class society of dominators and dominated.

Nove notes that real existing capitalisms, as distinct from Friedmanite models or Thatcher dreams, are in various combinations of market and plan. *Laissez faire* capitalism does not exist anywhere nor could it stably exist. Moreover, if it could (to speak counterfactually) it would be disastrous both economically and morally. What is needed, as Nove puts it, is a flexible combination of central planning, worker self-management, and local and small and typically private initiative.[23] In capitalist societies (actually existing capitalisms) there are deep disputes about where the boundary lines should be drawn between enterprises which should be market driven and those which should not. There would be similar problems for market socialism, though I do not think they would be as extensive and intractable as in capitalist societies. Be that as it may, there is general agreement in capitalist societies, all their ideology about *laissez faire* to the contrary notwithstanding, that some things should and indeed must be centrally planned. On the other side, as socialist societies move away from the Soviet models of a command economy, there is also a growing agreement that any viable socialist economy must be a mix of market and plan. Some things just must be centrally planned, others clearly shouldn't be and there is much dispute—and sometimes reasonable dispute—about where the boundary should be drawn.[24]

In both capitalist and socialist societies, in deciding what should be centrally planned and what not, we must distinguish between sectors. We need to look at economies of scale and at the location of the necessary information about needs and alternative sources of supply. Nove's favorite example of an enterprise that should be centrally planned is electrification: the generation and distribution of electricity. Modern societies all have an interconnected electricity grid. It would be insane to decentralize that and "grant powers to the managers of every power station to generate electricity by reference to the profitability of their own power station taken in isolation."[25] Nove goes on to remark that "the element of *system* is strong.

Furthermore, demand in such a circumstance can be, indeed must be, assessed at the center. Operational and economic criteria are best judged at that level, including the efficiency criteria applicable to specific generating stations."[26] Similar things should be said for the supply of water, oil, gas, steel and coal and, arguably, public transport, the post office, the telephone and telegraphic services. But the case is clearest with the supply of electricity and water. What we have here is something which

> ... is bound to be a monopoly and since any monopoly can improve its financial results at the customers' expense, price control becomes essential, as do some qualitative criteria (e.g., the avoidance of power cuts, the requirement to supply electricity to outlying areas, etc.). Also, investment decisions, involving addition to capacity, and choice between different forms of generation (gas, oil, coal, hydro) require the sort of information that is available only at the centre. This applies with equal force to capitalist and socialist economies. Market data, market prices, are, of course, an important element in decision making but not, in this instance, a decisive one. Quantitative assessment of future demand and a view as to *future* relative costs and prices, requiring knowledge and judgment—these are decisive. There are, needless to say, no "future markets" adequate for the purpose.
>
> Many of the same considerations apply to other energy sources—for example, oil and gas, and probably coal too. Nor is it an accident that giant firms, many of them multinational, dominate steel, chemical, aerospace and computer production in most capitalist countries. In all these instances, major investment decisions are taken at levels far above the individual factory or plant. There are big economies of scale, a long gestation period and very large expenditures on research and development.[27]

Here, with such industries, whether the society is socialist or capitalist, central planning is essential. Indeed anything else would be, to put it minimally, economic irrationality. Moreover, such large scale, centrally planned industries are, popular mythology to the contrary notwithstanding, usually more innovative than their smaller counterparts. A big oil company, unlike a small one, need not put all its eggs in one basket. It can afford experimentally to take risky ventures in a few areas, knowing that if they do not pan out the enterprise is protected by other ventures which are less risky. It also, because of its extensive wealth, can afford, and indeed find it both safe and profitable, to plow more money into research.

We have seen that many smaller scale industries (the clothing business, grocery stores, bike manufacturers, tent producers, travel agencies, watchmakers, wineries and the like, whether workers' cooperatives or privately owned firms) can, and should, operate within market parameters and thus within the discipline of the market. If they operate inefficiently they can and should be allowed to go under. But this can hardly be true of large scale industries that are centrally planned whether they have competitive markets or not. They are no more allowed to go into bankruptcy in capitalist states than in socialist ones. When they get into trouble they will be bailed out as Chrysler was bailed out in the USA and British Leyland in the UK. Some are natural monopolies: water supplies and electrification being paradigms. They also have a public service aspect. They are so vital to the society that they cannot be allowed to falter. Their provision is so essential that its continuing in place does not depend on its profitability. Clean water is a good example but so is electricity, health care, education, public transport, housing, roads and the like. But at least most of these things require coordination and long range conception and that, of course, necessitates central planning. With roads, airports, railway systems, rapid transit systems and the like there are "external economies (time saving, convenience) and diseconomies (congestion, pollution) and also elements of system, of network, which render the conventional marginal cost and marginal profitability analysis both misleading and irrelevant, and the public service aspect of high importance." [28]

Given the public service aspect of such enterprises, it is not only better that they be centrally planned but that they be publicly owned and controlled where the demand for profitability is not center stage. Where in some capitalist societies the postal service, railroads, the airlines or hospitals have been privatized and deregulated, the quality and extent of services has declined and the cost has gone up to the users of such services under the imperative for the operations in question to be profitable. In any society many enterprises must make a profit if wealth is to be generated in the society. But this need not and should not be true of those essential enterprises that have an important public service aspect. They should, of course, endeavor not to be wasteful but *need* should be the crucial criterion determining how they should operate. In the wealthy industrial societies, with many wealth generating industries, this can be, and should be, afforded.

However, there are a vast number of enterprises, usually middle range to small enterprises, where competition should exist and which should be governed, with some government regulation, by competitive market criteria. Construction industries, clothing industries, fishing tackle industries, most of the service sector, agriculture and commercial fishing are paradigms. Market socialists will argue that these, except where they are very small, should be organized as producer cooperatives where they are owned or at least controlled principally, if not exclusively, by their own workforce.

This, particularly where they are owned as well as controlled by their workforce, will keep the market efficiency of capitalist society while giving more people more control over their own lives, yield more equally distributed wealth, make more work meaningful, extend democracy into the workplace and by doing that make life more democratic, prevent the great disparities of wealth and power and the radically unequal life prospects characteristic of capitalist, even welfare state capitalist, societies. Thus market socialism, at least on Nove's model, the somewhat different models of John Roemer and David Schweickart,as well as the simpler models I have proffered, has at least most of the efficiency and economic rationality of capitalist societies along with providing the enhanced autonomy, equality, social justice and democracy of democratic socialism.

The considerations discussed above apply to both 3 and 4. What reason, if any, is there to prefer one to the other? The choice here is not clear. Perhaps there should be some mixture of forms of public ownership, all of it democratically controlled, some being state ownership and some fairly specific cooperative ownership. Where we have the latter type ownership, more power goes to the workforce in the particular workplace, enhancing workplace democracy, but it could be at the expense of consumers who are after all principally workers in other enterprises. Yet worker ownership, in addition to control, gives the worker more of a stake in her enterprise leading her to stick with it and to have a greater care for the firm's economic well-being. There are tradeoffs here to be judged not only by criteria of efficiency but as well by normative criteria both of fairness and of which would contribute most to developing the democratic character of the society including in that more extensive autonomy and equality in the society. Finally, by way of normative criteria, we can ask which would make for the most extensive well-being of the most people. Here is a place for social experiment and for trial and error, but whatever way we go here we have good reasons for believing that market socialism would be at least as efficient as capitalism while being a good deal fairer.

7

I will turn now to the second difficulty I raised for socialism. I want to consider whether market socialism has an adequate way around it. Even market socialism, as I conceive of it, to remain clearly a socialism, does not want much of a labor market, if any labor market at all. Only in the small private sector would labor power be purchased as a commodity.

But this would not, as in capitalist societies, be a pervasive feature of the society. How, if that did not obtain, would people get jobs? Would they just be assigned them? That does not—to understate it—seem to show much respect for individuals and their autonomy. For many jobs at least, market socialists will reply, they would compete for them and the most talented and those most able would be given the best jobs. The procedure would be similar to the way we now assign scholarships and fellowships in the graduate schools of universities. There can be reasonably, though hardly perfectly, objective criteria for who are the most talented, generally speaking the most able and who make best use of their talents and thus, putting those criteria together (e.g. ability and effective work), are the most entitled.

This procedure seems fair enough. It is, again to understate it, no more undermining of autonomy than our present procedures and its procedures would be favored by people believing in equality. People would compete for jobs for which they applied on the basis of competitive merit: merit clearly determined in large measure by the particular job in question. The people who did best would be offered the jobs. Those doing less well would be offered less desirable jobs. The most able workers would not be required to take the best jobs or indeed any jobs and the less able people would not be required to take the less desirable jobs or any jobs, though they would not have first shot at the best jobs. No one, that is, would be required to take a job if she did not want to. There would be from the state a provision—a guaranteed basic income—providing a minimum of money, but clearly a life sustaining amount, to be given to everyone including those who do not choose to work. No one, in normal circumstances, would be forced to work but no one would starve either. (I give below a circumstance, which is not normal, and where in such an unusual circumstance a limited term conscription might very well be justified.) Once in a job there would remain chances to compete for other jobs that come open and to leave your job, if you choose, for the new job if you win in a fair competition. You can, of course, leave your job in any event. Similarly, people in whatever jobs they work in would have to be rewarded in various ways, including monetary ways, for good work and could be fired for clearly bad work after suitable warnings.

For the jobs, if any, that require so little in the way of skills that they cannot be assessed in terms of merit criteria, people could have them by applying on a first come first serve basis or by lottery or some other such fair device. Again no one would be required to take them for there remains the minimum provision payment: a guaranteed basic income available to all. If someone chooses not to work she can rely on that. If everyone took that option the system would, of course, break down. But there is little prospect of that. Most people, where the conditions are reasonable, want to work. However, if the jobs are jobs, say garbage collection, that (let us assume) no one wants and moreover are jobs which are onerous, there could be a fair but limited term conscription for all able bodied persons in a certain age range, including people who did not want to work at all. It would be similar to conscription in the army or jury service. Alternatively to such a conscription, it could be a bit of work, for a few hours each month (say), that everyone, if able-bodied, at certain appropriate times in their lives would be required to do. In *that way* there could be job assignment in a socialist society. Everyone in such a society would be required to do their fair bit (*pace* Nozick) to take up the necessary burdens of the society. This would probably be not very efficient, but it could be done and we might want here, as an wealthy society could, to make the tradeoffs with efficiency.

Job assignment, even so fairly done, like conscription, is not likely to be popular. If people on careful reflection really do not want these things—and this would have to be settled by something like a majority vote—there is another rather more conventional way to get the necessary but distasteful jobs done. They could just command higher salaries and/or shorter working hours to compensate for the onerousness of the work. In this way we might stick to a voluntary system avoiding conscription and job assignment. I am confident that these possibilities do not exhaust the reasonable possibilities. But they are examples of fair ways, and at least seemingly not wildly inefficient ways, of handling these matters. Moreover, which system should be used should be decided by a democratic vote, after a reasonable display of the alternatives within the society.

If we opted, as perhaps might be desired, for a voluntary system with extra payment for onerous or dangerous jobs, inequalities in monetary award would surely arise but they would not be great enough to give rise to differences in power such that some could dominate others or that the whole life prospects of people, including children, would be significantly different. They would not give rise to a class society. Moreover, it is not anti-egalitarian for the higher salary compensates for a loss elsewhere, namely in the onerousness or danger of the job. The society would be a full employment society for those who chose to work, but people could and would be fired for bad performance and people would be differentially awarded in various ways for good work. Such devices would enable a market socialist society to avoid keeping in existence an extensive labor market and it would keep up the full employment ideal of a socialist society while still having a workforce in control of their own affairs who would work efficiently.

There remains the problem of how we can have, if indeed we can have, full employment in a technologically advanced society and efficiently utilize the labor power and make the firms run efficiently. Would we not have—as in the former Yugoslavia—too many people working at too few jobs? One solution, for a society of considerable wealth (the only place where socialism could work anyway), is to have shorter working hours. Work schedules could be staggered in various creative ways that would be to everyone's advantage. To the question of how the society is to generate the wealth to pay for all of that, the answer is that only when the productive forces of a society are extensively developed could socialism or anything like it be plausibly set forth along the lines being proposed here or indeed any lines. That is something that Marx understood very well. But in modern industrially developed societies the productive forces are so developed such that there is sufficient wealth about (wealth measured by the productive capacity of the society) to so arrange work. Moreover, and independently, there are all kinds of interesting and socially useful work in our society that needs to be done and is not being done. Various ways of cleaning up and improving the environment spring to mind. However, they, at best, only indirectly develop the productive forces and thus create wealth, so that we must also, and essentially, find work that does so. Science with its associated technologies is one such productive force. Many more people than are so employed now could be employed in scientific activities and with that employment there would be a development of the productive forces and with that the generating of additional wealth in the society.

8

Let me now turn to the third defect that I found in socialism and in socialist societies, namely to the difficulty I described as a mixed economic/normative one. Socialism, to be socialism, requires at least the public ownership of the major means of production. But the concept of public ownership is a troublesome one. Public ownership, of course, means ownership by the people. But what does that mean? Whatever everyone owns, it has been quipped, no one owns. In actually existing socialisms public ownership—ownership by the people—has come to mean *state* ownership but that has in effect meant ownership or at least control by a small privileged and dictatorial elite. Ownership, but not control, in fact become anomalous here. But the crucial point is that workers—people at large—have had very little to say, even in some broad democratic way, about what is to be done with "their property."

Market socialists and democratic socialists more generally have usually said that public ownership should come to workers' ownership and control of their own workplaces. But, as both Alec Nove and John Roemer have noted, if we leave it at that and if, as in market socialism, individual firms and enterprises compete with each other and prosper or lose, including some going completely under, as in capitalism, some enterprises, and thus some workers, will do much better than other enterprises and thus other workers. Moreover, some workers will be altogether on the dole when their firms go under as some surely will when we allow genuine competition. So inequalities will arise and related imbalances of power. Many of the unfortunate features of *laissez faire* capitalism will be reproduced here.

These difficulties could perhaps be met in several different ways. In one way that does not depart very much from what is done to capitalist enterprises in capitalist welfare states, the workers and cooperatives could be taxed so that part of the wealth is returned not just to the workers in their individual firms but to workers more generally. There are, of course, problems here. On the one hand, the tax might have to be considerable, for it would need to be enough to keep extensive inequalities from arising and (what may come to much the same thing) for the wealth to be spread widely and reasonably evenly in the society. But, on the other hand, the taxation must not be so considerable as to undermine the workers' incentive to make their enterprises excellent ones. This would take some nice balancing and trial and error fiddling. But some capitalist societies (Sweden, for example) have done very well with their capitalists being heavily taxed and yet still, in spite of extensive carping, have retained incentives to develop their enterprises. After all, Sweden is one of the most successful capitalist societies in existence, but it engages in a lot of such fiddling. Swedish industry is very efficient and yet individuals and the corporations that they own are heavily taxed and subject to extensive public service oriented regulation. It might also be said, though *market* socialists would not say that, that carping about taxation and demanding monetary incentives to work efficiently reflects a capitalist mentality from which socialist workers would be free. But in turn it should be replied that whatever may become true of genuinely "socialist persons" we are not there yet and starting from where we are we need incentives. Market socialism will not rely on strongly utopian motivations. And there they may follow Marx.

However, perhaps something more thorough than just using the state's powers of taxation should be deployed. Perhaps we need the enterprises to be only partly owned by workers working in the enterprise, but, as well, to be partly owned by the state where control proportionate to the state's part ownership would go to democratically elected representatives who represent the interests of the workers (all the workers) and not just the interests of the workers who work in these worker cooperatives: cooperatives they partly own. They, after all, with part ownership and control, can still, and rightly so, look after their own interests. The problem is would they be too exclusively concerned with their own interests? It is understandable that they might. This partial state ownership is meant as a check on what *might* be on the excesses of workers here. Moreover, it would give more reality to the public ownership claim than were it simply the case that the workers in the individual firms *solely* own the firm in which they work. Yet there is again a delicate balancing act to be played. The ownership should not be so generalized that the workers in the workplace could not reasonably think of it as their firm where they would take a keen interest in its prospering and efficiently producing and effectively distributing quality goods. I think it is reasonably evident that socialism needs to work out a more adequate conception of public ownership and control than it has as yet.[29] But I also think that it is evident that we are not utterly at sea here. We do not want the Soviet model of state ownership, construed as they construed it. But we also recognize that workers' self-management and their ownership of their own workplaces, while plainly an advance over the Soviet model, is also not without its problems.

9

I now want to consider some at least alleged political-ethical defects of socialism. One defect is in some not atypical Marxist uses of central normative conceptions, including, of course, ethico-political conceptions. Marx and Engels, particularly during the period in which they wrote *The German Ideology*, stressed the ideological nature of talk of justice, freedom, equality, and rights.[30] These conceptions, they stressed purport to give voice to universal claims that are in the interest of all humankind when in reality they, directly or indirectly, standardly serve the interests of the dominating class. In that way they are *status quo* protecting. Whatever the intentions of the moralizers who engage in such talk, such conceptions in fact function as instruments of class domination, though sometimes, when used as slogans of the challenging class, they serve those class interests instead while again, as in the more typical circumstance, purporting to serve the interests of everyone alike. In either case they are, Marxists have it, through and through ideological. Moral conceptions typically are not what they seem to be. They lack their claimed universal validity and in reality are verbal weapons in class struggle answering to the interests of one or another of the antagonistic classes.[31] The typical situation is one where moral ideas, as disguised ideological ideas, express the interests, or at least the perceived interests, of the dominant class while purporting, though, of course, falsely, to serve the interests of everyone alike.[32]

Thus in an important sense moral ideas tend to be expressive false currency; that is, they, as ideological ideas, are expressive of false consciousness: the distorted ideas of social reality of a dominated and ideologically bamboozled people in class society. In most instances our moral ideas are not reality tracking but distort our understanding of our social situation and typically reconcile us to the *status quo*—our station and its duties—and impede our emancipation from class society, not infrequently by failing, Marxists argue, to steel us to the hard tasks of class struggle, a struggle which will not be pleasant and in which the morality of turning the other cheek will dull the edge of native resolution for the revolutionary tasks ahead.

Soviet thought, prior to its liberalization, a liberalization that led to its demise, when thinking of bourgeois morality or, back of that, of feudal morality or the morality, as in Ancient Greece and Rome, of slave society, saw morality in the above sense as ideology while failing to note the ideological nature of their own moralizing inside of Soviet societies about their socialist duties and the tasks of Soviet people in Soviet society. Or at least this was true of those people in those societies who took their Marxism seriously. There are, they claim, their socialist duties in the building of socialism in their societies: in, the constructing, as some East German writers put it, sometimes sincerely, of constructing "their utopia." But, in reality, whether it is the intent of their ideologists or not, fundamental moral conceptions in Soviet societies get used manipulatively, as they not infrequently do in our societies as well. Rights talk and talk of duties and obligations in both societies not infrequently protects the elites of the respective societies. Claims of Soviet legality shored up the Soviet state as did claims about freedom, equality and social justice when there is very little of any of those things in that society or in its formerly dependent societies. But again parallel things obtain for our societies. The propaganda and deployment of ideology in our societies is different, and, as Noam Chomsky notes, more subtle and with that greater subtlety even more insidious.[33] Moral conceptions, that is, are used manipulatively and ideologically in our societies as well and often such moral ideology is very effective. Its sophistication makes it all the more effective.

However, and be that as it may, the point I wish to make here is that in Soviet societies morality was used manipulatively while more was being *claimed* for it. Indeed it could not be successfully used manipulatively if this were not so. Yet the underlying *theory* of morality, viewing morality as ideology (as ideological in its very nature), could hardly justify the claimed objectivity of Soviet moral injunction. The actual use in such societies in political domains of moral conceptions fits the iconoclastic theory that morality is ideology while Soviet theoreticians claimed that these moral conceptions—that is their own moral conceptions—were objective truths answering to the interests of great masses of people.

To take all morality, socialist morality included, as ideology impoverishes socialist conception.[34] Socialist conception asserts honestly that in capitalist societies workers are exploited by capitalists.[35] It also asserts that capitalism offends against the belief in moral equality, a belief which is pervasive across the political spectrum in modernizing societies.[36] In speaking of moral equality, I speak of the belief that the life of everyone matters and matters equally. Believers in capitalism, where they have much in the way of a sense of justice, are also typically believers in moral equality. But they, given the realities of capitalist society, any capitalist society, cannot consistently and knowledgeably hold that belief and claim that capitalist societies are or even can be just societies. In capitalist society, the claim goes, moral equality cannot be a reality. With the steep inequalities capitalism accepts as either fair or unavoidable such an ideal is merely ideological, for, from birth, the very life prospects of many people are so radically unequal that moral equality cannot be even reasonably approximated. There is just no possibility of a society remaining capitalist and securing moral equality.[37]

The socialist critique of capitalism is in part a moral critique and requires that its underlying moral ideas have a reasonable measure of objectivity. If talk of justice is just ideological twaddle socialism itself is undermined.[38] For socialism to be viable it must show that all capitalist societies, though in varying degrees (Norway is not the United States), are unjust exploitative societies in which wage workers are in an important sense unfree.[39] For this claim to be justified moral notions cannot be ideological through and through and capitalist societies must actually be exploitative and undermining of freedom without it being the case that there are sound counterbalancing moral arguments that, everything considered, makes capitalism the lesser evil. If no moral conceptions of any sort can be anything other than ideological distortions, we can have no rational basis for claiming capitalist societies are exploitative and unjust, but this undermines socialism's critique of capitalism.

There are analytical Marxists such as G. A. Cohen, Rodney Peffer, Kai Nielsen, John Roemer, Jeffrey Reiman, and Alan Gilbert who will argue just that.[40] They argue, that is, that capitalism is unjust and exploitative. But this requires a rejection of Marxist immoralism which claims that morality is ideological through and through. What such analytical Marxists can and should say is that we must distinguish between claims in the *sociology* of morals and in the *epistemology* of morals.[41] What Marxists and socialists should say is that when we consider the actual sociological function of morality in class society that we will see that it does typically function as ideology and as such usually distorts our understanding of social reality and supports class society. This is a thesis, and indeed an important one, in the sociology of morals.[42] But this sociological truth, if it is a truth, should not be confused with an epistemological thesis where it is claimed that something in the very nature of morality makes all moral ideals necessarily distortive such that, as the error theory claims, moral beliefs, and a belief in morals more generally, rests on intractable error. What the error theorists claim is that people very widely think, as J. L. Mackie put it, that moral claims can be objective but they are mistaken for in reality they are not and cannot be. They in reality are nothing but our projected emotions while we think, mistakenly, that there are objective moral properties. Belief in morals rests on a mistake. But, it should be responded, nothing in Marxian theory requires that meta-moral theory and if it were justified and if moral claims were necessarily ideological the socialist critique of capitalism would be hoisted by its own petard.

10

The last at least putative defect of socialism I shall discuss is the inadequacy of its conception of democracy in both theory and practice. Leninist conceptions of a vanguard party in which the communist party is to have a legally protected leading role in social life have not led to the hoped for and anticipated—at least among Marxist-Leninists—distinctive socialist democracy beyond the party politics and the class domination of capitalist democracies. Where democratic socialists have rejected this Leninist model or any model of a one party state, they have tended to replace it with the pluralist conceptions of liberal democracy. They have with the pluralism of liberal political democracy tried, without a change in underlying political conception, to add socialist conceptions compatible with those liberal conceptions which would, they argue, lead to an even more extensive democracy on that very liberal political conception.[43] In short, they claim that democratic socialism can deliver the goods of liberal democracy in a way capitalism cannot. But such a socialist conception of democracy makes little theoretical advance over liberal democratic conceptions of democracy.[44]

Democratic socialists, the above mentioned liberal turnings being the exception, have typically been suspicious of representative democracy and have advocated both direct democracy and participatory democracy.[45] By democracy they have meant, as Robert Ware puts it, "rule by the people, all of the people deciding everything themselves."[46] To speak of direct democracy is to speak of decision making by everyone with each person having the right to an equal say and to have her vote count equally. The usual criticism of both direct and participatory democracy is that in large and complex societies such as our own it is thoroughly impractical and in a bad sense utopian. Perhaps in certain contexts we can and should supplement representative democratic institutions such as parliaments with direct democratic decision making and put a stress, as well, on the active participation of citizens in face to face groups of a necessarily small size.[47] These citizens, on such a conception, should deliberate together about all kinds of local matters and make decisions on such local matters themselves. But there are many considerations that cannot be so settled such as the rate and nature of taxation, incomes policy, monetary policy, foreign policy, trade relations with other states and the like. Such matters need to be determined at a society wide level and with extensive discussion and debate. These are things that cannot be done by referenda or simply by engaging in discussion and decision-making within small groups. Direct democracy and participatory democracy mechanisms can only be supplemental, though still importantly supplemental, in the business of democracy. The main business of democratic ordering, the claim goes, must be done through representative institutions such as parliaments.

Where the argument against direct democracy is that it is impractical, defenders of direct democracy argue that it can be and sometimes is used in a number of areas, namely in the election of presidents or members of parliament seen now as *delegates* rather than as *representatives*. They so function in diverse matters of substance such as sovereignty association, gun control, length of term of legislators and the like. They simply enact the citizens' democratically determined beliefs here—beliefs determined by majority vote on such issues. However, where the argument is that direct democracy should *replace* representational democracy in modern complex societies, the argument seems to me very weak indeed. There are problems that need to be settled on something like a province-wide level or a nation-wide level or even, arguably, on an international level. They cannot be decided in a participatory way or reasonably settled by direct democracy without parliaments by the use of referenda even with accurate information perspicuously publicly displayed availing ourselves of all the devices of modern technology. These things will not replace the articulation of proposals, their discussion, investigation, amendment and revision after careful deliberation in parliament with people listening to each other and arguing out the relevant issues. But such a Millian and Habermasian idealization of parliamentary debate may catch little of the present reality of it. Modern parliaments are far from exemplifying the virtues of deliberative democracy. But it is still a reasonable picture of how a parliament *should* operate. Here we need parliaments and representational democracy. Direct democracy cannot replace that. Socialists have rightly stressed that those who oppose direct democracy often use good arguments for questionable purposes.[48] They have exaggerated the impracticalities of direct and participatory democracy in order to deny people access, say, in the workplace or in decisions about schools, that arguably should be theirs.

There is a further and distinct consideration that needs attending to. Plainly, as liberals standardly stress, there are some things which should not be up for democratic decision. Free speech rights or rights to privacy in the living of your own life where you are not harming others should not be treated as vote issues. Fundamental moral issues are not up for majority decision, even two-thirds majority decision. Basic moral issues are not vote issues. The last Jew hauled off to a concentration camp in a world composed otherwise only of committed Nazis would still have her rights violated. But arguments against direct democracy, workplace democracy and participatory democracy and for limiting democracy to representational democracy and for not having it in the workplace are not over such morally privileged claims and have in fact, whatever the intentions of the articulators, the ideological function of securing greater power for an elite few at the expense of the many.

Participatory democracy and direct democracy, rather than replacing representational democracy, should supplement it. Moreover, it can supplement it in a way that respects the rights of individuals and still extends democracy by giving more people in more areas of their lives greater control over their lives. With this obtaining our societies will be much more democratic than they are today without being individual rights-violating societies.[49] This includes importantly workplace democracy in worker owned and run cooperatives. It also includes, through public ownership and control of at least the major means of production, democratic decision making concerning the workings of major industries and of the economy more generally. Such devices will produce more democracy by making more things matters which will come up for democratic decision and, as well, set institutions in place which will give more people in more domains more control over their own lives.[50] Here a democratic socialist society will be more democratic than a capitalist democracy, even a good capitalist democracy (e.g., Finland), by, with the industrial and workplace democracy of such a socialism, giving more people more extensive control over their lives than without it. This can be achieved without it being the case that individual rights will be any more in jeopardy than in a well functioning capitalist democracy such as Finland, Denmark or Holland. The underlying aim should be to extend the ideals of liberty and equality to more and more domains of life. The idea is that they not only exist as ideals but that they, as Rosa Luxemburg stressed, be embedded in the practices and institutions of our societies. This involves, of course, the ending of gender, race and class subordination and the achievement of equality of condition of people no matter what their race, class, gender or sexual orientation.[51]

Notes

1 John Roemer, *Free to Lose* (Cambridge, MA: Harvard University Press, 1988) and Richard Miller, *Analyzing Marx: Morality, Power and History* (Princeton, NJ: Princeton University Press, 1984). For brief programmatic statements by each, see Roemer's "Introduction" in John Roemer, ed., *Analytical Marxism* (Cambridge: Cambridge University Press, 1986) and Miller, "Marx in Analytic Philosophy: The Story of a Rebirth," *Social Science Quarterly* 64, no. 4 (1983), 846-61. In Miller's case, he has abandoned his Marxian orientation without abandoning his socially progressive orientation. It is very important that "analytical Marxism" not be identified with a Marxian form of "rational choice theory." Some analytical Marxians are wedded to that methodology and some are not and that it is the right way to go to be at the

cutting edge of social science is anything but evident. See here Chandra Kumar, *Historical Materialism* (unpublished M.A. thesis, University of Calgary, 1990).

2 Jon Elster rightly derides its sloganeering use in "Orthodox Marxism" but beautifully exemplifies it in his own work. Jon Elster, *Making Sense of Marx* (Cambridge: Cambridge University Press, 1985) and his "Reply to Comments," *Inquiry* 29, no. 1 (March 1986), 65-77. Andrew Collier gives a straightforward and proper sense to "scientific socialism" in his "Scientific Socialism and the Question of Socialist Values" in J. Mephan and D. H. Ruben, eds., *Issues in Marxist Philosophy* 4 (Brighton, England: Harvester Press, 1981), 3-41.

3 In addition to Roemer, Miller and Elster see as well G. A. Cohen, *Karl Marx's Theory of History: A Defense* (Oxford: Clarendon Press, 1978), G. A. Cohen, *History, Labour and Freedom* (Oxford: Clarendon Press, 1988), Andrew Levine, *Arguing for Socialism* (London: Routledge & Kegan Paul, 1984), Andrew Levine, *The End of the State* (London: Verso, 1987), Kai Nielsen, *Marxism and the Moral Point of View* (Boulder, CO: Westview Press, 1989), Allen Wood, *Karl Marx* (London: Routledge & Kegan Paul, 1981), William Shaw, *Marx's Theory of History* (Stanford, CA: Stanford University Press, 1978), Daniel Little, *The Scientific Marx* (Minneapolis, MN: University of Minnesota Press, 1986), Erik Olin Wright, *Classes* (London: Verso, 1985), Philippe van Parijis, *Evolutionary Explanation in the Social Sciences: An Emerging Paradigm* (Totowa, NJ: Rowman and Littlefield, 1981). Three important collections of essays on analytical Marxism are: John Roemer, ed., *Analytical Marxism* (Cambridge: Cambridge University Press, 1986), Robert Ware and Kai Nielsen, eds., *Analyzing Marxism* (Calgary, AB: University of Calgary Press, 1989), and Jon Elster and Karl Ove Moene, eds., *Alternatives to Capitalism* (Cambridge: Cambridge University Press, 1989). In addition to the programmatic essays mentioned in the first note, see Erik Olin Wright, "What is Analytical Marxism?" *Socialist Review* 19, no 4 (Oct-Dec 1989), 35-56, Philippe von Parijis, "Analytischer Marxismus" in W. F. Haug, ed., *Kritisches Wörtenbach des Marxismus* (Berlin: Das Argument, Band 1, 1988), and Kai Nielsen, "Analytical Marxism: A Form of Critical Theory," *Erkenntnis* 39 (1996), 1-2.

4 Michael Buraway, "Marxism is Dead, Long Live Marxism," *Socialist Review* 20, no. 2 (April-June 1990), 7.

5 Editor's note, *Socialist Review* 20, no 2 (April-June, 1990), 5.

6 *Ibid.* Russell Hardin, "Efficiency vs. Equality and the Demise of Socialism," *Canadian Journal of Philosophy* (forthcoming).

7 Ferenc Fehér and Agnes Heller, *Eastern Left, Western Left* (Cambridge: Polity Press, 1987), chapters 1, 2 and 11. See also F. Fehér, A. Heller and G. Markus, *Dictatorship Over Needs* (Oxford: Basil Blackwell, 1983).

8 Claus Offe, *Contradictions of the Welfare State* (Cambridge, MA: MIT Press, 1984). See also note 9.

9 Frank Cunningham, *Democratic Theory and Socialism* (Cambridge: Cambridge University Press, 1987), Ernesto Laclau and Chantal Mouffe, *Hegemony and Socialist Strategy: Towards a Radical Democratic Politics* (London: Verso, 1984), Andrew Levine, *The End of the State* (London: Verso, 1987). Frank Cunningham and Andrew Levine have reviewed each other's books in *Canadian Journal of Philosophy* 19, no. 3 (September 1989), 455-76.

10 Alec Nove, *The Economics of Feasible Socialism* (London: Allen & Unwin, 1983) and Ferenc Fehér, Agnes Heller, and G. Markus, *Dictatorship Over Needs* (Oxford: Basil Blackwell, 1983).

11 Buraway, "Marxism is Dead, Long Live Marxism," 12.

12 See the article, including the interview, with Stanislav Shatlin in *The Gazette*, Montreal, October 6, 1990, B6.

13 *Ibid.*

14 *Ibid.*

15 *Ibid.*

16 *Ibid.*

17 *Ibid.*

18 *Ibid.*

19 See Alex Nove, *The Economics of Feasible Socialism*, Ernest Mandel, "A Critique of Market Socialism," *New Left Review* no. 15 (1986), 5-37, Alec Nove, "Markets and Socialism," *New Left Review*, no. 161 (Jan/Feb 1987), 98-104, Ernest Mandel, "The Myth of Market Socialism," *New Left Review*, no. 169 (1988), 109-119, Jon Elster and Karl Ove Moene, "Introduction" to *Alternatives to Capitalism*, 1-35, Richard Arneson, "Meaningful Work and Market Socialism," *Ethics* 97, no. 3 (Apr 1987), 517-545, John Roemer, "Market Socialism: A Blueprint," *Dissent* (Fall 1991), 562-572, John Roemer, "Can There be Socialism after Communism?" (unpublished manuscript), Boris Frankel, *Beyond the State* (London: Macmillan, 1983), 223-250, Alec Nove and Boris Frankel, "Debate on Market Socialism," *Radical Philosophy* no. 39 (Spring 1985), 24-35, Julian Le Grand and Saul Estrin, eds., *Market Socialism* (New York: Oxford University Press, 1989), and David Schweickart, *Against Capitalism* (New York: Cambridge University Press, 1993).

20 Even this socialism without *labor* markets or with labor markets in restricted domains, namely, where there is small-scale private ownership of productive property (family style restaurants and the like), may be too strong. As much as labor markets offend socialist sensibilities (including mine) we may have to live with them to achieve anything like socialism in the foreseeable future. John Roemer just takes this as a given for his blueprint of a market socialism. *Perhaps* we will have to just bow to such a thing to get an efficient organization and utilization of labor. This would require an amendment to my definition of socialism given in the first section. Condition (b) would have to be dropped and only condition (a) would remain. But, given the exploitative and class-forming nature of the labor market, I shall develop my model for a market socialism without extensive labor markets. If the Roemer-like moves in the direction of "realism" prevail then my model and conception of socialism will have to be amended accordingly. For further remarks on markets and market socialism see R. G. Peffer, "Marxism, Markets and the 'Sanctity' of Socialist Property Relations" and Kai Nielsen, "On Capitalism, Socialism and the Market" both in *Journal of Social Philosophy*, No. 1 (Spring 1991), Lane Kenworthy, "What Kind of Economic System? A Leftist's Guide," *Socialist Review* 20, no. 2 (April-June 1990), 102-124, Lou Ferleger and Jay Mandel, "The Economic Future of Socialism in Eastern Europe," *Socialist Review* 20, no. 2 (April-June 1990), 125-130, John Roemer, "Visions of Capitalism and Socialism," *Socialist Review* 3 (1989), Alec Nove, *Marxism and "Really Existing Socialism"* (New York: Harwood Academic Publishers, 1983), Ingnacio Ortuno-Ortin, John Roemer and Joaquin Silverstre, "Market Socialism," Working Paper Series No. 355, Department of Economics, University of California, Davis, March 27, 1990. For, in addition to Mandel, another dissident view, see Bertell Ollman, "Market Mystification in Capitalist and Market Socialist

Societies," *Socialism and Democracy* 11, no. 2 (Fall 1997), and Bertell Ollman ed., *Market Socialism the Debate Among Socialists* (New York: Routledge 1998).

21 Alec Nove, "The Role of Central Planning under Capitalism and Market Socialism" in Jon Elster and Karl Ove Moene, eds., *Alternatives to Capitalism*, 98.

22 *Ibid.*

23 Nove, *The Economics of Feasible Socialism*, 223.

24 See references in note 19. And see, as well, Rolf Dahrendorf, *Essays in Theory of Society* (Stanford, CA: Stanford University Press, 1968), 215-236.

25 Nove, "The Role of Central Planning under Capitalism and Market Socialism," 100.

26 *Ibid.*

27 *Ibid.*

28 *Ibid.*, 101.

29 There are other alternatives for public ownership as well. For one very suggestive one see John Roemer, *Free to Lose*, chapter 10 and John Roemer, "Public Ownership and Private Property Externalities" in Elster and Moene, *Alternatives to Capitalism*, 159-178. See also the two references to Roemer in note 19.

30 See Philip Kain's discussion of *The German Ideology* in his *Marx and Ethics* (Oxford: Oxford University Press, 1989) and my *Marxism and the Moral Point of View*, 43-97.

31 Kai Nielsen, "Are Moral Beliefs Ideological Deceptions?" in B. Parekh and T. Pantham, eds., *Political Discourse* (New Delhi: Sage Publications) and Kai Nielsen, "Truth, Morality and Moral Ideology" in J. Boulad-Ayoub, ed., *Politique et Culture et Verite* (Montreal: Université du Québec à Montréal Press, 1987).

32 Nielsen, *Marxism and the Moral Point of View*, chapter 5 and my "The Concept of Ideology: Some Marxist and Non-Marxist Conceptualizations," *Rethinking Marxism* 2, no. 4 (Winter 1989).

33 Noam Chomsky, *Towards a New Cold War* (New York: Pantheon, 1973), Chomsky, *Radical Priorities* (Montreal: Black Rose Books, 1981), Chomsky, *Necessary Illusions: Thought Control in Democratic Societies* (Boston: South End Press, 1987), Joshua Cohen and Joel Rogers, "Knowledge, Morality and Hope: Chomsky's Social Thought," *New Left Review* (1991).

34 Nielsen, *Marxism and the Moral Point of View*.

35 Cohen, *History, Labour and Freedom*, Part III and his "Review of Wood's *Karl Marx*," *Mind* 92, no. 367 (July 1983), 440-445, Jon Elster, "Exploitation, Freedom and Justice," *Nomos* XXVI (1983), 111-120, Jon Elster, *Making Sense of Marx*, 166-234, Jeffrey Reiman, *Modern Moral Philosophy* (New Haven, CT: Yale University Press, 1990), and Kai Nielsen, *Marxism and the Moral Point of View*.

36 *Ibid.*

37 Kai Nielsen, *Equality and Liberty: A Defense of Radical Egalitarianism* (Totowa, NJ: Rowman and Allenheld, 1984), Nielsen, "Capitalism, Socialism and Justice" in T. Regan and D. Van De Veer, eds., *And Justice For All* (Totowa, NJ: Rowman and Littlefield, 1982), 264-286, and Nielsen, "Justice, Autonomy and *Laissez Faire*," *The Windsor Yearbook of Access to Justice* X (1990), 40-91.

38 Cohen, *History, Labour and Freedom*, 239-304, Nielsen, *Equality and Liberty: A Defense of Radical Egalitarianism*, Nielsen, *Marxism and the Moral Point of View*.

39 Cohen, *History, Labour and Freedom*, 255-285.

40 See references to Cohen in note 35. R. G. Peffer, *Marxism, Morality and Social Justice* (Princeton, NJ: Princeton University Press, 1980). See references to Nielsen in notes 37 and 38. John Roemer, *Free to Lose*, Jeffrey Reiman, *Modern Moral Philosophy*, Alan Gilbert, *Democratic Individuality: A Theory of Moral Progress* (Cambridge: Cambridge University Press, 1990).

41 Nielsen, *Marxism and the Moral Point of View*, 26-33.

42 *Ibid.* and Nielsen, "Marx and Moral Ideology," *African Philosophical Inquiry* 1, no. 1 (Jan 1987), 71-86.

43 See references to Frank Cunningham and Ernesto Laclau and Chantel Mouffe in note 9. See also Chantel Mouffe, "Radical Democracy or Liberal Democracy?" *Socialist Review* 20, no. 2 (April-June 1990), 57-66.

44 Andrew Levine, *Liberal Democracy: A Critique of Its Theory* (New York: Columbia University Press, 1982), Samuel Bowles and Herbert Gintis, *Democracy and Capitalism: Property, Community and the Contradictions of Modern Social Thought* (New York: Basic Books, 1986), Jeff Goodwin, "The Limits of 'Radical Democracy'," *Socialist Review* 20, no. 2 (April-June 1990), 131-144.

45 Andrew Levine, *The End of the State*.

46 Robert Ware, "Socialism and the Circumstances of Democracy," (unpublished manuscript).

47 Richard Norman, *Free and Equal* (New York: Oxford University press, 1987). See his last chapter for interesting suggestions here.

48 Andrew Levine, *Arguing for Socialism* and *The End of the State*.

49 Frank Cunningham, *Democratic Theory and Socialism* and Kai Nielsen, "Rights-based Ethics: A Critique and Replacement," *The Windsor Yearbook of Access to Justice* 14 (1994), 162-196.

50 *Ibid.*

51 Kai Nielsen, "Equality of Condition and Self-Ownership" in Guy Lafrance, ed., *Ethics and Basic Rights* (Ottawa, ON: University of Ottawa Press, 1989), 81-99.

Part III
Applied Ethics

David Cooper

An Introduction to Applied Ethics With References to Contributions by Burleigh Wilkins

Introduction

To claim that someone has made contributions to a field of knowledge, one must have an interpretation of the field. My task, then, is to sketch out a plausible interpretation of "applied ethics" which can then be used to highlight some of Burleigh Wilkins' contributions. This may seem like a straight forward project, but philosophers are notorious for disagreeing about the nature of their own field of study. To emphasize this point, I will begin with a piece of personal history. In 1966 I was asked by my logic professor what area of philosophy I intended to choose as a specialty. I told him that I was interested in focusing on applied ethics. He scoffed and said: "If you want to do ethics, then go to the English department." I found this advice to be quite disconcerting. My B.A. was in English, and I had switched to philosophy precisely because I wanted to undertake a serious cognitive study of the practical implications of normative ethics. I told him that I had been taught that normative ethics was very abstract and theoretical, since it attempted to rationally justify background, universal ideals of the kind that inspired Thomas Jefferson when he wrote the Declaration of Independence.

> We hold these truths to be self-evident, that all men are created equal and endowed by their creator with certain inalienable rights, among these the right to life, liberty and the pursuit of happiness.

On the other hand, while these ideals may seem self-evident on the theoretical level, it is not obvious how they ought to be applied to local circumstances. Thus, it is impressive when we see someone like Socrates, who has the theoretical capacity to pursue universal ideals and the practical wisdom to conduct his concrete daily activities in a manner consistent with those ideals. Since I wanted to learn how to combine these two levels of wisdom in my own life, and since applied ethics investigates the best "means" for applying rationally based universal ideals to concrete local circumstances, it seemed to me that applied ethics was the right field to study.

My professor smiled, both at my youthful idealism and my naivete. He assured me that the logical positivists had undertaken a metaethical[1] study that conclusively demonstrated that traditional normative philosophies were not based on rational universal foundations that could be applied at the local level. His short speech went something like this:

Once ethics is boiled down, it amounts to no more than a series of subjective emotional preferences. Anyone interested in getting a teaching position in philosophy had better not advertise themselves as being interested in applied normative ethics. Universities are not going to be interested in hiring such people, because professional schools are removing subjective ethics courses from their curriculums in favor of training in practical research, logical analysis, and the technical skills required for competent practice. [This was, of course, pre-Watergate advice.]

Looking back, it is clear that my professor was a strong advocate of a logical positivist metaethical position called "emotivism," which I'll discuss in the next section. There are also a number of contemporary "postmodern" metaethical positions which have been used to attack the traditional Enlightenment belief that reason can help us discover and then apply universal ethical truths. Postmodernists are suspicious of so called universal moral values. They fear that they may just be tools of power used to oppress minority groups by forcing everyone to live in the same way as the people in power. Together, logical positivists and postmodern critics have provided some powerful reasons to be skeptical about traditional normative philosophy's ability to discover rational universal values let alone apply them at the local level. I will deal with these two challenges to applied ethics one at a time. In the course of the discussion, I will argue that Burleigh Wilkins has made contributions in ethics that can satisfy some of the concerns of both these metaethical positions.

The Role of Metaethics

The need for metaethical analysis in applied normative philosophy develops naturally when social life becomes sufficiently complex. During those periods in human history when people lived in homogeneous tribal societies, there was not much interest in metaethics. It was natural for tribal members to assume that the traditional background values of their tribe were objectively true absolutes. To apply their fundamental values, tribal members could appeal directly to traditional, concrete, institutional rules (e.g. "That is the way we have always done it and, of course, it is right.") As long as people lived in stable closed communities, this level of "conventional thinking" worked quite well, and there was no reason for anyone to challenge the legitimacy of local laws.

When cultures collide, however, it becomes possible to compare the legal arrangements found in different tribes. Comparisons can lead people to challenge the legal status quo, forcing those who wish to defend it to move up to a higher level of abstraction by appealing to those background principles that are used to justify legal systems themselves (e.g., life, liberty, and the pursuit of happiness). When agreement can not be reached about the principles that ought to regulate institutions, then people have to turn to an even higher level of abstraction. At this level, they appeal to background normative theories that are used to justify both a culture's favored principles and its way of interpreting concrete events (e.g. a theory of natural rights). Finally, when there is disagreement about the legitimacy of background normative theories, it is necessary to turn to the most abstract level of ethics and ask metatheoretical questions about the nature of ethical language and the structure of ethical theories themselves. Because of increased sensitivity to value pluralism in this century, meta-ethical discussions have dominated much of the recent philosophical ethical literature.

The metatheoretical assumptions found in early versions of logical positivism radically challenged traditional beliefs about the nature of concrete ethical claims. For instance, my emotivist logic professor claimed that A. J. Ayer (1952) had "proven" that "all" value statements are merely expressions of emotion which have the same logical structure as the exclamation "Hooray for our team!" Value expressions of this kind are not true or false, because they do not describe a state of affairs. Emotivists believe that "all" value statements have this same structure, thus, it is meaningless to ask about the truth of any particular value claim, including those in ethics.

This theory seems reasonable when used to evaluate concrete emotional utterances that amount to no more than a cheer for a team, but the theory seems less reasonable when applied to statements used to assert specific ethical claims. For instance, the theory reduces an ethical claim such as "Torturing babies is wrong", to being merely a sophisticated way of commanding everyone to say: "Boo for torturing babies." However, people who condemn torture believe it is "true" that torture is wrong, and they think they can prove it. On the other hand, emotivists believe these people are essentially confused about the logical structure of the statements they are using when they make such emotional moral claims.

Given this point of view, it makes sense that my logical positivist professor would send me to the English department for applied ethics. Because he thinks that normative ethics is grounded only in subjective emotions at all levels of consideration, he believes applied ethics can amount to no more than learning how to tell effective stories that will cause others to share the subjective feelings of the speaker. Since eliciting emotion is not the philosopher's task, if I want to stay in philosophy, I should stop looking for background foundations that can be used to convince people of the truth of ethical claims. I should instead use my logical, analytical skills to investigate the meaning of the terms ordinary moral agents use when they assertively express their feelings.

The Moral Point of View is Public Not Private

Of course, emotivism does not exhaust the possible ways to analyze the meaning of ethical claims. Consider the following motto: "Feelings do not justify moral positions, moral positions justify feelings" (Dworkin, 1971, p. 63). This slogan reminds us that ethical claims are practical "public" assertions about what everyone ought to do, they are not claims about "private" feelings. Participants in public discourse expect those who make public claims to have reasons for their assertions that will make sense to other members of the public. As the Scottish communitarian, philosopher, and economist Adam Smith said:

> A moral being is an accountable being. An accountable being, as the word expresses, is a being that must give an account of its actions to some other, and that consequently must regulate them according to the good-liking of this other (cited in Hope, 1984, p. 159).

Since a personal feeling is not a public argument, it does not provide a reason why "someone else" should think they are obligated to do anything. Unless our feelings about public matters are supported by good "public" reasons that can justify them, our feelings may amount to nothing more than a familiar prejudice or an outdated personal coping strategy that will not meet with "the good-liking" of those affected. This same point applies to the general social feelings that may be shared by a community. While social feelings are important to the members of a group, by themselves they do not provide a moral reason for action across group lines unless there are public reasons that can support them at the multi-group level. In pluralistic settings, the need to bring forth public reasons at the appropriate level of abstraction requires us to go beyond local social feelings to try and discover reasons for action that do not ideologically favor any particular group. This means that before all affected people will agree to the legitimacy of any particular universal ethical theory, they will have to reach a post-conventional,[2] metaethical consensus about an appropriate "moral point of view" from which to judge the public basis for the theories.

The most popular current metaethical consensus in Western ethics maintains that for ethical positions to be impartially justified, they must strive to 1) meet publicly acknowledged rational standards, 2) satisfy conditions of universality, that is, in principle be compatible with "the good-liking" of all honest people, 3) be impartial in the sense of self-critical rather than ideological, and 4) promote generalized empathy and respect between all people. Attempts to justify and satisfy public standards of this kind can provide a basis for rational inquiry. The logical positivists are right to insist that those who work in ethics ought to make use of metaethical analysis, but they are wrong when they insist that there can be no cognitive basis for the ethical judgments that emerge from rational, self-critical dialogue about the ethical standards that ought to regulate public life at the various levels of ethical consideration.

During the metaethical debates about the nature of ethical discourse, philosophers have had to develop a number of logical distinctions to help them cope with the complexity of ethics in this multicultural world. For instance, because ethical discourse that aims to provide a "justification" for background universal ideals is not of the same logical type as discourse that aims to "apply" the ideals in local contexts, it has become necessary in contemporary applied ethics to clearly distinguish between these two activities (see Gunther, 1993). Impartial discourse that aims to "justify" background universal norms for all groups restricts the complexity of discussion by ignoring local contingencies. Thus, at the theoretical level of consideration we use the *ceteris paribus* qualification, which means we ask: *"Other things being equal,* which background universal principles will seem most likely to meet with 'the good-liking' of everyone when considered from an impartial point of view?" As Wilkins (1970) points out, when we agree to consider an issue *ceteris paribus*, then an ethical claim is often placed in an agreed upon moral context where it can be treated as a noncontroversial assertion (p. 161). By holding contexts steady in this way, philosophers can reach agreement on general *prima facie* rights and duties that will serve as background norms that *at first appearance* can help to guide our ethical decisions (life, liberty, pursuit of happiness). As Wilkins (1994) says, "a *prima facie* obligation is understood to be an obligation for which there is a strong but not always conclusive reason for doing whatever the obligation requires" (p. 92). *Prima facie* norms represent the moral status quo from which we begin deliberations, so they place the burden of proof on anyone who would want to override them by claiming that the "other things being equal" (*ceteris paribus*) qualification does not hold in a particular situation.

Whatever the initial *ceteris paribus* consensus about theoretical *prima facie* universal norms, when people begin to apply them to concrete cases, then "other things are seldom equal." At the applied level, we have to shift focus and pay attention to all the features that are unique to the local context. The nature of the question asked has to become much more complex, thus application discourse asks: "*When all things are considered,* which of the universally valid *prima facie* norms previously justified under the *ceteris paribus* condition seems most appropriate in 'this' case right now?" That is, at the applied level of consideration where a specific situation is the focus of attention, a universal norm's "... appropriateness refers only to the particular features of this situation... ." (Farrel, 1993, p. x), and some of these features may provide a reason to override the usual moral status quo.

An Example: Abraham Lincoln[3]

Somehow universal norms must be applied without either distorting the norms themselves or doing violence to legitimate local arrangements. To make this abstract point clear, it will be useful to consider an historical example that demonstrates how difficult it can be to apply valid universal values when people are already embedded in concrete local systems that violate those universal values. Although Abraham Lincoln was clearly convinced about the truth of the "self-evident" universal norms mentioned in the Declaration of Independence (moral equality and equal rights to life, liberty, and the pursuit of happiness), as a practical politician he had the difficult task of trying to figure out how to protect everyone's universal rights without at the same time leading his nation into a civil war. He asked his fellow citizens to take the high road and dedicate themselves to the universal ideals that inspired the Founding Fathers.

> Let us readopt the Declaration of Independence, and with it, the practices, and policies, which harmonize with it. Let north and south—let all Americans—let all lovers of liberty everywhere—join in the great and good work. If we do this, we shall not only have saved the Union, but we shall have so saved it, as to make, and to keep it, forever worthy of saving... (Oates, p. 118).

Given that background ideals like moral equality and self-government (liberty) can be seen to be universally valid norms during the discourse of justification, how should they be applied to the controversy over slavery? In an historical context that allowed legalized slavery, Lincoln's appeal to such universal ideals seemed hopelessly theoretical to many people. Because of the existence of all kinds of concrete inequalities, pro-slavery advocates also insisted that the claims about universal equality in the Declaration of Independence were "lies." Judge Stephen A. Douglas, Lincoln's chief antagonist in political debates about the problem of slavery, said:

> When the Founding Fathers spoke of equality they meant equality among white people… and Negroes had nothing to do with it. Why? Because they were racially inferior and innately incapable of self-government (Oates, p. 133).

Lincoln publicly repudiated this interpretation of the Founding Fathers' ideals. He argued that the Declaration of Independence was not meant "…to declare all men equal in all respects. They did not mean to say all were equal in color, size, intellect, moral development, or social capacity" (Oates, p. 134). They intended to declare only the self-evident truth that all men were equal in possessing inalienable rights like those to life, liberty, and the pursuit of happiness [To emphasize universality, I think they would now say: "all people" rather than "all men"]. Of course, they were aware that people did not yet enjoy full expression of their equal rights. They were declaring, however, that these universal rights not only existed but were to serve as a standard for the establishment of policy in the future (Oates, p. 134). Lincoln also claimed that proslavery advocates were being illogical when they tried to use moral arguments based on the notions of self-government and local sovereignty to justify slavery. He said local sovereignty is inconsistent with the ideal of self-government when issues like slavery are involved.

> When the white man governs himself, that is self-government; but when he governs himself, and also governs another man, that is more than self-government—that is despotism. If the Negro is a man, why then my ancient faith teaches me that 'all men are created equal;' and that there can be no moral right in connection with one man's making a slave of another (Oates, p. 117).

To argue on the basis of local sovereignty was "… a fraudulent, insidious, and potentially devastating device… it reduced a momentous national issue—the existence and growth of human bondage—to a purely local matter, equal in importance to the cranberry trade" (Oates, p. 116). Lincoln pointed out that proslavery people declare slavery to be a very good thing, yet no one under the ideal of self-government has ever chosen to make himself a slave, good thing though it is supposed to be (p. 126). But what should be done about it?

Decisions in applied ethics are not simple. The application of universal principles has to take into account the realities of history, and we should not assume that ideal conditions exist when they do not. Because it takes practical wisdom to apply background ideals in an imperfect world, and because we do not all see local events in the same way, Lincoln had to struggle for years to find a realistic ethical approach to the problem of slavery. Early in his run for public office, when one of his Southern friends said that although slavery may be wrong from an abstract point of view he would rather abolish the Union than give up his right to own slaves, Lincoln responded that he was not asking his friend to give up his right to own slaves. He acknowledged that slavery was his friends' own business since this peculiar institution had constitutional standing. Thus, he said "I now do no more than oppose the extensions of slavery [into the new border states]" (Oates, p. 122).

As President, Lincoln did not want civil war, and he had taken an oath to uphold the constitution. It was not clear how he could both seek justice for slaves and be fair to local communities under the law. The historical circumstance of the war finally gave him the opportunity to use his war time powers to abolish slavery with a presidential proclamation, but without the war it would have been a long struggle to find a proper way to implement these justifiable ideals given the reality of local disagreements. One thing is clear, however. Without background universal values, Lincoln might not have been willing to stand firm on the slavery issue year after year. Like Douglas, he may have been tempted to accept unethical compromises on the nature of human freedom. The fact that application is difficult, however, is no reason to abandon the background ideals that guide our intuitions about what ought to count as legitimate ethical accommodations to local differences.

Lincoln's situation is dramatic, but in structure, it is also quite common. Clarity at the level of background values "other things being equal" is not synonymous with clarity about the best means for applying those values in a specific concrete situation "all things considered." Unlike the discourse of justification, application discourse requires a complete description of the entire context in order to determine which features of this specific case are ethically relevant. "This can involve a semantic analysis of the terms used in the norm, which are in turn ultimately dependent on an even more extensive (exhaustive) description of the situation" (Farrell, 1993, p. xi). At the applied level, then, both conceptual analysis and descriptive empirical research on specific cases become crucial, and philosophers will have to do much of the analytic work.

Wilkins' Analytic Contributions

Burleigh Wilkins is not a logical positivist, and his contributions to ethics move ethical understanding away from the positivist's metaethical stance. However, he has made a number of contributions at the level of conceptual analysis that can be admired by positivists. Since I cannot discuss all the issues he covers in his articles, I will simply review some of the major themes in his early analytic papers before turning to the normative contributions found in his later work.

Wilkins (1970) used semantic analysis of the "is-ought" controversy to show the importance of being sensitive to context when evaluating ethical claims at the level of application. The need to distinguish between "is" and "ought" statements arose in justification discourse when philosophers began to recognize that foundational claims about what "ought" to be can not be logically derived from facts alone, that is, from a complete list of statements about what "is" the case. "Ought" statements add something new to our understanding of the world, so there has to be some other way to prove the validity of foundational value claims than by simply listing all the facts. Some philosophers asserted that because there is an insurmountable logical gulf between facts and values, no matter what the level of ethical consideration it is impossible to ever derive an ought claim from statements that are only descriptive. In response, Wilkins (1970) argued that the logical gulf between descriptive factual statements (what "is" the case) and value statements (what "ought" to be) could be bridged in concrete settings as long as people confined their value claims to hierarchical moral settings where there is no reason to challenge the *ceteris paribus* condition. As Wilkins (1970) says, the "other things being equal" assertion is not itself evaluative

> ... in cases where reasons for denying *ceteris paribus* can't be given (such cases can't be uncommon, else injunctions like "*always* keep your promises" would

> lose all plausibility) and also in cases where, given a clearly structured hierarchy of moral institutions, one knows in advance of particular cases which duty or obligation will be honored under various kinds of circumstances (p. 162).

Thus, in a closed community of discourse, where people have already reached agreement on the meaning of normative terms in institutionalized moral hierarchies, there does not appear to be a gap at all. An exhaustive description of the facts of a case will automatically contain previously agreed upon understandings about how to deal with values, *ceteris paribus*. This early analysis shows an appropriate sensitivity to the fact that value claims at the applied level are often contextually constrained by prior institutional practices that give them a different logical structure than those claims made about foundational values. As we will see, such clarity about the importance of levels of abstraction and the hierarchical nature of value claims serves him well in his later applied ethics work.

In "Concerning 'Motive' and 'Intention'" Wilkins (1971) argued that motives and intentions "... face the future in different ways, with 'intention' marking the means and 'motive' the end" (p. 142). In this sense, an intention can serve as motive "...in that it involves a decision or choice to bring about a certain, rather specific future state of affairs" (p. 141). This clarity about the link between intention and a future state of affairs was used to resolve a conceptual problem in the applied legal ethics paper "Intention and Criminal Responsibility" (1985). Wilkins argued that in complex legal cases, to adequately account for our basic intuitions about criminal intent and responsibility we need to modify the way we have traditionally defined the relationship between these terms in the law. For instance, our sense of justice tells us that perpetrators of crimes should be held responsible for all the damages they caused, not just the very narrow set of consequences they desired as the explicit aim of their intended criminal activity.

> The problem is whether we can maintain the distinction between the consequences of an action which are desired and those which are not desired while also maintaining that at least some of the undesired consequences may nevertheless be spoken of as intended consequences (Wilkins, 1985, p. 272).

To maintain these distinctions, Wilkins suggest that we think of criminal intent as aiming at a "state of affairs" which perpetrators intend to bring about as a result of their actions (p. 273). In this way, we can hold them responsible for the entire set of consequences attached to the "state of affairs" that result from their harmful actions, even though they may not have explicitly desired some of them. This allows us to say that "...

an agent is willing to pay the price of bringing about an undesired consequence in order to achieve a consequence that he does desire, and it does not imply that he intends to bring about a consequence he does not desire. It is sufficient to say that he intends to bring about a state of affairs despite its having an undesired consequence" (p. 274). This approach has advantages over the traditional approach and "... supplies the requisite *mens rea* for murder, and it is sufficiently narrow not to allow murder to be confused with a homicide stemming from recklessness" (p. 277).

In 1993 Wilkins used semantic analysis in "Does the Fetus Have a Right to Life?" to clarify some of the issues in the abortion debate. He argued that because the fetus is a unique creature all analogies used to portray its moral status will miss the mark to a degree. This is the case with the analogies used by Fineberg and Benn to show that the potentiality argument is illogical. Their analogies are misleading since they tend to confuse potentiality with possibility (pp. 126-128). Wilkins favors Aristotle's interpretation of potentiality which, when applied to the case of the fetus, would assert that a fetus is potentially a person because if nothing external to the normal situation hinders its development, it "of itself" will become a person (p. 132). On the basis of its status as a potential person, Wilkins says there are substantive moral reasons to assert that the fetus has a right to life that is an actual right.

> What gives at least a nondefective fetus the right to life is, I believe, its potential to become a person and to experience the good things that virtually all persons experience at least occasionally, and what gives the terribly senile, the very painfully terminally ill, and the irreversibly comatose person a right to euthanasia is that the potential (the capacity, the power, or the ability) to experience such things is in their cases all used up (p. 130).

This actual right to life derived from the discourse of justification is not absolute, however, because it must be weighed against other valid rights and values in concrete settings. Since all births create risks and inconveniences that can turn out to be substantial, there will be occasions during the discourse of application where these other values may override the right to life of any potential person. On those occasions an abortion would not necessarily be a violation of the mother's duty to protect the right to life of the fetus. Who should decide which values are the most appropriate or have the most weight during a decision about abortion? Each case is uniquely complex and personal, and because this is an all things considered question, inevitably there will be errors in judgment no matter who decides. Thus, Wilkins argues that the decision must ultimately rest with the "person" who bears the greatest responsibility and is liable to the greatest risks, which of course means, the mother (pp. 134-137).

As Wilkins' analytic papers clearly show, philosophers with his logical skills are well positioned for making contributions in applied ethics when we need to analyze the conceptual complexities that arise at the level of application discourse. Meaning analysis is a necessary phase in developing cogent normative positions that can be consistently applied, especially when there is a gap between "is" and "ought" because disputes have arisen between different groups who have not previously reached agreement on the meaning of normative terms or the nature of the priorities that exist in moral hierarchies.

In 1984 Wilkins published two other metaethics papers that laid the groundwork for two different but significant 1990's contributions in applied normative philosophy. The first paper, "Can Terrorism be Justified?" initiated an investigation which lasted for about ten years into whether or not terrorism could ever be justified as a means to some legitimate moral end. In 1987 he elaborated on this initial metaethical analysis in "Terrorism and Consequentialism," which eventually became chapter five in his (1992) major applied ethics work, *Terrorism and Collective Responsibility*. In this text, Wilkins uses careful semantic analysis to dismantle the logic of the politically popular approach to terrorism that lumps terrorists in with all the unprincipled criminals who violate people, property, and the law for personal gain. He argued that terrorists, properly conceived, were desperate and powerless political actors who ought to be and often are governed by principle (p. 1-4). This implies that under certain circumstances, the activities of principled terrorists may be justifiable.

The burden of proof, however, is on the terrorists to justify their actions. As a methodological individualist, Wilkins (1992) argues that only individuals can have causal efficacy, and if we assign responsibility to a group or institution it is only to point to its "rules, norms, or standards which sanction or permit violent behavior by its members" (p. 9). Since individual agents are ultimately responsible for choosing to follow the rules, terrorists can not claim that because they are only agents of a group they bear no personal responsibility. It is also problematic to take apparently innocent individuals and harm them as though they were personally responsible for actions committed by other members of their group. Because terrorists apparently blame innocent members of a group for the policies and actions of leaders of the group, to justify their activities, terrorists have the burden of proving that all group members share to some degree collective responsibility for the policies and actions of their group leaders. This is not an easy burden to meet, and calls for an extended analysis of the nature of the collective responsibility of organized groups (Wilkins, 1992, see part 2). In the end, the ordinary conception of collective guilt can give us grounds for holding group members collectively responsible. But we must remember that:

> While liability for collective wrongdoing or injustice falls upon an entire group, the distribution of liability in the form of penalties may affect some of its members more than others. In view of these considerations, terrorists should take as much care as possible to avoid harming those individual members of a group who have played no part in some collective wrongdoing or injustice (p. 145).

In the end, then, there are cases where terrorism can be justified. For instance, during the holocaust when the Nazis used the apparatus of the German State to try and exterminate the Jewish people, terrorism as a defensive strategy would be justifiable. The following moral rule supports this claim.

> Terrorism is justified as a form of self-defense when: (1) all political and legal remedies have been exhausted or are inapplicable (as in emergencies where 'time is of the essence'); and (2) the terrorism will be directed against members of a community or group which is collectively guilty of violence aimed at those individuals who are now considering the use of terrorism as an instrument of self-defense, or at the community or group of which they are members (p. 28).

Because cases of legitimate terrorism are always instances of defensive political action for principled ends, terrorists have the moral duty to structure their action according to the appropriate norms. The following rules or conditions can help determine if a terrorist act is justified. It must aim at ending some injustice being committed by the targeted group, rational discourse and democratic procedures must have been tried and previously failed, it must bring the injustice to the attention of the public, the terrorist activity must be appropriate to the degree of the injustice being perpetrated against the terrorist's group, the targets must be carefully selected and morally appropriate (e.g. children are more innocent than military personnel), indiscriminate violence should be avoided, and the choice of target and means must be expected to contribute to ending the injustice (pp. 140-148).

As Wilkins' book on terrorism shows, philosophers can use valid background universal principles and careful conceptual analysis to justify actions that would appear heinous if looked at from a purely local point of view. Because it is possible to use esoteric philosophical skills for ideological purposes, many postmodern critics have become deeply suspicious of all attempts to use universal ethical norms to justify political decisions. I am going to argue that Wilkins' other 1984 metaethics paper "Principles for Individual Actions," initiated an extended dialogue with John Rawls' (1971) theory of justice that properly responds to some of the concerns of these postmodern skeptics. To make my case, I will first offer a sketch of Rawls' social contract theory. Next, I will outline some of the postmodern particularist criticisms of this kind of universalist theory, and then I will summarize Habermas' (1991) response to the particularists as developed in his theory of discourse ethics. I will finish by arguing that Wilkins' critique of Rawls is a response that is properly sensitive to the legitimate concerns of postmodern critics while remaining sympathetic to the spirit of universal theory as it is enunciated in both Habermas' and Rawls' latest work.

The Need for Universal Principles

The best contemporary normative theories build on the rational choice tradition in ethics which arose during the 17th and 18th century Enlightenment period in Europe. Whether philosophers of the Enlightenment relied on the divine light of reason, an appeal to natural laws, pure reason, a general will, or a theory about a sixth sense that could "see" moral truths, the goal was the same: to transcend social and cultural idiosyncrasies by discovering justifiable background universal principles that could lead to rational consensus about how to resolve disputes between cultural groups. We clearly see this kind of normative expectation in the preamble to the 1776 "Declaration of Independence."

> When in the course of human events, it becomes necessary for one people to dissolve the political bands which have connected them with another, and to assume among the powers of the earth, the separate and equal station to which the laws of nature and of nature's God entitle them, a *decent respect to the opinions of mankind* requires that they should declare the causes which impel them to the separation [Emphasis added].

This attempt to give a public justification of their actions so as to show "respect to the opinions of mankind," illustrates a background metaethical assumption about the public nature of an impartial universal ethics that was fully developed during the 18th Century Age of Enlightenment.

In a multi-cultural world, justifications will have to transcend some aspects of local cultural contexts, or they will not be impartial enough to satisfy the criterion of being at least in principle "to the good-liking" of all affected parties. Alasdair MacIntyre (1988) argues that the plurality of existing philosophical traditions since the Age of Enlightenment proves that philosophers were overly optimistic in believing that the search for a common universal standard would be fruitful.

> Both the thinkers of the Enlightenment and their successors proved unable to agree as to what precisely those principles were which would be found undeniable by all rational persons... Nor has subsequent history diminished the extent of such disagreement. It has rather enlarged it. Consequently, the legacy of the Enlightenment has been the provision of an ideal of rational justification which it has proved impossible to attain. And hence in key part derives the inability within our culture to unite conviction and rational justification (p. 6).

Because of the considerable formal agreement between Western traditions, I am not yet ready to abandon the Enlightenment's optimism. For one thing, I am impressed by the fact that whenever there exists a reasonable balance of power, so that one side in a dispute can not use force in an attempt to "ethnically cleanse" the other side, reasonable people always eventually conclude that all sides in the dispute must try to publicly justify any normative claims being made, and they agree that, other things being equal, agreements should be reached through negotiations that are fair to everyone involved. In light of contemporary research into moral development, however, it will be useful to modify the Enlightenment's search for absolute universal values so as to make it consistent with the process of moral development. Moral conflicts and the type of dialogue that results when force is not an option, seem capable of stimulating the development of postconventional forms of consciousness that can help us make sense of universal goals. At this level of abstraction, ethical dialogue shifts its focus from ethnocentric concerns about local group interests to a concern about the nature of the increasingly better transcendent "truths" that can emerge when cross cultural dialogue becomes a dominant means for resolving conflicts between local groups. Universal values do not have to be considered unalterable truths; they can be seen as the result of historical agreements that emerge out of the kind of dialogue that is based on respect for all parties in a conflict. The recognition that pluralistic cultures will need to engage in this type of justificatory discourse to reach consensus on transcendent background norms is the underlying normative insight behind John Rawls' social contract theory.

John Rawls' Theory of Justice

Wilkins (1992, p. 6) maintains that on the level of political theory he is in substantial agreement with John Rawls' (1971) seminal work, *A Theory of Justice*. Rawls argues that the logic behind social contract theory requires that morally legitimate agreements can not be based on power or force. Thus, everyone should participate in foundational justificatory discourse about the principles that ought to regulate political, economic, and social arrangements, and they must be "fairly" represented at the start of the discussions. This means, theoretically speaking, that since no one can have an advantage at the start, we must conceive of people as beings who are by nature free, rational, and equal. It is hard for all of us who are embedded in on going social systems to imagine what a beginning position of fairness would be like. For example, if you ask "How can the migrant farmer be considered to be equal to an industrialist?" you are being far too concrete. Such questions focus on irrelevant local contingencies, just as did the writer who wrote the columnist Ann Landers complaining that the Founding Fathers were wrong when they claimed "all men are created equal," because the world is full of people who suffer from all kinds of inequalities. [Remember, this same argument was also used against Lincoln by proslavery advocates.]

Those who think about ethical foundations in such a concrete manner will not understand the logic behind a postconventional, theoretical discourse that tries to give an impartial justification for background norms. A social contract is a postconventional conception, since it is a hypothetical speculation about which moral principles ought to be used to justify societies. The point is for us real people to speculate about what *would* be chosen, *if* all people were agreeing to principles *before* local contingencies gave anyone real social, economic, or political advantages and disadvantages, in short, before we were all a particular somebody with our politically biased point of view. To capture this idea, Rawls (1971) says we should use our moral imagination to think about what it *would* be like to have to choose principles of justice from behind a "veil of ignorance" [p. 132]. Such a veil would cloud our memory so that each of us could forget particular details about who we are. We would know general things about humanity but would not know personal things about ourselves. That is, we wouldn't know if we were rich or poor, male or female, black or white, old or young, and so forth. All personal knowledge about the self would be gone, yet we would still have to choose which background moral principles ought to regulate institutions to keep them as just as possible. What principles would a rational agent choose under hypothetical conditions that force her to assume that she might have to occupy any role, office, or station that is permitted?

Of course, an abstract metaphor like the "veil of ignorance" is ambiguous by nature, thus it can carry contradictory meanings depending on how the metaphor is used. Some critics of the theory think the veil of ignorance implies that we must choose like an isolated, socially unencumbered, fictional being. Such a creature would have no interests, thus it wouldn't be able to choose anything. Since this is ridiculous, it is probably a mistake to follow this interpretation of the metaphor. Instead, the veil metaphor ought to give us insight into what it would mean to proceed in the opposite direction. The moral point of view emphasizes impartiality, thus we have an obligation to become so encumbered by human possibilities that we become completely empathic. If I don't know who I am, but would like to do the right thing, then I have to feel empathy for all positions so that I can be impartial in the sense of taking all of them seriously. That is, the logic of the veil requires us to sympathetically consider every form of life with the same enthusiasm we would have if we were socially constructed to live in each of them. On a practical level, this means I should take steps to give voice to all perspectives, just as I would if I knew some perspective was my own. The logic of the veil metaphor, then, points to an obligation to make a serious attempt to listen to all kinds of differences, not ignore them as we would if we were an unencumbered empty vessel.

Some feminist critics of this liberal, social contract tradition argue that we would get better insights from this device if we abandoned the idea that contractees ought to be rational, self-interested, autonomous beings, and instead portrayed them as rational, interdependent, needy beings, that is, beings who have normal human frailties (see Onora O'Neill, 1989, p. 230f). Contractees would be properly concerned about the quality of human virtues and the types of relationships that ought to evolve in all societies only if they acknowledged their social vulnerability. I think the veil of ignorance takes care of this kind of concern. Since contractees could turn out to be anyone, they will have to sympathetically evaluate all the options concerning moral virtues as well as the potential for human relationships under all the different social arrangements. As Habermas (1991) says, "... the impartiality of judgment is expressed in a principle that constrains *all* affected to adopt the perspectives of *all others* in the balancing of interests. The principle of universalization is intended to compel the *universal exchange* of *roles* that G. H. Mead called 'ideal role taking' or 'universal discourse'" (p. 65). If we use the veil in the proper way, then, it should lead to an appreciation of all those virtues that are necessary conditions for a variety of human lifestyles.

Because social contract theory rests on the background assumption that mankind's moral nature is equal at the start, all local concrete inequalities are either accidents of nature or the result of conventional choices that have to be justified in accordance with the valid background norms that would be chosen by free and equal rational people with impartial empathy for all positions. In theory, people who are fairly represented at the start, with no time constraints and no ability to use force, will all agree to the same universal principles of justice. Rawls (1971) argues that the following two foundational principles would be chosen:

> First: each person is to have an equal right to the most extensive basic liberty compatible with a similar liberty for others. Second: social and economic inequalities are to be arranged so that they are both (a) reasonably expected to be to everyone's advantage, and (b) attached to positions and offices open to all [under conditions of fair equal opportunity] (p. 60).

Social contract theory is a fully decentered, abstract, postconventional theory about how to justify fundamental background universal principles of the kind that inspired Lincoln. However, decision procedures of this kind have to be used by real people, and the principles chosen must be applied by real people. Thus, postmodern critics are concerned that we biased humans will distort the intended consequences of such hypothetical, idealized procedures during actual ethical debates. That is, privileged powerful groups will force their own interpretation of what would be chosen on to everyone else, which will create an artificial oppressive conformity in the public sphere.

Postmodern Criticisms[4]

According to postmodern contextualists, we should give up completely on the search for universal, rationally justified, transcendent values, since transcendence of any kind is a hopelessly compromised notion. Differences in background culture and personal experience always cause people to "project" different interpretations of events into the world. That is, because different cultural groups are "always already" embedded in "taken-for-granted backgrounds" (McCarthy, 1984, p. xxvi) that amount to incommensurable ways of life, there can never be a transcendent perspective that gives some interpretations of the world privileged access over all the rest. Because the ideal of a transcendent perspective can not be achieved, Flax (1990) argues that we must abandon "... 'truth' enunciating or adjudicating modes ...[since there can never] be a perfectly adequate unified theory of the 'whole'" (pp. 4).

Walzer (1994) thinks that deontological universalists have become so confused that they have reversed the process of history and think that "Minimalism precedes maximalism; [as though] once we were thin but have grown thick." (p. 13) He is pointing out the obvious historical fact that people first become members of a tribal culture with its "thick" theory about how to live life [this is similar to what Rawls (1993) refers to as "comprehensive doctrines" (p. 13)], and only then do they begin abstract reflections about "thin" transcendent principles of justice (such as Rawls'' two principles of justice). But because we are "always already" thick, our choices about thin transcendent principles are "always already" infected through and through by our previous socialization into our own thick, local or parochial world views. Thin principles of justice are, then, simply biased abstractions. They are not and can not be impartially based, because they "always already" presuppose a thick "taken-for-granted background" that reflects the stereotypes of any privileged group that has historically controlled the evolution of legal norms and political policies. As an alternative to failed attempts to universalize a conception of justice, Walzer (1994) argues that we must always respect those thick, local, culturally rich, tribal conceptions of justice that are embedded in particular ways of life. This means we need only adopt one thin universal principle, that of tribal "self-determination" (p. 67).

Legitimate skepticism about transcendent universals is often allied with another criticism that is quite alarming. Some postmodern critics claim that the attempt to find universal justifications for policies reifies abstract ideals in such a way as to contribute to oppression. For instance, some feminists argue that Enlightenment fictions are part of a sexist world view driven by "fantasies of omnipotence" (Bordo, 1992, p. 162) and androcentric needs for "unity and control" (Young, 1990, p. 94) which lead to "totalizing", "homogenizing", "reductionist" programs that distort the reality of humanity's "embodied", "heterogeneous" existence (Young, 1990, p. 107f). As an alternative to using totalizing, universalist fictions, these critics recommend the adoption of a postmodern particularist story that explicitly rejects universal assumptions and acknowledges the relativity of all interpretations of reality. In a strong statement of this kind of thesis, Dancy (1992) points out that particularists understand that "... there is no room for [universal] moral principles, and that it is bad faith to try to make moral decisions by appeal to them" (pp. 462-63). Walzer (1994) adds that even if the impulse to promote a universal vision is well intended it should be resisted.

> ...sometimes, watching the tribal wars, some of us may yearn for the uniform repressiveness of imperial or even totalitarian rule. For wasn't this repression undertaken in the name, at least, of universalism—and, in the case of the communists, of a thick morality ambitiously intended to replace every sort of moral particularism (p. 81)?

History has shown us again and again that some of the fears of postmodern philosophers are legitimate. People consistently misapply the universal norms that emerge during the discourse of justification. Attempts to implement such abstract universals are especially vulnerable to a type of error in judgment referred to as the "standard person problem" (Narayan, 1992). This term draws attention to those occasions when some group assumes that its beliefs can accurately serve as a universal standard for judging everyone's experience just because historically the group's beliefs have always worked well for that particular group. We are all vulnerable to this tendency, since it is natural for people to use their own experiences as a standard when making judgments, whether it be male, female, black, white, and so forth. Thus, whenever some group has power over others and is immune to outside criticism, the powerful group will make rules for those others based on the biased assumption that the powerful group's point of view ought to serve as a standard for judging interests in general. This is a natural legacy of our ethnocentric or tribal heritage. Postmodern critics may be right, then, when they complain that all legal systems, even those which strive for universal impartiality, will inevitably become infected with the myopic point of view of privileged classes (not to mention that favoring impartiality may itself be a bias in favor of a liberal group's way of life). In short, we can expect even the most well meaning of practical interventions by privileged powerful groups to be tainted by the special history of the groups.

Problems with Particularism

The postmodern particularist solution to this problem has serious difficulties of its own. In the first place, both Habermas (1987) and Bernstein (1986) argue that many of the postmodern criticisms of attempts to make rational sense of universal values focus almost exclusively on a narrow interpretation of instrumental reason. MacIntyre (1981) points out that contemporary critics of the Enlightenment's attempt to discover rationally based universal values share assumptions about reason that are in tune with those Enlightenment theologians who denied that reason could ever give us access to ends. They believed that "Reason is calculative, it can assess truths of fact and mathematical relations but nothing more. In the realm of practice it can speak only of means. About ends it must be silent" (McIntyre, 1981, p. 52). This narrow conception of reason, however, is hardly compatible with the ethical agenda of impartiality that aims to transcend ethnocentric points of view. Since the use of reason in ethics is not supposed to be in the service of any local political agenda, in conception at least, at the level of justificatory discourse everyone must participate in an on going struggle against the ideological uses of reason (thus Rawls'emphasis on the veil of ignorance). This means reason should not be equated with the positivistic conception of instrumental reason which "always already" serves background agendas (sometimes acknowledged, sometimes not.) Gunther (1993, pp. 137-154) argues that many of the postmodern criticisms of universal reason do not work as criticisms of the impartial justification of universal values. They work better as complaints about the lack of a well developed application discourse that can tell people how to impartially apply universal norms.

Furthermore, we should not allow the quite legitimate doubts about metaphysical foundationalism in epistemology to precipitate an unnecessarily hasty anti-universalist movement in ethics, or else we will cut off our moral feet, leaving those of us who are opposed to oppression with no place to stand. It is true that all people begin embedded in "thick" cultural contexts, so we all have values unconsciously introjected into us during our socialization. We should not, however, automatically assume that all values that have been introjected into people should be given equal moral weight, as though they are all equally benign ethical values. For those interested in fighting oppression in all of its varieties, an unqualified acceptance of all positions is self-defeating, since it leads directly to what Louise Antony (1993) calls the "bias paradox" (p. 190).

Antony argues that if the postmodern positions are going to assert that all claims are equally biased, then any criticism of oppression is just another bias even though critics (including postmodern ones) want to be taken more seriously than those they criticize. In a similar vein, Huntington (1995) argues that poststructuralist feminism is "...stuck in the awkward position of being unable to differentiate naive from critical consciousness while nonetheless presupposing its own authenticity as contrasted with other positions" (p. 49). If there is nothing that is not an arbitrary interpretation against which to judge, then all choices among competing interpretations become arbitrary (Hiley, Bohman, Shusterman, 1991, p. 8). Particularism makes liberation itself just one more arbitrary option sitting side by side with the arbitrary option of oppression. In the end, then, the logic behind the postmodern criticism of the Enlightenment's attempt to find a universal ethic, implies that the postmodern criticism is itself based on arbitrary assumptions. This leaves us with no place to turn in the attempt to liberate ourselves and others from oppression. If those who are oppressed are to have any basis for distinguishing normal forms of cultural bias from the pernicious forms that oppress, they need more than descriptions of how context affects belief, they also need to make normative distinctions between types of contexts.

Many of those involved in the fights against oppression are also rightly uneasy about the underlying passivity in some particularist accounts of political consciousness. Huntington (1995) warns that we must not reduce attempts to achieve liberation "... to a form of stoic awareness" (p. 43). As Wilkins (1992) says when discussing the My Lai massacre, we have to "... consider the possibility that in some circumstances to be weak or convention-bound just is to be evil, or if this is contested, it is at least a way of allowing evil to occur" (p. 96). Characterizing group members as passive products challenges the very idea that people might choose to develop personally transcendent capacities on purpose in order to emancipate themselves from oppressive forms of socialization. Wilkins (1992) points out that "... the methodological individualist would insist that it is an individual's assessment of the logic of the situation in which he finds himself, his own determination of the options which are open to him, not the circumstances themselves, which are in the final analysis decisive" (p. 92). Because particularism tends to portray people as essentially passive recipients of the world view introjected into them by their language community, Huntington says postmodern philosophy needs to find a way to make sense of a postconventional consciousness that emerges from a sense of

> ...critical awakening as opposed to being tied necessarily into the existing symbolic (p. 47)... . [We need] a normative ideal of autonomy that is neither stoic (acquiescent before oppressive signifying practices) nor transcendent (in the sense of pre-linguistic) (pp. 43-44).

Why is it so important to seek a transcendent, self-critical, postconventional perspective? For one thing, in the 21st century the homogeneous nation state will become a thing of the past. Increasing value and cultural pluralism is the future. Since ethnic cleansing is unacceptable as a way of dealing with advancing pluralism, people everywhere are going to have to find more ethical ways to accommodate those who are different from them, both internationally and within the territorial boundaries of their own state. As Habermas (1997) says, "What generally seems to be necessary is the development of capacities for political action on a level above and between nation states" (p. 122).

Errors at the Level of Application

It is not enough, however, simply to hand people a list of justified principles. We also need a virtue ethics that will emphasize the importance of developing those emancipatory capacities that are so essential for practical wisdom in this complex, multicultural world. As mentioned above, it is difficult to understand the difference between justification discourses (which aim to give legitimacy to background ideals other things being equal) and application discourses (which aim to rationally apply the ideals in local contexts all things considered). When people lack the capacity to keep these two related but distinct activities logically separated, then errors in judgment can occur that will lead to the kind of oppression in the name of universal values that worries the postmodern critics. For instance, those who primarily use bureaucratic instrumental reasoning to make ethical decisions will not understand how to apply abstract ethical principles with appropriate sensitivity to local contexts. Because they tend to assume that justification discourse and application discourse are the same, they distort the purpose of valid universal values by favoring their own local perspective during application. Sometimes attempts to apply universal values can be so clumsy as to contribute to gross evil. As Wilkins (1992) points out with regard to the My Lai Massacre, "... all the evidence suggests, that Lt. Calley was an ordinary man, is he then simply an example of what has been called 'the ordinariness of evil'?" (p. 99).

Hannah Arendt (1963) was especially concerned with this kind of phenomenon. She invented the concept of the "banality of evil" (p. 287f) to give meaning to her strange experience of watching the Nazi officer Eichmann defend himself against the charge that he committed crimes against humanity during WWII. In an ultimate absurdity, Eichmann claimed that as a good Kantian, he lived by universal ideals and performed his duty for duty's sake regardless of consequences. According to his interpretation of Kantian ideals, he impartially applied the law to all persons equally without making local exceptions. What should we make of this? Was his participation in the Holocaust caused by overly principled universalist thinking? When bureaucrats adopt Eichmann's approach, universals are treated like concrete rules needing no interpretation. "A universalist ethics then appears as an abstract, obstinate rigorism blind to facts and of service to immoral intentions at any moment" (Gunther 1993, p. 6). But universal principles are not concrete maxims for action, they need to be impartially applied in context sensitive ways with due regard to the ideals contained in the universal principles. I think it is much more accurate to attribute blame in Eichmann's situation to a lack of universalistic thinking. Governed as he was by his personal ambitions and duties of station, he could not see beyond his own local context. Although he mouthed a commitment to universal ideals at his trial, in practice Eichmann was content to focus narrowly on the level of his own bureaucratic role. Since the bureaucracy he served was organized for evil, he himself was able to serve evil while thinking of himself in idealistic terms.

When we fail to distinguish between levels of abstraction or notice that universal moral duties are logically different from the local duties that attach to our legal stations, then we can become so hopelessly muddled as to distort the application of ideal principles. Finding fault with bureaucratic thinking is not about claiming that people who use it intentionally lie or attempt to deceive others. Instead, the moral drawbacks of this form of judgment refer "... more to a lack of care in considering the relevant facts, to an absence of sensitivity to the particular circumstances, and to an insufficient aptitude for choosing the appropriate course of action in view of the particular situation" (Gunther 1993, p. 4). Habermas (1991) argues that inability to understand these important conceptual distinctions results in harmful "deficiencies" in moral thinking which can lead to the kind of oppression in the name of universal values that worry the postmodern critics.

> I speak of *moral rigorism*, one such deficiency, when hermeneutic sensitivity to the problem of application is lacking and when abstract moral insights are mechanically applied to concrete situations... Max Weber's dichotomy between an ethics of conviction and an ethics of responsibility is based largely on this popular critique of Kant. I speak of *intellectualization*, another such deficiency, when moral abstractions serve as defenses. Gilligan tends to misconstrue these deficiencies as characteristic of a normal state of postconventional formalism (p. 180).

In his critique of Gilligan's (1982) work, Habermas emphasizes that we should not confuse moral motivation to do the right thing with the possession of the ethical skills (virtues) needed for practical wisdom. One can be motivated by moral duty, but still be deficient in the virtues needed to intelligently apply universal ethical norms in pluralistic environments. Gunther (1993) argues that even when

> ...action is based on a justified norm [it] is not enough because no norm can regulate all the cases of its own application (p. 2) ... we know in most action situations which assertions of fact are true and which action norms... [are] valid, and yet often enough act 'immorally' because we... overlook or incorrectly appraise certain aspects of the situation; or we underestimate the importance of particular precepts or prohibitions (worthy of recognition) in relation to the norms we then actually observe in the particular situation (p. 3).

Practical wisdom (phronesis) in the modern world, requires that agents become much more sophisticated than was necessary in the city state of the ancient Greek world, with its relatively stable, background vision of a good life. One strategy that helps is to distinguish clearly between the ethical choice of lifestyle (or the good life) and the moral choice of rights in matters of justice. The choice of the good life involves issues of personal identity formation which are more a matter of esthetic or clinical judgment than a matter of achieving justice between groups. Because the contingencies of lifestyle choice are personal, they are not amenable to universalization. Thus, Habermas follows Kant and restricts universal ethics to considerations of justice and human rights. This means questions about justice must first be resolved to everyone's good-liking, then all further ethical concerns about which life style to choose can be solved at the local level.

Because justice concerns universal norms, justice can not be reduced to a simple matter of obedience to law. As Wilkins (1994) points out, even though there is a *prima facie* general obligation to obey the law, individuals are still not relieved of the burden of evaluating specific cases of legal compliance. States may be just without being perfectly just. "Thus, there may not be an actual moral obligation to obey a specific law provided it can be shown that disobeying the law in question will not harm the state, or provided it can be shown that disobeying the law may succeed in making it a more just state, as, for example, in cases where civil disobedience may be justified" (p. 94). These kinds of distinctions help, but they can not eliminate the application difficulties. The modern world is so complex that even if we agree on general principles of justice, good people can still find themselves unprepared for many of the moral contingencies that can arise at the level of application.

> The realization that we can never know all the relevant aspects of a situation because we would never have sufficient time to consider all the aspects—this insight confronts us with a structural indeterminacy of application situations; because of this indeterminacy there remains only the alternative of once again attempting a rationalization of the application problem from the perspective of morally acting persons, or of completely changing the perspective and of no longer tackling the problem within the conceptual framework of moral action (Gunther 1993, p. 7).

Since the second choice of abandoning "the conceptual framework of moral action" will leave us ethically stranded, we need to choose the first option and create a new discourse of application that can facilitate the development of the right kind of practical wisdom. Because it is never easy to implement abstract universal norms, Habermas argues that all universal theories must confront the problems of application that concern the postmodern philosophers. He (1991) points out that since "moral norms do not contain their own rules of application," we need more than universal principles and motivation, we also need "contextual sensitivity" and "hermeneutic prudence at the level of application" (pp. 179-182). Thus, all universal theories need clearly worded "principles of appropriateness" to help moral agents figure out how to apply fundamental, universal norms in particular situations.

Discourse Ethics

Because mistakes at the level of application are too common and too often tragic, Habermas (1991) tries to reconstruct universal ethics so as to direct additional attention at the level of "justification" to the inevitable problems that will arise at the level of "application." He says that the point of a postmodern universal philosophy should be to show how it is possible to "… create some legitimate commonality among different forms of life, with 'legitimate' here carrying the sense of reciprocity and mutual respect" (Cited in S. White, 1988, p. 154). One approach that seems promising is to build on the universal norms that structure the logic of honest discourse. In his theory of discourse ethics, Habermas argues that all people have to learn the norms of language that make human communicative discourse possible or they will not be able to adapt to social life. Thus, every competent language user already shares a tacit, procedural understanding of the same norms, i.e., those that make all instances of honest communication possible. In other words, because serious discourse requires honest speech between members of a speech community, both the speaker and the hearer have learned to share the same legitimate, universal, normative expectations. Habermas argues that Kant was essentially right about humanity's moral nature. People not only do not want to be lied to and thus treated as a means only, but they also expect to be shown the kind of respect found in honest discourse. Honest communication acknowledges that people are autonomous participants in a language community, and this means that they are essentially social beings who, as ends unto themselves, expect to be treated in ways that are consistent with their informed consent.

Charlatans and confidence men are well aware of this logic, that is why they can work their tricks. They pretend to honor the valid expectation that public language will be used in ways that respect our nature as autonomous participants in honest discourse, and then they intentionally violate this kind of universal expectation by deceiving people into making agreements they would never have chosen under conditions of honest discourse. As Habermas (1991) says, the lie fills us with moral indignation, because it is a "… violation of an underlying *normative expectation* that is valid not only for ego and alter but also for all members of a social group or even, in the case of moral norms in the strict sense, for all competent actors" (p. 48).

People everywhere take these universal expectations for granted within their own cultural group. The problem to be overcome in application discourse is to find a way to make these universal norms come alive in communication across group lines. That is, given that we are individually embedded in particular historical circumstances, is it possible to impartially apply the universalizable, abstract, moral respect behind the ideal of honest discourse in ways that will help us continue to show such respect even when we confront differences during conflicts? Habermas (1991) believes that if the universal norms presupposed by actual, honest, practical discourse are explicitly emphasized in our foundational principles, then moral agents will be less likely to participate in the common abuses at the level of application that have caused such dismay in postmodern critics. He begins his theory with a "rule of argumentation" from "the logic of practical discourse" (p. 93) which specifies the conditions a norm must meet before it can be called a universal norm.

> *All* affected can *freely* accept the consequences and the side effects that the *general* observance of a controversial norm can be anticipated to have for the satisfaction of the interests of *each individual* (p. 93) (and these consequences are preferred to those of known alternative possibilities for regulation) (p. 65).

This valid universal rule of argumentation shows respect for all people, since it does not require them to stop being who they were socially constructed to be (unless of course, their construction has lead them into ways of life that are inconsistent with justice, i.e., the right of other people to live according to their own social construction and ethical choices). As a formal rule it does not prejudge the substantive regulations of any particular way of life. It is, however, not compatible with choosing an unjust way of life, since it implies that legal forms which are inconsistent with everyone's practical participation are illegitimate. The moral "ought" which emerges from this universal rule of argumentation protects the right of all affected parties to be actual participants in substantive decision making. Because substantive legal and moral principles are all chosen at the application level, we need to ensure that the actual choice of such substantive content will "... depend on real discourses (or advocatory discourses conducted as substitutes for them)" (p. 94). The foundational "moral" principle of discourse ethics, then, states that:

> Only those norms can claim to be valid that meet (or could meet) with the approval of all affected in their capacity as participants in a practical discourse (pp. 66, 93, 197).

At the level of application, affected parties must actually participate in real discourses whenever issues of justice are involved. The most fundamental practical need is to find a way to make shared power and real interactive dialogue between different people a practical reality. After all, "...nothing better prevents others from perspectivally distorting one's own interests than actual participation" (Habermas, 1991, p. 67). Since universal, impartially based theories of morality all presuppose informed consent, perhaps a *prima facie* right to actual participation should be added to the universal background ideals of all theories as the first of many principles of appropriateness to guide application discourse during subsequent discussions at more substantive levels. As Habermas (1993) says: "In discourses of application, the principle of appropriateness takes on the role played by the principle of universalization in justificatory discourses. Only the two principles taken together exhaust the idea of impartiality" (p. 37).

Normative Conclusions about Applied Ethics

John Rawls is also well aware of the concerns of postmodern critics. In his (1993) text *Political Liberalism,* he explicitly addresses the issue of cultural diversity by acknowledging that a heterogeneous population with a plurality of points of view is a permanent and desirable condition of democracy. Indeed, by their nature truly democratic institutions will promote a plurality of points of view by protecting the rights of minorities to political and social space. For instance, the right to be different is already protected in the U.S. Constitution, since the constitutional guarantee of freedom of religion recognizes that there will be different forms of life within civil society. Rawls argues that extended real discourses between people who are living under various reasonable, comprehensive doctrines (which contain the "thick" principles that Walzer argues regulate how members ought to live their life) should lead to an overlapping consensus on a political conception of justice that will protect their freedom to be different from each other. Rawls believes that liberty, equal opportunity, and concern for equality in the distribution of primary social goods are the types of "transcendent" principles that would emerge from attempts to reach an overlapping consensus between people with different comprehensive doctrines.

While Wilkins (1992, p. 6) says he approves of Rawls' universalist approach to issues of justification, none the less, [like Habermas] he would like to move Rawls' liberal theory toward an even sharper focus on the practical problem of how to protect diversity. As we have seen, Habermas argues that background moral equality at the level of justificatory discourse implies that at the level of application, other things being equal, all affected groups ought to be represented in practical deliberations at all levels of consideration. Likewise, in his most recent ethical work, Wilkins (1997) argues that Rawls needs to go further and explicitly protect religious diversity with a third principle of justice that would emphasize the need to protect the right of all people to participate in application discourse. I will end this long introduction to applied ethics with a brief survey of the friendly dialogue Wilkins has had with Rawls' theory that has lead him to his latest recommendation.

In "Principles for Individual Actions," Wilkins (1984) argued that Rawls was right to admit that his theory of justice was incomplete insofar as it "... does not extend to the choice of principles for actions by individuals" (p. 299). Wilkins believes that Rawls was wrong, however, to assume that such principles were beyond the scope of his social contract theory. Wilkins argues that the social contract impartiality procedures which lead to the two principles of justice could be applied also at the level of individual action to help us formulate lexically ordered principles for individuals.

> ...once we understand the full significance of why questions concerning the basic structure of society should take precedence over questions concerning principles for individual actions we will be in a position to see that Rawls' basic strategy for settling the priority issue concerning the two principles of justice will be applicable where principles of individual action are concerned, and that the results in the two cases will be harmonious (p. 300).

These considerations entail that rational contractees would chose to arrange principles for individual actions in the following order. First, natural duties of justice would be lexically prior to the obligations that emerge from promises and duties of station, and then these kinds of "... obligations should in turn be ranked above principles of supererogatory actions" (p. 303). Wilkins believes this ordering should be acceptable to Rawls' himself, given what he has said about principles for individual actions.

This concern about adjusting Rawls' theory so as to make it more useful at all levels of application emerged again in 1997. In "A Third Principle of Justice," Wilkins argued that despite Rawls' emphasis on achieving an overlapping consensus between people living under different but reasonable comprehensive doctrines, Rawls needs to supplement his two principles of general justice with a third principle that is explicitly designed to protect the right of minority groups to follow their own religious visions. In the original position from behind the veil of ignorance, contractees would know about the history of application difficulties. They would have practical concerns about protecting their specific heritage (whatever it might be) from those people with power who will inevitably be inclined to impose standardized solutions on others who are different. They would also worry that a liberal society that emphasizes neutrality would itself pose a threat to some reasonable comprehensive doctrines. Even "... laws 'neutral' toward religion may burden the free exercise of religious beliefs as surely as laws intended to interfere with free exercise" (Wilkins, 1997, p. 16).

> the problem for a theory of justice is how to protect religious communities not from all the slings and arrows of fortune but from those slings and arrows directly resulting from the policies of a secular state, which in principle seeks to be neutral among competing comprehensive doctrines, at least among the doctrines that are part of what Rawls calls 'reasonable pluralism.' How to be neutral without being inhibiting? (p. 15).

To guard against the standard person problem, the impact of liberal neutrality, and the tendency for bureaucrats to distort the intent of universal values, contractees would choose a principle specifically designed to protect those reasonable, cherished differences that make up each group's unique identity. According to Wilkins, Congress has already recognized the need for this kind of adjustment by passing the "Religious Freedom Restoration Act" of 1993 (Public Law 103-141). Because they were concerned about "... the impact of so-called neutral laws of general applicability upon the exercise of religious freedom" (p. 17), they mandated that "... the government should not substantially burden a person's exercise of religion even if the burden results from a rule of 'general applicability' unless it can demonstrate that the application of the burden is in furtherance of a compelling state interest" (p. 16-17). This is contrary to the spirit of Justice Scalia's opinion as expressed in *Oregon Employment Services Division v. Smith.* In effect, Scalia ruled that if we use the "compelling state interest" criteria to protect religious freedom, then we will usher in "a parade of horribles." Scalia is worried that "... anarchy would prevail if, for every state regulation that might have a negative impact upon some religion, the state be required to justify such regulation by appeal to some compelling state interest" (Cited in Wilkins, 1997, p. 18). In response to Scalia's concern, Wilkins says "Perhaps Scalia questions whether the pluralism in our society is after all reasonable in Rawls' sense" (p. 18). He contrasts Justice Scalia's approach with that of Justice O'Connor, who shows much more sensitivity to the need to protect diversity. She " argued in effect that such a [compelling state interest] justification was necessary if we were to be properly sensitive to the free exercise of religious conduct guaranteed by the Constitution" (Wilkins, 1997, pp. 18-19). He thinks her interpretation of the constitution sends the proper message to legislators, since it is in tune with a "Rawlsian—Dworkinian" (p. 19) approach that claims "... principle must prevail over policy even if this places a considerable burden upon the efficiency of government" (p. 18-19). In short, if we are to protect religious diversity, then the burden of proof should be on those who favor policies that impact on religious communities to show that the impact does not harm religious ceremonies and the requirements of a group's faith (p. 20). At the level of application, then, we must treat the claim of a religious community that it is being harmed as "... presumptively correct barring overwhelming evidence to the contrary" (p. 19).

So, what kind of substantive protection do we need? To give religious communities veto power over legislation is too strong, but it is too weak to merely grant them the right to be consulted before decisions are made (p. 20). We need to find an appropriate middle ground. Because this issue would be so important to contractees, they would want to start the protection at the level of justification discourse. That is, protection must be seen to be more than a policy decision at the level of application, or else some future legislative body might think it is legitimate to weaken the protection of religious freedom as a trade off for some other more popular local agenda. To emphasize the importance of this fundamental right, contractees would want a third principle at the level of justification that would serve as a background ideal to regulate all future moves legislative bodies might make at the level of application. Protection at this level would look something like the following principle:

> A constitutional regime, acting in accordance with the protection of the basic rights and liberties and equality of opportunity, shall insofar as possible avoid adopting rules with harmful effects upon those comprehensive doctrines which satisfy the conditions of reasonable pluralism. Such rules would include those which (a) may be directed against specific comprehensive doctrines or (b) may be of general applicability but which may result in unintended but foreseeable harms against some comprehensive doctrine(s). Any 'neutral' rule which substantially burdens comprehensive doctrine(s) can be justified only if it furthers a compelling state interest (Wilkins, 1997, p. 23).

I think a principle of this kind is appropriate, since we can expect many people with power to share Justice Scalia's fear of diversity. When people can only see diversity as a problem, they are apt to be inclined to marginalize those who are different in order to protect the version of the "neutral" status quo which feels most familiar to them. Even though social order could also be achieved by protecting the right of people to be reasonably different, their first impulse will be to protect social order by voting to impose constraints on those others who are different, even if the constraints may be considered quite oppressive by the group being constrained (This kind of standard person approach to diversity would also inevitably lead to the corruption of application discourse even though it is supposed to be guided by the ideal of impartiality).

As Wilkins' discussion about the need for a third principle of justice indicates, the most compelling issue in applied ethics for the foreseeable future may well be how to give adequate support to those reasonable groups who live in ways that appear deviant to the majority of conventional citizens in democratic states. Given that each new decade ushers in a new wave of ethnocentricism, a just society needs to provide constitutional protection against the possibility that those with a conventional mind set might use political power to try and oppress others who live under reasonable comprehensive doctrines with which they disagree. This means that constitutional protection at the level of application must be reinforced by background principles that emerge at the level of justification.

The major theories we have reviewed seem to agree on a general strategy for the impartial application of the ideal of moral equality. Actual participation in decision making by all affected parties ought to be provided at all levels, even if it interferes with the efficiency of policies designed to promote other agendas. This will not be easy, and as Habermas (1997) says, it may require the majority to give up its historical prerogative to always set the political agenda (p. 117) in order to protect the participation of minority communities. This sentiment is echoed by Wilkins (1994) when he says he hopes that majorities in democratic cultures will feel secure enough in their liberties that they will allow members of minority collectives "... a certain amount of slack" (p. 95-96) in terms of legal compliance with those laws the collectives find troubling to their conscience, for instance, in a situation where a religious group feels that it can not in good conscience take a loyalty oath, but is "... in other respects willing to obey the laws of the state" (p. 96). Diversity of reasonable comprehensive doctrines would not be a problem, if people would develop the transcendent postconventional forms of consciousness that help us accommodate diversity. Personally, although I am not complacent on this issue, I do take some comfort from the fact that philosophers with the stature of Habermas, Rawls, and Wilkins are working on solutions to the types of problems that arise at the level of application discourse.

Notes

1 Metaethics focuses on the logical or analytical study of the meaning of ethical terms, thus it does not of necessity lead to ethical prescriptions about what we ought to do and should not be confused with normative ethics which does prescribe behavior. For instance, much of this paper is primarily a metaethical study, since it is about the meaning of applied ethics. I will, however, make some normative recommendations about how we "ought" to solve practical conflicts toward the end of this paper.

2 This term comes from Kohlberg's (1973) developmental theory. People naturally "decenter" in ethics as they develop more sophisticated orientations. First they move from a preconventional egocentric level of understanding to an ethnocentric conventional level. When people experience social conflict in a pluralistic environment, then they also may develop a postconventional universal, theoretical orientation that builds on and then transcends the ethnocentric loyalties that developed at the conventional level.

3 The summary of Lincoln's dilemma and all quotations are cited in S. B. Oates (1997).

4 The following two sections are adapted from Cooper (1997).

Bibliography

Antony, Louise, M., "Quine as Feminist: The Radical Import of Naturalized Epistemology," *A Mind of One's Own*, ed. Louise M. Antony and Charlotte Witt (Boulder: Westview Press, 1993).

Arendt, Hannah, *Eichmann in Jerusalem, A Report on the Banality of Evil* (New York: Penguin Books, 1963), p. 287f.

Ayer, A. J., *Language, Truth and Logic* (New York: Dover Publications, 1952).

Bernstein, Richard, "The Rage Against Reason," *Philosophy and Literature*, No. 2, Oct. 86, pp. 186-210.

Bordo, Susan, "Review Essay: Postmodern Subjects, Postmodern Bodies," *Feminist Studies* 18, No. 1, Spring, 1992, p. 162.

Cooper, David E., "Citizenship and Postconventional Consciousness," W. Krawietz, E. Pattaro, A. Erh-Soon Tay, ed., *Rule of Law: Political and Legal Systems in Transition* (Berlin: Duncker & Humblot, 1997).

Dancy, Jonathan, "Caring about Justice,"s *Philosophy* 67, 1992, pp. 462-463.

Dworkin, Ronald, "Lord Devlin and the Enforcement of Morals," in Richard Wasserstrom, ed., *Morality and the Law* (Belmont, CA: Wadsworth Publishing Co. Inc., 1971).

Farrell, John, "Translator's Introduction," in Gunther, Klaus, *The Sense of Appropriateness: Application Discourses in Morality and Law*, Trans. by John Farrell (Albany: State University of New York Press, 1993).

Flax, Jane, *Thinking Fragments: Psychoanalysis, Feminism, and Postmodernism in the Contemporary West* (Berkeley, CA: University of California Press, 1990).

Gilligan, Carol, *In a Different Voice* (Cambridge, MA: Harvard University Press, 1982).

Gunther, Klaus, *The Sense of Appropriateness: Application Discourses in Morality and Law*, Trans. by John Farrell (Albany: State University of New York Press, 1993).

Habermas, Jurgen, *Justification and Application: Remarks on Discourse Ethics*, Trans. by Ciaran P. Cronin (Cambridge, MA: MIT Press, 1993).

———. *Moral Consciousness and Communicative Action,* Trans. by Christian Lenhardt and Shierry Weber Nicholsen (Cambridge, MA: The MIT Press, 1991).

———. "The European Nation State—Its Achievements and Its Limitations. On the Past and Future of Sovereignty and Citizenship," ed., W. Krawietz, E. Pattaro, A. Erh-Soon Tay, *Rule of Law: Political and Legal Systems in Transition* (Berlin: Duncker & Humblot, 1997).

———. *The Philosophical Discourse of Modernity*, Trans. by F. G. Lawrence (Cambridge, Mass., 1987) p. 314f.

———. *The Theory Of Communicative Action, Vol 1,* Trans. Thomas McCarthy (Boston: Beacon Press, 1984).

Hiley, David, R., Bohman, James, R., and Shusterman, Richard, ed., *The Interpretive Turn* (Ithaca, N.Y., Cornell University Press, 1991).

Hope, Vincent, "Smith's Demigod," *Philosophers of the Scottish Enlightenment* in V. Hope, ed., (Edinburgh: University Press, 1984).

Huntington, Patricia, "Toward a Dialectical Concept of Autonomy," *Philosophy & Social Criticism* Vol 21, no 1, 1995, pp. 37-55.

Kohlberg, Lawrence, "From Is to Ought: How to Commit the Naturalistic Fallacy and Get Away With It in the Study of Moral Development," in T. Mischel, ed., *Cognitive Development and Epistemology* New York: Academic Press, 1971).

———. "The Claim to Moral Adequacy of a Highest Stage of Moral Judgment," *The Journal of Philosophy,* 70, No. 18, October 25, 1973, pp. 630-646.

MacIntyre, Alasdair, *After Virtue* (Notre Dame: University of Notre Dame Press, 1981).

———. *Whose Justice? Which Rationality?* (Notre Dame: University of Notre Dame Press, 1988)

McCarthy, Thomas, "Translator's Introduction," in Habermas, Jurgen, *The Theory Of Communicative Action,* Vol 1 (Boston: Beacon Press, 1984).

Narayan, Uma, "Non-Standard Vulnerabilities: The Legal Protection of 'Non-Standard' Vulnerabilities," AMINTAPHIL conference, Oct. 1992.

Oates, Stephen B., *With Malice Toward None: The Life of Abraham Lincoln* (New York: Harper & Row, 1977).

O'Neill, Onora, *Constructions of Reason: Explorations of Kant's Practical Philosophy* (Cambridge, MA: Cambridge University Press, 1989).

Rawls, John, *A Theory of Justice* (Cambridge, MA: Harvard University Press, 1971).

———. *Political Liberalism* (New York: Columbia University Press, 1993).

Walzer, Michael, *Thick and Thin: Moral Argument at Home and Abroad* (Notre Dame: University of Notre Dame Press, 1994).

White, Stephen, *The Recent Work of Jurgen Habermas* (Cambridge, Ma: Cambridge University Press, 1988).

Wilkins, Burleigh, "Concerning 'Motive' and 'Intention'," *Analysis,* Vol 31, March, 1971, pp. 139-142.

———. "Can Terrorism Be Justified?", *Assent/Dissent,* ed. J.White, (Dubuque, Iowa, 1984).

———. and Zelikovitz, Kelly M., "Principles for Individual Actions," *Philosophia,* Vol XIV, December 1984, pp. 299-319.

———. "Intention and Criminal Responsibility," *Journal of Applied Philosophy,* Vol II, 1985, pp 271-278.

———. "Terrorism and Consequentialism," *Journal of Value Inquiry,* Vol 21, 1987, pp. 141-151.

———. "Does the Fetus Have a Right to Life?," *Journal of Social Philosophy,* Vol XXIV, 1993, pp. 123-137.

———. "The Moral *Prima Facie,* Obligation to Obey the Law," *Journal of Social Philosophy,* Vol. 25, No. 2, Fall 1994, 92-96.

———. "A Third Principle of Justice," *The Journal of Ethics,* 1997, (accepted and forthcoming).

———. *Terrorism and Collective Responsibility* (New York: Routledge, Chapman and Hall Inc., 1992).

———. "The 'Is-Ought' Controversy," *Ethics,* Vol 88, No. 2, January, 1970, pp. 160-164.

Young, Iris, "Part Two: The Politics of Difference," *Throwing Like a Girl and Other Essays in Feminist Philosophy and Social Theory* (Bloomington: Indiana University Press, 1990).

Aleksandar Jokic

What is Wrong with Potentialism?

Back in 1991 while I was working on a paper dealing with fetal rights "Why Potentiality Cannot Matter," to my surprise, I discovered that my then dissertation supervisor Professor Burleigh Wilkins (and this is how I called him then) was working on his paper "Does the Fetus Have a Right to Life?." To my even greater surprise and concern, he was advocating a position exactly on the opposite spectrum from mine. Not that we had never disagreed before, but one can easily imagine how odd (and perhaps dangerous) things could get for a student about to graduate who happens to radically disagree with his mentor on whatever topic of interest. And I was so confident that I had it right! But there was nothing to fear when Burleigh was in question. In fact, we had many interesting discussions that helped both our endeavors, and I earned a honorable mention in his paper and he in mine. However, I was never quite able to persuade him that there was something wrong with his views. Let me try again.

Let us call Potentialism the view based on the so called strict potentiality criterion according to which the fetus can correctly be said to have rights because it is a potential adult human being. An obvious generalization of this criterion is that *all* entities with such potential are to be granted the status of right-holders. This prompted an argument, of the slippery slope variety, against potentialism. The argument states that the potentiality criterion leads straight to absurdity: if rights are to be extended back to fetuses in virtue of their potential, rights must by parity of reasoning be extended back also to ova and spermatozoa in virtue of their potential. It is common for Potentialists to think they can block this *reductio* by invoking the concept of identity. Jim Stone most explicitly employs this strategy.[1] The idea is that while the fetus is identical to the adult human being it will result in, if it develops normally, a sperm or an egg is not a potential adult human being, for the relation of identity cannot hold between either of them (nor, of course, both of them) and the adult human animal that will develop if pregnancy proceeds without problems from a zygote which would be brought into being *after* the sperm penetrates the egg.[2]

I find this strategy confusing in more ways than one. For example, it seems to suggest that (in the imagined circumstance) when I am in a laboratory where an attempt at artificial fertilization is about to take place, observing under the microscope the designated sperm and I utter "This is a potential human being," I fail to say something true. For "potentiality language" that could (in this case) generate true propositions, starts at the level after the sperm penetrates the egg, and they form a zygote. Maybe the suggestion is that I have uttered something obviously false, or perhaps that I have said something that cannot be evaluated in terms of the categories of truth and falsehood? However, this problem of interpretation does not concern me here. Instead I want to focus on the apparent suggestion that the idea of identity is to play an important role in the dispute, because the concept of identity is allegedly a constituent, or a part, of our concept of potentiality. The above strategy, namely, licenses as legitimate only that piece of potentiality discourse when the relation of identity would hold between the object of which some potential is attributed and the object which would come into being if the potential were to be actualized. In other words, Stone and others who adopt his strategy (including Wilkins in the end) must (and indeed do) say that the "is" in the statement,

(1) "In the case when the fetus will develop into an adult human being it *is* the resulting human being,"

is the "is" of identity. This is suggested by the manner in which fetal potential is expressed by these authors.

Stone's formulation is a typical example[3]:

(2) "If the fetus grows normally there will be an adult human animal that was once the fetus."[4]

The *close* connection between the assertion (1) and the statement (2), when seen as a way to explain what is meant by potentiality in this case, could strike one as obvious, although it may not be easy to capture in words what exactly it amounts to. But whatever the precise way of spelling it out, this way of looking at things seems to prescribe that the analysis of the concept of potentiality is to be carried out, in an important way, in terms of the concept of identity.[5] It is this suggestion that I want to challenge in what follows.

Those who see the "close connection" between (1) and (2) as a way to appreciate something true about our concept of potentiality are suggesting, I think, two things: (a) that the "is" in (1) is the "is" of identity, and (b) that (2) is a (correct) way of expressing the fact 'the fetus is a potential human being,' because it incorporates the idea of identity (identity between the fetus and the being it develops into, if it grows normally). The connection can be somewhat clarified if it is recognized that (b) appears to be a sufficient condition for (a). But, clearly it is not a necessary one, for (a) may be true even if the concept of identity in fact plays no role in the analysis, or our understanding of the concept of potentiality. Consequently, if (b) entails (a) then refuting (a) is sufficient to refute (b). It would appear, then, that the most effective way to rebut the above strategy would be to show that (a) is false. However, a direct attack on (a) is not the only option. Another way would be to show (or at least raise some doubt) that the concept of potentiality is not to be analyzed in terms of the concept of identity, i.e., by attacking (b). This latter line of argument is open to us because a response to the reductio argument, such as Stone's, which appeals to the idea that the adult is identical to the fetus from which it developed can be a successful defense of the potentiality principle only if this idea is appropriately connected to our concept of potentiality. That is, in order to obtain a successful response it must be established that the fact expressed in (a) (that the adult is identical to the fetus from which it developed) is part of what is said when a potential to become an adult human is attributed to the fetus. That would be achieved if a conceptual link between potentiality and identity were established, i.e., if it were shown that (b) is true. There are, I think, good reasons to believe that this link might not hold.

The central issue, therefore, is the question of whether the correct analysis of the concept of potentiality must be carried out in terms of the concept of identity. So we now turn to this. First I proceed by offering, what I shall call, a 'partial analysis' of the concept of potentiality. It proves sufficient for our purpose. Next I explore the question of what would be the natural role for the concept of identity to play within this analysis. I propose an argument that there can be none. Finally, I consider two possible objections to my approach and show that although, according to one objection, it might be possible to accommodate the concept of identity in the analysis, this particular way of doing it could be of no use to the defender of the potentiality criterion. I also reject the other objection, and conclude that the above strategy fails.

What does it mean, then, to affirm that the fetus is a potential person, or, more generally, that some object *a* is potentially anything, say *H*? (The question is put in general terms for we want an answer that can go beyond this one case of predicating a potential to the fetus. Yet, although the answer to be proposed has this feature, our main concern here will be with the fetal case.) I conceive of potentiality in terms of possibility and quantification over future times. This is what I would call a 'partial analysis' of the concept of potentiality. Whatever a full analysis might reveal, the concept, I contend, involves these two elements. It seems obvious that potentiality involves possibility, since any potential state of affairs is also a possible state of affairs, but it is more than just possibility. It also involves the quantification over future times.[6] This is obvious enough from expressions such as (2), which is clearly future oriented.[7]

Thus we may try the following simple definition (which provides what I call a 'partial analysis') of what it is for an object *a* to be potentially *H*, i.e., '*Hp*' (which is to be read '... is potentially such and such') involving the possibility operator '◇', the future tense operator '**F**' (which simply reads 'it will be the case that'), and 'U' as a place holder for whatever is needed to upgrade the 'partial analysis' of the concept of potentiality to its full analysis[8]:

(D1) $\forall x \, \{Hpx \leftrightarrow \{\Diamond \mathbf{F} \, [(\exists y)\, (\boldsymbol{I}yx \,\&\, Hy)] \,\&\, \mathrm{U}x\}\}$

Now, our interest is to evaluate the contention that the concept of potentiality involves the concept of identity. To make things simpler we may dispense with 'U' since it does not seem to be a natural place for the concept of identity to come into play, and concentrate on the following conditional, which is in fact a necessary condition for an object *a* to be potentially *H*:

(NC) $Hpx \rightarrow \Diamond \mathbf{F} \, [(\exists y)\, (\boldsymbol{I}yx \,\&\, Hy)]$

In English we have:

(NC') An object is potentially *H* only if there might come to be an *H* that bears ***I*** (better, is identical) to it.

(NC) suggests a clear role for the concept of identity. Namely, isn't the place-holder relation symbol '***I***' most naturally interpreted as identity? In fact, if the supporters of the strict potentiality criterion are to be right, this relation *must* be that of identity. However, I will show that potentialists owe us an argument where they attempt none, and that they might be wrong after all. To see this, let us note that the following is a theorem of modal logic:

(T) $\Diamond \mathrm{P} \leftrightarrow [\mathrm{P} \leftrightarrow ({\sim}\mathrm{P} \,\&\, \Diamond \mathrm{P})]$

It is not difficult to see that the component formula $\ulcorner({\sim}\mathrm{P} \,\&\, \Diamond\mathrm{P})\urcorner$ expresses the notion of the *merely possible* ("P does not obtain [in the actual world], but it might have obtained" is exactly what mere possibility amounts to).

Let us pause for the moment to clarify this notion by giving an example of a merely possible object. I quote from Nathan Salmon:

> Everyone of us is among the elite group of Elect whose gametes did manage, against all odds, to unite in the normal manner and develop into a human individual. Let *S* be a particular male sperm cell of my father's and let *E* be a particular ovum of my mother's such that neither gamete ever unites with any other to develop into a human zygote. Let us name the (possible) individual who would have developed from the union of *S* and *E*, if *S* had fertilized *E* in the normal manner, 'Noman'.[9]

The assumption here is that there is a unique individual who would have resulted from the union of *S* and *E*, if *S* had fertilized *E* in the normal manner. We may call this the 'uniqueness requirement'. This assumption, it may be appropriate to note, does not require the idea of a quantifier that purports to quantify over merely possible individuals.[10]

Now that we are familiar with the notion of the merely possible, let us use a diamond with an 'm' inside '$\Diamond_m$' to represent this notion. Moreover, note that the concepts of possibility and mere possibility are interdefinable as follows:

(D2) $\Diamond_m \Phi =_{def} {\sim}\Phi \mathbin{\&} \Diamond\Phi$

(D3) $\Diamond\Phi =_{def} \Phi \leftrightarrow \Diamond_m\Phi$

Given the latter of these definitions we can rewrite T as follows:

(T*) $\Diamond \mathrm{P} \leftrightarrow (\mathrm{P} \leftrightarrow \Diamond_m \mathrm{P})$

And given T* our partial analysis (NC) of "*x* is potentially *H*" becomes:

(NC*) $Hpx \rightarrow \{\mathbf{F}\ [(\exists y)\ (\boldsymbol{I}yx \mathbin{\&} Hy)] \leftrightarrow \Diamond_m\mathbf{F}\ [(\exists y)\ (\boldsymbol{I}yx \mathbin{\&} Hy)]\}$

In English we have:

(NC*') Either there will be an object *y* such that *y* has *H* and bears the relation ***I*** to *x*, **or** this is merely possible, i.e. there will be no object *y* such that *y* is *H* and bears relation ***I*** to *x*, but there might have been such a future *y*.

This analysis gives us a concept of potentiality which is analyzed in terms of a disjunction. Ascribing to an object a potential of some sort, therefore, may be seen as ascribing a complex, disjunctive property to it. The two disjuncts have different ontological commitments: one disjunct, of an *Hp*-property predicated of some object *x*, purports to be about some object with the relevant property *H* which *will* exist in the actual world and is appropriately related to *x*, i.e. a *future object* which is ***I***-related to *x*, while the other disjunct purports to be about an object ***I***-related to *x* which is only *merely possible*, that is, it is merely possible that *x* will be *I*-related to a human—the future object *y* may actually exist but will not be *H* (or will not bear *I* to *x*). Hence, to have some property potentially is to have a disjunctive property, which is to be accounted for in terms of the two (expressions stating the) alternatives of the disjunction having a future object and a merely possible object (i.e., an object for which it is merely possible it would have requisite features) respectively as their semantically determined satisfiers. Hence, our concept of potentiality is such that concepts of a future object and a merely possible object come packaged in it. Does the concept of identity also have a role in the analysis of the concept of potentiality?

This, of course, is only a sketch of the analysis; a great deal more would have to be said to make it stand.[11] (In particular, it would have to be explained what it means for a phrase to purport to pick out a *nonexistent* entity.[12]) Yet as sketchy as it is, the proposal suggests an answer to our question. I will try to make this clear by using a two-part demonstration: I will first offer an argument that the place-holder relation symbol '***I***' *could not* be interpreted as 'identity'; then I will show that this argument proves too much to be a conclusive refutation of potentialism, but that, nevertheless, it indicates clearly where this doctrine fails. That is, even though I cannot establish that '***I***' couldn't possibly be identity, which would conclusively refute potentialism, it will turn out that proponents of the strict potentiality criterion have no recourse to show that '***I***' is identity, and in absence of an argument to this effect their position remains the victim of the *reductio* argument.

The first thing to note is that the relation ***I*** figures in both disjuncts. That is, put more precisely, '***I***' in both instances stands for the same relation, whatever it is. So a premise of the argument will be that ***I*** is the same relation in both disjuncts. Now, when the first disjunct obtains it is not fully implausible to think that the relation ***I*** is identity. Namely, if there will in fact exist an adult human being which will have developed from *this* fetus, then it is not clear, at least not without further argument, that the fetus is not identical to the individual that develops from it. (In my diagnosis, the apparent intuitiveness of this point is the very source of the strategy which attempts to salvage the potentiality criterion by appealing to identity.)

However, when we consider the case when the second disjunct obtains the assumption that the relation ***I*** is identity leads very close to a contradiction. To say that the second disjunct obtains is to say that there will be no adult human being which developed from *this* fetus, but that there might have been such a human being. Let us name this (unique) merely possible individual 'Nobe'. To take '***I***' in the second disjunct to be identity would be, in this case, to say (*de re*) of the fetus that it is identical to Nobe, and thus affirm a contradiction. For it is to affirm of an actual object (the fetus) that it is identical to an object which is *forever* merely possible, i.e. either never actualizes or if it does then it is not *H* (or does not bear ***I*** to the fetus). Consequently, given our premise, if the relation ***I*** cannot be interpreted as identity in the case when the second disjunct obtains it cannot be so interpreted in the context of the first disjunct either.

Now if this were a good argument it would prove too much. To see this consider the sentence 'Mary (a 20 year old athlete) is a potential (90 year old) geriatric.' Consider now the case when Mary dies in her youth. We could run the argument through, attempting to name the merely possible geriatric who Mary might have become: 'Nancy'. The above argument shows that Mary is not Nancy. But this is surely wrong. We can and do write stories *about* those who die young describing what might have become of them, and suitable referring phrases in those stories refer to the very people who did in fact die young. To deny that 'Nobe' names a fetus (when the fetus fails suitably to develop) might appear also to deny that a fetus can ever be identical with the adult human being it might have become (the opposite of what we have tentatively agreed to two paragraphs above). Of course, something must underwrite the identity of Nobe with the earlier fetus just as something underwrites the identity of Mary with Nancy. In the latter case, they are clearly the same human being. As Wiggins would put it, 'human being' here is a substance sortal, terms like 'geriatric' are presumably phase sortals—and some substances simply do not ever reach the stage where a given phase sortal applies. Presumably 'adult human being' is also a phase sortal; those who die as children were nonetheless human beings. Now some substance sortal like 'human being' must be offered to us by the defenders of the strict potentiality criterion as the kind term that underwrites the claim to identity of fetus and subsequent adult human being. They must give us (i) some kind term true of both fetus and adult, and (ii) furthermore the kind of thing in question must be such that it is a possible possessor of rights. This twin requirement is not going to be easily satisfied by potentialists. In particular, I am inclined to think that there is nothing available for potentialists to rely on in order to satisfy the requirement (ii).

Thus, to attack potentialism one would need to show that there is no common kind to which fetus and adult could both plausibly be said to belong, thus undermining the fatal parallel with the Mary/Nancy example. To produce an argument of this sort would be to refute potentialism conclusively. Rather than pursue this line of argument, I will simply point out that at this stage of our argumentative exchange the onus of proof is on the friends of the strict potentiality criterion. They need to produce an appropriate kind to which fetus and adult both belong, and to which it makes sense to attribute rights. 'Human being' and 'person' are not open to them, except on pain of begging the question. Potentialism's attractiveness comes precisely from the fact that it would enable us to bypass the vexing questions of whether fetus is a person or a human being. Potentialism claims that fetus has a right to life not because it is a person but because it is a *potential* person. To introduce the concept of person this late in the game would be to abandon potentialism and switch to a different position. The same goes for 'human being.' It is up to potentialists to tell us what other sortal could be used here in order to block the *reductio* argument. But, some less committing biological term, such as "organism" will not do either, for not all organisms are possible possessors of rights.[13]

One way to oppose the above argument is to challenge the premise that both occurrences of '***I***' in (NS*) depict the same relation. After all, was it not admitted as plausible to interpret '***I***' as identity in the context of the first disjunct? Why not say, then, that '***I***' stands for identity in the case of the first disjunct, while it obviously cannot be so interpreted in the case of the second? Certainly there are ways to argue against this proposal, but even if it is granted it does not serve the purpose of the defender of the potentiality criterion. For now the issue of fetal potential vanishes altogether. The outcome is that the fetus is to be seen as a right-holder, if at all, not *qua* potential adult human, but *qua* future individual. That is, we are given a reason to include the fetus among the sort of beings which can have rights when the first disjunct is true. But this fact has nothing to do with the property of the fetus that it is *potentially* an adult human being. We are simply told that the fetus which *will* develop into an adult human being has rights. And this may be entirely uncontroversial.[14] But the question, for the sake of which identity was invoked in the first place, of whether the fetus can be a rights-holder by virtue of its potential remains unanswered.

A different and more radical objection would come from the skeptics who take the position that an individual cannot be dubbed until it comes into existence. Thus examples about 'Noman' and 'Nobe' would have to be reinterpreted. But how? Perhaps, contrary to my way of presenting things, these were not cases of naming merely possible individuals. What are these names, then, names of? The only available answer is to say that they are names of actual objects. So my attempt to name a unique possible individual, which would have developed from *this* fetus had it been allowed to grow normally, using the name 'Nobe' resulted in (re)naming the fetus; and 'Noman' would be a name of, what else, the (actual) scattered object consisting of *E* and *S*. The result, therefore, is a suppression of all talk about future and merely possible individuals. But as Kaplan rightly pointed out "we often wish to speak *about* such unnameables ... through the use of 'denoting phrases' as Russell termed them."[15]

We may, therefore, conclude that until potentialists produce evidence that identity plays a role in the analysis of the concept of potentiality the *reductio* argument stands. The mistake here uncovered, then, is that the defenders of the strict potentiality criterion assume, without argument, that identity is a part of the concept of potentiality when in fact it might not be.

Notes

1. J. Stone, "Why Potentiality Matters," *Canadian Journal of Philosophy* 17 (1987).
2. *Ibid.*, p. 816.
3. *Ibid.*, p. 815.
4. I want to stress immediately that (2) does not strike me as a fully acceptable way of expressing the fact that the fetus is potentially an adult human being. For this purpose the counterfactual construction is more suitable:

   (3) If the fetus were to grow normally there would be an adult human animal that was once the fetus.

   (3) is better because it emphasizes the modal import of 'potential.' My analysis of the concept of potentiality, to be presented latter in this paper, will substantiate this claim. Our present concern, however, is with a particular response to the *reductio ad absurdum* argument against the potentiality criterion which employs (2) rather than (3). Consequently, in our reconstruction (and evaluation) of this response we must focus on (2).
5. As a special sort of identity (through time and possible worlds.
6. I argue in detail in favor of this way of conceiving of the concept of potentiality in my "Why Potentiality Cannot Matter," *Journal of Social Philosophy* Vol. 24, No. 3, Winter, 1993. *Cf.* note 11 below.
7. The counterfactual version listed as sentence (3) above in note 4 clearly illustrates both the temporal and the modal aspects of potentiality.
8. According to some proposals potentiality is to be analyzed in terms of a capacity, a power, or an ability on the part of the object of which some potential is predicated. (Cf. Wilkins, B. "Does the Fetus have the Right to Life," *Journal of Social Philosophy*,

V. 24, No. 1, Spring, 1993). Others want to analyze it in terms of probability. (CF. J.T. Noonan, "An Almost Absolute Value in History," in *The Morality of Abortion*, ed., Noonan; Cambridge, 1970.) These look like the sorts of candidates for the interpretation of U. These views indicate that potentiality involves something more than just possibility and quantification over future times. Since they might be right I included 'U' in definition (D1). However the argument of the present paper need not commit to any interpretation of U. This is why I refer to (D1) as the partial analysis of the concept of potentiality.

9. N. Salmon, "Existence" in J. Tomberlin, ed. *Philosophical Perspectives I: Metaphysics* (Atascadero, 1987) pp. 49-50.
10. For an argument to this effect see N. Salmon, *op. cit.* note 1, p. 98, and references listed there.
11. An attempt to do that is offered in my "Why Potentiality Cannot Matter" *Journal of Social Philosophy* V 24, No. 3, Winter 1993. There I have argued, in a less technical manner, that the analysis of the concept of potentiality has the consequence that whether a fetus will live to adulthood determines whether it has rights now. I defend an anti-potentialist position: that what we cannot say of the fetus we will be able to say he had as a fetus when he is an adult. In the present paper I want to substantiate this view further by pinpointing where exactly the mistake in potentialism is.
12. On this, and some alleged problems with the naming of future and merely possible individuals see Kaplan "Afterthoughts," in J. Almong, J. Perry and H. Wettstein (eds.) *Themes from Kaplan* (Oxford, 1989) pp. 605-10.
13. I should add here that in correspondence Timothy Williamson has suggested to me that "'potential adult human' is all the sortal one needs," however he is quick to add "but [this] is controversial."
14. In fact I argue that this is exactly what we should say about future individuals, that they are presently possible possessors of rights, in my "Ethics and Ontology: Present Rights of Future Individuals and Property Instantiation" *Journal of Philosophical Research* XXIV, 1999, pp. 473-486.
15. *Ibid.*, pp. 607-8.

MARGARET GILBERT

Considerations on Collective Guilt

'The problem of collective guilt... is surely one of the *murkiest* and *least explored* topics in moral philosophy'.[1]

Introduction

Recent history resonates with the names of groups in conflict. In the course of these conflicts atrocities of various kinds are often committed. If we are to avoid such events, or to keep them to a minimum, we need to explore the question of who or what is responsible for them.

In fact there are two relevant kinds of responsibility, causal and moral. I may be causally responsible for something, breaking a vase, say, without being morally responsible or blameworthy. My breaking the vase may have been an accident.

If I am morally responsible, then I am at least in part causally responsible. Several different agents may share the blame for something; each then played a role in bringing it about.

Sometimes a government issues an apology on behalf of a nation. It implies that the nation is blameworthy; that it is guilty of some improper action.

It is not only the leaders of *nations* who speak of collective guilt in the sense of collective moral responsibility.[2] The newspapers and everyday conversations are full of statements implying the guilt of one group or other. Thus one might read or hear, for instance, 'The union is to blame for the strike'; 'The department was wrong not to have given a farewell party for so-and-so'; 'Our family acknowledges its guilt in the matter'.

Though such statements and avowals are common in everyday life, philosophers and other theorists have expressed much skepticism over the idea of collective guilt.

Philosophical Skepticism about Collective Guilt

Philosophical skepticism about collective guilt can take one of two main forms. In order to explain what these are, I shall use a hypothetical example.

Imagine that a certain nation wages an aggressive war in which thousands of people are killed. I shall call this nation Badland. Now suppose someone claims that Badland is guilty of these deaths.

The Reductionist Critique

The first form of skepticism construes this as the claim that *every single citizen of Badland is personally guilty in relation to these deaths*.[3] It may immediately be observed that when the claim that Badland is guilty is so understood, it is unlikely to be *true*. For many citizens are likely to be morally blameless in relation to the wars their nations undertake. Some of its citizens may not know the war is taking place. Others may attempt to stop it, and so on. In spite of this, the claim that Badland is guilty *could* be true, on this construal. And it is perfectly intelligible.

The skepticism about collective guilt to which this construal gives rise may be couched as follows: If what we refer to as Badland's guilt is simply the personal guilt of each of Badland's citizens, then in an important sense there is no such thing as *collective* guilt. That is, there is no such thing as the guilt of *a group itself*, as opposed to the personal guilt of the group's members.[4]

I shall call the first form of skepticism about collective guilt *the reductionist critique*. This is because it stems from the thought that so-called collective guilt *reduces to*, or is simply a matter of, the personal guilt of a group's individual *members*.

The Anti-holist Critique

The other form of skepticism takes a different view of the claim that Badland is guilty of the war deaths. Rather than taking this as a claim about the personal guilt of all of Badland's citizens, it takes it at face value: to claim that Badland is guilty is precisely to claim that the *nation* is guilty, the nation as opposed to any or all particular citizens.

The argument then proceeds as follows. It is hard to see what it could be for a group to bear guilt, that is, a group itself *as opposed to any or all of its citizens.* After all, what *is* a group, over and above its individual members? What could it be for a *group* to act, as opposed to some or all of the groups' members acting? As the great sociologist Max Weber roundly stated, "there is no such thing as a collectivity which acts."[5]

On this view, to speak of collective guilt smacks of 'holism'. That is, it treats groups as if they were wholes or real units, as things that exist in their own right. To speak this way—it is argued—is philosophically suspect, if it is not simply unintelligible.

I shall call this form of skepticism *the anti-holist critique*. It takes collective guilt to require that groups are in some sense 'wholes' or real units, an implication that it finds doubtful at best.[6]

A Positive Approach to the Idea of Collective Guilt

I believe that both the reductionist and the anti-holist critique misrepresent collective guilt. To put it more carefully, I believe that there is a viable idea of collective guilt that does not reduce to the idea that all group members are personally guilty. Indeed, it has no implications with respect to the personal guilt of the group's members. It is holistic, but not, I believe, in an unacceptable way.

In order to argue this, I first ask what it is for an individual person to be morally responsible for doing something bad. I then argue that groups can be morally responsible in much the same way. Finally I consider the connection between personal and collective guilt. I should add the appropriate caution that much more can be said on all of these topics than I shall venture here.

Personal Moral Responsibility

When is an individual person morally responsible for something? Let us approach this question informally and intuitively.

Think of the times when you feel it is right to take the blame for something. Perhaps you agree that you can properly be blamed for ignoring your best friend Jane at the party you both went to last weekend. You knew a lot of people at the party and Jane didn't. She had asked you to introduce her to some people and you'd said you would. In the event you were having such a good time you decided to ignore her. Jane left early feeling that you had let her down.

What are the crucial features of this case? First of all, *you did something*, you (knowingly) ignored your friend. Second, *you knew it was wrong* to ignore her. Third, in ignoring your friend, *you acted freely*, at least in the sense that no one forced you to ignore her. Your uncoerced decision to ignore her is what led you to do so.

In this case, then, you freely did something you knew to be wrong. This seems to sum up the intuitive basis for saying that you are to blame for what you did, or are morally guilty in this matter.

The Moral Responsibility of Groups: Preliminaries

What, then, of groups? Can groups, as such, be morally responsible in the way individual people can? This seems to break down into the following three questions. First, can a group act, or do things? Second, can a group know that a certain act is wrong or immoral? Third, can a group act freely in the sense of being uncoerced?

First, then, *can* groups act, or do things? Well, we talk about groups doing things all the time. I spoke earlier of a nation, Badland, starting a war. Starting a war is surely an action. So is declaring war and invading another country's territory. Both are ways in which a country might start a war. We also talk about groups believing and knowing things. And we talk about them being coerced or uncoerced.

Philosophers and other theorists have, though, seen a problem here. They have questioned what these ways of talking amount to and whether they really make sense.

The problem is reflected in the critiques of collective guilt that I have discussed. The reductionist critique suggests that a group's action is nothing but a collection of the actions of individual group members. The anti-holist critique suggests that a group's act—were one to occur—would be something other than this.

One can see where these divergent conceptions of group action come from. On the one hand, it may be hard to see what a group's action could be if it is not simply the sum of the actions of individual group members. On the other hand, to say that a group acts appears to make a claim about something other than individual group members. In short, it seems to make a claim about the group itself! If we agree that a group's act is indeed a *group's* act, as opposed to the act of any individual people, we may despair as to the very intelligibility of group action.

It seems, then, that we need an account of a group's action before we can decide whether a group as such can be morally responsible. And we need some purchase on what it is for a group to know or believe something.

Group Action: a Philosophical Account

Introduction

Let us start with group action. How does a group get around to doing something? Must everyone in the group contribute to the group's action with some relevant action of his or her own? That seems doubtful, since it seems that in some cases only officials, for instance, are involved. But can it be enough for one or more officials to do something? How can the actions of those people amount to the action of the group rather than, purely and simply, their personal actions?

I shall now present a general account of a group's action. I shall be drawing on a number of previous discussions of my own, but will not assume any knowledge of those discussions.[7]

Walking Together

Consider three people who are out on a walk together. We can think of them as constituting a small group. They could be referred to as the 'walking party' or the 'group of walkers'.[8]

What is it for people to be out on a walk together? One might guess, at first, that it was enough for them to be walking along side-by-side, each with the intention of continuing this way for a certain period of time. But this is clearly not enough. Three people could meet these conditions, but just happen to be walking along in tandem, with similar intentions.

What is lacking in this case? Some of you may know the rhetorical question raised at one point in the Bible, "Shall two people walk together except they have agreed?"[9] I say this is rhetorical because it seems to imply that an agreement is a prerequisite of walking together. In my view something like this is right.

Typically, when people go for a walk they make some sort of arrangement first. This may be very casual and informal. For instance, one person says to the other two "Shall we go for a walk?" and the others nod or say "Sure," or whatever. Or one person may be out walking and two others come up to him and say "May we join you?" The first person indicates that they may.

Now in these cases the parties do enter into an agreement. Each could later say, "We agreed to walk together." But people can end up walking together without an agreement proper being in place. Consider the following case. A man is leaving his house on a walk and his wife, realizing what is happening says, "Just a minute, I'll join you." He doesn't say anything, but waits for her. Soon she reappears with her coat on and they go out together without further discussion.

I don't think one can say that these people *agreed* to walk together, even though clearly the right understanding was set up by what transpired between them. One might speak of a tacit agreement here, but since we've already decided that there was no agreement, we will need to explain what a tacit agreement amounts to. Indeed, if we want a certain depth of understanding, we need to know, in any case, what an agreement amounts to.

Joint Commitment

At this point I want to introduce a technical term of my own. I believe that what goes on in all these cases is this: Something I call a joint commitment is set up. I must now explain what I mean by a joint commitment.

The idea of a joint commitment can be understood by reference to the idea of a personal decision. If I decide to go to the beach, for instance, I commit myself to going to the beach. It's true that I can change my mind, but while the decision stands I am committed. This means that, at least, I have reason to go to the beach. All else being equal, I should go to the beach.

The idea of a joint commitment is the idea of a commitment *of several people*. Generally, and a little roughly, given that two or more people have mutually and openly expressed their willingness to be jointly committed in a certain way, the relevant joint commitment is brought into being. It then applies to each of the parties and can only be rescinded by them all, since it is *their* commitment. It is not a set of distinguishable personal commitments, one for each of the parties.

In my book *On Social Facts* I argued that, intuitively, the parties to any joint commitment thereby constitute a social group in a central sense. The joint commitment binds the members together. It can be argued to create a 'real unity' of sorts, providing the basis for an innocuous form of holism.

Why have joint commitments? What are they good for? A joint commitment is a very useful tool for several people all of whom wish to advance towards a particular goal.

The Role of Joint Commitments

Suppose three people personally wish to enjoy one another's company on a walk. Each could personally decide to pursue this goal as best possible, perhaps telling the others of his or her decision. But they will all do better if they enter a joint commitment to pursue the goal together or *as a body*. In that case two important things are achieved.

First, the goal in question is shared in the sense that each of the parties is subject to a commitment to aim at it. Second, none of the parties is at liberty unilaterally to give up this commitment. Thus each has some security, in doing and planning to do his or her part, that the others will be acting accordingly. If all cease personally to want the goal to be achieved, they may rescind the joint commitment together. They are therefore not stuck with it irrespective of all their wishes.

There is, of course, an obvious cost involved, which is that if some one of the parties ceases to want to go on walking, he (or she) cannot unilaterally remove any commitment he has to doing so. He can always act contrary to the commitment, but then it will have been violated and the other parties have a basis for complaint.

This lack of personal freedom is simply the other side of the coin of the security in relation to others' actions that a joint commitment provides.

In my view, when people speak of 'our' goal or 'our' intention, what is at issue is, often, not a goal that each party personally espouses, but, rather, a goal they are jointly committed to pursuing as a body. Given that we have a goal, in this joint commitment sense, each of us will naturally attempt to reach that goal, coordinating as best he can with the others involved.

I have now provided the background tools for a rough general account of group action. Here it is:

> There is a group action if and only if the members of a certain population are jointly committed to a goal, and in light of this joint commitment relevant members (perhaps not all) successfully act so as to fulfil the goal in question.

What makes a group action, in this sense, is not simply the acts of the members who together bring the goal about. The underlying joint commitment plays a crucial role. It is in light of that commitment that the members act, or must act, if we have a clear case of a group action.

Before leaving group action, I should mention an important aspect of the account I have given. This helps to explain how one can speak of a group acting even when some members were not aware of what was happening.

Members of a population may be jointly committed to allowing some person or body to make set goals for the population as a whole, and to organize their implementation. Thus a leader and his henchmen may formulate and carry out a plan in the group's name, without most members even knowing about it. After the fact all of the members are in a position properly to say of the group as a whole 'We did it'.

Group Belief

I now turn, briefly, to group belief. My account of group belief follows the approach to group action that I have outlined. There is a group with a belief if and only if the members of a certain population are jointly committed to believe something as a body.

What I take this to imply is that the people in question must, at a minimum, express the relevant belief to one another. One or more of them may not personally have that belief. If they wish to express the contrary belief, however, they must do so using some qualifier such as 'personally', as in, for instance, "Personally I don't think astrology is worth anything." [10]

Collective Moral Responsibility

Here, then, is an account of collective guilt in the sense of collective moral responsibility. A group has adopted a certain goal, and acted so as to achieve it, without any external pressure (as from another group, say). At the time the group believed that it was morally wrong to do what they did, but decided to do it anyway. In these circumstances it seems to make sense to say that the group in question is morally responsible for what they did. The group is guilty of acting immorally, if indeed the act in question was morally wrong.

If we accept this account, we are not forced to say that, given collective guilt, each member of the group in question is personally morally blameworthy. In order to decide on personal guilt, we need to know precisely who did what, why they did it, and what they knew of its moral status.

Similarly, we are not forced to deny that any of the individual members bear guilt. Some may indeed be personally guilty. Again, it depends on what a given individual did, why he did it, and what he knew of its moral status. A leader may have understood that the war was immoral, a follower might not have—or vice versa. And so on.

This account appears to have avoided, then the Scylla of the reductionist critique, and the Charybdis of the anti-holist critique. A central aim of the present paper was to show that this is possible.

The Importance of Collective Guilt

At this point someone might wonder: what is the point of saying a group is guilty, if as yet we know nothing of the guilt of any individual members? What difference does it make to anything?

I would say that if the conditions I have specified hold, then that is an important fact about the world. Here is a group which acted badly, indeed culpably. Is there anything which can and should be done about this?

Perhaps I am a member of the group, and I see that this kind of thing is likely to be repeated. Then, if this is a realistic option for me, I may wish to leave the group. If it is not a realistic option, I may wish to work for change within the group. I might even work to have it disband. If I do none of these things, I may at least accept that my group is not perfect, and that a certain humility in relation to its actions is in order.

If a group has acted badly enough, or badly enough in relation to others, outsiders may decide they have to act. Perhaps they will attempt to do away with the group. This does *not* in itself mean doing away with the individual members. As noted, a group may disband. Perhaps it can be incorporated into a larger group, or split up into smaller groups.

If one accepts that there can be collective guilt without personal guilt, or with little personal guilt among group members, then one is perhaps more likely to adopt a humane posture towards the group members of a clearly bad group, failing any cast-iron evidence of personal evil.

One is likely to be concerned about the character of the group as such, and as insider or outsider, address the possibility of relevant change, such as change in values or goals.

Clearly, according to my account of them, a group can have a character of its own: it can have beliefs, including values, both of which are crucial to character. These beliefs and values need not be the personal beliefs and values of the group members.

A group that is guilty may be capable of a change in character. If this is what is needed to improve its actions, then it will be well if its members are able reflectively to consider its character and to work for the necessary changes. It will be well, as a prompt to this, if both individual members and the group itself are able to acknowledge, with remorse, that the group has indeed acted culpably.[11]

In short, the idea of collective moral responsibility seems not only to be theoretically respectable but of great practical importance. If so, it is important that it receive a warmer welcome from philosophers than it has in the past.[12]

Notes

1 Burleigh Taylor Wilkins, *Terrorism and Collective Responsibility*, Routledge: London and New York, 1992, p. 19. My emphasis. I shall not attempt to review or explore here the details of Wilkins' interesting and sensitive discussion of collective guilt in the pages that follow the quoted passage (pp.19--27). Central points of agreement are our desire to take the idea of collective guilt seriously and our connecting it with something that might be referred to as 'solidarity'. 'Solidarity' also features in relevant recent writings of Joel Feinberg and Larry May. Nor shall I attempt any kind of detailed literature survey or discussion of the literature in the present paper. The aim of my discussion is rather to sketch a relatively precise account of collective guilt that appears to be proof against a variety of philosophical doubts (see section 2 below).

2 In what follows I shall generally interpret 'collective guilt' in this way.

3 Cf. H. D. Lewis, 1948, 'Collective Responsibility', *Philosophy*, vol. 24, reprinted in *Collective Responsibility*, 1991, Larry May and Stacey Hoffman, eds., Rowman and Littlefield. See also, Daniel Goldhagen, *Hitler's Willing Executioners*, 1997, foreword to the German Edition, Abacus, p. 481.

4 One may think that the so-called guilt of Badland must be a matter simply of the personal guilt of Badland's citizens, because one *assumes* that there is no such thing as the guilt of a group as such. Either assumption can lead to the other, though the latter could lead to a variety of different construals of Badland's guilt. For instance, it could be construed as a matter of the personal guilt of those citizens who were directly involved in developing and implementing the nation's war aims.

5 See Max Weber, *Economy and Society*, Part I (reference to be completed).

6 An alternative formulation might speak of the involvement of 'reification', treating groups as things in their own right, indeed as agents in their own right.

7 A central reference is Margaret Gilbert, *On Social Facts*, 1989, Routledge (1992, Princeton University Press). Some other references are given in later notes.

8 I discuss this example in detail in 'Walking Together: A Paradigmatic Social Phenomenon', 1990, reprinted in my book *Living Together: Rationality, Sociality, and Obligation*, 1996, Rowman and Littlefield.

9 Reference to be added. This is of course a translation from the Hebrew and may not capture it's every nuance.

10 Extended discussion of this account of group belief can be found in several places including *On Social Facts*, Chapter 5, and *Living Together*, Introduction and Chapters 7 ('Modelling Collective Belief') and 14 ('More on Collective Belief').

11 See my paper 'Collective Remorse', forthcoming, for discussion of what it is for individual group members to feel remorse over their group's action, and what it is for a group itself to feel remorse over its act.

12 Thanks to Keya Maitra for helpful comments on a draft of this paper. Thanks also to the lively and perceptive audience at Providence College, where I presented a version of the paper in April 1998.

Part IV
Philosophy of Law

Brenda M. Baker

Wilkins on Intention and Responsibility, and The Obligation to Obey the Law

Intention, Foresight and the *Mens Rea* of Murder

When Mrs. Hyam in 1974 stuffed a petrol-soaked cloth into the letterbox of her ex-lover's mistress's home and set it alight, causing a house fire in which two of the woman's daughters were killed, she could not have foreseen the impact of her actions on debates about the criteria sufficient for criminal liability for murder. The case of *Hyam v DPP*[1] occasioned extensive analysis and reexamination, by the highest courts of law and by many legal theorists, of what was needed to satisfy the *mens rea*—malice aforethought—requirement for murder. According to Hyam, her intention was simply to frighten the woman so that she would leave the neighborhood. Hyam's case raised the question of whether performing a risky or dangerous action with foresight of probable or highly probable harm or death to someone, or performing a risky or dangerous action which was highly likely to cause grievous bodily harm or death without foreseeing this, could amount to the malice or intention to cause grievous bodily harm or death that would, if death ensued, result in being guilty of murder rather than manslaughter.

A host of more specific questions presented themselves. Was acting with foresight or knowledge of inevitable or 'morally certain' harmful consequences that would be produced if one carried out one's intentions 'tantamount' to intending these consequences as well? What did the judgment of 'tantamountcy' come to? Was it claiming that the notion of intention could be extended to cover, by describing them as intended or intentional, the agent's relation to these foreseen harmful side-effects? Or perhaps making the more limited claim that malice or intention for the purposes of murder could be so extended, or that the traditional category of recklessness with respect to highly probable grievous or fatal effects should be displaced as a sufficient basis for intention? Or was it claiming that, even if these were not properly subsumable under the scope of the agent's intentional/intended action, the agent was nonetheless as fully responsible for them as he or she was for intended effects? How important is it, in defining the requisite mental conditions for murder, to adhere to the contours of ordinary notions of intention, desire and responsibility that are familiar in everyday ascriptions of action? Was the fact that a foreseen certain or highly probable harmful consequence was not desired, but unwanted, relevant in determining the kind or degree of responsibility that the agent had for this side-effect, or whether it could appropriately be thought of as intended or intentional? And what about the fact that the foreseen harmful consequence was perceived, either by the actor or by society generally, as the unavoidable side-effect of some action that was otherwise permissible or obligatory or directed at some good end—was this relevant to its status as being intended or intentional, or to the nature of the actor's responsibility for it? From the viewpoints both of the law of murder and the agent's general moral responsibility, how should we regard highly probable or virtually certain harmful side-effects of a course of action that were unaccountably not foreseen or appreciated by an actor who brought them about when carrying out some other primary intention? Can we analyse what is required for the *mens rea* of murder purely in terms of some permutations and combinations of mental states and stances such as agent intention, foresight or knowledge, desire, and choice, or must we also include in the analysis factors bearing on the overall rightness or wrongness (culpability) of the action done, such as possible justifications and excuses, aggravating and mitigating circumstances?

Burleigh Wilkins undertakes a case oriented discussion of *Hyam* and *Regina v. Moloney*[2] in which he looks at consequences that are foreseen as (morally) certain or highly probable, and asks when these should be treated as intended by the agent or as consequences which the agent is as responsible for as he is for his intended consequences. Wilkins thinks it is important to respect ordinary language differences in meaning between intending a consequence and merely foreseeing one. In ordinary speech, foreseeability is a necessary but not a sufficient condition for intentionality. Most of our actions have inevitable or highly probable consequences that are not thought of as intentional or intended by us, even when they are known or foreseen by us. (272-3) We know that movements of our bodies, for instance, agitate adjacent air molecules and certainly cause changes in the retinas of any observers, but we do not therefore consider these effects to be intended or brought about intentionally. In Wilkins' view, it is more important to preserve a connection between what is intended and what is desired. He thinks that we need to explain how an agent can be considered responsible for a certain or highly probable consequence that is not intended and not desired, and responsible in a way that is comparable to his responsibility for intended consequences. His solution is to enlarge the range of results that an agent can be said to intend, by talking about a state of affairs that incorporates the foreseeable effects of his action including both desired and undesired effects, and then explaining how an agent can intend this state of affairs by reference to the balance of his desires regarding the overall state of affairs.

So we are asked to suppose that the state of affairs which an agent intends to bring about consists of at least one desired consequence and one undesired consequence. Wilkins holds that the agent intends this state of affairs as a whole "if he desires his desired consequence of his action more than he desires to avoid the undesired consequence of his action." (273) This allows us to avoid saying that someone intends to bring about a specific consequence which he does not desire, while permitting us to say that he "intends to bring about a state of affairs *despite* its having an undesired consequence." (274)

Wilkins' thesis appears to assume that the agent was cognizant of both the desired and undesired consequences in question, for otherwise the comparative judgment could not be made. So I take him to be considering only effects foreseen or known by the actor.[3] I believe he intends his analysis to determine when an agent's bringing about a state of affairs which includes foreseen harmful consequences should be sufficient to amount to the malice or intention (the *mens rea*) required for murder in the criminal law. According to his analysis, establishing that someone intended a state of affairs that included the causing of grievous bodily harm or death (even though this effect may have been unwanted) would suffice to establish the intention needed for murder. The crime of murder is the context that generates his analysis, and he defends it as superior to Lord Hailsham's analysis in *Hyam* because it is committed neither to holding that an agent intended a consequence that she did not desire nor that intention in murder required an action that was aimed at a particular person. Whether he means his analysis to be restricted to consequences that are foreseen as certain or highly probable or to include consequences with lesser degrees of probability, or whether he means it to reveal when agent responsibility (or culpability) is equivalent in nature and seriousness to an agent's acting with an actual intention to cause death or serious bodily harm as a means or end, is less clear.[4] In my remarks, I will assume that Wilkins' thesis is confined in the former way. I will discuss later some complexities about the role that responsibility-attributions may play in accounts of the *mentes rea* of criminal offenses like murder.

Two questions about this thesis come to mind straightaway. The first asks what would be needed to satisfy the proposed test for an intended states of affairs? Would it be enough that the agent reflected on the desirability of the anticipated consequences and made a judgment about his preference, or what he would choose, without actually acting on a chosen course or choosing what to do? Or would the test be satisfied only by his choosing the course of action, or choosing not to do it? In other words, is this account distinguishable from an account which emphasizes choice as a basis for deciding when causing known or foreseen highly probable bad effects should amount to malice or intention in murder?

The question is pertinent because the literature contains other explanations of why an agent's responsibility for foreseen certain or probable untoward side-effects of an intended action is nearly equivalent to his responsibility for those effects that he does specifically intend as means or end. One such explanation is given by Hart in "Intention and Punishment,"[5] who emphasizes that in the case of both intended effects and foreseen side-effects brought about by an agent, the agent "had control over and may be considered to have chosen the outcome [between the victims' dying or living], since he consciously opted for the course leading to the victims' deaths." (121-2) Hart's point is that the common element of agent control over the outcome through choice is important in explaining why we think the agent's responsibility in these two kinds of case are very similar in kind and strength. This explanation of the nature of an agent's responsibility for an effect in terms of the nature of the agent's control over the occurrence of that effect is quite plausible. One wonders if Wilkins' analysis in terms of 'the balance of desires' is intended to emphasize other factors distinct from control as being important to agent responsibility, such as the agent's attitudes towards or level of concern about others' lives? More generally, should we think of the choice and the desire accounts as offering competing explanations of agent responsibility for foreseen highly probable or certain side-effects?

A second question concerns the ability of Wilkins' account to handle the facts in *Hyam*. Mrs. Hyam claimed that her aim in starting a fire was simply to frighten her former lover's mistress away from the neighborhood, and that she did not aim to cause bodily harm, much less death, to anyone. A major issue addressed by the court was whether malice aforethought in murder would be established by proving that when doing the act which led to death the accused knew it was highly probable that death or serious bodily harm would result from carrying out her intention. Yet it was never settled with certainty that Mrs. Hyam did know that this was a highly probable consequence of setting fire to the cloths she stuffed into the letterbox. Although we might think that the act she did had a moral certainty or high probability of burning down the house and/or causing death or serious bodily harm, it is not clear that Mrs. Hyam was thinking clearly enough to foresee those as side-effects of her action. This raises a question about exactly how, on Wilkins' account, we are to determine the undesired and desired consequences that the agent is expected to weigh against one another. Are we to use a full-blooded subjective test, based on what the agent actually believed, foresaw, aimed at, or should we use some more objective test to determine the relevant consequences to be considered, such as the test of what a reasonable person would have foreseen as certain or highly likely consequences? If we use the former, then the agent's beliefs about the likely consequences of her action, even if confused or ill-thought out, will provide the content for a 'balance of desires' judgment. Suppose Mrs. Hyam didn't think that starting a fire in the letterbox was highly likely to burn down the house, or thought confusedly that she could cause the house to burn without a high probability of causing death. If so, she thought she could carry out her intention without a high probability of burning the house or causing death, and we could not say that in acting she desired to avoid killing someone (burning down the house) less than she desired to rid the neighborhood of her rival. Nor could we say that she intended a state of affairs which included bringing about the deaths of some persons. If instead, we suppose that Mrs. Hyam must be taken to have foreseen serious harm or death as very probable because of the inevitability or closeness of these effects to her action, or because maintaining minimal standards of tolerable behavior requires that supposition, and so on, then we will identify as a undesired consequence that of very likely causing serious harm or death, and the intended state of affairs will be correspondingly more grave.

Wilkins' text is equivocal about which of these approaches, the subjective or the objective, his thesis is supposed to endorse[6]. Adherence to a strict subjective perspective might show that Mrs. Hyam was not guilty of murder at all, but only of manslaughter. There is no space here to consider the relative merits of these two approaches. My more limited purpose has been to point out an unclarity or uncertainty in Wilkins' solution as it applies to Hyam's case.

Others have proposed accounts very similar to Wilkins'. R. M. Chisholm, in "The Structure of Intention"[7], says if a person who acts with the intention of bringing about a state of affairs believes that by bringing about *p* he will bring about the conjunctive state of affairs *p* and *q*, then he does act with the intention of bringing about the conjunctive state *p* and *q*. The consequence *q* is part of what he intends. While Chisholm's account does not mention desire, it does like Wilkins' expand the object of intention to incorporate foreseen consequences, even if not directly intended and possibly unwanted, within a larger whole. In his book *Intention, Agency and Criminal Liability,* R. A. Duff also develops an account of intention for legal purposes which has several affinities with Wilkins' own. Duff holds that although highly probable or certain harmful consequences are not intended by an agent who foresees them as consequences of an action, if he causes them to come about by his (intended) action then he *brings them about intentionally*, meaning that he is unqualifiedly their agent and is fully responsible for them. If Barrett was certain that the bomb he devised to aid his prison escape would cause death, and he set it off with resulting deaths, then "his intention encompassed those deaths" (76) and we can say he brought about those deaths intentionally. Duff thinks that both intended killings and intentional killings (deaths brought about intentionally) should amount to murder, and that intentional agency is often sufficient for criminal liability. The legal notion of intention contains "two different shades of meaning" of intention, corresponding to what we intend and what we bring about intentionally.

There is much in this approach that would appeal to Wilkins. Both Duff and Wilkins would agree that it is incorrect to say that I intend every effect which I am morally certain will occur as a result of what I do, and that legal intention can encompass many foreseen effects that are neither intended nor desired. However, Wilkins would likely disagree with Duff's use of 'acting intentionally' to describe the agent's relation to foreseen side-effects. He would object, as he does to Bentham's talk of "indirect intention," (273) that this attempts to bridge a conceptual gap between foresight and intention by means of a "linguistic fiat" which runs plainly counter to the ordinary meaning of intention.

The disagreement is symptomatic of deeper differences in approach. Wilkins thinks it important to preserve our ordinary language distinctions in thinking about action and responsibility, and to respect these as far as possible in establishing agent conditions for legal guilt and liability. Duff, on the other hand, argues that we should look beneath ordinary usage to "moral notions of responsibility and agency" in order to understand how intention operates in the law. And it is clear that Duff's account of "what an agent brings about intentionally" depends on a prior understanding of what we think an agent can be properly held responsible for. Two examples should illustrate this. In explaining why we do not say that my foreseen making of marks in the snow by walking through it is brought about intentionally, Duff says that this is due in part to conversational conventions and in part to the fact that marking the snow by walking through it is not the kind of situation/side-effect for which I am held responsible. "We are held responsible for effects for which we are liable to be blamed" if we do not have some adequate justification or excuse, and more generally when we properly can be called upon to explain our actions by giving reasons for them.[8] (78) In contrast, if the anticipated side-effects provide reasons against doing the action (as they do when they entail harm or death to another), and I do perform the action, I bring about these side-effects intentionally "since I am properly held responsible for them"—they are properly ascribed to me as their responsible agent. (79) At another place Duff is discussing our judgments about the scope of a person's responsibilities as a teacher, and whether these include responsibility for certain foreseen effects (hurting a student's career) of an academic action such as failing the student's thesis. He spells out how such judgments bear on what a person intends as contrasted with what a person does intentionally. *What a person intends*, he says, depends on the *actor's* view of the relevance of an effect to her action. She intends it only if it provides part of *her* reason for acting. However, *what she brings about intentionally* "depends on whether *we* think it is something to which she should attend as a reason against acting thus." (84) (emphasis mine) We may disagree with her about this.

As I hope these excerpts make clear, Duff stretches the notion of 'acting intentionally' well beyond its ordinary language boundaries, so as to make it reflect our judgments about what a person is properly responsible for. His thesis often looks correct as a thesis about what a person is responsible for, but not about what a person brought about intentionally. In everyday life, you and I may disagree about what responsibilities attach to a certain role held by Jones, and so disagree about what effects Jones is responsible for in that capacity. But we would not characterize our difference as one about what Jones brought about intentionally. And if I, or society generally, think that R is a reason against Brown's doing A while he does not think it is, we may disagree about what he is responsible for, but this implies nothing about what we, or he, think(s) he did intentionally.

But perhaps Duff's thesis is more plausible as a thesis about how the criminal law conceives intention for purposes of liability? It is certainly true that for many offenses, though by no means for all, the criminal law does not discriminate between the knowing or foreseen bringing about of very probable harmful consequences and their intended production, but regards both as sufficient for the *mens rea* required for guilt. Sometimes this is described by saying that often the law recognizes knowledge or foresight, and recklessness, along with intention as alternative sufficient grounds of agent liability. However, these legal facts have been explained by other accounts which try to spell out how these 'agent conditions' are connected with strong forms of responsibility for prohibited harms.[9] Without further investigation of these other accounts, it is not clear that an account like Duff's, which tries to assimilate all strong forms of responsibility to the model of responsibility for our intended actions, is superior. I will return to this question later.

With Duff's account in hand, it is interesting to return to Wilkins' analysis of when foreseen consequences can be considered to be part of an agent's intention. When we do this, we find that Wilkins manages to secure much the same results as Duff does, by means of the use he makes of 'undesired consequences' and 'desired consequences'. If we allow the idea of 'desired consequence' in Wilkins' account to stand for a consequence which there is a positive reason to bring about, and 'undesired consequence' to stand for a consequence that there is a negative reason against bringing about (a reason not to bring about),[10] then Wilkins' thesis entails that where an agent intends a state of affairs, that state of affairs includes producing at least one consequence that there is a reason not to bring about. For if the agent desired to avoid the undesired consequence of his action more than he desired the desired consequence of his action, he would choose not to do this action at all. There would then be no state of affairs produced. In this way, Wilkins' analysis of intended states of affairs embraces just those cases where an agent acts *despite* there being some reason for him[11] not to bring about some consequence included in that state of affairs.

In short, while Duff's account of broad intentionality depends explicitly on the idea of a context where it is appropriate to consider whether someone should be held responsible and liable for an untoward outcome, Wilkins' analysis of intended states of affairs quietly implies such a context. This invites us to ask two things. First, just how much work is the idea of attributing events to agents as their responsibility doing in both of these accounts? And secondly, are there other factors that go unmentioned but are nonetheless playing a part in the answers that Duff and Wilkins reach?

In order to answer these questions, let us first look at the idea of when we can properly hold persons responsible for untoward outcomes or effects of their behavior. Persons can properly be held responsible for, and liable to blame for, unforeseen and unintended harmful effects that they ought to have foreseen, but bring about through negligence or carelessness. There is nothing in the idea of 'what a person can properly be held to be responsible for' that limits it to side-effects which the agent contemplated the occurrence of. Indeed, the norms of responsibility operative here are objective ones about standards of reasonable behavior that persons are expected to meet. They do not take the subjective perspective of the agent and what that agent believed, desired or foresaw. Persons who cause death or serious harm as side-effects can properly be held responsible for manslaughter as well as (forms of) murder. So the idea of 'what can be attributed to an agent as his or her responsibility' is not precise enough to sort out the intentional and knowing ways of bringing about bad side-effects from other ways of bringing these side-effects about. This means that Duff's appeals to our practices of attributing responsibility do not, despite appearances, compel specific conclusions about 'what we bring about intentionally'.

But suppose we focus instead on agent responsibility of some robust and full-blooded kind, that would make an agent 'fully responsible' for a harmful side-effect or 'unqualifiedly the agent' of that effect.[12] This kind of responsibility can be found if we narrow our field of investigation to certain kinds of agent-involvement, by focusing on side-effects that are known or foreseen as highly probable or certain by the agent. It will include effects that are done purposefully, with intention, after deliberation and choice, and that are produced knowingly or with foresight of their likelihood.

In fact, both Duff and Wilkins restrict their discussions to *foreseen* effects that are morally certain or highly probable. In answer to the second question I put above, this is a factor that is independent of responsibility and that is at work, though not highlighted, in the answers they reach.

Even if we restrict ourselves to the more limited range of cases where the effects are foreseen or known beforehand, there is still not one single model of 'full agent responsibility' which all these cases satisfy. The field still includes more than one way in which personal agency can be mediated or given effect, and the nature of a person's responsibility for certain effects can vary depending on how he or she as agent is involved in the occurrence of these effects. Many authors regard effects which we aim or intend to bring about as the clear paradigm of effects which we as agents are *most fully responsible for*, and regard our responsibility for foreseen side-effects as somewhat less tight than our responsibility for what we intend. The reasons for this have to do with the force of intention in initiating or motivating and guiding our actions, and in providing us with the main reason for acting as we do. Foreseen side-effects, whether certain or not, do not initiate action but 'ride in' on the back of an intended plan of action that one has. Their occurrence requires, if it does not wholly depend on, the agent's carrying out his intentions. They become the object of practical deliberation, if at all, because of the intentions and aims that the agent has. Their non-occurrence does not constitute a failure of the agent to do what he aimed to do.[13] These ways in which agent intentions structure the context for identification of and deliberation about foreseen effects explain why we think a person's responsibility for their intended actions is clearer and fuller than for foreseen effects they bring about.

If this is right, then we cannot simply argue from the idea of 'full or robust agent responsibility' to the conclusion that it is exhibited equally in intended effects and foreseen effects. The nature of an agent's responsibility for these two kinds of effects is similar but not identical in quality. Can we then defend the law's treating them as 'equivalent' for purposes of criminal liability? I think we could defend this in one of several ways. We might say that although responsibility for intended effects is greater than for foreseen effects, both pass a threshold of agent involvement that the law deems sufficient for establishing the intent (or *mens rea*) needed for criminal liability. Or we might try to show that the affinities between responsibility for intended effects and foreseen effects are greater than we have yet brought out. When persons bring about an adverse effect knowingly or foreseeably, they cannot plead ignorance or unawareness of the effect. Once they realize that this will be an effect of their action, they are faced (or should be faced) with a more complex action decision than they had initially. They will need to make a judgment about whether the intended effects or ends are of sufficiently great importance or worth to outweigh or override the bad foreseen effects. They will need to make what is really a fresh judgment about a combination of effects, and whether they are prepared to bring these about on balance.

We are now able to see more clearly what is important about Duff's stress on reasons sometimes being "reasons not to do an action." Failure to bring about foreseen side-effects does not amount to failure to do the action intended, but the prospect of bringing about foreseen harmful side-effects is a positive reason not to do the action intended, and one that enlarges (or should enlarge) the topic of the agent's practical reasoning. It should also be clear that Wilkins' analysis correctly recognizes the enlarged subject matter for practical reasoning when he speaks of an "on balance" judgment about whether to bring about a state of affairs including these effects. Furthermore, his analysis of the resulting state of affairs as intended is appropriate, in view of the fact that the agent's producing it should be the product of a fresh, or separate, decision on whether to initiate a more complex set of outcomes. The kind of control, through choice, that an agent has in relation to this state of affairs is very similar to that he had over the initial action that he intended to do.

A complete account of agent responsibility for foreseen and intended effects would need to say more about the surrounding situation or context of choice, and the opportunities or limitations for choice that it presents for the agent. It would also need to consider the goodness or badness (moral character) of the agent's ultimate ends or aims. What I hope to have shown here is that Wilkins' account provides some genuine insights about how agents are responsible for foreseen consequences of what they do.

Do Members of a Just State have a *Prima Facie* Obligation to Obey Their Law?

There is nothing in the nature of a legal system itself which gives rise to a *prima facie* moral obligation to obey what is the law simply because it is the law, if by a '*prima facie* obligation' we mean 'a strong but not always conclusive reason for doing whatever the obligation requires'. (92) Therefore, it is plausible to hold that if there is a *prima facie* obligation to obey the law, it must be derived from some other more basic *prima facie* obligation, such as the obligation to keep promises or to obey just institutions.

When we turn to review the standard justifications offered for our having a *prima facie* moral obligation to obey the law, they appear to follow this pattern. They attempt to defend that obligation by grounding it in some more basic *prima facie* moral obligation, such as consent of the governed (the promise model), gratitude or reciprocity for benefits received, or a duty or obligation of fair play.[14] But these standard arguments fail to establish an obligation that extends to every legal system or to every law or legal subject. The conditions required for these justifications are not satisfied in the case of some, or sometimes all, of a social population, and where they are satisfied, it is not always clear that they warrant the specific outcome of an obligation to obey the law.

The case for a *prima facie* obligation to obey the law might be thought to be stronger if we restrict the range of legal systems to which it is held to apply, by requiring that those legal systems meet certain basic moral requirements. The *prima facie* obligation to obey the law could be derivative from some more basic obligation to respect the moral requirements which the legal system embodies.[15] The claim that we have an obligation to obey the law in the case of legal systems that are just, or that are based on just institutions, is of this kind. It is this argument that Wilkins discusses in "The Moral *prima facie* Obligation to Obey the Law,"[16] and that I will consider here.

Even if we restrict ourselves to legal systems which are thought to be just or to be based on just institutions, this restriction cannot ensure that there is an actual obligation to obey every law in such a system. But what do such examples show about a *prima facie* obligation to obey the law? It seems there could be a *prima facie* obligation to obey the law that is derivative from a *prima facie* obligation to obey just institutions, but that this would not entail any actual moral obligation to obey every law in the system. The fact that certain laws can be shown to give rise to no moral obligation to obey them does not, then, disprove the existence of a *prima facie* obligation to obey the law in a society where the law is based on just institutions.

Wilkins raises this sort of question about just how much is shown by certain familiar examples that are enlisted in hopes of establishing that there is no *prima facie* obligation to obey the law, even where that law is based on just institutions. One typical example is whether there is any obligation to stop at a red light which one encounters in the middle of the night in a remote area where no other drivers or persons are about. Here many would say that there is no obligation to obey this law in this situation, and that the reason for that is because the social benefits that would be reasons for observing it in the usual case do not obtain in this particular situation. It is, further, implausible to suppose that reinforcement of a general habit of obedience to law is an independent reason for complying in the instance where all of the usual reasons for compliance are not present. People's habits of compliance can be more sensitively and intelligently maintained than by the means implied by that argument.

Suppose we agree that there is no obligation to obey this traffic rule in this situation? What does this show? Wilkins thinks that we can admit that such laws can be disobeyed without questioning at all the existence of a *prima facie* obligation to obey the law (or to obey just institutions). What the example illustrates is a relatively trivial case where the reasons why obedience to a particular law is generally warranted are not present in an individual situation to which the law applies. While it may have been technically possible to narrow the scope of the law so as to exclude this kind of situation, doing so would not usually be administratively cost-effective or worthwhile. According to Wilkins, this sort of example shows only that there is not an *actual* moral obligation to obey the law in situations of this sort, not that there is no prima facie obligation to obey the law when it is based on just institutions. We need an example where there is no obligation to obey a more central or important law if we are to be able to use it to raise questions about the existence of a general prima facie obligation to obey a system of law that is reasonably just.

Suppose then we consider more seriously unjust laws in a legal system based on just institutions, and ask what these show. It is not difficult to find examples of more seriously unjust laws in systems that are overall just. The features that make for justice at the level of the system, even if these systemic features include certain charters protecting individual rights and other restrictions as to justice in content, will not be able to guarantee that every law introduced or ratified in the system will itself be just. Even the fairest procedures, directed at trying to respect the worth of individual citizens, will sometimes lead through error or ignorance to the endorsing of laws which are seriously unjust because they are discriminatory, or permit some unfair inequality, and so on. Examples of such unjust laws include democratically supported legislation which denies recognition of rights expressive of sexual orientation, or progressive taxation which nonetheless provides few or inadequate remedies for the very poor or disadvantaged.

Of course, as Rawls points out, we may have a duty to obey unjust laws that is based on our duty to comply with just institutions. This duty or obligation can obtain as long as these unjust laws do not exceed certain limits of injustice. (353-4) However, there is nothing to exclude the possibility (given the looseness of fit between legal systems and their implementation) of the system yielding individual laws whose content is sufficiently bad or wrong to outweigh any *prima facie* obligation to obey that is attributable to the character of the system within which the law was generated. Rawls would consider that laws which result in loss of basic liberties, or which fail to distribute fairly evenly the costs of unjust policies, do not require our acquiescence. Judged from an independent moral standard or set of moral principles such as these, we may think there is insufficient moral reason to support a moral obligation to obey such laws.

But once again, this example does not show that there is no *prima facie* obligation to obey such laws, but simply that any such *prima facie* obligation that there is is overridden by a greater obligation to avoid injustice, so that there may be no actual obligation to obey such seriously unjust laws.

What would then undermine the *prima facie* obligation to obey the law where it was reasonably just? Perhaps there would need to be some more deep seated and systemic moral failing in the legal system. It might incorporate a pernicious belief in the inferiority of one sex, with this belief being reflected in denials of a battery of civil and political rights to members of that sex, and denials of equal protection or equal standing in the criminal law. Or perhaps the legal system's scheme of penalties might be barbarously cruel and unduly severe throughout, although the law's prohibitions on conduct to which these penalties attached were reasonable enough. It is not clear whether such moral failings would weaken or undermine any *prima facie* obligation to obey the laws of this system or not. Perhaps we would sometimes think that this general obligation had been destroyed, because the law could no longer be thought just or thought to reflect just institutions. In other cases, such moral failings might be held to undermine only a *prima facie* obligation to obey those parts of the law that were 'infected', leaving other rules of law with some claim on subject obedience, insofar as they were just or reflected just institutions.

Wilkins wants to argue that there can be a *prima facie* obligation to obey the law that is derived from a *prima facie* obligation to obey just institutions, and that such an obligation can hold for any member of a society provided that that society meets certain moral standards, such as basic principles of justice. I have two concerns about his position. First, unless it can be shown that a state which qualifies as a just institution cannot tolerate the existence of some members (even a very small minority) who receive none of the important benefits of state ordering, then I do not see how such members could be shown to have even a *prima facie* moral obligation to obey the law, much less an actual obligation to obey it. The argument that they do have such an obligation just because the state is generally just, and regardless of whether they enjoy any of the major benefits of its justice (perhaps they are impoverished homeless people unable to effectively exercise any 'rights' they may have), seems unacceptable. In other words, I think that the obligation to obey or comply with the law varies with persons and their situations, so that one cannot establish a uniform and stable obligation to obey the law that applies to every citizen in a society.[17] Secondly, Wilkins' argument for his position looks incomplete at one stage. He argues that citizens have such an obligation because their not abiding by the laws and policies of the state could make the state unable to provide benefits and protections for its members.

But this argument does not go to the duties of the individual citizen. Provided that enough other citizens comply, my compliance is not required for the state to promote the common good, and therefore I have, by Wilkins' reasoning, no *prima facie* obligation to comply. In order to avoid this loophole, Wilkins' argument needs supplementation by some principle about individuals assuming a fair share of responsibility for maintaining collective beneficial practices.[18]

While the second difficulty here can be rectified, I do not think that the first objection can be answered. So although it may be true that many, or most, of the citizens of a just state have a *prima facie* obligation to obey many of the laws of that state, not every citizen may have such an obligation. And those who do have it do not have that obligation simply in virtue of their state membership alone. There need to be additional moral reasons to ground even a *prima facie* obligation to obey the laws.

Notes

1 [1974] 2 All E. R. 41

2 "Intention and Criminal Responsibility", *Journal of Applied Philosophy,* V. 2, No. 2, (1985), pp. 271-8

3 See note 6 below.

4 Some remarks on this second distinction are provided later in this comment.

5 *Oxford Review,* No. 4, 1967. Reprinted in *Punishment and Responsibility,* Oxford, 1968. Citations are from the latter.

6 On p. 273, Wilkins says that the expanded state of affairs can include a consequence that an agent did not desire but that this consequence need only be foreseeable, not actually foreseen, by the agent. This suggests that an objective or 'reasonable person' test can be used to identify those undesired consequences that may be brought about. But how is this compatible with Wilkins' 'comparative desirability' test, which seems to require a comparison of subjectively determined desired consequences and undesired consequences?

7 *Journal of Philosophy* (1970), pp. 633-647.

8 "To say that A killed B intentionally (to hold him responsible for B's death) is to say that he is to be blamed for killing B unless he can justify (perhaps as self-defense) or excuse (perhaps as due to insanity) his action of 'killing B'. To ascribe responsibility is not yet to blame the agent; it is rather to say that he must justify or excuse his action as thus described if he is to avoid blame for it." *Intention, Agency and Criminal Liability,* p. 78.

9 See earlier discussion of Hart above.

10 This is a big 'if.' One might well object to Wilkins' analysis that in concentrating exclusively on 'desire' it ignores the complexity of different kinds of reasons that persons can have for and against doing certain actions, and the different ways in

which such reasons (e.g. reasons of duty or obligation, role responsibilities, virtue, concern for others, etc.) can bear on the actor's responsibility for an outcome that was chosen on a balance of such reasons.

11 I am assuming that in order to make sense of an agent's desiring one consequence more than another where both cannot be secured by the same action, the agent must be aware of these consequences and their incompatibility. Although Wilkins does not explicitly specify that the agent must know of or foresee the relevant consequences, and occasionally speaks of these consequences as being foreseeable but not necessarily foreseen (273), I cannot see how his test of comparative desire can operate except where the agent is cognizant of the desired and undesired alternatives.

12 Duff, p. 76.

13 Considerations of these kinds lead G. Dworkin to argue that, when our action is done for good ends, our responsibility for foreseeably adverse consequences is less as compared with that for similarly bad consequences that we intend as means to such ends. This is, he thinks, because of the value we place on the freedom to act for good ends. If we compare a case of bringing about foreseen bad effects with a case of intending similar effects as a means, Dworkin thinks that the "quality of our will" is certainly not worse, and perhaps better, in the first of these. It is not "more callous or malevolent or cruel." "There is not less room (but more) to be glad that the harm did not in fact eventuate. There is not less ability (but more) to alter one's plans so that the end can be achieved at less cost." See G. Dworkin, "Intention, Foreseeability and Responsibility" in *Responsibility, Character and the Emotions,* ed. F. Schoeman (Cambridge Univ. Press, 1987), pp. 351-2. Some of the contrasts proposed by Dworkin diminish to vanishing point as the probability of our foreseen consequences increases to complete certainty.

14 A thorough examination of arguments in this form can be found in Joel Feinberg, "Civil Disobedience in the Modern World", *Humanities in Society,* Vol. 2, No. 1, (1979), pp.37-60.

15 Joseph Raz thinks that laws which satisfy sound moral reasons for compliance with them give us reasons to conform to the law, that is, to act as it requires, but they do not give us reasons to obey the law. In acting on these reasons, he says, one would not be obeying the law but would be acting, e.g. on the doctrine of justice, and so on. See J. Raz, "The Obligation to Obey: Revision and Tradition," *Ethics in the Public Domain,* p. 326.

16 *Journal of Social Philosophy*, Vol. 25, No. 2, Fall 1994, pp. 92-6.

17 A detailed argument of this kind is developed by Raz, with respect to his idea of obedience to law, in the paper cited in note 13 above. Raz believes that the extent of the duty to obey the law in a reasonably just state varies from person to person and from one range of cases to another, and although there is probably a core of cases where everyone has an obligation to obey, beyond this core obligations vary widely.

18 See Colin Strang, "What if Everyone Did That?" *Durham University Journal*, No. 53, (1960); and M. B. E. Smith, "Is There a Prima Facie Obligation to Obey the Law?" *Yale Law Journal*, No. 82, (1973).

EDMUND WALL

Coercion, Voluntariness, and Valid Consent

There is no question that Joel Feinberg's *Harm to Self: The Moral Limits of the Criminal Law* has made a valuable contribution to the problem of legal paternalism. In his defense of soft paternalism, he finds that whether the state has a right to prevent an agent from pursuing some dangerous self-regarding activity hinges on whether the agent's action is sufficiently voluntary. This leads Feinberg to offer an account of coercion and compulsion, as they are among the things that can undermine an agent's voluntariness. Feinberg's book has proven to be very instructive for those of us attempting to clarify these challenging concepts. In this essay, Feinberg's analysis is critiqued. This critique is intended to shed some light on the nature of voluntariness and its relation to morally and legally valid consent.

Feinberg distinguishes compulsion from coercion in the following way:

> We can reserve the word "compulsion" for cases where options are closed, in the sense that some alternative, or all alternatives, to a given act are made impossible, whether the closing is brought about by natural, social, or internal causes, working either directly on one's body, or indirectly on external facilities.[1]

Feinberg offers examples illustrating the three possible causes that he believes to be indicative of compulsion. A blizzard compelling someone to miss an engagement is an example of natural causes blocking one or more of an agent's alternatives. A gang compelling someone to go to a certain destination by dragging him to it is an example of social causes at work. Internal causes can eliminate the options of someone who suffers from obsessions that compel him to repeatedly entertain some troublesome thought. According to Feinberg, compulsion proper exerts irresistible pressure that necessitates movements or experiences. Such forces, in his estimation, do not produce genuine actions.[2]

Feinberg maintains that even though coercion proper may arise from the same three sources which produce compulsion proper, the two conditions are to be distinguished by considerations about an agent's access to options. He believes that compulsion renders one of a victim's alternatives impossible, whereas coercion does not destroy an alternative but only increases its cost to the victim.[3] Feinberg maintains that when someone is coerced he is still able to choose. He chooses to comply with a coercer's demand, and in so doing performs a genuine action. This is not the case, we are told, when someone is compelled to do something. In such cases a victim is said to be unable to act. He is moved or restricted in his bodily motions by an initiator.[4]

Feinberg believes that compulsive pressure on agents can be either resistible or irresistible.

> The same miscellany of forces that in other circumstances render alternatives impossible exert compulsive pressure, but when the pressures are resistible they do not necessitate movements or experiences; they simply render alternatives difficult, inconvenient, troublesome, or costly... A snowstorm may not compel me to miss an appointment, but it may require me to leave inconveniently early... [In such examples] a person is subjected to compulsive pressures short of compulsion proper.[5]

Feinberg's suggestion here that compulsive pressure can be both resistible and irresistible appears to be untenable. As we have seen, he also has said that the distinction between coercion and compulsion turns on whether pressure on a victim is resistible or irresistible. If the pressure is resistible, he finds coercion; if irresistible, compulsion. However, Feinberg goes on to distinguish compulsion *proper* which leaves a victim without a choice from compulsive pressure which may either do the same or may allow for choice. According to Feinberg, a person who is blown over by a hurricane wind has fallen prey to compulsion proper, whereas the person who must muster all his strength to hold his window shutters closed in the face of a very strong wind is a victim of compulsive pressure. Unlike compulsion proper, compulsive pressure is not necessarily sufficient to determine its victim's movements.[6]

If compulsive pressure can refer to pressure that is not sufficient to destroy an alternative or to eliminate choice altogether, then how, given his distinction between compulsion proper and coercion proper, is Feinberg to identify cases of *coercive* pressure? He does not appear to be in a position to distinguish coercive pressure from resistible compulsive pressure.

To illustrate coercive pressure Feinberg refers us to the hiker who chooses one route rather than his normally preferred route because he learns that the latter may have been blocked by a landslide. Here the hiker opts for the lesser of two evils.[7] We are told that

> Even though there is no personal coercer in this example, the determinative pressure, operating on the hiker's choice, is more like coercive pressure than

> compulsive pressure, and had better be classified as such. On the other hand, if the hiker opts for the dangerous path, and is knocked down a hill by a falling boulder, or forced to turn back by an uncrossable fissure in his path, then his movements are determined by natural compulsion, that is, irresistible compulsive force that bypasses his "choice" altogether.[8]

Notice, however, that there is no relevant difference between the hiker who supposedly is coerced by a landslide and the wind-stricken home-dweller who suffers from one of the resistible forms of natural compulsion. In each case a choice can be made between alternatives. In neither case is the pressure irresistible. In the quote directly above, Feinberg contrasts coercive pressure with irresistible compulsive force. This approach reflects his initial distinction between coercion proper and compulsion proper, but does nothing to assist us in classifying those activities that exert only resistible compulsive pressure.

If Feinberg's attempt to classify compulsive pressure is unacceptable, what are our options? We could limit compulsive pressure to pressure that eliminates alternatives altogether, and then contrast that with coercive pressure, but that would be too drastic. Certainly human beings can experience substantial compulsive pressure short of the type that is sufficient to vitiate choice. The other option is to allow for the broader range of compulsive pressures but to contrast coercion and compulsion according to new criteria. That is precisely my suggestion.

Rather than to distinguish coercion from compulsion based on access to options (i.e., the former rendering an alternative costly and the latter eliminating alternatives altogether), let us view the *source* of the pressure as the criterion for the distinction. After all, coercive pressure can be every bit as persuasive as compulsive pressure. What distinguishes coercion from compulsion is that unlike the latter, coercion involves a threat by another human being. There can be no coercion without coercive threats, and there can be no coercive threats without agents who are capable of engaging in purposeful behavior designed to control other purposeful agents. Such cases are to be distinguished from Feinberg's hiker and home-dweller examples in which the pressure arises from natural conditions or circumstances. The victims in those cases experience compulsive pressure. If we allow pressure that arises from impersonal sources to count as coercive, we lose sight of the basic distinction between coercion and compulsion.

Feinberg's approach forces him to confront what he considers to be "hard cases." He is not sure if the following is to be classified as coercion or compulsion. The case involves an arm wrestling match. We are to suppose that one contestant called Groan is gradually forcing down the arm of the other contestant, Grunt. We also are to assume that only through great strain can Grunt keep the match alive. When the pain of resistance eventually becomes intolerable, Grunt decides to relax his arm, thus ending the match.[9] Feinberg finds that

> Groan's physical pressure on Grunt is both compulsive (but resistibly so) and coercive in its effect, and the deliberate choice to succumb to compulsive pressure on the grounds that continued resistance is possible only at too great a cost is to give in to *coercion* by choosing the lesser evil.[10]

Feinberg maintains that the threat in this case is tacit, that from the context of the case Grunt recognizes Groan's implicit message: "Either cease resisting or I will continue to cause you pain."[11] It is obvious that if Grunt prolongs the match, he will continue to suffer physical pain. However, this is not to say that Grunt has been threatened, tacitly or otherwise. Groan has not coercively threatened Grunt. Groan does not induce Grunt to believe that if he continues with the match, Groan will continue to cause him discomfort. Groan does not attempt to do anything like this. He is simply trying to force Grunt's arm down for a victory. Grunt is the victim of resistible compulsive pressure brought about by the circumstances.

However, suppose that during the match Groan catches Grunt's attention through some purposeful gesture or statement. Groan may very well be attempting to break Grunt's will to win. At this point, Groan would be attempting to convey the message attributed to him by Feinberg. He would be trying to induce Grunt to believe that he will continue to inflict pain on him unless Grunt gives up. This would constitute a coercive threat.[12]

What about Feinberg's contention that the compulsive pressure on Grunt is coercive in its effect? If Feinberg is to distinguish compulsive pressure from coercive effects, then he must also say that every form of resistible compulsive pressure has coercive effects. But then resistible compulsive pressure that has coercive effects and coercive pressure become indistinguishable. As long as we acknowledge that compulsive pressure is not always sufficient to eliminate choice, there is nothing to be gained by referring to the 'coercion' of Grunt.

Feinberg says that for this case, and many others, it will be very difficult to determine when compulsive pressure is resistible and when there is an "irresistible psychologically compulsive force to give in."[13] Feinberg argues that there is a fine line between a victim's choice to submit to intense pressure and submission that is a product of "automatic responses of the nervous system independent of one's conscious control."[14]

Feinberg asks us to envision a scenario in which intolerable pain forces Grunt to relax his resistance to Groan's downward pressure. Feinberg also refers to cases in which a kind of psychological paralysis causes a victim to submit to some pressure. Feinberg finds such cases of extreme psychological compulsion very hard to distinguish from resistible compulsive pressure.[15] Why does Feinberg find this determination difficult? He explains that "there are few behavioral differences between sudden automatic capitulation and [a] sudden choice to capitulate."[16]

Here Feinberg ought to distinguish between third party verification of an agent's experience and the experience itself. Even though it may be difficult for third parties to determine whether a victim is fully compelled or just strongly influenced, this says nothing about the *victim's* knowledge of these matters. Gathering empirical evidence for such a determination may, indeed, be quite a chore, but such travails offer no reason to doubt the validity of the distinction. Moreover, it is not obvious that such determinations by third parties are all that difficult. In pathological cases, the extreme compulsion that Feinberg refers to is not likely to manifest itself merely on one occasion. There would most likely be a wealth of odd behavior attributable to an individual in such a condition. For legal purposes, one assumes that an accused does make a genuine choice and is legally responsible for his actions. The burden would be on the accused to establish that the pressure was literally unbearable. At that point, the court would consider the nature of the accused's behavior and the circumstances surrounding it as evidence for such an extreme condition. The law does not have to settle on purely external criteria, criteria that ignores an accused's capacity to choose and act. Even if it did adopt purely external criteria, however, the inaccessibility of legal evidence would not alter the philosophical dimensions of compulsion.

These criticisms notwithstanding, Feinberg offers valuable lessons on coercion and compulsion. For one thing, we are encouraged to distinguish personal threats from pressure that arises from impersonal sources. This is helpful, even if Feinberg does not trace out its implications. If we examine proposals that are made by purposive agents who are attempting to influence other purposive agents, and contrast this with natural or social circumstances that exert pressure on purposive agents, we are in a better position to make moral judgments. Someone who contributes to a social predicamant that leaves its victims with drastically limited options is not to be judged in the same way as the person who is, say, blackmailing another individual. In the first type of case, we would point to the person's contributory negligence, their indolence, their lack of empathy, or even their evil cunning in manipulating the circumstances. In the other type of case, however, we would say that the blackmailer is trying to threaten his victim into compliance. We would identify his distinctive intention to hold the prospect of harm over the victim's head, a harm the occurrence of which is taken to be conditional on the victim's compliance. Unlike cases in which one is victimized by natural or social circumstances, or by the mere manipulation of others, the blackmail victim has actually been threatened. Coercion arises from personal sources and centers on an intention to use the prospect of harm to exact compliance. These are the defining elements of coercive threats.

Another lesson arising from Feinberg's discussion is his insistence that there is a significant psychological dimension to voluntariness. In his estimation, voluntariness is closely related to the amount of pressure exerted on an individual. Thus he also maintains that voluntariness can be a matter of degree. These are valuable points. Let us examine his account of voluntariness in some detail.

Feinberg introduces what he calls "variable standards of voluntariness."[17] He maintains that voluntariness should be thought of as a continuum between complete freedom on the one hand and total involuntariness on the other.[18] The cut-off point for identifying a sufficiently voluntary action depends, according to Feinberg, on the context of the given case and on its moral and legal ramifications.[19] He insists that as an individual's conduct becomes more risky, more voluntariness is required if that conduct is to be permitted.[20] Likewise we are told that as the risked harm becomes more irrevocable, more voluntariness is required before the conduct will be permitted.[21]

Feinberg turns to Hart and Honore's analysis of moral and criminal responsibility to support these points. Hart and Honore ask us to compare the case of an individual who gives money to an armed robber in order to save his life to a case in which someone reveals his nation's vital plans to an enemy in order to save his life. Hart and Honore decide that the hold-up victim gives up his money involuntarily, whereas the soldier gives up the vital plans voluntarily.[22] Feinberg adopts Hart and Honore's conclusion that value judgments play a key role in the determination of voluntariness. Contrasting the two cases, Feinberg writes:

> The threatened consequences to the chooser [i.e., the hold-up victim] are much more harmful than those of the alternative allowed him, so the cut-off point

> where involuntariness begins is low on the scale. In the wartime example, the issue is criminal responsibility for the chooser himself, and while the harm threatened to him was equally great, the harm to others resulting from the alternative allowed him was catastrophic, so the cut-off point at which involuntariness begins is much higher.[23]

Feinberg agrees with Hart and Honore that the national interest is to be given more weight than the interests of the hold-up victim. The soldier's action involves considerably more risk to human life. It follows, according to Feinberg, that the degree of voluntariness required to find the traitor's action voluntary is considerably less than it would be for the hold-up victim. In Feinberg's estimation, moral considerations require that the traitor suffer considerably more pressure than the hold-up victim before the relevant threshold of involuntariness is reached.[24]

Here we should insist on a distinction between voluntariness and moral or legal responsibility. In the traitor's case, Feinberg finds an action with a low degree of voluntariness to be voluntary. In truth, the traitor's action is largely involuntary, but, nevertheless, morally reprehensible. It would be better to maintain that although the traitor's action is minimally voluntary, this is sufficient to render his action—in light of acceptable moral and legal criteria—one for which he is seriously accountable. Given that so much was riding on the traitor's action, he should have tried harder to avoid divulging national secrets. But this is a point about effort and how much of it we can reasonably expect in the two different cases. It is not a point about voluntariness *per se*.

Feinberg is treating voluntariness as a variable concept. According to him, determinations of voluntariness are based on variable thresholds that reflect the circumstances of the case at hand, including the moral and legal purposes to be served by the investigation of voluntariness.[25] In other words, voluntariness determinations are to be derived from the very same considerations used to determine moral and legal responsibility. I agree with Feinberg that voluntariness is a matter of degree, but I also believe that determinations regarding it should be made logically prior to ascriptions of moral and legal responsibility. An action may be more or less voluntary, but such determinations are not implied by considerations of that action's legal or moral effects. The traitor's action is not *more* voluntary because it has potentially disasterous effects; and although it is true, as Feinberg acknowledges, that the traitor's attempt to offer an excuse would require a greater degree of involuntariness than would be required in garden variety cases, moral and legal excuses are not defining elements of voluntariness.

Moral responsibility is to be determined, among other things, by the degree of voluntariness with which an agent performs an action. However, the entailment does not hold in the other direction. Moral determinations do not provide even a partial basis for determining voluntariness. Voluntariness is a variable concept, but it bends only in relation to the effects of empirical conditions on an agent.

Feinberg rejects a purely empirical approach to voluntariness. In his view, there are at least two different standards of voluntariness, the proper selection of which depends on moral or legal objectives.[26] One standard is applied to an agent's acts or choices against an unrestrictive or normal background, whereas the other is tailored to the actual background against which a specific agent chooses. The latter requires an analysis of a person *talis qualis* or "exactly as he is," to use Feinberg's terminology. The former requires an analysis made against a background of normal circumstances.[27]

In his examination of the following three cases, Feinberg provides an initially plausible account of his two standards of voluntariness. We are to suppose that:

(1) B is a patient who is seriously ill. B's physician informs him that he will not live long unless he has an operation which he has only a 50% chance of surviving.[28]

(2) A is a malicious gunman who tells B that unless B jumps from the third floor of a building A will shoot him. B realizes that he has only a 50% chance of surviving the fall.[29]

(3) B is on a boat during such an intense storm that he knows he must either jettison his cargo or else drown.[30]

Feinberg finds that the patient's consent to surgery would be voluntary, but that B's consenting to jump out of the window would not be voluntary. Feinberg advises us to go beyond an agent's mental states when determining the voluntariness of his consent. Such determinations, he argues, reflect judgments of comparative responsibility among individuals. He insists that we incorporate evaluative considerations about the actions of others into our judgments about consent.[31] Given the moral appropriateness of the physician's actions and the moral inappropriateness of the gunman's actions, Feinberg finds that B's consent to the surgery would be voluntary, whereas his consent to jump out of the window would be involuntary. Feinberg refers to the pressure on B in the three cases as coercive pressure. I already have explained why I do not believe that pressure arising from natural sources (as in cases (1) and (3)) can be coercive. Let us therefore refer simply to the pressure on B, or, following Feinberg, to his freedom.

Feinberg specifies that the amount of B's freedom in cases (1) and (2) is identically minimal. In either case, B must perform some risky action or else die. However, despite the fact that in each case the pressure on B is identical, Feinberg concludes that, for legal purposes, only the patient's consent should be considered voluntary.[32]

Feinberg draws some further comparisons. We are told that in the third case where a storm may force B to jettison his cargo, it is nature that threatens B with death, and not, as in the second case, a gunman. In this respect, the first case is more like the third. In the first and third cases, Feinberg locates impersonal nature as the source of the pressure on B. Feinberg says that in the first case, the disease is the source of the pressure; the physician does not threaten B in any way. Feinberg accepts as given that the terminal disease is a compulsive force, and that there is no pressure on B beyond what is brought about by the disease.[33] According to Feinberg, the absence of any voluntariness-reducing factors beyond that which is given indicates that the patient grants voluntary consent to the surgery.

> To deny that B's acceptance of medical assistance in his plight is voluntary would be like denying that a drowning swimmer's rescue was freely consented to, on the ground that the swimmer, after all, had no alternative to his rescue but death. To be sure the swimmer had "no choice" but to accept the rescue, but that is hardly a reason for denying him the rescue he seeks![34]

When Feinberg points to the absence of pressure on the patient beyond that which arises from the deadly disease, he is applying his *talis qualis* standard of voluntariness. The standard is applied against a background that consists of the patient's circumstances exactly as they are. We are likewise instructed to apply the same standard to the drowning swimmer. This indicates that the drowning swimmer also grants voluntary consent to assistance. The *talis qualis* test, a test that factors out the pressure exerted on an agent by unfortunate circumstances, indicates that both the patient and the swimmer grant voluntary consent.

For the gunman case, unlike the patient and drowning swimmer cases, Feinberg decides to apply the normal or unrestrictive standard of voluntariness. According to this test, the gunman's conduct is to be viewed "as an intervention on the stage rather than part of the stage-setting," that is, we are instructed to determine whether the gunman's intrusive behavior, as judged against the background of normal, everyday living, forces the victim into compliance.[35] Why does Feinberg apply the unrestrictive standard to the gunman case? Feinberg says that for a legal grasp of the factors which tend to defeat voluntariness, a coercive threat is regarded as an obtrusive intervention, rather than as an assumed background.[36]

In this way, Feinberg builds his case for two standards of voluntariness, one which tables certain voluntariness-reducing factors because it accepts those factors as given (i.e., the *talis qualis* standard) and another that includes those voluntariness-reducing factors - provided those factors would be absent under normal circumstances (i.e., the unrestrictive standard). Since, for legal purposes, an obtrusive threat should not be treated merely as an aspect of the given, but a mortal disease should, the former leads to involuntary consent, whereas the latter allows for voluntary consent.

We certainly want to join Feinberg in affirming the validity of both the patient's consent and the drowning swimmer's consent. We also share Feinberg's belief that the victim does not grant valid consent to jump out of the window. Feinberg's standards offer a method for retaining and factoring out those voluntariness-reducing factors that may shape our ultimate judgments about consent. For instance, in the patient's case, we were invited to factor out the voluntariness-reducing factors associated with the disease, thus inviting the preferred conclusion that the patient's consent is valid. If Feinberg's approach were adopted, it would provide a covenient way to make determinations about voluntariness and consent.

Let us scrutinize this approach, however. It is one thing to gauge the extent to which an agent's action is voluntary. It is quite another to make determinations about the validity of consent. Feinberg makes reference to the impersonal source of the pressure on the patient and on the seaman. He contrasts these two cases with the gunman case and decides that the unlike the other two cases, he will apply the unrestrictive standard to the gunman case. He argues that the personal and obtrusive intervention by the gunman should not be tabled, and that a normal, everyday background should be assumed. What he does not notice is that the source of the pressure is not necessarily related to voluntariness; it may or may not have bearing on the extent of the pressure on a victim. A particular agent may be especially sensitive to the specific source of the pressure, and this may result in "additional" pressure on the agent, but then, again, it might not. Voluntariness is determined solely by those psychological and empirical conditions that affect an agent's ability to choose. The issue of moral legitimacy does not arise in these determinations.

Although the source of the pressure is not necessarily tied to questions of voluntariness, it does have direct bearing on the *validity* of an agent's consent. The validity of consent is derived from two considerations. The first is the degree of voluntariness by which an agent forms an agreement. The second is the determination of relevant rights in relation to that agreement. This is where the source of the pressure comes into play. If a gunman is the source of the pressure, the status of the agreement is rightfully subjected to moral scrutiny. Moral considerations are relevant in establishing the validity of consent, but they do nothing to establish the voluntariness of consent.

In the patient's case, the source of the pressure indicates that the patient grants valid consent to the surgery. If the doctor were to act coercively, however, we would then call the physician's motives into question. An investigation of the source of the pressure on the patient would then be required. For instance, suppose the physician threatens to drop the patient's case if the patient rejects the surgery. Under these conditions the validity of the patient's consent to surgery would rightly be called into question. This reservation occurs precisely because the physician may be making a coercive threat. The source of the pressure would have direct bearing on the validity of the patient's consent. After all, the patient has certain rights. These rights may be violated by coercive threats made against him.

The moral bearing of the distinction between coercive pressure (i.e., pressure arising from personal threats) and compulsive pressure (i.e., pressure arising from impersonal sources) is not captured by Feinberg's approach which allows coercion from impersonal sources and compulsion from personal sources. If the distinction is drawn along the lines I suggest, special attention is afforded the rights of victims. Unlike compulsion, coercion arouses a strong suspicion that there is a moral villain. The occurrence of a personal threat distinguishes coercion from compulsion, and this distinction is very important in determinations of the validity of consent. The wrongful intervention of a coercer can be identified without recourse to an unrestrictive standard of voluntariness. Moreover, the *talis qualis* standard implies that a noncoerced individual (such as the patient) acts voluntarily. In fact, the patient's action is likely to be involuntary - to some extent. After all, the disease exerts compulsive pressure on him.

There are other problems with Feinberg's two standards of voluntariness. Consider the third case involving the seaman. Feinberg claims that the seaman would not be acting voluntarily if he threw his cargo overboard.[37] However, instead of explaining how his two standards of voluntariness might apply to this case, he moves on to the drowning swimmer case. Recall that in the drowning swimmer case, Feinberg instructs us to apply the *talis qualis* test, thus inviting the conclusion that the swimmer's consent to be saved is voluntary. Since the swimmer's case is to be accepted just as it is, limited options and all, there remain no acknowledgable voluntariness-reducing factors. Given his treatment of this drowning swimmer case, one would have to assume that for the seaman case we are also to apply the *talis qualis* test, since these two cases involve very similar natural predicaments. Indeed, Feinberg seems to confirm that he would choose the *talis qualis* test for this case. He says that the patient case, which we are to examine according to the *talis qualis* test, should be afforded the same treatment as all of his cases involving pressure from natural sources.

> That the physician gave a warning only, and not a threat to make things worse on his own, distinguishes this case from the other two-person examples in which direct threats of coercion are made by gunmen, and assimilates this case in principle to those one-party cases where the "threats" of death come from nature itself.[38]

Feinberg acknowledges that his seaman case is one of those "one-party" cases involving a natural "threat" to human life. However, he says he bypasses the seaman case in favor of the drowning swimmer case because the actions forced on the seaman are not acts involving consent to the particular conduct of another person. The drowning swimmer case, on the other hand, is likely to involve such consent.[39]

Feinberg is, of course, correct. The drowning swimmer may be in a position to grant consent to some third party, whereas the unfortunate seaman is not. Nevertheless, we could still examine the voluntariness of the seaman's action, a point that is not acknowledged by Feinberg. We can ask whether the seaman's act of jettisoning the cargo is voluntary. Feinberg wants to say that the seaman does not jettison his cargo voluntarily. But I do not see how he could comfortably arrive at this conclusion by means of his *talis qualis* test. Since Feinberg admits that the seaman case is similar in relevant respects to the patient case, it appears Feinberg would use the *talis qualis* test for the seaman case just as he did for the patient case. If he does this, however, he cannot arrive at his conclusion that the seaman acts involuntarily. Instead, he would be led to conclude that the seaman jettisons his cargo voluntarily. Under the *talis qualis* test, we would accept the raging storm as given, just as we would accept the patient's disease as given. Granted, consent is not the issue in the seaman case, but his actions are, and under this test he jettisons his cargo voluntarily.

What if we ignore Feinberg's suggestion and apply his other test, the unrestrictive test? If we do this, we can certainly arrive at his conclusion that the seaman does not act voluntarily when he jettisons his cargo. The storm would now be seen as an imposing voluntariness-reducing factor with regard to the seaman's behavior. The obvious problem, however, is that there appears to be no relevant difference between the seaman and patient cases. There appears to be no justification for the use of a different standard for each case.

Feinberg does have a response to this problem, however. He writes that "the choice of assumed backgrounds or perspectives is ours, to be determined by our purposes in undertaking the inquiry."[40] His position is that even though the facts of any two cases may be similar, the choice of voluntariness standards may vary depending on the purposes behind the inquiry. Indeed, Feinberg believes that we are free to apply his two standards to the very same case, thereby yielding answers to two different sorts of inquiry.

He asks us to consider the case of someone who is threatened at gunpoint to sign a will.[41] Feinberg applies his unrestrictive standard to this case. Not surprisingly, he concludes that the testator's action is insufficiently voluntary to indicate any responsibility on his part.[42] Feinberg finds that the unrestrictive standard is helpful in delineating the legal parameters of this and similar cases. We are told that the will signed by the victim at gunpoint may be invalid, given a normal or unrestrictive background.[43]

What is it that the *talis qualis* test could tell us about this and similar cases? Its application, according to Feinberg, can reveal that "a person may deserve credit for good judgment, coolness under fire, and courage, in a context that deprived his action of legal effect."[44] Here Feinberg is referring to the advantage of being able to evaluate someone's conduct, even though the individual may not be morally or legally responsible for that conduct.

Feinberg contends that his two standards of voluntariness afford the flexibility required in answering legal, moral, and personal questions concerning voluntariness. For instance, if we inquire into the legal obligations of the testator who was threatened at gunpoint, we would use the unrestrictive test. Of course, we would find that he would not be morally or legally obligated to follow the terms of the will. If we inquire as to his coolness under fire, on the other hand, we can apply the *talis qualis* test which would reveal his personal character in the face of ominous circumstances.

All of this may seem helpful, but let us inquire as to our purpose for examining voluntariness. In the patient case, Feinberg focused his inquiry on the patient's decision to have surgery. There we were asked to apply the *talis qualis* standard and to imagine that the patient was not subject to the ominous pressure of a life-threatening disease. In doing this, we concluded that the patient voluntarily consents to surgery. With the seaman, on the other hand, we examined his decision to jettison the cargo against a background of normal sea-going circumstances. In doing this, we found his action to be involuntary. Given Feinberg's point that the *talis qualis* test is normally used for character assessment and the unrestrictive test for moral and legal assessments, what could Feinberg possibly say about the patient and seaman cases? Was the purpose behind his use of the *talis qualis* test for the patient's case the personal one of assessing his coolness under fire, as opposed to asking the relevant moral and legal questions? This obviously was not the case, since the question was whether the patient grants voluntary and valid consent, and clearly that is an ethical and legal inquiry. Applying the *talis qualis* test for voluntariness to the patient's case, we are asked to ignore the pressure of a life-threatening disease in order to apply a test that is normally aimed at estimates of personal character, but which in this case is to be used to decide the moral and legal issue of consent to surgery. Such an approach is unacceptable.

I suggest that we examine all voluntariness-reducing factors through one consistent method of inquiry. We should not channel these factors into two separate investigations. For example, we should not attempt to factor out the ominous pressure of a life-threatening disease when trying to determine the voluntariness of a patient's consent to surgery. We need a comprehensive approach that can capture any and every voluntariness-reducing factor. We need a test that will acknowledge all of the empirical factors that may diminish or undermine voluntariness. Only then will we be in a position to determine voluntariness and, in turn, the validity of consent.*

Notes

1 Joel Feinberg, *Harm to Self: The Moral Limits of the Criminal Law* (New York: Oxford University Press, Inc., 1986), p.190.
2 Ibid.
3 Ibid., p.191.
4 Ibid., p.192.
5 Ibid., p.190.
6 Ibid., pp.190-1.
7 Ibid., p.193.
8 Ibid., pp.193-4.
9 Ibid., p.194.
10 Ibid.
11 Ibid.

12 Edmund Wall, "Intention and Coercion," *Journal of Applied Philosophy*, Vol.5, No.1 (1988), pp.75-85.
13 Feinberg, op. cit., p.194.
14 Ibid.
15 Ibid., p.195.
16 Ibid.
17 Ibid., p.117.
18 Ibid., pp.104-5; 117-8.
19 Ibid., p.117.
20 Ibid., p.118.
21 Ibid., p.120.
22 H.L.A. Hart & A.M. Honore, *Causation in the Law* (Oxford: The Clarendon Press, 1959), p.147.
23 Feinberg, op. cit., pp.390-1, n.18.
24 Ibid.
25 Ibid., p.117.
26 Ibid., p.122.
27 Ibid.
28 Ibid., p.148.
29 Ibid.
30 Ibid., p.146.
31 Ibid., p.148.
32 Ibid.
33 Ibid.
34 Ibid.
35 Ibid.
36 Ibid.
37 Ibid.
38 Ibid., p.149.
39 Ibid.
40 Ibid., p.122.
41 Ibid., p.123
42 Ibid.
43 Ibid.
44 Ibid.

* I will always be grateful to my mentor, Burleigh Wilkins, for his valuable suggestions on this topic. In addition to his enduring lessons on excellence in scholarship, he offered genuine encouragement to me and other students to persevere in the development of our research. It is unlikely that we will be fortunate enough to meet someone like him again.

Part V
Theory of Justice

Thomas Pogge

On the Third Principle of Justice Proposed by Burleigh Wilkins

Introduction

In a recent paper, Burleigh Wilkins has suggested that Rawls's criterion of justice—his famous two principles—should be complemented through an additional, lexically subordinate principle of justice, which Wilkins formulates as follows:

> *Third Principle:* A constitutional regime, acting in accordance with the protection of the basic rights and liberties and equality of opportunity, shall insofar as possible avoid adopting rules with harmful effects upon those comprehensive doctrines which satisfy the conditions of reasonable pluralism. Such rules would include those which (a) may be directed against specific comprehensive doctrines or (b) may be of general applicability but which may result in unintended but foreseeable harms against some comprehensive doctrine(s). Any "neutral" rule which substantially burdens comprehensive doctrine(s) can be justified only if it furthers a compelling state interest. (TPJ 369)[1]

The present essay discusses some of the important issues raised by Wilkins's proposal and by his arguments for it.

Let us begin with a brief outline of *justice as fairness*—Rawls' conception of justice—which Wilkins seeks to amend. Rawls' project is to propose and defend a *criterion of justice*, that is, a criterion for the moral assessment of *institutional structures* for societies. His central claim is that we should morally endorse that criterion of justice which parties in the *original position* would endorse prudentially. He imagines these parties to deliberate in behalf of prospective members—but behind a *veil of ignorance*, so that they know nothing specific about the particular persons they are supposed to represent. The parties are made to assume, however, that every prospective member has three interests, which Rawls sees as closely connected to their role as citizens in a democratic society (and hence as not being partisan to any particular religious, philosophical, or ethical world-view or way of life). Rawls calls these the *three higher-order interests*, suggesting both that they are interests in the content and fulfillment of other interests (like second-order desires are desires about desires) and also that they are deep, stable, and normally decisive. The first two higher-order interests are interests in developing and exercising *two moral powers* (PL 74), which Rawls characterizes as

> a capacity for a sense of justice and a capacity for a conception of the good. A sense of justice is the capacity to understand, to apply, and to act from the public conception of justice which characterizes the fair terms of cooperation. Given the nature of the political conception as specifying a public basis of justification, a sense of justice also expresses a willingness, if not the desire, to act in relation to others on terms that they also can publicly endorse.... The capacity for a conception of the good is the capacity to form, to revise, and rationally to pursue a conception of one's rational advantage or good. (PL 19)[2]

The third higher-order interest is "to protect and advance some determinate (but unspecified) conceptions of the good over a complete life" (PL 74), that is, the interest to be successful in honoring and promoting one's fundamental values, projects, and ambitions.

Rawls claims that the parties would deliberate pursuant to the *maximin rule*: that they would evaluate each candidate criterion of justice by reference to the worst life prospects a person might face in societies in which it is the governing public criterion of justice. The parties would endorse the criterion that would secure the best worst outcome (maximum minimorum)—specifically: the criterion that would secure the highest floor for the fulfillment of prospective members' higher-order interests.

Rawls holds that the parties would then endorse the following criterion of justice:

> *First Principle:* "Each person has an equal claim to a fully adequate scheme of equal basic liberties, which scheme is compatible with the same scheme for all; and in this scheme the equal political liberties, and only those liberties, are to be guaranteed their fair value." (PL 5)
>
> *Second Principle:* "Social and economic inequalities are to satisfy two conditions: first, they are to be attached to positions and offices open to all under conditions of fair equality of opportunity [the *opportunity principle*]; and second, they are to be to the greatest benefit of the least advantaged members of society [the *difference principle*]." (PL 6)

These principles are to be understood as *lexically ordered*, so that the first principle takes precedence over the second and, within the second principle, the opportunity principle takes precedence over the difference principle (TJ 302f).[3] The word "lexical" is short for "lexicographical" (TJ 42f.). The paradigm case of a lexical priority is this: When arranging words alphabetically, as in a lexicon, one gives precedence to the first letter over the second, to the second over the third, and so on. For example, one lists all words beginning with an "a" ahead of all words beginning with a "b" regardless of the second and subsequent letters—as when "azure" is listed ahead of "baal." Rawls conceives the priority of one principle over another along the same lines: In the comparison of institutional structures, an advantage in terms of a lexically prior principle overrides any disadvantage in terms of lexically subordinate ones.

The Status of the Third Principle

Reflection on the lexical structure of a Rawlsian criterion of justice immediately raises the question whether Wilkins has given his proposed Third Principle a high enough status when he proposes to rank it lexically *below* Rawls' own principles. It is easy to see how the Second and Third Principles might come into conflict: A certain religion may forbid the mixing of men and women in the same workplace and its adherents may then want to run single-sex companies in violation of the opportunity principle. The members of another religion may believe in their obligation to preserve intact an uncultivated and now very valuable tract of land of great significance to the history of their faith while being unable to fulfill this obligation without a sizable property tax abatement that would violate the difference principle by instituting an economic inequality that makes the lowest socio-economic position lower than it might otherwise be. Wilkins is quite effective in arguing for his Third Principle by appealing to the importance of religious obligations such as those displayed in these two hypothetical examples. And he can draw support from Rawls' own acknowledgment—both in his argument for equal liberty of conscience (TJ 32) and also in his explication of the third of the higher-order interests on which the parties in the original position are to base their choice of a criterion of justice[4]—that citizens may consider religious obligations to be fundamental to their self-conception. The question is then whether Wilkins might be underestimating the strength of his own arguments when he allows claims based on such profound religious convictions to be overridden in the name of the Second Principle.

I would answer this question in the affirmative. Knowing that citizens may have very profound religious commitments and are deliberating pursuant to the maximin rule, the parties in the original position would not endanger possible religious commitments of those they represent for the sake of improving their socio-economic prospects. To be sure, the parties' alternative options have their own difficulties: If the parties rank (something like) the Third Principle *above* the Second, they run the risk of eroding the Second Principle. And if they try to find a compromise that permits some limited overall shortfalls from fair equality of opportunity, and some limited overall departures from optimal social and economic inequalities, in order to accommodate the most important claims based on values that are central to some citizens' comprehensive doctrines, they run the risk of instability by burdening judges and administrators with the task of deciding about very difficult and potentially divisive trade-offs. Still, the proposed lexical priority of the Second Principle over the Third would seem to involve a worst-case scenario that is worse for persons characterized through the three higher-order interests than the worst-case scenarios citizens might face under either of the two alternative options.

Why then is Wilkins prepared to subordinate his Third Principle to the Second without even raising the question of whether it should not perhaps be given greater weight in the envisioned Rawlsian criterion of justice? His reason is, I believe, that he takes very important concerns of his Third Principle to be already accommodated in Rawls' First Principle. Thus he writes: "Once we provide that basic liberties such as freedom of thought and association are given what Rawls calls their 'fair value' (so that their value is the same for all citizens) then the free exercise of religious liberty is guaranteed" (TPJ 363) and later again refers to "Rawls' idea that we must see to it that all citizens enjoy basic rights and liberties at their 'fair value'" (TPJ 371). If the First Principle did include such a guarantee of the fair value of the basic liberties, then the more important conflicts between religious commitments and socio-economic justice might indeed be preempted. But the First Principle, as explicated by Rawls, includes such a fair-value guarantee solely for the basic political liberties.[5] Rawls repeatedly and very explicitly rejects the idea of extending this fair-value guarantee to the other basic liberties as well (TJ 204f, PL 329f). He suggests that the socio-economic primary goods governed by the difference principle can serve as a suitable proxy for the value of these other basic liberties and then considers inequalities in their value to be justified insofar as those least able to take advantage of their non-political basic liberties are still better able to do so than they would be under any more egalitarian arrangement (TJ 204). In specific reference to the equal basic liberty of conscience, he writes:

> Some persons may count among their religious obligations going on pilgrimages to distant places or building magnificent cathedrals or temples. To guarantee the equal worth of religious liberty is now understood to require that such persons

> receive special provision to enable them to meet these obligations. On this view, then, their religious needs, as it were, are greater for the purposes of political justice, whereas those whose religious beliefs oblige them to make but modest demands on material means do not receive such provision; their religious needs are much less. Plainly, this kind of guarantee is socially divisive, a receipt [recipe?] for religious controversy if not civil strife" (PL 329f).

Let me sum up my discussion thus far. One main provision of Wilkins' Third Principle prohibits the adoption of rules that, although of general applicability, result in unintended but foreseeable harms against some comprehensive doctrine(s). Wilkins seems to believe that much of what his principle forbids is already excluded by a general fair/equal-value guarantee attached to all the basic liberties covered by Rawls' First Principle. But this is not so. In its current form, Rawls' conception of justice provides no protection against general and universal rules that result in disproportionately harmful burdens on the adherents of specific comprehensive doctrines.

Here it may be objected that a fair and democratic process, as required by Rawls' First Principle, may provide some protection by allowing any endangered doctrinal community to appeal to the good will of their fellow citizens. But such appeals may, of course, fall on deaf ears. And what is worse, it is quite possible that a majority of citizens, even if they wanted to adopt special legislative provisions designed to accommodate the fundamental values of some specific group(s), would not be permitted to do so on pains of violating Rawls' Second Principle. This is illustrated by my two examples above: The opportunity principle may require rules that outlaw single-sex workplaces, thereby dramatically reducing the employment opportunities of those whose faith prevents them from working alongside members of the opposite sex. And the difference principle may well require a general tax on property, proportioned to its market value, which would make it impossible for some ethnic or religious groups to preserve assets of great historical importance to them.[6] Rawls' conception of justice, in its current form, may well then *require* rules of precisely the sort that Wilkins' Third Principle is designed to exclude.

The Significant Elements of the Third Principle

Leaving the matter of priority behind, let us now turn to the content of Wilkins's proposed principle. The Third Principle prohibits the government from adopting rules that substantially burden, or have harmful effects upon, comprehensive doctrines—for example, by making it hard for such doctrines to win and hold adherents or hard for such adherents to live in accordance with their doctrine. The term "rules" here is intended to include not merely legislated rules (laws and statutes) but also those laid down by the executive and judicial branches on all levels of government, insofar as they are backed by coercive state power.[7] Wilkins clarifies that the prohibited burdening or harming of specific comprehensive doctrines might come about in two ways: (a) through rules specifically directed against particular comprehensive doctrines or (b) through rules of general applicability whose imposition results in unintended but foreseeable harms to particular comprehensive doctrines. The Third Principle makes this prohibition subject to five qualifications:

(1) The design of rules must be in accordance with the protection of the basic rights and liberties and equality of opportunity. This qualification restates what we already know: that the First Principle and the opportunity principle constrain the design of all coercive rules and lexically outrank the Third Principle.[8]

(2) The prohibition protects only against "harmful effects" or "substantial burdens." These terms require explication in two respects. Something must be said about when negative effects or burdens are to count as large enough to qualify as harmful or substantial. Moreover, the notions of a harm or burden indicate a loss of some sort and thus raise the question what the benchmark is against which losses (and gains) are to be measured. That Wilkins expresses his principle as a constraint on the *adoption* of rules suggests that the relevant question is whether a doctrine is in substantially worse shape than it was before the adoption of the rule. But on this reading it would be perfectly permissible to continue the imposition of an old rule that is especially odious to the Muslim faith, say, or to replace such a rule by a new one that is no more odious to this faith as its predecessor. I doubt that this is what Wilkins had in mind. Wilkins's reference to ostensibly neutral rules suggests the second possibility of measuring gains and losses relative to the rule's effects on other doctrines: The effects of a rule on any one doctrine must not be substantially worse than its effects on other doctrines (others on average?, the doctrines for which the rule is most advantageous?). The problem with this reading is that it would allow the adoption of rules that have severely negative effects on many or all doctrines alike. A third possibility would be to focus on the question whether a rule leads to some doctrine being in substantially worse shape than it would be in the absence of that rule. This seems to me to be the most promising reading, but it still needs

refinement. It is often quite unclear how we should think of the "absence" of some rule—what, for instance, would the world be like in the absence of the rule of driving on the right? What is clear, in any case, is that the Third Principle needs some further explication on these points.

(3) Disregarding the prohibition can be justified only if rules it would otherwise prohibit further a compelling state interest. The "only-if" formulation—esp. in conjunction with "*can* be justified"—indicates that the furthering of some compelling state interest may sometimes not suffice to overcome the prohibition. This, of course, is as it should be. But much more guidance is surely needed for the decisions that will have to be made pursuant to the Third Principle: What is to count as a compelling state interest? When is the (greater or lesser) furtherance of some (more or less) compelling state interest important enough to justify the imposition of some (more or less) substantial burden on some comprehensive doctrine(s)? Should the "furtherance" expected from a rule be assessed relative to the absence of this rule or also relative to alternative rules that impose lesser burdens? Wilkins rightly points out (TPJ 365) that questions like these have been addressed by U.S. Supreme Court opinions. But these opinions where written not in the light of a Rawlsian criterion of justice—they were certainly not informed by a commitment to the fair value of the political liberties or to the difference principle, for example—and they were written in the light of many constitutional provisions and historical precedents that are extraneous to, if not inconsistent with, any such criterion. So we can surely not assume that the meaning a term like "compelling state interest" has acquired in the context of U.S. judicial history (including a long period of anti-communist anxiety) is appropriate also to the context of a Rawlsian criterion. In any case, saying that the interpretation of a principle of justice should be governed by the standards and ideas that the supreme court of a particular country has developed in some particular period is surely getting things backward. The meaning of the principle must be specified independently so that the principle can then govern the formulation and interpretation of the constitution. Wilkins implicitly accepts this demand by assuming that his modified Rawlsian criterion of justice (i.e., the First, Second, and Third Principles in lexical order) would have to be justified through the original position. If the parties in the original position seek to protect the comprehensive doctrines of those they represent by adopting something like Wilkins's Third Principle, they will also be concerned to make this protection effective by reducing the risk of abusive appeals to such rubbery phrases as "furthers a compelling state interest"—either by avoiding or by explicating such phrases. The Third Principle

needs then a clear and self-contained explication comparable to the explications Rawls provides for the principles he has proposed.

(4) The prohibition is to be observed "insofar as possible." I don't see the point of this qualification, but assume that it does not go beyond the first and third qualifications and thus is redundant.

(5)The prohibition protects only those comprehensive doctrines that satisfy the conditions of reasonable pluralism. The remainder of this essay examines this fifth qualification in detail.

The Problem of Unpalatable Doctrines

What does it mean for a comprehensive doctrine to satisfy the conditions of reasonable pluralism? Following suggestions by Rawls (PL xvi-xvii), one might plausibly take this to mean that the doctrine (a) accepts the fact of reasonable pluralism: accepts that there is a plurality of incompatible and yet reasonable religious, moral, and philosophical doctrines, (b) recognizes the fact that this plurality could be overcome only through the oppressive use of state power, and (c) endorses the essentials of a democratic regime—in particular, the basic liberties enshrined in Rawls' First Principle—and therefore opposes an oppressive use of state power for the purpose of overcoming reasonable pluralism.

By speaking to how a doctrine and its adherents relate to and conduct themselves toward their social environment, these three conditions leave the content of the doctrine wide open; a doctrine can satisfy these three conditions and yet prominently include commitments to pedophilia, animal sacrifices, polygamy, nudism, drug use, and such like. Should a just society be concerned to shield such doctrines from special burdens; and should it in this regard show equal concern for these as for more palatable doctrines?

In reaction to this query, one might tighten Wilkins'sfifth qualification by adding that a comprehensive doctrine satisfies the conditions of reasonable pluralism only if it is itself a reasonable doctrine. This addition picks up a restriction Rawls himself imposes, albeit not as part of his principles.[9] We would then read the Third Principle as protecting only doctrines that, in addition to conditions (a)-(c), also fulfill the conditions of reasonableness (PL 59), that is, (d) satisfy the demands of theoretical reason by being consistent and comprehensible, (e) satisfy the demands of practical reason by giving clear guidelines for conduct and/or character development, and (f) change over time only in ways that are plausible from the inside.

By taking all six conditions together, we can narrow the set of comprehensive doctrines eligible for protection and thus through a Rawls-Wilkins combination do better than either has done on his own.[10] But I am afraid that we will still not be able to do well enough. It is not hard to imagine versions of the unpalatable doctrines adduced above—prominently involving commitments to pedophilia, animal sacrifices, polygamy, nudism, drug use, and such like—that satisfy both the conditions of reasonable pluralism and those of reasonableness in Rawls' narrow sense. The question is then whether justice really requires full tolerance of such doctrines by prohibiting the adoption of any rules that are directed against them or, though neutral on their face, are especially burdensome for them.

Seeing no further way of strengthening the criterion that determines which comprehensive doctrines are to be eligible for the protection of the Third Principle, I conclude that this protection would extend to many unpalatable doctrines: A group committed to pedophilia could protest statutory-rape laws; a religion committed to animal sacrifices could object to laws against cruelty to animals; 19th century Mormons (and homosexuals) could complain against marriage laws that offer legal recognition only to heterosexual twosomes; nudists could protest laws that require people to appear in public only when clothed; and various native Indian religions could object to general anti-drug laws. To be sure, Wilkins may well believe that some of these complaints would be justified. He may believe that some of the others could be turned away by reference to a compelling state interest. And he may also believe that some of the unpalatable views I have given as examples do not (fit into larger outlooks that) deserve to count as comprehensive or partly comprehensive doctrines. I do not mean to suggest, then, that his Third Principle is fatally flawed on account of the protection it extends to unpalatable doctrines. My main point is rather that we need more details in order to assess the meaning and import of this principle. An additional point is that these difficulties are not unique to Wilkins's proposal, because Rawls' conception as it stands clearly fails to deal adequately with the problem of unpalatable doctrines.

Testing for Stability

Let me offer one final point that may help us think further about the Third Principle and about how it might be modified to cope better with the problem of unpalatable doctrines. Wilkins sees one important reason in favor of his Third Principle in the need for stability: In order to work well over time, *a conception of justice and the institutional structure it favors*—or, as I shall write from now on, *a justice scheme*—must engender strong moral support for itself among its participants (TPJ 356-57).[11] And, in order to engender such support, it must be compatible with, and preferably even be supported by, the comprehensive doctrines held by these participants. But how, exactly, are we going to test a justice scheme for stability? I see four main answers to this question:

I. The stability test takes into account, presumably equally, all possible comprehensive doctrines. In light of the indefinite number of possible such doctrines, it would be entirely impossible for anyone to conduct such a test. And, to the extent that such a test could yield a meaningful result at all, it would presumably be negative for all conceivable justice schemes: For each such candidate scheme, we could *ad libitum* construct comprehensive doctrines whose adherents would reject it. If given enough time, one could dream up millions upon millions of hypothetical religions, say, whose adherents would strongly—and, in light of their doctrine, quite reasonably—oppose the justice scheme under consideration.

II. The stability test takes into account, presumably equally, all possible comprehensive doctrines that are in some sense recognized by the justice scheme under consideration. Since candidate justice schemes vary in regard to what doctrines they recognize (as well as in regard to what such recognition consists in), they would here be tested against specific sets of doctrines, narrower than the amorphous and indefinite set of "all possible doctrines" used by type-I tests indiscriminately for all schemes. Such a type-II test could nevertheless lead to the same difficulties as type-I tests. The Rawlsian justice scheme, as it has emerged from our discussion in the preceding section, for example, would "recognize" all doctrines satisfying conditions (a)-(f) and would thus still be faced with an indefinite number of (hypothetical) recognized doctrines and, worse, with an indefinite number of (hypothetical) strongly hostile recognized doctrines. Our Rawlsian justice scheme would thus presumably fail the test. And yet, unlike type-I tests, type-II tests can be passed. In order to pass, a justice scheme need merely employ a simple trick: It must confine its recognition to comprehensive doctrines that are supportive of itself. But this is a little too convenient. For whether a justice scheme achieves stability must surely depend not on how it gets along with the doctrines it recognizes, but how it gets along with the doctrines it actually faces in the society in which it is authoritative.

Stability tests of the first two types are not, then, the ones we ought to be concerned with. They miss the crucial point that the stability of a justice scheme does not in any way depend on whether it would be supported by hypothetical adherents of doctrines that never have been and never will be held by any human being whatsoever. Any type-I test is inadequate because it fails justice schemes on the ground that they lack such ethereal support; any type-II test is inadequate because it will pass some justice schemes on the ground that they have such ethereal support. An adequate stability test must then incorporate some sort of distinction between actual and fictional doctrines and must focus on the former while leaving aside the latter. There are two fundamentally distinct ways of drawing such a distinction: We could define "actual" solely in reference to the social reality that would exist if the justice scheme under consideration were realized (III) or in reference also to the social reality of the here and now (IV).

III. The stability test takes into account all comprehensive doctrines that could actually survive under the justice scheme under consideration. Doctrines that could not survive under it are irrelevant, because they would not have any adherents whose disgruntlement might affect its stability. The question is then to what extent any doctrines that could survive would do so only with hardships and difficulties, which might make their adherents feel hostile to the justice scheme and disinclined to support it vigorously, and to what extent surviving doctrines would thrive, which might incline their adherents to support the justice scheme with zest. In running such a type-III stability test, one would presumably take into account the predicted numerical strength of each of the surviving doctrines. The more adherents a doctrine would have under some justice scheme, the more important it is that it and its adherents be supportive of this scheme. So understood, a type-III test would show whether a proposed justice scheme is *practicable*.

IV. The stability test takes into account the comprehensive doctrines that actually exist in the society in which the justice scheme under consideration is to be implemented. Here one would presumably focus not on how the Protestant faiths, say, are presently understood by their adherents in the U.S., but on how they would over time come to be understood by their U.S. adherents once the candidate justice scheme will have been realized. So understood, the stability test may yield diverse results for a single justice scheme because the set of doctrines it tests against is relative to the specific society that might come to be governed by this conception—in particular, relative to the comprehensive doctrines that have emerged and survived in the course of its history. A justice scheme passes the stability test with respect to a particular society, S, then, if and only if its gradual realization in S would cause the main comprehensive doctrines now existing in S to evolve, without coercion and excessive strain, so as to become supportive of this justice scheme. A type-IV test of this sort would show whether a proposed justice scheme is both *practicable* and *realizable*.

Type-III stability tests have one very disturbing feature. There would always be two contrary responses to any discovery that a comprehensive doctrine would be disinclined to support some justice scheme: One could try to make the justice scheme more hospitable to the doctrine in question so as to increase the support it is likely to give to this scheme. Or one could try to make the justice scheme *less* hospitable to the doctrine in question so as to ensure the doctrine's demise (with few or no adherents it is of little or no relevance to the scheme's stability). This suffices to show, I believe, that type-III stability tests are too weak. Imagine a justice scheme proposed for the U.S. is challenged on the ground that believing Christians could not possibly accept it. It is no satisfactory answer to this challenge to point out that the justice scheme under consideration is in fact so undermining of Christianity that the implementation of the scheme would reduce the number of believing Christians to irrelevancy. This answer might show that the scheme is practicable. But it would also show that it is not realizable, cannot be implemented, in this country.

So what about type-IV stability tests? Wilkins seems to envisage the test along these lines when he occasionally understands his concern for (religious) doctrines as a concern for religious communities (esp. TPJ 361 and 363-64). After all, when a religious doctrine has no adherents, then there is no corresponding religious community.

Though Rawls does not explicitly address the issue, he also seems to have a test of type IV in mind when he insists that the stability test he envisions constitutes a *second stage* of justice as fairness, strictly separate from its first stage in which the content of the conception is formulated and justified. On the basis of this strict separation he wants to be able to claim that the content of the principles of justice

> is not affected in any way by the particular comprehensive doctrines that may exist in society. This is because, at the first stage, justice as fairness abstracts from the knowledge of citizens' determinate conceptions of the good. So while a political conception of justice addresses the fact of reasonable pluralism, it is not political in the wrong way: that is, its form and content are not affected by the existing balance of political power between comprehensive doctrines (PL 141).

This passage strongly suggests that one point of the strict separation of stages is to ensure that the first-stage formulation and justification of the criterion of justice not be influenced by information about which comprehensive doctrines exist and how strong they are. Evidently, the separation is needed to serve this purpose only if the stability test conducted at the second stage *does* take account of this sort of information. If the stability of a justice scheme were assessed without regard to such information (a mere practicability test), then such assessments could be thrown in together with all the other considerations that bear on the choice of one criterion of justice over its competitors.[12]

It is worth pointing out that Rawls' separation of stages does not quite achieve its advertised purpose. To see this, suppose that the criterion of justice emerging from the first stage fails the stability test of the second. Rawls would then have to go back to the first-stage drawing board. In doing so, he faces a fatal dilemma: He could either 'forget' the result of his previous first-stage efforts and its failure at the second stage or he could 'remember' and learn therefrom. If he forgets, he will presumably—unless there are some random elements in his first-stage deliberation—arrive once more at the same solution and fail once more at the second stage. He will repeat the same attempt over and over again like a broken record. If he remembers, or if his solution is changed on account of random elements, then information about which comprehensive doctrines exist and how strong they are will have played a role after all. This information did in fact filter out candidate criteria of justice that would have won out, if different doctrines had been prevalent in the society for which a justice scheme is sought. Rawls's best response to this difficulty may be to concede the point and express the hope that his very first proposal emerging from the first stage, the two principles, will pass the stability test of the second stage. Yet, even if he turned out to be lucky in this way, it would still be rather incredible that his work at the first stage should not have been affected by an (at least unconscious) desire to accommodate especially the comprehensive doctrines of his fellow citizens (not to speak of his own!) and the more widely held ones at that. A justice theorist engaged in the first-stage exercise cannot possibly proceed without being influenced by the values and aspirations, conceptions of the good, in whose midst he is spending his whole life.

Great (and thus far unappreciated) complexities are involved then in the questions how stability is to be understood and measured and how the concern for stability should enter into the design of a justice scheme. Two things have convincingly, I believe, emerged from the discussion: that the stability of a justice scheme matters greatly and that the only sensible understanding of stability is along the lines of a type-IV (practicability and realizability) test. The advertised stability-enhancing powers of Wilkins's Third Principle should then be understood in terms of a type-IV test, and the Third Principle itself be interpreted in light of this purpose. Interpreting it in this light would suggest that the protections guaranteed by the Third Principle are narrower than its wording might indicate. To be eligible for protection under the Third Principle, a comprehensive doctrine must not merely satisfy the conditions of reasonable pluralism, but it must also satisfy an actuality condition (which might be added as a sixth qualification or else be worked into the fifth).[13]

How should this actuality condition be formulated? Clearly, comprehensive doctrines that have never had and never will have any adherents in the society in question are not eligible for protection by the Third Principle. One might say that such doctrines are, in the relevant sense, non-existent (though they may, of course, have present, former, or future adherents abroad). This is a plausible result in light of the fact, pointed out in connection with stability tests of type-I, that no justice scheme could possibly avoid the hostility of all conceivable comprehensive doctrines.

The difficulty in specifying the Third Principle lies then in the questions whether the social importance of a doctrine should be considered relevant to its eligibility for protection—and, if so, how social importance should be defined and how it should be brought to bear. To get a sense of this problem, we do best to begin with the second question. The social importance of a doctrine might be defined in terms of up to four variables: how important a role the doctrine in question has played in the (especially more recent) history of the society in question, how many persons are now committed to the doctrine, how strongly these citizens are committed to it, and how significant these citizens are (thanks to their wealth or political influence, say) as potential supporters or opponents of the justice scheme under consideration. Insofar as the point of the Third Principle is to fortify Rawlsian justice schemes in preparation for a type-IV stability test, it would seem that social importance should be taken into account. By allowing rules to be blocked in the name of doctrines that are almost non-existing (having just a handful of adherents, perhaps), the Third Principle would impose a heavy burden on the legislative process and would thereby probably reduce rather than enhance the stability of Rawlsian justice schemes. Insofar as the point of the Third Principle is (pursuant to maximin reasoning) to protect citizens against some very bad outcomes, however, it may be implausible to declare the social importance of doctrines irrelevant: Being subject to rules that go against my comprehensive doctrine or harm its prospects for survival is no less (and quite possibly more) burdensome to me when my doctrine is socially quite marginal and close to extinction.

The social importance of existing doctrines could be made relevant as a threshold, for example by requiring that, to be eligible for protection, a doctrine must have at least a quarter of one percent of all citizens as its adherents. This understanding of the actuality condition would lead to vexing discontinuities as doctrines just above the threshold could be treated quite differently from doctrines just below. This would give all doctrinal communities a strong incentive to ensure the requisite minimum strength, which might lead to a divisive competition over potential adherents. Alternatively, the social importance of existing doctrines could be made relevant in some scalar way, so that a doctrine's degree of protection under the Third Principle would be in some way proportional to that doctrine's social importance. Such a proportionality could, for example, be incorporated into the weighing that determined whether the substantial burden a rule imposes on some doctrine is or is not justified by the compelling state interest furthered by this rule. A straightforward way of effecting this incorporation is by using the number of a doctrine's adherents as one (multiplicative) factor in assessing the substantial burden imposed by a rule (the burden, that is, which must be outweighed by the rule's furthering a compelling state interest). This proportionality solution could again lead to a divisive competition for adherents, and it might well render the political process (what Rawls would call) political in the wrong way.

Conclusion

Burleigh Wilkins has proposed amending Rawls' conception of justice as fairness by adding to its criterion of justice a third, lexically subordinate principle. This is an important and interesting proposal which deserves detailed examination and discussion, especially in the context of Rawls' later work on public reason, pluralism, and overlapping consensus. My very preliminary examination suggests that the values secured by the Third Principle may well deserve a more prominent place in a Rawlsian criterion of justice than Wilkins himself suggests (by subordinating these values to the First, opportunity, and difference principles). I have further indicated a number of respects in which the Third Principle must be further explicated and specified if it is to provide clear guidance within a criterion of justice. And I have sketched a way of filling in one important argument Wilkins has made for his proposal—the argument that it will make it easier for a Rawlsian conception of justice to pass the test of stability.

Notes

1 Numbers preceded by "TPJ" will refer to Burleigh T. Wilkins: "A Third Principle of Justice," in *The Journal of Ethics,* Vol. 1 (1997), pp. 355-374.

2 Numbers preceded by "PL" will refer to pages in John Rawls: *Political Liberalism* (New York: Columbia University Press 1993).

3 Numbers preceded by "TJ" will refer to pages in John Rawls: *A Theory of Justice* (Cambridge MA: Harvard University Press 1971).

4 For example: "Citizens in their personal affairs, or within the internal life of associations, ... may have attachments and loves that they believe they would not, or could not, stand apart from; and they might regard it as unthinkable for them to view themselves without certain religious and philosophical convictions and commitments." p. 545 in John Rawls: "Kantian Constructivism in Moral Theory" in *Journal of Philosophy*, Vol. 77:9 (September 1980), pp. 515-572.

5 "Those similarly endowed and motivated should have roughly the same chance of attaining positions of political authority irrespective of their economic and social class" (TJ 225); "the worth of the political liberties to all citizens, whatever their social or economic position, must be approximately equal, or at least sufficiently equal, in the sense that everyone has a fair opportunity to hold public office and to influence the outcome of political decisions" (PL 327).

6 Here granting some group(s), or even all groups of a certain kind, a special abatement would be impermissible because it would introduce socio-economic inequalities that are not to the greatest benefit of the least advantaged members of society. Of course, it is an *empirical* question whether or not such special treatment is to the greatest benefit of the least advantaged. It does not seem probable at all that the social and economic inequalities introduced by all the extensive special tax breaks currently granted to religious organizations and their benefactors in the United States are part of the best strategy for optimizing the lowest socio-economic position. But in a society in which religious organizations spent much of their resources on truly charitable projects (benefiting the least fortunate), special breaks for such organizations could be justifiable, and even mandatory, under the difference principle.

7 "The rule [the Third Principle] refers to legislative statutes, administrative findings and decrees, and court decisions which govern the activities of the state, and the Principle aims to protect comprehensive doctrines at all levels of government activity." (TPJ 369).

8 It is curious, though, that Wilkins does not mention the Difference Principle in this context. This may indicate some doubt on his part about whether the Difference Principle, as well, should have lexical priority over his own Third Principle.

9 He writes: "It is unreasonable for us to use political power, should we possess it, or share it with others, to repress comprehensive views that are not unreasonable" (PL

61).

10 Note that Rawls' statement quoted in the preceding note cannot possibly be maintained in the face of the problem of unpalatable doctrines. Even a doctrine prescribing human sacrifices could easily fulfill conditions (d)-(f). So Rawls must surely require more from a comprehensive view, if its repression is to be unreasonable, than merely that it be reasonable, or "not unreasonable," in his narrow sense. At one point, he writes: "Political liberalism also supposes that a reasonable comprehensive doctrine does not reject the essentials of a comprehensive regime" (PL xvi). One could read this as a (false) empirical supposition. But Rawls's more recent work suggests that he is strengthening the notion of a reasonable doctrine so that, to count as reasonable, a doctrine must satisfy the conditions of reasonable pluralism. See his "The Idea Of Public Reason Revisited" in *The University of Chicago Law Review,* Vol. 64/3 (Summer 1997), pp. 765-807.

11 A conception of justice may prescribe different institutional structures for different societies, depending on their climate, culture, and level of economic development. There could, for example, be quite diverse utilitarian justice schemes, each consisting of the same utilitarian conception of justice combined with the institutional structure favored by this conception for some specific society. It is clear, then, that what is to be tested is not a conception of justice as such, but a conception of justice combined with the institutional structure it favors in some specific context. To be sure, some conception of justice might turn out to be stable, or unstable, in all contexts. But in order to ascertain this, we would still have to go through all these contexts and test this conception as paired with the institutional structure it favors for each of them.

12 Note also that, if the stability test determined only the practicability of a justice scheme, then Rawls would need yet a third stage for testing whether a proposed justice scheme is realizable from where we are now. The fact that Rawls never suggests such a further test is evidence for my conjecture that her thinks of his stability test as a type-IV test, which assesses both practicability and feasibility.

13 I say "eligible for protection," because it is always possible that a doctrine will not actually be protected by the Third Principle because of one of the other three qualifications built into it: because protecting it would run afoul of Rawls's First or opportunity principle (1), would go against a compelling state interest (3), or would be impossible in some other way (4).

J. Angelo Corlett

Collective Moral Responsibility*

Professor Burleigh Taylor Wilkins was the first to teach me to do my very best at advancing plausibly and constructively philosophical knowledge and analyses. This paper is both dedicated to him, and to his style of the Socratic search for truth.

In *Terrorism and Collective Responsibility*, Wilkins argues that:

> I cannot provide a list of necessary and sufficient conditions for holding a collective responsible for the faulty actions of some of its members, but I can perhaps do some of the reflection, which would precede the creation of such a list.[1]

In this paper, I shall address the question of what are some of the necessary conditions of collective moral responsibility.

What *are* the conditions of collective moral responsibility? Furthermore, *do* any collectives satisfy these conditions? Consider the *Principle of Collective Moral Liability (PCML)*: It is justified for one to ascribe to a conglomerate *moral liability* with respect to an outcome or a state of affairs *to the extent that*:

(i) That conglomerate is an intentional agent concerning that outcome, i.e., that its action or inaction (say, in cases of negligence, where "negligence" is construed as the creation of an unreasonable risk of harm to others) is caused by its wants and beliefs;

(ii) That conglomerate is a voluntary agent concerning that outcome;

(iii) That conglomerate is an epistemic agent concerning that outcome;

(iv) The responsible conglomerate did the harmful thing in question, or at least that its action or omission made a substantial causal contribution to it (i.e., that it is responsible for the harmful outcome in the causal sense);

(v) The causally contributory conduct must have been in some way faulty (i.e., that it is responsible for the harmful outcome in the blame sense);[2] and

(vi) If the harmful outcome was truly the fault of the conglomerate, the required causal connection must exist between the faulty aspect of its conduct and the outcome.[3]

As with individuals, we want to know whether or not conglomerates may be morally liable for their inactions (omissions) as well as for their actions as they are causes (of one kind or another) of outcomes or states of affairs.[4] I disclaim any intention to deal with (iv)-(vi) in the present paper. Instead, I will try to solve a limited number of questions regarding (i)-(iii). Among the most important matters here are whether or not (i)-(iii) are (independently) necessary conditions of collective moral responsibility, whether or not a conglomerate *can* act or omit to act intentionally, voluntarily, and/or knowingly, and whether or not a conglomerate *does* act in such ways. Let us take on each of these important matters in turn.

Are (i)-(iii) jointly or independently necessary conditions of collective moral responsibility? This is an important question in that one might argue that intentional, voluntary, and epistemic action are required for *individual* moral liability, yet deny that such action is required for *collective* moral liability.

Now it might be objected that the PCML wrongly construes collective moral responsibility in terms of what constitutes individual moral responsibility. For example, Virginia Held argues that "It is not clear … that the best way to decide about corporate responsibility is by adopting the criteria for individual personal responsibility to corporations. We might well need to analyze corporate responsibility on its own terms."[5] Perhaps, moreover, Held is correct in claiming that

> … we cannot get by deduction from such judgments as "the corporation did *X*" or "corporation *C* is responsible for *X*," to judgments about individual responsibility. From judgments about collective entities, nothing follows logically about what any members of such a collective did or is responsible for. We have to know about the internal structure of the collectivity, and about the roles and activities of its individual members, to assign responsibility to individuals for what corporations do and are responsible for.[6]

Held's arguments for such a view about collective responsibility are the following. First, she argues that

> If it makes sense to say that the corporation 'should have known' and hence can be 'held responsible,' perhaps we should conclude directly what this means for corporations, without the detour of analyzing what it means to say of individual persons that they 'should have known,' and then applying this to a corporation.[7]

She continues to argue that

> For the corporation to be responsible, we may have to suppose the outcome was such that the corporation 'could have done other than it did' in some sense. But establishing this may be quite different for corporations than it is for individual persons.[8]

Moreover, Held claims that

> What to think about corporate intention is complex and difficult. Corporate intention may well be very different from personal intention, and yet it may make perfectly good sense to speak of a corporation intentionally doing something, or having an intention to do something.[9]

It is noteworthy, however, that in light of Held's three statements her own claim that "'Responsibility' may be something which is quite different for corporations than it is for individual persons"[10] is dubious. For not only does Held not explicate precisely *how* collective and individual responsibility differ, analytically speaking, Held's own claims seem to *favor* an analysis, not unlike Moral Liability Collectivism, which analyzes individual and collective liability by way of the *same* conditions. For Held's "should have known," "could have done other than it did," and "intentionally doing something" criteria are congruent with the fundamental analysis of Moral Liability Collectivism's conditions of collective knowledge, voluntariness and intentionality, respectively. Thus it seems misleading, if not false, to argue that collective and individual responsibility ought to be analyzed differently. For how else ought collective responsibility to be analyzed if not in terms of intentional, voluntary and epistemic action? And what is the reason for thinking that collective responsibility ought to be analyzed in terms significantly different than these? Held's own statements, then, seem to indicate a basic agreement with the analysis of collective responsibility in terms of intentional, voluntary and epistemic action.

Thus to the extent that a collective satisfies the conditions set forth in the PCML, then it is a plausible candidate for moral liability ascriptions. It is possible for certain collectives (namely, highly organized conglomerates such as nations and corporations) to satisfy such conditions. However, I believe there are empirical factors which tend to undermine any claim to the effect that such collectives *do in fact* typically satisfy such conditions (at least in a strong sense). Consider three related problems with such a claim: the Problem of Collective Intentional Action, the Problem of Collective Voluntariness, and the Problem of Collective Knowledge. Each of these difficulties makes it difficult to justifiably say that a certain necessary condition for moral liability is satisfied by even the most highly organized collectives. Let us consider each of these problems in turn.

A collective (intentional) action is an action the subject of which is a collective intentional agent. A *collective behavior* is a doing or behavior which is the result of a collective, though not the result of its intentions. A *collective action* is caused by the beliefs and desires (wants) of the *collective* itself,[11] whether or not such beliefs and desires can be accounted for or explained in individualist terms. Although species of collective action include "shared cooperative activity" involving as few as two parties,[12] I am concerned with whether or not it is justified to ascribe intentional action to conglomerates of a numerically larger sort such as (large) nations and (large) corporations. If such conglomerates are not intentional agents, then they are not proper subjects of moral responsibility attributions.

Necessary, but perhaps insufficient, conditions of collective intentional action or omission include: official representatives of the collective engaging in a valid rule-governed, goal-oriented (putatively collective), decision-making procedure designed to "act" (or not act, as the case may be) for the conglomerate. This procedure should permit a conglomerate to admit and expel members at will according to its valid rule system. This affords the conglomerate the freedom to determine the boundaries of its own membership. Moreover, such a goal-oriented, decision-making procedure must be recognized by the official rule system of that conglomerate, be it a corporate or national charter, a legal system, etc. Thus if a conglomerate has a rule-defined, goal-oriented, decision-making procedure, then it can be said to have the capacity to do things or refrain from doing them.

But doing things and acting intentionally are quite different. For a conglomerate's doings to be plausibly construed as actions it is essential that that conglomerate act intentionally. So if the rule system of the conglomerate eventuates in a decision by official representatives of that conglomerate, and if that decision is an action which is caused by the wants and beliefs of that conglomerate (Assuming the plausibility of the fundamentals of Alvin I. Goldman's theory of human action), then that conglomerate may justifiably be said to have acted (as a secondary agent) intentionally. Moreover, if the weight of moral reason supports that conglomerate's being held liable to sanctions as a result of the action or omission, then it is justified to ascribe moral liability to that conglomerate for that action or omission.

David Copp argues that a theory of collectives must be compatible with the claim that collectives *can and do* perform actions.[13] He goes on to argue that "collectives are moral agents" (a moral agent is an entity to which intentional agency can plausibly be ascribed, and where the content of one's action is moral).[14] I agree with Copp that certain collectives, namely conglomerates such as nations and corporations which have rule-governed and highly structured decision-making capacities, *can* be (re-structured to qualify as) intentional agents. However, there are difficulties, which face any claim to the effect that such collectives commonly *do* act intentionally such that they might qualify as moral agents.

If one necessary condition of moral liability is that the party is an intentional agent, then it is important to ask whether or not conglomerates are plausible candidates for ascriptions of intentional agency, including omissions to act.

It might be thought that conglomerates do not act intentionally, and for two reasons. First, they do not act *intentionally* as individual humans often do. Instead, individual constituents of the conglomerate act on its behalf. Another reason why it might be thought that collectives do not act intentionally is that, it might be argued, it is possible to reduce ascriptions of collective 'agency' to attributions of individual agency in congruence with recognized rule systems[15]—without loss of cognitive meaning. This sort of reasoning would lead one to adopt some version of Moral Responsibility Individualism. For if ascriptions of collective 'agency' are problematic, so are attributions of collective moral responsibility since moral liability requires intentional action by or on behalf of the morally liable agent.

It seems clear that aggregates and ethnic groups (*qua* ethnic groups) do not act intentionally because they do not function according to a recognized formal or informal rule system. Raimo Tuomela, however, argues that even crowds and rioters *can* properly be said to act:

> Crowds ... can be said to act in virtue of their members' actions .... Thus in a riot the members of the collective typically perform their destructive actions *as members* of the collective without acting on its behalf. So we are here dealing with groups without much or any structure (and divisions of tasks and activities), ... with respect to the goals and interests of the group.[16]

The difficulty with Tuomela's position is that rioters and aggregates such as crowds altogether lack common goals and interests, though their respective members can and do possess goals and interests. Rioters and crowds are aggregates, and aggregates are simply a loose collection of individual human persons. It seems, then, that such collectives are not plausible candidates for intentional action attributions.

But perhaps certain other sorts of collectives (namely, those of the conglomerate type) *can* act intentionally. In fact, nations and corporations act, though not in a primary way. They are secondary agents. A primary agent is one who has the capacity to act on her own, intentionally. A secondary agent, as I said earlier, is one for whom another acts according to a legal or moral rule system, intentionally. In the case of secondary agency, both the one on behalf of whom the action is performed and the one performing the action 'in her name' are intentional agents, but in different respects. The secondary agent, for whom the act is carried out, must have the capacity to have the action carried out according to her beliefs and desires. The one acting 'in her name' must be capable of performing 'her action' such that her own doings are caused by her wants and beliefs. For example, an attorney acts on behalf of (or 'in the name of') her clients, and states, corporations, and even nations have attorneys. This makes at least some conglomerates secondary agents to the extent that those who properly represent their putative aims and purposes (according to an official rule system).

Moreover, there seems to be no conceptual barrier to construing secondary agents as intentional ones. This means that if it is possible to reduce the language of collective action to that of individual action, this poses no logical problem for the justifiedness of collective agency ascriptions.[17]

In light of this consideration, it might be objected that to deny the very possibility of collective moral responsibility fails to take into account the fact that some conglomerates, such as corporations, *do* act intentionally *via* their respective Corporate Internal Decision Structures.[18] These structures are official regulations concerning the way in which the corporation should operate.[19]

Now to this line of argument it might be replied that there is no doubt that nations and corporations (and other highly organized collectives) often *behave* (without intention) according to official rules of their respective systems. But it is unclear that behavior resulting from such decision-making is the result of the intentionality of the conglomerates themselves, or whether it is the consequence of the intentionality of certain powerful decision-makers in those collectives.[20] What the first objection needs is an independent argument adequatly supporting the claim that such *collectives* do in fact exhibit intentional agency.

Against this reply it might be argued, as Copp does, that some collectives such as nations (in signing treaties) act "for a reason," which is sufficient for a collective's acting intentionally.[21] However, this counter does not suffice as an answer to the previous query. For what is questioned concerning collective intentionality also arises at the level of collective 'reasons.' That is, how does one know whether it is the collective itself which 'acts for a reason,' or whether it is merely a certain powerful individual representative or member of that collective (or group of them) who 'acts for a reason?' Furthermore, the plausibility of this notion of what is sufficient for intentional action is contingent on the plausibility of G. E. M. Anscombe's theory of intentionality.[22] Thus it requires an independent defense of Anscombe's overall theory. However, if we assume as I do, that intentional action is that which is caused by the beliefs and desires of the agent,[23] then the Anscombian view of intentional agency (as acting 'for a reason') is not clearly warranted. This means that even if collectives such as nations and corporations can and do act 'for a reason,' it is not obvious that this is sufficient for collective intentional action.

Nor will it do to argue, as does Copp, that some collectives in fact act as secondary agents:[24] If a corporation's attorneys successfully defend that corporation against all suits brought against it for it's alleged corporate wrong doing, then it is not misleading to say that the *corporation* vindicated itself in the midst of such charges.

But even if Feinberg is incorrect in arguing that this line *is* misleading,[25] and even if it does make some sense to say that the corporation vindicated itself from the said charges leveled against it, it does not necessarily follow from this that what the corporation did constitutes an *action*. At best it is a doing or a doing-related event. Actions entail intentionality, doings do not. And Copp's point, even if well-taken, requires an independent argument to show that what a conglomerate does amounts to an *action*, i.e., that what it does is caused by its *own* wants and beliefs, and not merely the wants and beliefs of certain powerful individuals of that conglomerate. For only then can such a collective hope to satisfy the conditions of being the subject of justified retrospective moral liability ascriptions.[26]

Another attempt to rescue the notion of actual collective intentional agency argues that collective intentional agency *supervenes* on individual intentional agency. The argument states: "actions by collectives supervene on the actions of the operative members of the collective."[27] This view may be construed as a response to my previous point requiring an argument for the claim that collectives have their own wants and desires requisite for intentional agency. Tuomela argues that "I accept that collectives may be said to have wants and beliefs and to act for a reason, the concepts for these mental states seem to acquire their meanings basically (or at least to a great extent) from the individual case."[28] Moreover, he argues, the actions of a collective supervene on the actions and joint actions performed by its members or representatives, and this involves two claims. First, whenever the collective does something, it does it *via* some actions of its members. Secondly, suitable actions by the members or representatives of the collective will (conventionally, legally, etc.) determine the collective's action. Tuomela intends his view to apply to both organized and unorganized collectives (or to what I refer to as "conglomerates" and "aggregates").[29] Thus, Tuomela argues, the properties of collectives—such as intention, belief, desire—are "embodied in" and "determined by" the properties of individual members or representatives of that collective.

However, Tuomela's position is problematic. For he begs a crucial question pertaining to the problem of collective agency: Do collectives act intentionally, do their own beliefs and wants cause their actions? As Tuomela himself admits, he *assumes* that collectives have the intentional properties of belief and desire. But the moral responsibility individualist demands that collective intentionality be proven by independent argumentation, and this requires the establishing of *collective* beliefs and desires which cause a collective's doings, forming a collective action. And this holds true whether or not collectives are construed as primary agents or as secondary agents. As Max Weber writes, "Social action is not identical either with the similar actions of many persons or with actions influenced by other persons."[30] Even as a secondary agent, a collective must have the capacity to believe and desire such that members or representatives may act for it, in its name.

Tuomela's argument for collective action is based on his analysis of "we-intentions."[31] But for his argument to succeed in showing that *collectives* act intentionally, it must be successfully argued that such collectives also have "we-beliefs"[32] and "we-wants" (or "we-desires") which can and do somehow causally generate a collective's doings and "convert" them into actions.[33] Thus it is still unclear whether or not conglomerates as a class of entities commonly act intentionally. In turn, it is not clear that they are (typically) legitimate candidates for moral liability ascriptions.[34]

But even if a solid case could be made for the claim that some conglomerates are commonly intentional agents, it is doubtful that the typical nation or corporation is a morally responsible agent. The reason for this is that collective intentionality is at best only a necessary condition of collective moral responsibility. Significant levels of collective voluntariness and knowledge are also needed.

If, as Harry G. Frankfurt argues of individual moral agents, having a higher-order volition is necessary for acting freely and sufficient for moral responsibility,[35] then, I would argue, conglomerates must have the capacity for having such volitions if they are to be seen as plausible candidates for moral liability attributions. And this holds true even if conglomerates are viewed as secondary agents.

One might argue that the sometimes highly sophisticated and complex goal-oriented decision-making structures of certain conglomerates like democratic nations and corporations are indicative of a kind of higher-order cognition. For in such processes, certain choices are weighed and balanced against others, where in the end a higher-level decision is reached between competing lower-level alternative desires. This implies that some collectives do act freely and thus are morally responsible agents.

But this line of reasoning runs into the same trouble, which arose in regard to intentional agency. How does one know whether the putatively higher-order volition or metamental ascent which is present in such conglomerates is that of the conglomerates themselves, or merely that of certain powerful individuals acting within the rules of the conglomerates' decision-making structure? If the former is true, then it seems justified to ascribe higher-order volitional action to some collectives. But if the latter is true, then it is unclear to what extent, if any, collectives are volitional agents. What is required by the moral responsibility collectivist is an independent argument rendering plausible the claim that conglomerates are volitional agents in the requisite sense.

Thus there seem to be at least two skeptical concerns with the position that collectives are indeed morally responsible agents. The first is that it is unclear that the intentionality present in conglomerate activities is the intentionality of the conglomerate itself (conceived of in the "strange entity" sense). Second, it is difficult to understand how to separate conglomerate voluntariness from the voluntariness of certain powerful decision-makers in the conglomerate.

But even if collective intentionality and voluntariness obtained in a given circumstance, collective moral responsibility would *not* accrue unless some significant measure of *collective knowledge* also obtained therein. To the extent that acting knowingly is a condition the satisfaction of which is crucial for moral liability, it is unjustified, normally, to attribute moral liability to such collectives. I say "normally" because there are cases where a moral agent's ignorance does *not* exculpate.[36] However, this point is not inconsistent with the fact that collectives are *not* clearly epistemic agents at all, at least in a sense which qualifies them as agents which act knowingly. To the extent that collectives are not clearly epistemic agents, they are not morally liable ones.

Concerning collective belief and truth (belief and truth are normally considered to be conditions of human knowledge), Margaret Gilbert writes that "there is no obvious reason to think that group beliefs in general have a high probability of truth, or that they are likely to be superior in this respect to the beliefs of individuals."[37] More specifically, there is the "Problem of Social Epistemic Reliability." This is a problem for collective knowledge attributions. There are at least three empirical problems with the claim that collectives such as conglomerates are plausible candidates for knowledge or belief acquisition based on collective decision-making, rendering problematic any collectivist account of social knowledge, which is based on the reliability of collective decision-making. Collectives can adversely effect the decisions of individual cognizers in at least three ways, which question the reliability of collective decision-making: by the group polarization effect; by pressure toward group consensus; or by deindividuation.[38] The Problem of Social Epistemic Reliability poses a difficulty not only for a conglomerate's satisfying the collective knowledge condition ((ii)), it also poses a challenge to the collective intentionality condition ((i)) in that intentional action is caused (in part) by the agent's *beliefs*.

Thus there exist three widespread difficulties with any claim that group knowledge or justified belief arrived at on the basis of group decision-making is likely. For this reason, I argue that conglomerates typically do not act as epistemic agents. This does not, however, deny the *possible* epistemic status of some conglomerates.

The upshot of the Problem of Social Epistemic Reliability is that there is good reason to doubt the plausibility of group beliefs being reliably produced by a collective decision-making process. If collective knowledge depends in part on collective belief (and assuming, as many contemporary analytical epistemologists argue,[39] that belief is a necessary condition of knowledge), and if justified collective responsibility ascriptions are contingent on there being collective knowledge, then collective moral responsibility attributions are dubious to the extent that collective knowledge and belief are doubtful. So even if Gilbert is correct in arguing that some attributions of *beliefs* to certain collectives as "plural subjects" is justified or reasonable,[40] it would not follow that such collectives are epistemic subjects in the requisite sense of their acting *knowingly*.

It is unclear, then, that it is justified to ascribe intentional action, voluntariness, and knowledge (or belief) to conglomerates such as nations and corporations. Again, I do not deny the *possible* epistemic status of conglomerates. So it is not that conglomerates such as nations and corporations *cannot ever* satisfy the conditions of justified collective moral liability ascriptions. Rather, it is that, given a certain prevalence of a social cognitive nature, it is unclear that such conditions *do* (commonly) obtain when it comes to epistemic agency.[41]

Notes

* The analysis will be congruent with, for the most part, the views set forth in J. Angelo Corlett, "Corporate Punishment and Responsibility," *Journal of Social Philosophy*, Vol. XXVIII (1997), pp. 96-100; "Collective Punishment," in *Encyclopedic Dictionary of Business Ethics*, Edited by Patricia Werhane and R Edward Freeman (London: Blackwell, 1997), pp. 117-20; "Collective Responsibility," in Werhane and Freeman, pp. 120-25; "Corporate Responsibility for Environmental Damage," *Environmental Ethics*, Vol. 18 (1996), pp. 195-207; "Collective Punishment and Public Policy," *Journal of Business Ethics*, Vol. 11 (1992), pp. 207-16; "Corporate Responsibility and Punishment," *Public Affairs Quarterly*, Vol. 2 (1988), pp. 1-16.

1 Burleigh T. Wilkins, *Terrorism and Collective Responsibility* (London: Routledge, 1992), p. 97.

2 This condition is related to the notion of collective feelings of guilt based on collective wrong-doing. For an incisive discussion of collective guilt, see Margaret Gilbert, "Group Wrongs and Guilt Feelings," *The Journal of Ethics*, Vol. 1 (1997), 65-84.

3 This notion of collective fault ((iv)-(vi)) is borrowed from Feinberg's notion of individual liability (See Joel Feinberg, *Doing and Deserving* (Princeton: Princeton University Press, 1970), p. 222).

4 For an incisive discussion of shared moral responsibility for inaction, see Larry May, "Collective Inaction and Shared Responsibility," *Nous*, Vol. 24 (1990), pp. 269-278; Larry May, *Sharing Responsibility: Expanding the Domain of Moral Responsibility* (Chicago: University of Chicago Press, 1992); David Copp, "Responsibility for Collective Inaction," *American Philosophical Association* (Central Division), 1990; and Gregory Mellema, "Shared Responsibility and Ethical Dilutionism," *Australasian Journal of Philosophy*, Vol. 63 (1985), pp. 177-187.

5 Virginia Held, "Corporations, Persons, and Responsibility," in Hugh Curtler, Editor, *Shame, Responsibility, and the Corporation* (New York: Haven, 1986), p. 164.

6 Ibid., p. 164.

7 Ibid., p. 165.

8 Ibid., pp. 166-7.

9 Ibid., p. 166.

10 Ibid., p. 161.

11 This is a Goldmanian account of collective action based on the analysis of human (individual) action of Alvin I. Goldman. For suggestive remarks about whether or not collectives are intentional agents, see Alvin I. Goldman, *A Theory of Human Action* (Princeton: Princeton University Press, 1970), p. 226. For a helpful discussion of the plausibility of collective beliefs, desires and intentionality in light of Daniel Dennett's "intentional stance," see Austen Clark, "Beliefs and Desires Incorporated," *The Journal of Philosophy*, Vol. XCI (1994), pp. 404-425.

12 Michael Bratman, "Shared Cooperative Activity," *The Philosophical Review*, Vol. 101 (1992), pp. 327-41; "Shared Intention," *Ethics*, Vol. 104 (1993), pp. 97-113; "Responsibility and Planning," *The Journal of Ethics*, Vol. 1 (1997), pp. 27-43.

13 David Copp, "What Collectives Are: Agency, Individualism and Legal Theory," *Dialogue*, Vol. 23 (1984), p. 250.

14 Copp, "What Collectives Are: Agency, Individualism and Legal Theory," p. 268.

15 Such collective rule systems may be enacted formally, as in a national or corporate charter, or informally, as when the rules of the system are unwritten but understood and abided by members of the collective (as in the case of an academic association or society such as the American Philosophical Association).

16 Raimo Tuomela, "Actions By Collectives," *Philosophical Perspectives*, Vol. 3 (1989), p. 476.

17 Copp writes: "A collective, one might say, could not have any "immediate impact" on the world, but can only have impact "through" the actions of persons. Alleged actions of collectives can always be explained ultimately in terms of the actions of persons. The question here, of course, is why should we regard this as showing that collectives do not act, rather than merely as showing how their actions can ultimately be explained?" (See David Copp, "Collective Actions and Secondary Actions," *American Philosophical Quarterly*, Vol. 16 (1979), 178).

18 Larry May, *The Morality of Groups* (Notre Dame: Notre Dame University Press, 1987), p. 65f.

19 Peter A. French, *Collective and Corporate Responsibility* (New York: Columbia University Press, 1984), Chapter 4.

20 This point against French's argument for the moral responsibility of some corporations is found in J. Angelo Corlett, "Corporate Responsibility and Punishment," *Public Affairs Quarterly*, Vol. 2 (1988), p. 4. (For a more recent assessment of French's theory of collective responsibility, see J. Angelo Corlett, "Corporate Punishment and Responsibility," *Journal of Social Philosophy*, Vol. 28 (1997), pp. 86-100). This argument counts also against Larry May's argument for a version of Moral Responsibility Collectivism, where he asserts that the key to corporate intentionality lies in the redescriptions of actions of corporate-individuals into acts of corporations themselves (See May, p. 65f.).

21 Copp, "Collective Actions and Secondary Actions," p. 178.

22 G. E. M. Anscombe, *Intention* (Ithaca: Cornell University Press, 1969). For a critical assessment of Anscombe's idea of intention, see Cora Diamond and Jenny Teichman, Editors, *Intention and Intentionality: Essays in Honour of G. E. M. Anscombe* (Ithaca: Cornell University Press, 1979).

23 Goldman, p. 71.

24 Copp, "Collective Actions and Secondary Actions," p. 178.

25 Feinberg, *Doing and Deserving*, p. 227.

26 Ladd argues that there is a "logical" way to distinguish collective actions from those of its constituents, especially in highly organized collectives (See Ladd, "Morality and the Ideal of Rationality in Formal Organizations," pp. 492-496). However, this logical distinction is blurred in the actual world of collective decision-making, where it is often difficult to distinguish between a conglomerate and its constituents as intentional or as teleological (goal-oriented) agents. To the extent that this is true, the notions of collective intentional action or teleological agency are proble- matic as a foundation for Moral Responsibility Collectivism, that is, where such a view pertains to a collective's *actually being* an intentional and morally responsible agent.

27 Tuomela, "Actions By Collectives," p. 494.

28 Raimo Tuomela, "Collective Action, Supervenience, and Constitution," *Synthese*, Vol. 80 (1989), p. 243.

29 Tuomela, "Collective Action, Supervenience, and Constitution," pp. 254-255.

30 Max Weber, *The Theory of Social and Economic Organizations*, Translated by A. M. Henderson and Talcott Parsons (New York: The Free Press, 1947), p. 113.

31 Raimo Tuomela, "We Will Do It: An Analysis of Group-Intentions," *Philosophy and Phenomenological Research*, Vol. 60 (1991), pp. 249-277.

32 The plausibility of collective belief attributions is considered below.

33 It is assumed, of course, that the Goldmanian notion of human action is an adequate model for collective intentional action.

34 It might be argued that collectives themselves need not act intentionally for collective intentional action ascriptions to be justified. Instead, one might argue, collectives are intentional agents to the extent that their members share an intention. However, this point assumes the plausibility of the idea of the intersubjectivity of intentions, a notion which is itself problematic (See Wilfred Sellars, *Science and Metaphysics* (London: Routledge & Kegan Paul, 1968), p. 217f.).

35 Harry G. Frankfurt, *The Importance of What We Care About* (Cambridge: Cambridge University Press, 1988). See Keith Lehrer, *Metamind* (Oxford: Oxford University Press, 1990) and "Freedom, Preference, and Autonomy," *The Journal of Ethics*, Vol. 1 (1997), pp. 3-25 for a competing higher-order or "metamental" compatibilist theory of freedom. For discussions of freedom and moral responsibility, see John Martin Fischer, Editor, *Moral Responsibility* (Ithaca: Cornell University Press, 1986); John Martin Fischer, *The Metaphysics of Free Will* (London: Blackwell, 1994); John Martin Fischer, "Responsibility, Control, and Omissions," *The Journal of Ethics*, Vol. 1 (1997), pp. 45-64; John Martin Fischer and Mark Ravizza, Editors, *Perspective on Moral Responsibility* (Ithaca: Cornell University Press, 1993). See also *The Journal of Ethics*, Vol. 3 (1999), forthcoming.

36 Holly Smith, "Culpable Ignorance," *The Philosophical Review*, Vol. 92 (1983), pp. 543-571.

37 Margaret Gilbert, "Modelling Collective Belief," *Synthese*, Vol. 73 (1987), p. 198.

38 For an account of the difficulties of collective knowledge see, J. Angelo Corlett, "Social Epistemology and Social Cognition," *Social Epistemology*, Vol. 5 (1991), p. 140f. This constitutes part of my reply to Frederick Schmitt's excellent critical comment (see note 11) on J. Angelo Corlett, "Epistemology, Psychology, and Goldman," *Social Epistemology*, Vol. 5 (1991), pp. 91-100. Also see J. Angelo Corlett, "Goldman and the Foundations of Social Epistemology," *Argumentation*, Vol. 8 (1994), pp. 145-156; and J. Angelo Corlett, *Analyzing Social Knowledge* (Lanham: Rowman and Littlefield, 1996).

39 For example, see Roderick Chisholm, *Theory of Knowledge*, Third Ed. (Englewood Cliffs: Prentice-Hall, 1989); Alvin I. Goldman, *Epistemology and Cognition* (Cambridge: Harvard University Press, 1986); Keith Lehrer, *Theory of Knowledge* (Boulder: Westview, 1990); John Pollock, *Contemporary Theories of Knowledge* (Totowa: Rowman & Littlefield, 1986).

40 Margaret Gilbert, *On Social Facts* (Princeton: Princeton University Press, 1989).

41 I am grateful to Steve Barbone, Joel Feinberg, Robert Francescotti, Margaret Gilbert, Keith Lehrer, James Nickel, Thomas Pogge, Mark Wheeler and Burleigh Wilkins

for helpful comments on earlier sections or drafts of this paper. A section of this paper was presented at the Conference on War, Collective Responsibility, and Inter-Ethnic Reconciliation, University of Belgrade, Belgrade, Yugoslavia, 27 June 1998. Another section was presented to The Serbian Philosophical Society, 1 July 1998. I am grateful to the participants of each session for their valuable comments, especially those from Jovan Babic, David Cooper, David Crocker, Aleksandar Jokic, Natalija Micunovic, Michael Slote, and Svetozar Stojanovic.

PART VI
Replies and Literary Postscript

Burleigh T. Wilkins

Replies and Reflections

Most of us want to believe that we have lived a good life. We point with pride, or at least I do, to family and friendships, and sometimes to community service and work. Philosophy is a strange kind of service and work to point to. Many readers of this book will have had some experience with the inconclusiveness of philosophical debate and the divisiveness among philosophers. Philosophical community may seem as much a misnomer as the so-called international community, and yet in both cases progress has occurred, for example, in the treatment of human rights. In my lifetime as a philosopher, I have observed that the distinction between continental philosophy and analytic philosophy has lost much of its earlier significance, and that there has emerged, often from within the ranks of analytic philosophy, the distinction between pure or traditional philosophy and the newer applied ethics. In a way I have lived through these distinctions, as the essays in this book and in my responses which follow illustrate. I have written about some of the great historical figures such as Hegel and Burke but from an analytic point of view. And as an analytic philosopher I have worried about the problem of explanation in the historical and the social sciences before moving on to do work in applied ethics. All of these activities have involved the exploration of the relationships between the individual and the community. Although I seem constitutionally incapable of sitting through a single city council session or even a philosophy department meeting without discomfort I have found a place for myself in the discussion of the moral conditions and objectives of our lives in various forms of activity. As a liberal, I can proudly point to a basic distinction which political liberalism emphasizes, namely the distinction between the political community and state and the various organizations and associations which occur within it. Helping resolve, either on the level of theory or practice, the tensions arising from membership in these various communities would I think constitute a significant part of a good life.

Popper once remarked that the philosophy of science is like a horse race: no matter what they think they are doing, philosophers of science are really betting that a certain horse, a certain way of actually doing science, will win the race. Popper's point, although exaggerated, captures the normative aspect of much of philosophical inquiry and not just in ethics, or applied ethics. Have I bet on the right horse where my various historical interpretations of great philosophers are concerned? Have I bet on the right horse where my various proposals in applied ethics are concerned? Most importantly, have I addressed the right questions? I can only hope so, but I am certain that I have kept good company in the community of scholars whose essays I will discuss in the following pages.

Frederick G. Whelan

In one of his essays Harold T. Parker wrote that erudition endures. My own view is somewhat bleaker, but still I confess to being delighted that Professor Whelan believes my natural law reading of Burke will endure. I am especially pleased that Whelan endorses the parallels I noted between Burke and Hume, and that he believes these parallels stand independently of any impact Hume's epistemology may have had upon the foundations of natural law theory. In this reply I wish to follow Whelan's example and comment briefly upon some recent developments in Burke studies. Connor Cruise O'Brien, in particular, has dismissed all efforts to construct a system of Burke political philosophy out of what he calls the "hollower components of his rhetoric and the common places of his education." Remarks like this suggest that political philosophy is too important to be left to literary critics. In any case, Burke's rhetoric was not the rhetoric of an unthinking school boy reciting the common places of his education, but in its better moments was the reflection of a mature politician trying to combine political theory with his considerable experience of historical reality. Starting with Leo Strauss, there has been an alarming tendency to focus too much on the stylistic idiosyncracies of political philosophers at the expense of what they actually said. Where the reading of texts is concerned, what really matters is whether, for example, Alasdair MacIntyre's reading of Burke as the champion of a dying traditionalism, which has no place for self criticism, is correct. I think it is not correct because he has exaggerated the importance of Burke's contrast between tradition and reason, and between the stability of tradition and conflict. For Burke tradition in a viable constitutional regime is the product of successful conflict resolutions over many generations, and neither death nor stagnation need occur so long as we have changes and piece meal reforms in which practical reason does not neglect the historical circumstance of a people. MacIntyre's own communitarianism is ill-served by his repudiation of Burke and by his failure to take seriously Burke's strictures, in the context of Burke's criticisms of Warren Hastings of the East India Company, of what he called "geographical morality" or relativism. This represents a substantive difference between MacIntyre and myself, and so far as I can see it has nothing to do with rhetoric or literary style. Whelan notes that my approach to the reading of texts is old-fashioned, and I think his is, too. Indeed, his essay is an example of traditional critical historiography at its best.

Paul Redding

Although most of these essays were available to me before I wrote my "intellectual autobiography," I refrained from reading them, wanting my memory of things past to be free from their potentially distorting effect. But now I have to re-write my intellectual autobiography, at least in part, in the light of Redding's placing me among a group of younger scholars, including himself, who read Hegel in a non-metaphysical way. Charles Taylor's *Hegel* appeared the year after my book on Hegel's philosophy of history and it cast Hegel as a dogmatic metaphysician with history serving as God's biography. But I, in company with Redding and others, have seen that metaphysics would never be the same after Kant and that Hegel understood this. Here, my initial failure to understand Hegel's account of the variety of historical writing stood me in good stead, because it enabled me eventually to see how Hegel built his philosophy of history from the ground up. Hegel's teleology of history would not, I think, be intelligible if it were not preceded by his analyses of the variety of historical writing, beginning with accounts of contemporary events by historians and continuing with histories involving an ever increasing distance on the part of the historian from the events he was recounting. Kant saw the problem here, and again, I was lucky: I had written an essay on Kant's teleology of history years before tackling Hegel. However, Kant was from the Hegelian perspective superficial in his conclusion that teleology serves mainly to account for the variety of perspectives or points of view historians or others may take toward the past. Hegel claimed that if we arranged histories in terms of their increasing generality, we would see the teleology latent in the historical process itself unfold and thus we would have a factual basis for answering the question of what is the purpose of the historical process. If Redding, Pippin Robert and Terry Pinkard are correct, the key to Hegel's philosophy is Hegel's idea of recognition, or *Anerkennung*. Hegel, as I recall, saw religion as a kind of mirror by means of which we projected human aspirations "upward" toward the divine, and history serves as an ever widening exploration of how we have come to have the aspirations we share. On this view, history provides a fully rational form of self-understanding, as on my view American history has involved the working out in our historical and especially our constitutional experience of an ever fuller realization of what was involved in Jefferson's idea of equal moral worth. What is important here is the emphasis placed by Redding and his colleagues upon the fact that for Hegel recognition is community based. Community takes a variety of forms, and historical scholarship is an expression of the community of historical scholars. Instead of a romantic craving for a lost past, we can see the past in an evolving present. Instead of bemoaning some conspiracy to use history for present political purposes, we can see the past as a necessary condition for present forms of social recognition. Where my own intellectual autobiography is concerned, Redding helps me understand better why I chose to write on Burke and Hegel. Previously I saw these books mainly as exercises in historical reconstruction, but although I failed to realize it at the time, what attracted me is in hindsight fairly obvious. Both Burke and Hegel were accused of historicism , relativism, and romanticism. By helping rescue them from these allegations I could help preserve their insight that philosophy, especially political philosophy, must be grounded in historical reality, in an ongoing tradition, and in a sense of community while at the same time it must avoid surrendering entirely to the demands of a particular moment in history.

Johnatan L. Gorman

Apart from his generous assessment of my contributions to the philosophy of history, Professor Gorman traces accurately and with sensitivity the role that the philosophy of history has played in Anglo-American philosophy. He correctly finds that before Hempel's classic paper on the function of general laws in history there was very little attention paid to the philosophy of history by British and American philosophers. The result of this neglect was that historians in reflecting on historical methodology had to devise their own philosophical responses to problems having to do, for example, with the reliability of testimony and other historical evidence. I should add here, perhaps, that a fuller intellectual autobiography would take note of the fact that I was most influenced by the writings of the historian Carl Becker, by the writings of R. G. Collingwood, especially his *Autobiography,* and then by Hempel's paper on the covering law model of explanation. I found Becker to be very stimulating, but I found his relativism unacceptable. I found Collingwood's account of historical explanation in terms of empathic reconstruction to be beguiling, but it seemed to me to partake of too much subjectivism. I was somewhat relieved to find Hempel's paper as something I could finally agree with. Hempel noted that historians don't have covering laws in their explanations, but he noted that historians do use explanation sketches which often contain a very high level of generality. For Hempel explanation proper consists in deducing statements about the occurrence of a particular event from statements of either a universal or probabilistic law conjoined with statements to the effect that the antecedent conditions in a given law are satisfied. Objections to Hempel came essentially from two quarters. First, there was an objection about the nature of explanation itself. Explanation on this view was said to be essentially pragmatic in nature, i.e. the unfamiliar was explained in terms of the familiar. I have not been impressed by either the importance or accuracy of this criticism. The second criticism of Hempel had to do with reasons for acting. It was argued that reasons for acting explained the actions of historical actors. I think Hempel was right in pointing out that this is true only if reasons for acting are regarded as good reasons for acting by historical actors themselves. Hempel's covering law model was not so much refuted as it was superceded by the emergence of an entirely new way of looking at the philosophy of science. This took the form of Thomas Kuhn's book *The Structure of Scientific Revolutions.* The main point of Kuhn's book is that science is not a progressive enterprise, but that science is a succession of scientific revolutions, each bringing with it what he called its own paradigm, and the important thing about revolutions in science is that the theories that bring about these revolutions are radically incommensurable with one another. However, if so -called paradigm shifts occur in the philosophy of science as well as in science itself, it should be noted that incommensurability seems not to be a problem. Pre-Kuhnian and post-Kuhnian philosophers of science seem to have little difficulty in communicating with one another. This is borne out, for example, by Aleksandar Jokic's important book on scientific discovery, which is a clearly written criticism of Carnap and other pre-Kuhnian philosophers of science.

David Cooper

I can assure Professor Cooper that just about everyone working in the area of applied ethics has his own horror story to tell. Mine concerns the time when a colleague looked me straight in the eyes and said, "There's no such thing as applied ethics." I believe that Cooper's essay is perhaps the best account we have of why applied ethics should be taken seriously and why there is a radical incompleteness if we stop simply on the level of ethics proper, after, for example, we have decided whether Kant is better than Mill or vice versa.

The problem which I think is central to applied ethics is roughly the following. Universal principles while laudatory in themselves are insufficient where the actual living of an ethical life is concerned. There has always been a tension noted by philosophers like Burke and Hegel between the universal and the concrete in the form of the history and institutions of a given people. Universal principles by themselves do not tell us what to do in particular situations. Kant remarks that an action is not good or bad in itself, but only good or bad under some description, and this is why specifying the content of what Kant calls maxims of actions is so crucial. What exactly is the action that we are considering? I suppose that Eichmann is the most hideous and tragic example of a misapplication of principles. Eichmann claimed that he was a good Kantian, doing his duty and obeying the law. Well, he certainly was obeying the law, and this may seem a defensible maxim of action, but when the action is further specified so the law involves the extermination of millions of people on grounds having to do primarily with race, we can see the absolute importance of getting our act descriptions right. This may be the appropriate time to mention what I take to be a major concern of philosophers working in applied ethics over the last several decades, which has been to give avoice to the victims of our society including people who have been sacrificed in various ways on the altar of the misapplication of universal principles. There is a tendency in the moral life towards something called moral rigorism which involves an insensitive application of abstract principles to concrete situations. Thus, for example, where the principle of equality of opportunity is concerned, so long as our laws forbids discrimination, many people are prepared to say that nothing further needs to be done on behalf of people who have historically been discriminated against or disenfranchised in various ways. But this, I think, shows that the ruling class in our society has, as it were, hijacked certain laudatory principles and has used these principles at the expense of groups of people who have in various ways been victimized, historically speaking. The problem which has concerned most of us working in the area of applied ethics is how to give a voice to those who are silent or oppressed without infringing upon the rights of others. I'll have more to say about this in my reply to Professor Pogge's critique of my paper proposing a third principle of justice.

C. Behan McCullagh

Just when I feared I was about to be canonized, I read Professor McCullagh's lively polemic against things I said and against things he thinks I said. It is hard to tell from McCullagh's essay which he dislikes more, liberalism or the covering law model of explanation, both of which I espouse in my *Has History Any Meaning*?. Liberalism is often under attack from the left and from the right. McCullagh's criticism is from the left, and he finds that liberals like me are willing to tolerate what he considers an unacceptable level of social and economic inequality. Apparently, he would relegate liberals to the eighteenth century, and while this is certainly not the century that I would most fear being relegated to, I believe that the eighteenth century contained serious inequities. Slavery was still a legal institution in the West, and there were serious injustices arising from social class and gender. Liberalism, in the twentieth century, has tried with varying degree of success to alleviate inequalities connected with race, social class, and gender.

McCullagh is adamant in stating his conviction that the covering law model of explanation is crude and inadequate, but the alternatives he espouses, such as explanation in terms of tendencies, dispositions, and reasons for acting, have been shown in the literature not to be serious alternatives to explanations in terms of the covering law model. McCullagh writes: "Wilkins' main concern in this book is to defend a generalization about the conditions which make for scientific progress." How he arrived at this conclusion escapes me. What I did was to offer an example of a putative covering law which would explain how scientific progress is possible. And here there is a crucial difference between a law and a generalization. McCullagh says that my "generalization" does not take account of the fact that science seems to have developed in the West but not so rapidly in India and not at all in aboriginal Australia. But if you look at my law it says something like this: Scientific progress occurs in the presence of certain conditions, such as open inquiry, and in the absence of certain other conditions, such as religious mysticism. My law may have only one instance, namely Western society or Western societies. But in any case, to say that it doesn't apply to non-Western societies is just a way of saying that some of the antecedent conditions in this putative law are not satisfied in these societies. This says nothing about the importance of the law as such.

I think what is really bothering McCullagh is his mistaken belief that I have made scientific progress the key to the meaning of history. He writes, "Wilkins does not want merely to suggest an interpretation of history, rather he wants to impose an interpretation upon us, so that we will see history in terms of the values and processes which his interpretation presents. Wilkins wants to use history as propaganda, as a conservative liberal, and would probably justify doing so on moral grounds. If people focus upon the growth of science and technology, life will become less miserable in due course." I believe McCullagh gets carried away in this quotation. I do want to suggest an interpretation of history, but not the one he imputes to me. I certainly don't want to impose any interpretation upon anyone, and given my commitment to the open society and to the basic rights and liberties in Rawls' first principle, it is hard to see how I could do this even if I wanted to. As for the use of history as propaganda, I don't think there is anything I have said about the meaning of history as being self-referential, or anything I have said about the nature of the historical process, which would in any way prevent us from distinguishing between history as propaganda and history as a factual account of certain features of the historical process. As for whether, if people focus on the growth of science and technology, life will become less miserable in due course, this may or may not be true. I think it is clear, however, that a fair minded reading of my book would show that I see science and technology as only potentially valuable means to the end of promoting a society that is both more open and more just.

Brenda M. Baker

Professor Baker has kindly contributed two essays to this volume. In her first essay she examines my paper on the moral *prima facie* obligation to obey the law. I sought to derive this obligation from what Rawls calls the natural duty to uphold just institutions. She claims there is a loophole in my argument. I don't think there is, but undoubtedly a comprehensive account of the obligation to obey the law would have to consider the free rider problem she calls attention to. Her other objection is more interesting. She doubts whether there can be an obligation to obey the law which is constant and uniform over all citizens. She offers the example of impoverished homeless people who she says cannot effectively exercise any of their rights as being a class of people who would have no obligation to obey the law. Here I think we have to distinguish between *prima facie* and actual obligations. In the *A Theory* Rawls remarks that people who benefit most from a reasonably just society have a stronger obligation to uphold the laws of that society. This seems to me correct, but it would only be coherent if we were talking about actual obligations. It seems to me to make perfectly good sense to say that people who fare badly under a reasonably just society have less of an actual obligation to obey the law than more fortunate members of that society. However, this seems consistent with saying that there is a *prima facie* obligation to obey the law, in all but the most severe cases where there has been a systematic and deliberate discrimination against a group; and under these circumstances we will in all likelihood not be dealing with a reasonably just society.

Baker's criticism of my paper on intention and criminal responsibility is very probing and thoughtful. Of all my papers this was the one that left me most dissatisfied, and I thank her for giving me the opportunity to have a second chance at clarifying the proposal I made. The paper was a response to two British cases, the more important being one in which a Ms. Hyam set fire to a letter box in a house occupied by a woman and her children. The woman in question was a rival of Ms. Hyam's for the affections of some gentleman, and she and her children perished as a result of the fire Ms. Hyam set. Ms. Hyam denied that she intended to kill her rival, and I constructed a scheme which would acknowledge that Ms. Hyam may have been telling the truth, and at the same time hold her responsible for something she did intend, namely the bringing about of a state of affairs aimed at the achieving of one desired consequence, frightening her rival into leaving that part of town, and one consequence that she neither desired nor intended. I argued that a person could be said to have intended to bring about a state of affairs consisting of a desired consequence and an undesired consequence, if on balance the agent in question preferred to bring about the desired consequence more than the agent preferred to avoid the undesired consequence. Baker wonders if this is simply a subjective test, or if it represents an unstable mixture of subjective and objective components. In a footnote she says that a state of affairs intended by an agent could, according to me, include a consequence that an agent did not desire, but that this consequence need only be foreseeable and not actually foreseen by the agent, and this suggests that an objective or reasonable person test could be used to identify those undesired consequences that may be brought about. How is this compatible she asks with my comparative desirability test which seems to require a comparison of subjectively determined desired consequences and undesired consequences? I think there are certainly cases when an agent makes the comparative desirability test where he foresees both the desired consequence and the undesired consequence, and is willing to continue to attempt to bring about the desired consequence because he desires this consequence more than he desires to avoid the undesired consequence. This kind of case I think is not interesting, and it can either be captured by my scheme of intending to bring about a certain state of affairs or by other means. But looking back on the Hyam case, and on my comparative desirability test, I think it is possible to mix both subjective and objective considerations. The reasonable person test can serve to identify the undesirable consequence or consequences which might follow an action initiated to achieve a certain desired consequence. Presumably, the extent to which we hold someone responsible may well depend in large part upon calculations of probability as to various outcomes of an action. The important thing about the reasonable person test is that it represents an objective fleshing out of the probable and possible consequences that may follow an action which an agent knows to be risky, but which are not foreseen by her, at least not as specific consequences of her action. The proposal I make therefore involves a mixture of what an agent foresees with what a reasonable person foresees. My scheme should help us capture cases where an agent knowingly runs a risk without stopping to calculate what undesirable consequences may follow from the risky action in question. I take it that it is typical of people like Ms. Hyam to know that they are doing something risky, but to refuse to consider exactly what the outcome of their risky conduct might be. I just didn't stop to think, I didn't intend such and such. These are familiar plaintive cries from people accused of certain kinds of criminal conduct. What my proposal involves is a spelling out by the reasonable person test of what the consequences of risky action may be. Once these are spelled out I think it becomes more plausible to say that someone who engages in risky conduct intends to bring about the state of affairs with the two components that I've mentioned.

Thomas Pogge

I'm glad that Professor Pogge finds my proposal for a third principle of justice to be important and interesting, and I return the compliment where his comments are concerned. I wish to begin by clarifying some things that I said in the postscript to the paper. Pogge is correct in pointing out that the idea of enjoying rights and liberties at their "fair value" is limited by Rawls himself to the enjoyment of political rights and liberties. Rawls says that going beyond political rights and liberties could be divisive. For example, suppose members of one religious community see attendance at religious observances at a far distant holy shrine as an essential part of their religion, while members of other religious communities do not. It would be divisive, Rawls writes, to give money to the first group and do nothing for the other groups, and I think he is probably right about this. However, there are problems with the idea of "fair value," even in the restricted sphere where Rawls saw it as being useful. Rawls believes that we should enjoy our political liberties in a substantive way: "mere formal equality" is not enough. Rawls attaches great hopes to campaign reform so that the financing of political campaigns could be undertaken by the public sector. I think he is unduly optimistic here about what this would accomplish. Maybe the problem is that as long as Rupert Murdoch owns lots of newspapers and I don't even have one, substantive equality may be hard to come by. There is an obvious analogy between this problem and the religious exercise example cited by Rawls. My second thought on "fair value" is that although this idea may be a necessary supplement to any Rawlsian account of justice, much more needs to be done in working out the implications of this idea.

I wish now to say something about the third principle and its motivation. Pogge interprets the third principle in terms of its contribution to what he calls the "stability problem." In other words, the third principle is intended to keep religious doctrine, or any comprehensive doctrine, from having destabilizing effects upon the institutions of political liberalism. That is certainly a large part of what I was after. But another part is the idea that we want to be fair to all communities, especially religious communities, that have decided to abide by the terms of reasonable pluralism and that are committed to the institutions of political liberalism. In other words, we don't want, even if it weren't destabilizing, for these communities to suffer unfair burdens at the hands of the liberal state. So one idea behind the third principle was that where the liberal state does or contemplates doing something with harmful foreseeable consequences to these communities, this can be justified only where there is a compelling state interest. Scholars familiar with American constitutional history know that the compelling state interest test has been very difficult for the state to satisfy, and rightly so.

I think we can see some of the strength of political liberalism if we consider two examples. One is the example of snake handling as a part of religious ceremonies, and the other is the refusal of members of some religious communities to accept blood transfusions. The liberal state has decided that snake handling is illegal, but that the refusal of transfusions is not. What is the difference, since both may involve harm and even death? I think the explanation is that political liberalism is able to make a distinction here which neither paternalism as a comprehensive doctrine nor liberalism as a comprehensive doctrine could make. Paternalism, presumably, would outlaw both practices while liberalism would allow people to do pretty much anything they wanted, provided they did not harm others. The liberal state makes a principled distinction here. In the snake handling case individuals undertake a deliberate risk of harm. Snake handling offers a kind of empirical test for these individuals as to whether God is present. If God is present in a particular person who handles snakes, he either won't be bit or he will suffer only minor injuries. There is no deliberate risk-taking in the case of the religious refusal to allow blood transfusion. The refusal reflects certain beliefs about the importance of preserving the purity of the blood. No one says he will refuse to take a blood transfusion and see what happens. And certainly no one in this religious community is saying that if someone survives without the transfusion this shows that God was present. Thus, I think there is a principled way that the liberal state has of making distinctions between two activities which many of us may find unpalatable. Also, I think it is important that the liberal state be the final arbiter of what constitutes harm. As I understand it, pedophiles think they are doing children a favor by introducing them to sexual activity as soon as possible. However, there is a body of social science which strongly indicates that early sexual activity on the part of children can have devastating psychological consequences. Here it is going to be the liberal state which prohibits pedophilia on the grounds of objective harm, as opposed to some strange doctrine which insists that no harm is actually being done.

Pogge worries that I may not have attached enough importance to the issue of what to do about religious communities, but this I think is not true. I think Pogge's reasoning is potentially subversive of any Rawlsian effort to lexically order principles for basic institutions. Lurking behind my concerns here is the specter raised by Joel Feinberg in an early review of Rawls' *A Theory of Justice* where Feinberg said that intuitionism as an account of principles for the basic institutions of a just society may be all that we can have. One of Pogge's worries is that religious communities may be allowed to limit employment opportunities, for example, in their church offices (see *Church of Jesus Christ of Latter Day Saints v. Amos*). Pogge believes that significant gains in employment opportunities could be achieved at some minuscule sacrifice where one of the liberties in Rawls' first principle is concerned. That may be true, but here I think we should recall Rawls' metaphorical insistence that the basic rights and liberties must be seen as a family and that even a seemingly small sacrifice may adversely impact the entire family in important ways.

Aleksandar Jokic

This is one of three sophisticated papers written by Professor Jokic in which he attempts to refute a doctrine which he calls potentialism. He describes potentialism as being based on the so called strict potentiality criterion "according to which the fetus can correctly be said to have rights because it is a potential adult human being." The paper he has included in this volume is an attack upon J. Stone's version of potentialism which claims that in cases where the fetus will develop into an adult human being it simply is the resulting human being, and this 'is' is the 'is' of identity. I find this worrisome because if the fetus simply is the adult human being, then it is hard to distinguish Stone's potentialism from the Catholic position, which maintains that the fetus has a right to life because it already is a person. I believe Jokic has successfully refuted Stone's version of potentialism. However, I have some reservations about the methodology that Jokic uses. He tells us that the concept of potentiality consists of three things. First there is the idea of possibility. Then there is the idea of quantification over future time, and finally there is something that he marks by the dummy letter 'U', where 'U' attempts to explicate potentiality in a way that goes beyond possibility and quantification over future time. Jokic believes we can do without a full analysis that would require us to take 'U' into account, because as he puts it, "to make things simpler we can dispense with 'U' since it does not seem to be a natural place for the concept of identity to come into play." But as he acknowledges in a footnote 'U' may contain concepts other than identity such as the one in my analysis of potentiality as a power, a capacity or an ability. Jokic uses his partial analysis to divide fetuses into two categories. In the first we find the fetus that not only represents a possible adult human being, but will become an adult human being. In the second category we have a fetus that is a possible adult human being, but which fails because of a natural or a manmade abortion to become an actual human being. As a distinction, this certainly is viable, but what Jokic builds on it seems to be dubious. Where the fetus that is merely a possible human being is concerned, Jokic says it has no right to life, since merely possible existents can't have rights. Where the fetus that is both possible and which is quantified over time so it becomes an adult human being, Jokic has no trouble in saying it has a right to life. But of course we can't pick out in advance the fetus that will become an actual adult human being, so the upshot of Jokic's partial analysis seems to be that we cannot say of any particular fetus in the real world that it has a right to life. This seems to me counter-intuitive. Another way of putting my point is that the right to life is a claim right. If we say that fetuses as a class have a claim right to life, then we know how to proceed to protect this right by pointing to the parties who have a correlative duty to respect the fetus' right to life. On the other hand, if we say that a sub-class of fetuses, namely those that will become adult human beings have a right to life but we can't know which ones these are until after the fact, then we can't provide for the protection of any claim they might have to the right to life.

Margaret Gilbert

I am in substantial agreement with much of what Professor Gilbert says in her clearly written essay. Her claim that collective moral responsibility can be modeled on personal moral responsibility is well taken. You knowingly perform an action, you know it is wrong, and you act freely. This is enough to establish individual culpability. If Gilbert is right, this modeling goes a long way in helping to establish group responsibility. Her example of walking together as an example of a group action is well taken, and I like her idea that what distinguishes a group action is what she calls a joint commitment. I am, however, troubled by her claim that joint commitment is revocable only if all of the parties to a joint commitment can agree to rescind the commitment in question: "It is not a set of distinguishable personal commitments, one for each of the parties." It seems to me that perhaps the requirement of unanimous consent before a joint commitment can be rescinded sets too stringent a requirement.

Once we move from an account of relatively simple group actions like taking a walk together to more complex group actions, there is a host of problems which arise from the fact that we delegate authority to, say, a leader and his henchmen, and these people may carry out a plan in the group's name sometimes without some or most members even knowing about it. Still, "after the fact all of the members are in a position properly to say of the group as a whole: 'We did it.'" The problem however, is to make sense of the notion that we, as a collective did things that we as individuals did not know we were doing at the time. (See my following response to Corlett's paper.) This brings us back to the problem of individual culpability. Gilbert writes that before we decide whether the individual members of a group are personally morally blameworthy we need to know more about the individuals involved, who did what, why they did it, and so on. But I think she would still want to agree with Feinberg that ascriptions of group liability may involve a weakening of the fault condition required in ascriptions of individual liability. A moral individualist would say that there is at least a moral contradiction in blaming individuals simply because they are members of the group that is held blameworthy for some action. In *Terrorism and Collective Responsibility*, I suggested a practical way around some of the difficulties which arise from Feinberg's conclusion that blame for a collective action is distributive over all the members of a collective. I proposed that sanctions or other forms of punishment be designed to impact most heavily upon those members of a group most responsible for a collective action we deem blameworthy.

J. Angelo Corlett

This paper is a useful addition to the literature on collective moral responsibility. Corlett notes two problems. The first problem arises when we are deciding whether an action by an organized collective is intentional and voluntary. Here and elsewhere Corlett has asked how do we know whether a collective has acted intentionally and voluntarily or whether it is simply that certain powerful individuals in a collective have chosen to do certain things. Then there is the problem of epistemic reliability in regard to how a collective has come to have the beliefs or knowledge that it possesses. And this problem reflects back on the question of whether a collective is acting intentionally, since on the common account intentional action is the result of beliefs and desires. Corlett concludes that typically, but not always, collectives in the real world fail to satisfy the necessary conditions he has set forth for ascriptions of collective moral responsibility. This worries me. It seems to me that we don't want conditions that are so stringent that they make ascriptions of collective moral responsibility unduly contingent upon questions having to do with the nature of the decision procedure which obtains in any given collective. First I want to note that the difficulty Corlett poses where intentional and voluntary collective action is concerned also occurs where the formation of beliefs by a collective is involved. The formation of beliefs can reflect the activity of powerful individuals within a collective so that we have as much reason to wonder whether the beliefs in question really reflect the beliefs of the collective as we did when we were concerned about whether the actions of a collective are really reflective of intentionality and voluntariness on the part of the collective. I think that perhaps the question of how a collective has come to have the beliefs and the intentions it has is to a large extent separable from the question of whether a collective has acted intentionally, voluntarily, and as an epistemic agent. Tentatively I offer the following solution to Corlett's problem: A collective may be said to have acted intentionally if the actions of some of its members or agents were in some way authorized by the collective in question. Perhaps something like Hart's "rule of recognition" is all we need to determine whether an action has been duly authorized by a collective. Usually, actions by so-called loose cannons do not count as collective actions unless it can be shown that they were encouraged or permitted by the collective in question. A collective may be said to have acted voluntarily in the absence of compulsion or coercive threats. Coercive threats may originate with powerful individuals within a collective or they may come from other collectives or powerful individuals outside a particular collective. A collective may be said to have acted as an epistemic agent even if it acted on the basis of beliefs created or encouraged by powerful individuals within the collective, and we do not have to decide upon the truth or falsity of the beliefs held by a collective in order to determine that it acted as an epistemic agent. If the above points are correct, I think we can preserve Corlett's insight as to the importance of intentionality, voluntariness and epistemic agency without limiting ourselves to the thesis that typically most organized collectives in the real world do not satisfy the conditions for ascriptions of moral responsibility.

Susan Meld Shell

Professor Shell's essay is an important contribution both in the history of philosophy and in our understanding of Kant's philosophy of history. Kant believed in all seriousness that a rigorous predictive science of human progress was possible. For Kant this predictive science would turn on three variables: republicanism, enthusiasm, and honor. Republicanism for Kant is conceived of in terms of the quest for just constitutions which will protect the rights of citizens The quest for a just constitution for Kant will always excite enthusiasm on the part of the people. The enthusiasm for a just Constitution will, according to Kant, be supported by the idea of honor.

Although honor has its roots in martial affairs and was originally conceived of as the prerogative of a ruling class, Kant argued in effect that the concept of honor had been democratized. According to Kant, the fact that human beings, and human beings alone, take honor seriously mediates between the physical realm in which we hardly matter, and the moral realm in which we matter absolutely. For Kant honor has a central role in the civic education of a people and the moral enlightenment of mankind.

What are we to make of Kant's belief that he had found the keys to the inevitable moral progress of mankind? It would be easy to dismiss Kant's position as a touching faith. We, for example, have seen how the language of republicanism and the language of honor have been debased to cover some very dark enthusiasms indeed in the twentieth century. In fairness to Kant, however, it is clear that he was not as naive as one might initially suppose. Kant was very much aware of the distinction between a quest for honor and the quest for honors. He saw the quest for honors in contemporary England, for example, as being very debased. The fact that we are able to distinguish with greater sophistication between formal acknowledgments of republicanism, as for example in the Constitution of the late unlamented Soviet Union, and the reality of republicanism, and the fact that we are able to distinguish between enthusiasms for good causes and totalitarian causes, show that we are not hopelessly at sea where moral progress is concerned. While talk about honor may have become the last refuge of scoundrels in our time, it is important to remember that the idea of honor in Kant is accompanied by other ideas having to do with equality, dignity, and the rights of mankind. Thus, honor is to be seen as one of a cluster of concepts, and arguably, taken as a whole, this cluster of concepts is doing very well indeed in the international arena. The quest for just Constitutions and for the adequate protection of human rights is one of the most encouraging aspects of our times. Whether the trend in the direction that Kant hoped for will continue is still up for grabs, but arguably Kant did succeed in identifying three crucial variables which are necessary conditions for human moral progress. If we add conditions specifying the absence of success on the part of totalitarian parties in hoodwinking people into giving up their basic rights, and further conditions stipulating that people will not be seduced by the quest for honors, or for celebrity status, or for excessive wealth, then it may be that we have here the basis for a list of separately necessary and jointly sufficient conditions for the occurrence of the moral progress that Kant predicted.

Kai Nielsen

Kai Nielsen was the first philosopher I ever talked with and the first philosopher to encourage me to pursue further work in philosophy. He was a teaching assistant in the first course I took in philosophy, a course in American philosophy nearly fifty years ago at Duke University. I haven't seen him since, and I am greatly honored that he has contributed an essay to this volume.

I share Nielsen's horror at the effects of severe economic inequalities upon the moral and intellectual growth of individuals. Unlike Professor Nielsen, however, I do not believe that problems arising from severe economic inequalities can be traced to the fact that labor is treated as a commodity. Nielsen has offered, in my opinion, a utopian proposal to the effect that there be a minimum wage for everyone. He assumes that everyone would really like to have a job, specifically a job that would pay more than the minimum income that he has in mind. My response to this is that it depends upon what kind of job we are talking about. It is not only garbage collectors who have onerous jobs, it is the people who work in the chicken processing plants on the Eastern Shore of Virginia and Maryland, and it is a fact about our economic life that most people don't like the jobs they have and work only for the money these jobs provide. This may change as we move toward more challenging jobs in an age of technology. But I seriously doubt that most people will ever cherish the work that they do.

I think Rawls' difference principle addresses the severe economic inequalities that concern Nielsen, although I may be unique among liberals influenced by Rawls in the significance I attach to this principle. Any principle that takes distributive justice seriously may well involve sacrifices where economic efficiency is concerned, and the question is how much in the way of inefficiency is tolerable before this inefficiency has a destabilizing effect upon a society. Nielsen greatly admires the Scandinavian societies with their mixed economies, and their ability to have effective redistribution of incomes without sacrificing basic rights and liberties. I think the contrast here with the Soviet Union where inefficiency approached the point where severe destabilization was the result should be kept in mind. Nobody who takes justice seriously can ignore the problem of stability, and what you had in the failed Soviet experiment was a state of affairs where a wide spectrum of basic rights and liberties was sacrificed to the achievement of an alleged equality and where inefficiency was so rampant that this inefficiency taken in conjunction with corruption led to the collapse of the Soviet system. Like Marx, Nielsen believes that socialism is possible only in comparatively wealthy societies. My conjecture is that it is precisely in these societies that we don't need socialism. In other words, distributive justice can proceed by means of the difference principle and by a judicious use of the tax structure to alleviate the more severe consequences of economic inequality. Further evidence of Nielsen's utopianism concerns the question of when central planners might allow small farmers and small businesses such as bookstores to hire workers. The idea here is that so long as these farms or businesses are suitably small, this would be acceptable from a socialist perspective. It seems to me, however, that whether you work on a one to one basis with a farmer or bookstore owner, or whether you are one of a hundred employees, your labor is still being treated as a commodity and I don't think size in any way necessarily alleviates the problems that concern Nielsen. I fail to see anything wrong with the idea of labor as a commodity, provided laborers receive adequate wages and are treated fairly.

Nielsen is dismayed not only at the collapse of socialism, but the almost total disappearance of loyalty to socialism in countries that were previously committed to the socialist ideal of equality. My conjecture is that the almost overnight disappearance of loyalty to socialist ideals reflects the fact that people who lived in these societies had become, on various levels of consciousness, masters at understanding what Marx and others have called false consciousness. They were taught to believe that under socialism all men were equal, but as they saw the big shots go by in their limousines they knew that this was false. They were taught that they owned the means of production, but they had virtually no control over decisions affecting the means of production.

Nielsen hopes that so-called analytical Marxism will be able to overcome some of the deficiencies in earlier versions of Marxism. In the beginning of his essay he quotes Roemer to the effect that central planning can be distinguished from command/administrative allocations. Roemer and Nielsen rightly point out that the terms aren't coextensive. However, so long as they and other analytical Marxists believe that the collapse of the Soviet system shows only the failure of the command/administrative apparatus and doesn't reflect the failure of central planning, I'm not sanguine about the prospects for analytical Marxism. While we can distinguish conceptually between central planning and a command/administrative apparatus I see an analogy with a phenomenon that we find in the philosophy of law. Conceptually we can distinguish between a law and a sanction, and it may be that a command theory of law is inadequate, as various critics of legal positivism have pointed out. It is nevertheless the case that the point of having a law is that people can be expected to obey the law in question. Analogously, the point of having central planning is that the plans arrived at will be implemented by some sort of command/administrative apparatus. Central planning and law making have this in common: they are not academic exercises, but are aimed at controlling the lives of people in various important respects. If the command/administrative apparatus system of the Soviet Union and other socialist countries failed, this failure seems to me to reflect the inadequacy of central planning. If we read philosophers like Popper on the difficulties involved in holistic engineering as compared with piecemeal engineering, I think we can better understand why the failure of the Soviet system was a failure on all levels, and not just the result of some idiosyncracies involving the command/administrative apparatus.

Some years ago I co-taught a course on analytical Marxism and was impressed by the intellectual rigor of analytical Marxists, and their familiarity with modern economic theory. I was not impressed by their resolve to face seriously problems concerning central planning and problems arising from concentrations of power in some central planning agency. I recall reading that Lenin at one point had to decide whether members of the Communist Party should receive special treatment in the department and grocery stores in the Soviet system, and he decided that they should receive special privileges. This was a mistake of great consequence, and he could have decided otherwise. The important thing, however, is that there was nothing in the institutions of the Soviet system which would have prevented his unwise decision to treat Communist citizens differently from non-Communist citizens. What was frightening about the Soviet system was precisely the absence of a system of checks and balances. When political and economic power become indistinguishable and are concentrated in a central bureaucracy, I think it is just a matter of time before totalitarianism and inefficiency become the order of the day. I know it is fashionable to say that if only Stalin hadn't been Stalin, things might have gone differently. The point is, however, there was nothing t keep Stalin from being Stalin, and I think this is the moral to be derive from the collapse of the Soviet system.

Edmund Wall

In an earlier published paper Wall rebutted Robert Nozick's "baseline" account of coercion, and there is a full length manuscript on coercion by Wall. These two works in conjunction with the present essay on Feinberg on coercion will, I think, establish Wall as our preeminent commentator on coercion as it relates to moral and legal responsibility. I want to begin with two observations. The first is that Wall is too generous in describing my contribution to his analysis of coercion. I was at most a literary midwife, helping Wall present his analysis of coercion. The second observation I want to make concerns the question of whether or not progress is possible in philosophy. When I compare the work of my teacher, Joel Feinberg, on coercion and Wall's analysis of coercion, I believe that progress has occurred. Wall has built upon the work done by Feinberg, but has departed from him significantly. Wall, I believe, offers a simpler and more persuasive analysis of coercion than we find in Feinberg. If Wall is correct, we lose the point of the distinction between compulsion and coercion if we allow compulsion to yield results which are said to be coercive in effect. According to Wall, compulsion is always the result of impersonal forces, and coercion always occurs in an interpersonal relationship in which a coercer attempts, by the use of threats, to make another agent do something that the agent in question doesn't want to do. Roughly speaking, for Feinberg the difference between compulsion and coercion turns upon the effect they have upon the alternatives or options available to an agent. Compulsion eliminates alternatives or options. By contrast, coercion simply narrows the range of alternatives by making certain alternatives more costly. According to Wall, coercion like compulsion may in some cases altogether eliminate the possibility of alternatives. If this is true, then we must look to the source of compulsion and the source of coercion if we are to find significant differences between the two.

The significance of Wall's work for moral and political philosophy is, I think, the following: Philosophers and social commentators have often appeared genuinely perplexed over whether a political or economic system is properly described as compulsive or coercive. Wall's answer is that are properly described as compulsive, and certainly it would o picture an economic system as being designed to force to labor at low wages under the threat of unemployment, employment may well be a consequence of workers' refusal low wages. On the other hand, it is not as clear to me that stems are not coercive. People speak of the coercive state, they ether the minimal state is coercive, and so forth. More specif- al systems employ sanctions or penalties to force compliance that at least some individuals may choose to violate. More ds to be done on the question of whether legal systems resemble of interpersonal relationship that Wall has in mind when he coercion, but I don't think it is a stretch to say that lawmakers t least some institutions with the idea of sanctions or penalties as a threat where non-compliance is concerned.

l finds Feinberg's account of voluntariness significant in two re- Feinberg rightly emphasizes the psychological aspect of voluntari- nd he also rightly insists that voluntariness is a matter of degree. rg, following Hart and Honore, concludes that the moral and legal cations of an action affect our decision as to whether an action is ently voluntary. It is at this point that Wall takes significant exception at Feinberg is doing. If we compare a traitor and a holdup victim, of whom yield to coercive threats, then according to Feinberg we to say of the traitor that the coercive threat involved a much higher of pressure before we are willing to impute involuntariness to the or. Wall's position is that we want to say of the traitor that while his on was largely involuntary, it is nevertheless the case that what he did morally reprehensible. All that we need to say here, according to ll, is that, given the magnitude of what is at stake when a traitor rays his country, the traitor should have tried harder in resisting coercive essure. I am persuaded that Wall's "empirical test of voluntariness" is l that is needed here, and that decisions as to the voluntariness of an ction are logically prior to our considering any of the legal and moral amifications of a particular action.

Postscript

I am greatly indebted to Aleksandar Jokic for compiling this volume of essays in my honor. I am indebted to all the contributors for the high quality of their essays. They have reminded me of the absolute importance of the issues that I have been concerned with for nearly half a centur And they have reminded me that I couldn't possibly have lived a mo exciting life than the life I have lived. None of the contributors who wro about my own work is known to me personally. I suppose this guarante some measure of impartiality on their part, but it saddens me that I haven known them or some of the other contributors personally, because I ar convinced that their friendship would have enriched my life considerably

The poetess H.D. has a poem which begins with her saying that whe the world has come to an end, we will go to the Eastern Shore to sit an remember. When I can no longer do research or teach my world will hav come to an end, and I hope to return to the Eastern Shore where it al began. To sit and remember. I shall take this volume with me, and I will reread it many times.

3

v.
e
e
s
t

Burleigh T. Wilkins

Epilogue

A stereotype of a professional actor is that he is someone who never wants to leave the stage. He steals encores, he refuses to surrender the microphone, he may even "retire" several times. Just when you thought you were done with me I spring back on stage with an epilogue. Joe White has contributed a kind and perceptive essay on my unpublished fiction, which since it is unpublished can at best give me the status of a serious but amateur author. White is a former student of mine who is chair of the philosophy department at Santa Barbara City College, and he is a published writer of screenplays and fiction. If my unpublished novel, *Mr. Jefferson's Chair*, is, as White thinks, semi-autobiographical, its protagonist, Richard Webb, in his Hollywood period, has certain parallels with White, though his vices are distinctly his own. More seriously, what White fails to understand, or at least is too modest to acknowledge, is that he exemplifies far better than I do the connections between "llfe," philosophy, and literature he and I think are important.

Heidegger said that the main problem which confronts the cosmopolitan person is his search for a place that he can call home. In my case the problem is even more complex. I have a place I can call home, but as time passes it recedes, and my effort to recapture it each summer is less successful than it was the year before. So my visits become a pilgrimage to a lost past more than a bridge to a meaningful future. I become a tourist in my own land, someone who observes the lives of cousins and distant relatives who grow more distant. And every year I become more of a cosmopolitan, which I'm not all that fond of being either. There is nothing more abstract than the abstractions of philosophy, unless you count math or physics, and there is nothing more concrete than following a mule or later, as progress prevails, driving a tractor through the fields on a hot summer day. And there often seems to be no way of reconciling the two.

But this melancholy picture is not without some relief. The concrete world, I believe, is the world philosophy was meant to serve, and while I have honed my analytic skills as best I could I have had a larger purpose in mind, which is why my recent work and my visits to Belgrade have meant so much to me. Returning to my "career" as an author of fiction, I think that instead of being a distraction it has proved useful to my career as a philosopher. Not only has it helped keep me from seeing philosophy as an academic experience, but also, since most of my stories have been "Southern," it has been a way of going home, in some ways more satisfying and reflective than the real thing. I return to philosophy renewed and refreshed, which may help explain why, as I said at the beginning, I've been writing for a long time. Now it's your turn, Professor White.

JOSEPH WHITE

Two Voices – Philosopher and Writer

To quote Burleigh Taylor Wilkins, "I've been writing a long time."[1] As we know, most people haven't. Though a significant number of people will write for awhile, only a small percentage actually write for a long time. The reason I believe Burleigh has written for a long time is that he is a writer, which is not to overlook, nor to be confused with, the fact that he is also a philosopher. Nor is it to under-appreciate the cynical remark of Richard Webb in *Mr. Jefferson's Chair*, "...there was something pat, and familiar-sounding about that writers should write business." (p. 251—All pages references are to Burleigh's novel *Mr. Jefferson's Chair.*)

First and foremost Burleigh is a philosopher, a professional, respected, academic philosopher. Professional, academic philosophers do not consider themselves, nor do they introduce themselves, nor are they introduced as, writers. When queried as to profession, particularly by the nonacademic public, academic philosophers have a tendency to introduce themselves generically as professors unlike the tendency amongst physicists, mathematicians, historians etc. Such a generic title, at least initially, avoids those all too predictable, quizzical looks. Simon Blackburn, a contemporary academic philosopher, has cleverly taken to describing himself as a conceptual engineer[2], thus avoiding that predictable perplexity by utilizing a scientific sounding title, something familiar, something more culturally *au courant*. This ploy, I suspect, would not be Burleigh's style.

Writers, unlike most philosophers, particularly analytic philosophers, tend to find fascination first in specific or unique examples of humanness, and perhaps even more so today in seeming counter-examples of humanness. Purported counter-examples to humanness are reminders of our contemporary perplexity, at least amongst first world intelligentsia and artists, that generalizations or rules or abstractions about being human, about human nature, are suspect and highly problematic. Literary counter-examples have tended to include the alienated, the disenfranchised, the loners, the odd, the bizarre, the rebels without a cause, or as some would have it today, without a clue, but always they are essentially the different and always in literature the focus is upon the particular, specific human character, human event or human relationship in its storied context.

In his semi-autobiographical novel, *Mr. Jefferson's Chair*, Burleigh is primarily fascinated with the Webb family, as seen through the "eyes" of Richard Webb. Richard is held fast within the web (pun intended) of family relationships however, in the first twenty pages, as family members are variously introduced, Richard is principally preoccupied with Ben, his "odd," perhaps "retarded," uncle, a sort of counter-example amongst all the various family members, whatever their eccentricity. Not only is Ben odd, but Richard is himself a loner, an only child, an intellectual in a religious, rural world who "...had no interest in fishing...no patience or aptitude for games... but hungered and thirsted for knowledge of the outside world." (p. 27) He and Ben shared their oddness. As an amused Richard watched his perplexed Aunt Libby react to another of his verbal repartees with Ben, Richard remarked, "Aunt Libby looked from one of us to the other, as though wondering which of us was crazier. It's the same moon, I wanted to tell her: he's the dark side, and I'm the bright side, but it's the same moon nevertheless." (p. 217)

Richard, in these opening pages, tries to understand what it is that makes Ben "so different." Was it Ben's falling in a ditch, the beatings Ben received at school from his own sister, the teacher, or was it his birth—being the "last pup in the litter?"— or was it in his genetic structure? There is no clear, easy answer to Richard's perplexity over this difference in his uncle and then there remains his own lifetime ambivalence of being caught between two worlds and never fully in one. There seems no easy resolution between his deep-seated inclination to remain on the farm while also needing to venture out into the outside world. This ambivalence in Richard's character seems one of the autobiographical touchstones to Burleigh's life when his father would not allow him to return to farming after he had finished his undergraduate degree. In both *An Intellectual Autobiography* and *Mr. Jefferson's Chair*, we find a father telling his son, after the son decides to return to farming, "There is no money in farming." But with the betraying (?) additional remark in *Mr. Jefferson's Chair* that Richard "likes the nicer things" and these are not what a life of farming can provide.

Burleigh initially illustrates the writer's focus upon the particular through Richard Webb's first attempt at writing a story. Here Burleigh has Richard paraphrasing, while critiquing his own story, the familiar insight of Aristotle's, "Yet, on the whole, I think I had the essentials down pat, too pat undoubtedly, but it was the essentials Aristotle must have had in mind when he wrote that poetry is truer than history."(p. 137) However once Richard moved on to Duke University he makes a significant (life altering) choice to study English while an undergraduate. (Duke being another autobiographical touchstone.) Studying English takes Richard onto his adult career as a screenwriter in Hollywood, (not an autobiographical touchstone, I think), but Richard's choice to study English is again an expression of the writer's need for specific humanness. Richard remarks, "English was hardly a science, but in comparison with religion it had a certain concreteness and captures more fully, I thought, the uniqueness of our lives." (p. 154)

Analytic philosophers, on the other hand, tend to have a love/hate relationship with examples, particularly counter-examples. The clever, and sometimes least constructive, among professional philosophers seems naturally drawn to the counter-example, the exception. Genuine counter-examples are very potent as they can kill a philosophical claim, since philosophical claims tend to be abstract and general in scope. The devastating counter-example may be a significant part of a philosopher's legacy. One might think of Edmund Gettier. Ludicrous, bizarre, remotely possible, barely conceivable fictional counter-examples sometimes consume and irritate the imaginations of philosophers. As some philosophers read these remarks they have spontaneously and excitedly generated counter-examples to what I am claiming here. This activity brings an abiding, familiar, intellectual pleasure and sometimes a smile of self-conceit.

Writers, as conventionally understood to be the authors of literature, celebrate the specific human character, specific human event, human relationship, even the human story which are all, so far at least, non-philosophical. For they are neither abstract nor general. The acquisition of those qualities takes much delicate literary labor. In part, because of its specificity, some philosophers have expressed an indifference to, if not disdain for, literature. In their disdain, they share a certain affinity with their granddaddy, Plato, as Burleigh might remark, if I may be so bold. However, such disdain for, or indifference to, literature is perhaps but a reflection of their academic, if not ontological, (as with Plato), provincialness.

For writers, both ordinary and great, the example, or counter-example, is something which points beyond itself. It points beyond itself to what Robert Frost called wisdom, to what Joseph Conrad called the aeternitas veritas. For Frost pointing to wisdom distinguished literature (art) from entertainment since entertainment does not point beyond itself. While literature may thus become philosophical, since philosophy literally means the love of wisdom, literature is not philosophy. It is not philosophy in the academic, analytic sense as such philosophy does not point beyond itself. Nevertheless, philosophy is not entertainment either, as some would argue.

This difference in intellectual pursuits, in intellectual fascination and method, are rarely expressed in the works of one person. Occasionally one will find academics within English departments who, with varying degrees of success, are also writers. More rare is it to find the chemist, mathematician or philosopher who also has the voice of a writer. Burleigh is both philosopher and writer, though it appears as though these two voices may not have always spoken so distinctly.

His first book, *Carl Becker: A Biographical Study in American Intellectual History* by its very title is a mixture of the personal with the abstract intellectual. As Burleigh remarks in his *An Intellectual Autobiography,* "I realized that in writing about Becker I was, without knowing it, also writing about myself." I suspect Burleigh would say much the same thing in his writing about Richard Webb in *Mr. Jefferson's Chair,* or Bill in *A Partridge in a Pear Tree,* or the unnamed protagonist in *Judge Not*, though I also suspect in these literary contexts he would say he knew he was writing, to some extent, about himself. For his second scholarly book, Burleigh again focuses upon an individual, this time Edmund Burke, but now with a more purely philosophical twist as it is focused upon *The Problem of Burke's Political Philosophy*.

The transition from philosophical issues arising out of a specific individual's work to the more abstract, purely conceptual continues in Burleigh's academic writings with such books as *Hegel's Philosophy of History*, and *Has History Any Meaning? A Critique of Popper's Philosophy of History* to the 1992 publication of *Terrorism and Collective Responsibility*. In the latter work, the focus is pure philosophy as it is an analytically rigorous critical discussion of such abstract concepts as deontological and consequentialist justifications of terrorism. Particular cases, examples, are used, counter-examples considered, but these cases, particularly the individuals involved in the cases, are not the primary focus. The primary focus is conceptual, abstract, and "rigorously critical," as the reviewer for *Ethics* remarked.

It seems Burleigh's literary voice began to speak more distinctly somewhere in the early to mid-1970's, perhaps after the Popper book. His novel, *Mr. Jefferson's Chair*, while commencing with stories told by young Richard Webb, who is in college during the Korean War, concludes at around 1977. I, personally, began receiving short stories from Burleigh, apparently first penned, in the mid-1980's. As to the writer's voice and its concern with the particular, we find in Burleigh's literary work, beyond what was previously said regarding *Mr. Jefferson's Chair*, such short story titles as: *Grandfather Scott, The Runaway, Sam, E., and Sally, A Friend of the Family*. Personal stories about specific incidents in particular character's lives.

On a final note regarding this ambivalence between the voice or fascination of the philosopher and that of the writer, it seemingly blends for Burleigh is in his respect for John Rawls' work and his own contributions to Rawlsian scholarship. As most would readily agree, Rawls is one of the late 20th century's finest philosophers not only in terms of brilliance and scope of understanding but also in humanness. This humanness is, I believe, one of Rawls' strongest attractions amongst philosophers, the learned in general and Burleigh in particular. As Kai Nielsen once remarked to me, "Rawls will stand up to history. He is not a smart silly." (for smart silly read: clever fabricator of exotic counter-examples).

In *A Theory of Justice*, Rawls has contributed profoundly, and thus historically, to the centuries old political tradition of liberalism. Through his articulation and defense of his Difference Principle, Rawls has brought the fundamental principles of traditional, or pre-industrial, liberalism into a powerful contemporary model of distributive justice. According to Rawls' Difference Principle certain inequalities in society are just or warranted only if those inequalities are to the benefit of "the representative worst off man." Here we find a deep philosophical concern for human well-being, human well-being for any x which is both a man -generically—and the representative worst off.

A deep concern for the representative worst off man and his/her plight under conditions of justice seems a terminus for the dichotomy between the philosopher/writer in Burleigh. The representative worst off man is never any particular Ben, Richard Webb, Sam Smartley, Eliza Wise, Uncle Edmund, Carmelita, Frederico, or any specific person. (All of those named above are characters taken from a number of Burleigh's stories.) It is in this abstract concern for human well-being that Burleigh seems most involved as a philosopher, and it is here in a concrete concern for, even fascination with, human well-beingness that Burleigh the writer writes and searches for understanding. Philosophical language, even at its most humane, cannot provide a language for the voice of the writer. It is in particular relationships among families, e.g. uncles, aunts, husbands, wives, grandparents and grandchildren and in his novel, *Mr. Jefferson's Chair*, between parent and child, that Burleigh explores his concern with specific humanness in the language of the writer.

Burleigh's "long time writing" thus spans both of these worlds. His work as both writer and philosopher is something I believe both philosophers and writers should emulate. This is not to suggest that philosophers who attempt to write literature are worthy of publication as writers, (though Burleigh would be an exception), nor that writers attempting to write philosophy should reasonably expect to be published in philosophical journals. Few are so talented as to be able to speak or write in both languages so well. However, few would also disagree that much contemporary, professional philosophy seems lost to the concerns of real people in the real world. This is ironically the case even with discussions in applied ethics. Most people would also agree that much of the sophomoric, if not insipid, popular literature—especially the cinema—would greatly benefit by some commitment to, if not respect for, intellectual sophistication and refinement. If both writers and philosophers did incorporate such practices then perhaps G.B. Shaw's denigrating remark that we get the art we deserve would be less denigrating.

I have read nearly a dozen short stories and one novel by Burleigh though I believe he has written more than these. However, I suspect I may have the most extensive private collection of Burleigh's literary writings. These writings for the most part are peppered with autobiographical references, as previously mentioned. Some are explicit: *A Friend of the Family; Ten Days That Didn't Shake the World;* and some quasi- or semi-autobiographical: *Mr. Jefferson's Chair; Grandfather Scott; Sam, E and Sally.*

Consistently throughout his stories, for the most part things happen to or around Burleigh and/or his protagonists. While sometimes engaged in the events of the story neither Burleigh nor his protagonists are conventional protagonists whose passions consistently propel the drama forward. There are not the traditional dramatic story elements of beginning, middle and end. Scenes are not intricately crafted to tantalize and foreshadow. Such crafting, I suspect, would be seen as manipulative or artificial, perhaps even disingenuine, by Burleigh. Denouements, when present, are never magnificent but are instead quiet, understated and in the case of *Mr. Jefferson's Chair*, alone, secret. Rather, what we find is the telling of what some refer to as lyrical as opposed to dramatic stories.

In the case of the short stories, we find lyrical "slices of life" in which some incident seemingly points beyond itself. This most clearly occurs in *Ten Days That Didn't Shake the World But Moved Me.* Here, Burleigh, nearly in anecdotal travelogue format, describes a series of events that happen to him while visiting Belgrade, Yugoslavia, to attend a philosophy conference. After visits to ancient monasteries, solo ramblings around Belgrade, at one point trying on a $2700 Versace suit between visits to the local museum, Burleigh concludes this story with, "Two weeks into my Virginia vacation Versace is killed in Miami, and I wonder whose country is on the verge of collapse, and if you can collapse without knowing it."

In *Mr. Jefferson's Chair,* the story is a narrative of Richard Webb's growing up. Richard is a bright, curious, adventurous young boy, an only child, from an isolated—no phone, no electricity—rural, Virginia farm who becomes a middle-aged, somewhat jaded, worldly Hollywood screenwriter living at one point, until a fire, in Malibu. His existentially fatigued adult soul seems divided between the apparent honest, simple connectedness of rural life down on the farm and the want, the need for adventure and literary success which is only possible in a more complex urban life. As Richard remarks, "...to this day I have not seen a home where there was so much love and devotion, but even as a child I sensed that love and devotion can take us only so far. To Richmond or Charlottesville perhaps, but if we want to hear Tebaldi sing her heart out at LaScala and then fly on to Egypt to enjoy the silence of the pyramids then a certain amount of pretense, irritability, and plain, old-fashioned neurosis may stand us in good stead. I think that even as a child I somehow knew this and understood that the great things were available in large supply on the other side of the thicket." (p. 31)

Burleigh's stories are primarily the reports of a witness, a literary voyeur, though not completely disinterested, as journalists pretend. Rather, his interest is betrayed by the fact that many of his stories seem to end with a discrete, quiet smile, and whether genuine or forced, it is always gracious and always expectant of yet another story. Perhaps Burleigh-the-witness is the result of Burleigh's own sense of growing up "overwhelmed" by the shadows of the greatness of Washington, Jefferson, Madison, and living in Virginia, a State he has described as marked by a sense of complacency. A sense of great deeds already done, of major work finished, in a state of complacency, these are not traits of a proactive protagonist in a traditional dramatic story but rather the traits, now more typical, of a contemporary protagonist feeling trapped by history, lulled and lost in mass media culture yet needing and searching for an authentic voice. More on this shortly as Richard Webb's own conflict reflects this so vividly as he is a television writer, dealing with insipid television productions and producers, while being constantly pulled back to historically rich (or suffocating) roots in Virginia.

Being variously autobiographical, these stories for the most part are set within a rural and southern context, often Burleigh's Virginia. Unlike Twain, Burleigh does not attempt to capture the local dialect or cadence syntactically. Those sorts of details are not his concern. In his most extensive piece of writing, *Mr. Jefferson's Chair*, there are no detailed physical descriptions either of people or of locations. Lovers, first kisses, such intimate encounters, while present, are not dwelled upon. One doesn't come away with a vivid picture of faces, fashions or locations. One doesn't smell the farm or touch the rural life but one gets glimpses. In Richard Webb's case, he has one marriage, but we don't learn his wife's name for three pages, and then it comes in dialogue with his father and this dialogue doesn't involve her but is only about her. There is also an extended affair on two continents with "his script girl" but we are never given her name. Instead, Burleigh's focus is upon what happens to people, more specifically on the thoughts and feelings of his protagonist(s). These are largely protagonist-centered pieces in terms of that individual's inner life.

His short stories *A Friend of the Family* and *Ten Days That Didn't Shake the World But Moved Me* might well serve as approximate bookends for Burleigh's literary writings. *A Friend of the Family* appears to be one of his earliest writings while *Ten Days* is probably one of his more recent, as I know Burleigh's trips to Belgrade, the subject of *Ten Days*, first started just four years ago. Serving as bookends, they seem to reflect much of Burleigh's literary style and concern, thus introducing us to what we find in between.

A Friend of the Family is not only set within a family, the preferred arena for Burleigh, but is sprinkled with Burleigh's humor and the inevitable philosophical reference. The story opens with, "An old man is just a bag of anecdotes. Thus spoke Sartre." We get not only Sartre but a jab at Nietzsche. Told that the story has "the disadvantage of being true," we quickly learn that our unnamed protagonist is visiting his "ex-wife and current children, children are never ex..." Ever the witness, our protagonist notes, "I remembered Tampa when it was just a sleepy Southern town and my ex-wife when she was just a sleepy Southern girl. Both sultry, but now they are both very efficient and I marvel at the transformation."

Here, too, we find "the farmer" out of sync with the urban world. Having developed back problems, he takes his ex-wife's recommendation to go see a doctor-friend, Charles. Upon examining him, Charles suggests the back problems might have some psychological cause. With his rural suspicion of things urban, our protagonist, in talking the diagnosis over with his ex-wife, remarks, "Your friend wanted me to think I had psychological problems and I crowed gleefully: I wanted to tell him I came from a long line of old farmers who never had a psychological problem in their lives. That's because they didn't have consciences, she said. I let that little insight pass: she was my ex-wife and a good woman, and it was only a scratch."

The story ends with Charles, once harried and one of the "most successful doctors" in Tampa having suffered permanent brain damage from a freakish auto accident. Burleigh concludes the story, "Here was a man who no longer gave orders, or made diagnoses, and without his white smock he looked more like a Charlie than a Charles. I was driving into the sun when it happened, he told us, and I never saw a thing." Burleigh doesn't leave Charles/Charlie in despair but with a new job, one less stressful, and a position incapable of generating arrogance or that harriedness where one's patients so often become merely data on a chart for the ever so more important doctor. Charles became Charlie as he drove off into the sunset. The irony both in terms of literary and philosophical genres is inescapable. At the end of the story one senses a discrete, genuine smile from Burleigh over how life seems to happen to us.

The other bookend, *Ten Days That Didn't Shake the World But Which Moved Me*, is, as previously mentioned, a kind of travelogue narrative describing one of Burleigh's recent conferences in Belgrade. Though going to Belgrade to read a paper and give a seminar at an academic conference, when introduced to the patriarch of a local family, whom Burleigh meets while touring through the countryside, Burleigh describes himself not simply as a visiting professor but as "a peasant too," and then ponders toward the end of the story, "My farm is in Virginia, and my job is in California but for awhile my heart will be in Serbia."

As Burleigh, the farmer/philosopher, writes about his tour of one of Serbia's prized historical monasteries, a nun, whom he describes as pretty, remarks, "the saintly bones that are still preserved, are truly a miracle, otherwise they would have decomposed." While such a remark would prove a red flag for a young bull philosopher, the wise, the seasoned merely nods, perhaps graciously smiling. The nun, as Burleigh reports, recognizes him as a foreigner and approaches to speak with him. Burleigh writes, "What does he do, she asks my host. Tell him if he studies the life of Saint Sava he would give up philosophy and become a priest..." "The nearest I will get to God is philosophy and beautiful women like you, and that is close enough," is Burleigh's sprightly response. Following this playful encounter with the nun, Burleigh reminisces about his mother and her faith, her "monastic" isolation on a rural Virginia farm. Again, the recurrent themes of family, those ties that powerfully, but never perfectly, bind; the conflict in longing for the rural while traveling to a city as a guest lecturer at an international academic conference; and of course the humor.

In the middle writings, with the exception of *North of the Border*, which is the story of a young Mexican field worker who longs to be with his pregnant wife but is set up for the murder of a gringo, and *The Runaway*, where a fellow who has mysteriously fled to Rio to start a new life is unwillingly pulled back into some previous life of violence, all of the other stories are tinged with autobiographical elements. And yet again, one never quite knows where Burleigh begins or ends in this literary blur. *Sam, E., and Sally* starts by telling us that "Sam Smartley was a philosopher who cruised the bars looking for an argument the way other men look for more worldly pleasures... One day Sam met his match in one E. Wise, at least that was how she signed her name to journal articles, for who would take seriously an article signed Eliza and who would be able to resist making puns about a certain Wise woman? Though their arguments became legendary... Sam never nailed her once." There are many puns in this story.

In *Sam, E, and Sally*, Burleigh briefly explores, through Sam, the possibility of philosophical argument being sufficient for a "heavenly relationship." As Eliza stumbled one evening, nearly falling, Sam raised the issue of free will and determinism. The next morning, Sam found a note from the now departed Eliza, "I am so tired of arguing with you that I could puke!" So much for heavenly relationships and philosophy. More generally, as with other stories including *Mr. Jefferson's Chair* and *A Partridge in a Pear Tree,* is the theme that such intellectual cleverness, in the sense of intellectual cuteness or intellectual pretentiousness will, at most, allow one only a superficial-level of flirtation in a relationship. Genuine love is not possible for a character who only has such intellectual pretense in his repertoire of affections since true love, so it seems, must be found elsewhere and requires much more. More will be said shortly on love and the limits of character as it is also an essential feature of Richard

Webb's many futile relationships.

A Partridge in a Pear Tree finds Bill, an academic, a Southerner, specifically a Virginian, alone at Christmas in a university town somewhere in Massachusetts. As in Burleigh's story *Judge Not*, we find in this story a cynicism toward, along with the taint of moral corruption within, the life of one of our essential social institutions. In *A Partridge in a Pear Tree* it is academia as opposed to the judiciary in *Judge Not*. Similar attitudes toward academia surface in *Mr. Jefferson's Chair* as well. As *A Partridge in a Pear Tree* opens, Bill has recently been accorded the Fulton Award, "which is not quite the Pulitzer Prize," as Bill regularly reminds us. Having been invited by the university president's flirtatious wife, Anna, to a Christmas party, Bill attends as "the token Southerner" or so he says. The president is legendary for his drinking. Bill's department chair is also in attendance and ever suffocatingly conventional with his "tweed jacket, elbow patches but mercifully, there was no pipe, just an aftershave lotion which somehow reminded you, if the sunwrinkled face did not, that here was one helluva outdoors fellow not afraid to follow in the footsteps of Hemingway and all the other outdoorsy types who just happened to write great stuff when the fish weren't biting and the bulls weren't running."

At the party, Bill, for a moment, ponders the fate of that "representative worst off man" when he contemplates, "The buffet was awesome, with enough food to feed hundreds of homeless, but let them eat cake. For us there was caviar, and lots of it. The wine was imported, and, oh, how it flowed." There is extravagance and a hint of moral duplicity as Anna requests that Bill sit next to her at the table. The drinking continues with one Dean singing, "Four professors, my true love gave to me, should be hanging from a pear tree." A reference, we are told, to a group of faculty who opposed an administrative initiative.

At the dinner, the drinking builds to a crescendo, the flirtation increases with Anna teasingly, jokingly suggesting that she and Bill should leave the next day for Peru to join the communist Shining Path Revolutionaries. Bill responds, "Well, maybe. I sang softly in her ear, a partridge in the pear tree beats the KGB." Sensing himself caught in some degrading, corrupt charade Bill's mind races, "Oh God, I thought, let it end, and then I said to myself, make it end now and excused myself from the table." Anna followed him to the door telling him she would call.

The next day, Bill calls his colleague Jerry in Gainesville. Bill wants out of his present world but Jerry informs Bill that his own wife has just left him, he's been drinking all day but Bill should come down, read a paper to Jerry's department. Jerry has a graduate student "who is just made for Bill. In fact, he just made her himself." There seems no way out, as Jerry castigates Bill, "Oh, don't be so pious, you're too young to be a statesman. Come on down, the weather's great." Bill hangs up. The next day, Anna calls. End of story.

Mr. Jefferson's Chair was once titled *Carry Me Back* as well as *The Ties That Bind.* Titling is a mysterious but determinant process which operates according to no known laws. Each of these titles is appropriate in its own way for this novel but *Mr. Jefferson's Chair* is, in that mysterious way, closer to the mark. As previously mentioned this is the novel-length story of Richard Webb, son of a Virginia farmer, who evolved into a screenwriter living in Hollywood but who remains regularly on the move either working on location, living in LA or returning "home" to Virginia. Once married to a scholar, who finally "wandered into the Huntington Library never to return," as Richard quips with a new girlfriend, Richard spends most of his adult life perplexed by the Socratic dictum, "Know thyself," though this is never stated in the novel.

In Mr. *Jefferson's Chair*, we again find Burleigh's style of mixing the autobiographical and the fictional to a fine blur. Autobiographically, Richard Webb is an only child, raised on a Virginia farm, was on a debate team in high school which won one title but lost two others, and each of Richard's debates were on topics identical to those Burleigh defended in his boyhood. Additionally, Richard attends Duke, worries over his Korean war deferment, and at one crucial point in his life chooses to return to the farm only to be turned away by his father. Like Burleigh, Richard is in awe of Thomas Jefferson, finding Monticello a sacred place. As to Richard's extended family, the Webbs and Soames, as to his screenwriting career, his many women and few, if any loves, all of whom but his first wife, Hannah and last love, Maggie, go unnamed, as to the Polo Lounge deal making and worldly travels these seem the fabrications of a literary imagination. As to the adult character of Richard Webb, he is a character that points beyond himself to something that Burleigh as a philosopher and writer has worried about. Richard ultimately seems to be Burleigh's creation of contemporary man, of a character highly self-conscious of his strengths but more defined by his weaknesses, a character feeling trapped in ordinariness, a part of no world yet yearning for authenticity, for some sort of deep, genuine, redemptive involvement.

Richard Webb is a complicated character but as remarked earlier he is a character to whom things happen, primarily. As he describes his own family's plight, "There are, it is commonly believed, people who make history, people like the Carters, and then there are people to whom history is something that happens; reflecting the egocentric predicament, I have in mind not the downtrodden masses but people like the Webbs..." (p. 226) Richard carries the heavy, sometimes crippling, burden of history as fellow Virginian George Washington had already set the standard for practical wisdom, while Thomas Jefferson defined intellectual power wedded to the real world, and Robert E. Lee provided the archetype for the honorable, stoic gentleman. (p. 200) What was left? At some level, Richard Webb too, wants to be such a god yet he fully understands his finite, somewhat ordinary, humanness. He is rooted in the moment not in the eternal. He yearns futilely, "Perhaps, like Jefferson, I could farm and write, and talk philosophy when the sun went down...but that, too, would pass, and I would again be standing in the marketplace once more a topical topic in hand." (p. 251)

Richard, I think, speaks to many of today's twenty-somethings, even thirty-somethings. Unrooted in any particular world, seemingly caught somewhere between hunter/gatherer or early agriculture—or today, granola hippies living in a redwood tree—versus the lure of the fast, titillating, urgently convenient existence in the gleaming metropolis of a mass media culture. Most of Richard's adult life is spent going "home" to Virginia, not that he loves his extended family and if he does love them he doesn't wax poetic about it. Rather there is something in the rural way of life that pulls him from his career which is one of those popularly envied careers—the screenwriter. A career which allows him to buy his Ferrari, travel the world, own exotic homes but requires that he exist in an unreal world, a "fantasy town," (p. 258) a place of geniuses, frauds and psychopaths (p. 192), a place where he belongs, according to his mother. (p. 202).

Unable to find a world, Richard ponders, "On the plane I would sit drinking martinis and thinking here I am suspended between the future, California, and the past, Virginia." (p. 185) Ever alone, Richard's lack of connection seems to also render him incapable of love. How can one find another when one can't find oneself? His first marriage apparently dies a silent death of neglect. "Hannah [first wife] quietly boarded a plane for New York. I wasn't there to see her off, or to care much one way or the other, but Hannah did everything quietly, and I suppose this was no exception." (p. 183) Then there's a series of relationships in which the young ladies are sometimes brought home to Virginia but when "I saw myself and my companion through my parents' eyes, the practice of bringing a friend was discontinued." (p. 185) The "long" relationship with "his script girl" never yields her name nor any physical description but Richard does discover through this relationship the three act structure for love.

"Love is a three act play entitled: *You Don't Know Me.* Act One: You don't know me yet, but you will. Love conquers (almost) all, let me tell you about myself. Act Two: You don't know me, said accusingly, let me try again. Act Three: You don't know me, thank God Almighty, and you never will." (p. 208) Richard is at his most seemingly contemporary here in being the resentful victim. YOU—the other—have failed. Let ME tell you. Let ME try again to tell you. You never will understand ME. Never is the question asked, who are you? What do you need? Or what should I do for you? Is love possible for such an ego?

In making Richard a screenwriter, Burleigh gives us a lost soul at the center of mass culture and shows that the ordinary tangible and conventionally lusted for items are not enough to sustain this lost and self-centered soul. Ultimately, Richard discovers that one must decide, one must choose to be something and in that choosing there is hope that the choice will be genuine, redeemingly unique, a self-authenticating choice and in this way perhaps one can become, for that moment, god-like. In that moment of choice one escapes the ubiquitous web of antecedent conditions that determine one's character. And what character was most clearly defined in *Mr. Jefferson's Chair* by some complex, mysterious set of conditions but Richard's "different," "retarded" uncle Ben. Hence Richard's lifelong fascination with his uncle, the dark side of the moon to his light side, this difference marked only by degree and not kind. Ben was the key to Richard's own self-awareness.

By the end of the story, having buried many of his relatives including his father and Ben, Richard moves back to the farm, burnt out with Hollywood and his work there. Even his mother agrees, after a spell, to lease the farm to him the following year but none of this brings contentment. Maggie, his most recent and perhaps most deeply felt relationship, is in Charlottesville and that seems unfinished, perhaps unfinishable as he again is drawn and repulsed. Drawn by the woman and her Virginianness but repulsed by the prospect of a life in academia into which he believes she would inevitably pull him.

Finally, in his quest for an act of authenticity, for an act of genuine choice, Richard discovers, "There is nothing so exhilarating, I told myself, as an act done out of character." This is not an act out of character in the sense that it is a clear reflection of a deep-seated, pervasive disposition.

Rather, and most significantly, it is an act out of character in the sense that it is unanticipated, it is something out of the norm for this character, something new, an existential counter-example. The philosopher Immanuel Kant might just consider such an act a possible reflection of a genuinely free will though much more would need to be known.

Richard's exhilarating acting out of character came in returning his uncle Ben's purported Campechie chair to Monticello. The chair that his uncle Ben, in his twilight years, had boasted once belonged to Thomas Jefferson. Having "stolen" the chair from his now dead uncle's boarded up house, out of a sense of revenge over his uncle's unfair will, Richard, not ultimately caring whether the chair actually had belonged to Jefferson, finally finds himself sauntering (swaggering) back to his van after depositing the chair on the porch at Jefferson's own Monticello.

Now heeding his Uncle Edmund's advice, "Maybe none of us is really needed, except the great geniuses, and from what I understand they're seldom wanted or made welcome. But you're a writer, and writers should write, if you want my opinion." (p. 249) Though next morning Richard was a bit suspicious of the advice as "Uncle Edmund had been a bit too articulate... I suspected him of being a secret reader of books, no vice when taken by itself to be sure, but disturbing when one is looking for folk wisdom, the wisdom of the blood, in its purest, least adulterated form. And there was something pat, and familiar sounding, about that writers should write business." (p. 250)

Richard does take the advice and having returned Mr. Jefferson's chair decides to go back to California. "I read all sorts of symbolic significance into what I had and had not done in returning Mr. Jefferson's chair, without having sat in it, I was rejecting a ready-made past. And I had big plans for the future..." (p. 261) No more collaborative writing, Richard would be his own man. He leaves Virginia not with his own self-made loving ties that could bind, for he reconciles himself to the fact that "Maggie, I'm sorry, but you were for the long haul, for the difficult and arduous passage through time and I'm for the short run." (p. 264) Finally, "California is the land not of past, present, or future, but of *now or never.* I didn't need a ready-made past or a ready-made family or any kind of past or family, not where I was going. Where I was going every man is his own father and his own son. In other words, every man is a self-made man; and, as we all know, they're the very worst kind." (p. 264) And so concludes *Mr. Jefferson's Chair*.

We leave Richard Webb, not returning to Virginia but enroute to California seemingly free of the burden of history, free of the familial ties that bind and now with no need to be carried back. He is at this moment enraptured by that California mirage of worlds converging in endless possibilities on a limitless horizon of the future. This brings us back to Burleigh's philosophical worries about history, moral respect, fairness and justice which are all at their essence concerned with relationships of humanness. Richard Webb is not a moral man. Richard Webb's sole point of reference remains the first person singular pronoun. Richard Webb has yet to learn his lesson. I would hope that, as John Updike did for his Rabbit trilogy, so Burleigh will do for Richard Webb. In Burleigh's literary world, the future will bring Richard's mother's death and that inevitable call of the farm to his soul. He has not and he cannot escape history.

Though *Mr. Jefferson's Chair* ends with Richard unredeemed, perhaps readying us for the sequel, this novel along with many of the short stories does retain that quality of ending with a discrete, quiet smile, and whether genuine or forced, the smile is always gracious and always expectant of yet another story, which I mentioned earlier. This deep feature of Burleigh's writing reflects his own sense of being lucky in life and an optimist, which he describes in his *An Intellectual Autobiography*. On a final note, Burleigh utilizes a recurrent date in a number of his stories which is also a traditional symbol for deep-rooted optimism. This date is Burleigh's favored holiday, Christmas.

From *Grandfather Scott*, "On Christmas Eve of 1916 my mama came home with a soldier from the camp at Berlin, my father, a young lieutenant, and anyone could tell that Wicomico wasn't going to be Yankee free much longer just from the way my mama held his arm and looked up into his unmistakably Yankee eyes." *A Partridge in a Pear Tree* takes place almost entirely at a Christmas party as Bill seeks his freedom. In *North of the Borde*r, Jesus, after being set-up for the stabbing of a gringo, writes to his wife, optimistically, anticipating that things will change for the better, "Dear Carmelita, there has been an incident at the camp tonight, and I may be delayed in my return, but I will be home by Christmas for sure."

In *Mr. Jefferson's Chair*, Richard remarks, "To me August was a special time, a break from the almost unrelieved loneliness of summer vacation and a chance to live fully ..." (p. 27) August was also the month in which Richard's father died along with the patriarch of the extended Webb family. However, the first mention of August comes at page twenty-one while the first mention of Christmas occurs much earlier at page six. While August is featured six times through out the story, Christmas is featured twelve times and it is near Christmas, not August or the hot summer, that uncle Ben, Richard's literary doppelganger, dies. It is at Christmas that Richard and his first wife celebrate their arrival in California, a place that comes to define much of his soul. It is also near Christmas, though never explicitly stated, that Richard makes his final departure in the novel from Virginia to California.

The role of Christmas throughout these stories is not that of a religious holy day as in some simple or obvious Christian sense. Rather it seems deeper in a more ancient, and I suspect unarticulated, sense of the past which is rooted in our sense of the seasons changing, of shorter days, of the sun dying but anticipating, hoping for, the rebirth, a new sun, life returning. That period now marked by Christmas, a date which Catholics annointed for apparently non-religious reasons in the fourth century A.D., has primarily represented in the northern hemisphere a time of profound transition when the time of dying gives way to the new beginning. It is a sense of transition more ancient than Christianity or Saturnalia. Here, I believe Burleigh's regular use of Christmas as a story pivot is an indicator of the depth of honesty which Burleigh brings in giving voice to the writer, and in this particular case, a voice which resonates with some optimism, if not the joy of feeling lucky that is so deeply associated with Christmas.

Ending on a personal note, a few years back, when I was a young man attempting to build a career, and being rather new to the career world, I found myself facing some very frustrating and surprising (naive me) forces. Burleigh consoled me pointing out that I must be more prudent in my choice of surroundings as first-class people surround themselves with first-class people while second-class people surround themselves with third-class people. I've since been more conscientious and have always prized and been honored by Burleigh's friendship as he's first-class in so many ways. There are now many more varied and strong, even first-class, voices in the world thanks to Burleigh's mentoring and encouragement over these many years.

References

1. Wilkins, Burleigh. *An Intellectual Autobiography.* Festschrift., Peter Lang Publishers, New York, 2001, p. 1.
2. Blackburn, Simon. *Think*. Oxford: Oxford University Press. 1999. p. 2.

Contributors

Brenda M. Baker (Philosophy, Calgary University)

David Cooper (Philosophy, Northern Michigan University)

J. Angelo Corlett (Philosophy, California State University ,San Diego)

Margaret Gibert (Philosophy, University of Connecticut, Storrs)

Jonathan L. Gorman (Philosophy, Queen's University, Belfast)

Aleksandar Jokic (Philosophy, Portland State University)

C. Behan McCullagh (Philosophy, La Trobe University)

Kai Nielsen (Emeritus, Calgary University)

Thomas Pogge (Philosophy, Columbia University)

Paul Redding (Philosophy, University of Sydney)

Susan Meld Shell (Political Science, Boston College)

Edmund Wall (Philosophy, East Carolina University)

Frederick G Whelan (Political Science, University of Pittsburgh)

Joseph White (Philosophy, Santa Barbara Community College)

Burleigh T. Wilkins (Philosophy, University of California, santa Barbara)